MARK TWAIN IN NEVADA

"GOVERNOR" MARK TWAIN, 1863

MARK TWAIN

IN

NEVADA

BY

EFFIE MONA MACK

ILLUSTRATED

CHARLES SCRIBNER'S SONS, New York
CHARLES SCRIBNER'S SONS, LTD., London
1947

V.

TO

LEON ANDERSON MACK

MY BROTHER

LIEUTENANT, AIR FORCE

WORLD WAR I

PREFACE

THE LIFE AND WORKS OF MARK TWAIN is a story of perpetual interest. This book was written to recapture the flavor, the rhythm, the tempo, the frenzy of an amazing period in American history. What was the *mise en scène* when Sam Clemens arrived in Nevada Territory? Who were his fellow actors? What were the circumstances which moved him to write in the vein he chose for recording his reactions to the social, the political, and the industrial conditions of frontier society?

He has told a great deal of the story in *Roughing It.* Many people who read this book take it for exaggeration; some writers explain it—one is tempted to say dismiss it—as a flight of fancy, on the ground that no community was ever so fabulous as Mark Twain's Nevada. This writer thought so, too, until she searched the records, examined family archives and manuscripts, read the newspapers, visited the places in Nevada where Sam Clemens had lived, interviewed contemporary participants in Sam Clemens' world, and checked and rechecked his descriptions, allusions, and insinuations.

Of all the books that have been written on the literary career of Mark Twain, this one should have appeared first. It was in this territory that he incubated; it was in Virginia City that he became a full-fledged writer. The many books written about this humorist would seem to have squeezed the orange dry. Yet no book covers exclusively the three years, 1861–1864, which he spent in Nevada. He belonged to this part of the United States as much as he did to Florida and Hannibal, Missouri, to Keokuk, Iowa, or to San Francisco, California. These chapters are a study of a neglected aspect of the area in which he flowered.

In Nevada, Sam Clemens wrote under two pseudonyms, "Josh" and "Mark Twain." In this Territory, he progressed from an obscure visitor about the streets of Carson City, to a timber claim owner and mill hand in the Humboldt and Esmeralda Mining Districts, and finally to a reporter on *The Territorial Enterprise,* one of the most influential newspapers on the Pacific coast. During these years

vii

his personality took on definite characteristics. These attributes were reflected in his writings—they were carefree, unrestrained, vigorous, and dynamic. The variations of theme in his satire, burlesque, and serious commentary attest that he lived his life fully. Unrestrained he tried out his literary talent.

Sam Clemens' early life, his jobs on several newspapers, his early attempts to write, and his years on the Mississippi River conditioned him for his life in the West. He was already informed about it, for he had seen thousands of emigrants, argonauts, and Zionites pass through the river towns en route west. Many articles had appeared in magazines, and a number of books had been written on Western life. His descriptions and stories have some similarities to those of writers who preceded him. They, too, seem to be written in hyperboles, but frontier Nevada was hyperbolic.

Never before nor since in any part of the world, not even in the Gold Rush to California, was there such an extravaganza put on as in the Rush to Washoe. And there never has been a writer before or since Mark Twain who has left such a vivid picture of it. During these years he was Nevada—restless, bibulous, jocular, speculative, boisterous, rough, crude.

Several quotations from articles written by Mark Twain and some excerpts from writings of his contemporaries are included in the text of this volume. Most of them are in books beyond the reach of the general reader. Additional quotations are placed at the end of this volume. Over a period of years the writer has collected a number of contemporary sketches and pictures of places where he lived and of people he knew when he was in Nevada. Some of them are reproduced here for the first time.

The writer became interested in Mark Twain at the time of his death. A scrapbook of Clemens items was begun; men and women who knew him personally in Carson City and Virginia City were interviewed, and every place he lived in in Nevada and California was visited and revisited many times. These travels extended even to the Monkey Pod tree he planted when he was on the Island of Hawaii in 1866. It has also been the privilege of the writer to read unpublished family records, some material from which cannot be included in this book. Relatives of his Nevada associates have been most co-operative in loaning correspondence, photographs, and col-

PREFACE

lected data. Several scrapbooks, containing early Virginia City items compiled by some person or persons unknown to the writer, were given to her several years ago. They have been invaluable in filling gaps in the lost newspapers of this period.

Scores of persons have contributed important data to this book. For all of them the author is deeply appreciative. Individual credit is given to the persons who have loaned specific items. To the officers and attendants of the Bancroft Library, University of California, to the Librarians of the University of Nevada, the Nevada State Library, the Nevada State Historical Library, the Washoe County Library, to the Secretary of the Iowa State Historical Society, to the Secretary of State of Nevada, and to the attendants of the Mark Twain Museum, Hannibal, sincere thanks are extended.

The writer wishes, also, to acknowledge with thanks permission from Harper and Brothers to make extensive quotations from the published writings of Samuel L. Clemens; permission from Alfred A. Knopf to quote from *San Francisco's Literary Frontier,* by Franklin Walker; and permission from the University of North Carolina Press to quote from *Mark Twain, Son of Missouri,* by Minnie M. Brashear.

EFFIE MONA MACK

Reno, Nevada
May, 1947

CONTENTS

BOOK I
THE SCHOOL OF HARD KNOCKS

BOOK II
MATRICULATION

BOOK III
UNDERGRADUATE DAYS

BOOK IV
WASHOE SCHOOL OF JOURNALISM

CONTENTS

ILLUSTRATIONS

ILLUSTRATIONS

BOOK I

*THE SCHOOL OF
HARD KNOCKS*

THE LAND OF WASHOE

"I WAS SIRED BY THE GREAT AMERICAN EAGLE . . ."[1] Thus began the burlesque of a Fourth of July oration delivered by a Nevada politician[2] in the summer of 1862. It was written by the flickering light of a miner's candle in a cabin in Aurora, situated on the barren eastern wall of the Sierra Nevada Mountains, and sent to the editor of the *Territorial Enterprise* of Virginia City. It brought a job and later fame and fortune to its author, signed "Josh." His name was Samuel Langhorne Clemens.

He was twenty-six years old when he wrote this satire on a speaker whose clichés were so well known to him that he didn't even have to attend the address. At twenty-six, Sam Clemens had been in the land of Washoe, the western part of the Territory of Nevada, almost a year. He had twice paid dearly "to see the elephant." With all of his own money gone, his credit exhausted, and a great deal more money spent that his brother Orion had sent him, he was willing to give up mining and try his hand once more at writing.

This time the article he sent to the *Enterprise* "clicked" with the editor, Joseph Thompson Goodman, the discoverer of Mark Twain. For his discovery the world is richer and so was Sam Clemens. During the three years 1861–1864 he spent in the land of Washoe, he observed how men lived in frontier society, how they behaved in their frenzied quest for gold, how mightily they dreamed and how bitterly they were disillusioned in their fool's paradise. In shrewd and biting satire he laid bare the sham, the corruption, the artifices of bunko steerers. His grotesque parodies were written in defense of human justice.

If the Nevada literary productions of Sam Clemens are unique, it is partly because no other section of the United States is geographically like Nevada. This oddest of all our States is for the most part the floor of an enormous elevated sink commonly called the Great Basin. It is entirely walled around by high mountains. Clouds blown inland from the Pacific Ocean pile up in great masses against the ponderous barrier of the Sierra Nevada. Repelled by this hulk, the clouds break in rain, snow, and hail. Only a small part of the moisture gets through the mountain serrations. Sometimes a powerful "Maria," brought in by a terrific wind known locally as a "Washoe zephyr," sweeps over the top of the barrier and deposits great depths of snow, or sends torrents of rain to the valleys below. The storm rarely has the force to carry its moisture into the Great Basin.

The land to the east of the Sierra Nevada is by force of nature a barren desert. So barren that Sam Clemens wrote of it in one of his first letters home to his mother: "I overheard a gentleman say, the other day, that it was 'the d—dest country under the sun'—and that comprehensive conception I fully subscribe to. It never rains here, and the dew never falls. No flowers grow here, and no green thing gladdens the eye. The birds that fly over the land carry their provisions with them. Only the crow and the raven tarry with us." [3]

From the year when history is black, the red man has eked out only a slender living in this land of little rain and limited food supply. It was so difficult to get a living that each tribe had its well-defined food domain. The Washoe Indians claimed the land on the immediate eastern slope of the Mountains. And after this tribe, the mountains, the lake, the valley, and the surrounding land to the east was named, from the days of Forty-nine, "the land of the Washoes." The highest peak in the Washoe range was Sun Mountain, later christened Mount Davidson. The people living on its slopes refer to it simply as the Great Mountain.

The melting snows in the mountains cascade down the cañons to the valleys below, flow out into the desert for a hundred miles or so, then end ignominiously in brackish, treeless lakes, or vanish unbelievably in desert sand. Their oddity has been accounted for by an old prospector and mountaineer who told Dan De Quille,[4] Sam Clemens' close friend and literary associate in Nevada, how they were formed by the good Lord who "at the time he was creatin' and fashionin' of this here yearth, got along to this section late on Saturday evening. He had finished all of the great lakes, Lake Superior, Michigan, Huron, Erie and them—had made the Ohio, Missouri and Missippi rivers, and, as a sort of wind-up, was about to make a river that would be far ahead of anything he had yet done in that line. So he started in and traced out the Humboldt River, and Truckee River, and Walker River, and Reese River, and

all the other rivers, and he was leadin' of them along, calkerlatin'
to bring 'em all together into one big boss river and then lead that
off and let it empty into the Gulf of Mexico or the Gulf of California,
as might be most convenient; but as he was bringin' down and
leadin' the several branches—the Truckee, Humboldt, Carson,
Walker, and them—it came on dark and instead of trying to carry
out the original plan he jist tucked the lower ends of the several
streams into the ground, whar they have remained from that day
to this." [5]

A slender margin of green fringing these streams contrasts
sharply with the weather-beaten ridges along their banks. Looking
eastward from Sun Mountain, the eye sees no end to the scarred and
treeless mountain ranges. A hundred or more of them roll on to the
Wasatch Mountains. Sagebrush, bunch grass, scrubby pine, and
small cedar trees, scattered over the hills and mountains, hide the
raw bones of the rocky ridges. Only the tarantula, horned toad, rattle-
snake, and jack rabbit survive the severe heat in summer and the
extreme cold in winter.

Indeed so formidable was this Basin area the lowliest Indian
barely survived in it. His red brothers around the rim advised the
explorers against entering it. It was, therefore, the last area of these
United States to be explored by a white man. They had gone north
of it, south of it, and along the eastern border, but not into it. However, by geographic necessity, it had to be crossed to reach California
by the most direct route.

Indeed as late as 1835, the year Sam Clemens was born, there
were few records of any white man in the Great Basin. Only the
bravest had overcome the fear of its formidable reputation. No one
remained longer than was necessary to trap along its streams or to
pass through it. The emigrant parties recorded their hardships and
their losses of life, both human and animal. They cursed the bad
water, the burning alkali dust, and the long and trackless wastes.

Over this route to the Pacific Coast went the history-making
parties. Those intrepid souls who survived the ordeal were proud
of their strength and endurance. There is no episode in all history
of mankind quite like the first wave of exploring, trapping, and
trading Americans who swept across the Great Plains, over the
Rocky Mountains, through the Great Basin, and on to the Pacific
Coast. It is today a part of the flesh and blood of the generation

which has descended from those hardy pioneers. Proud indeed is the man or woman who can say, "My grandfather was the first man to explore this section," "My great-grandfather trapped on this stream," or "My ancestor traded on this trail."

When the Clemens family moved to Hannibal, Missouri, Sam began to learn of the great West. His formal education started at the time when the first organized emigrant party set out for California in 1841. In this year the Bidwell-Bartleson party, the first one to travel with wagons, answered the injunction of other Americans who had gone to California.[6]

Had the inquisitive youngsters of that time looked into the wagons of these travelers, they would have seen boats—or the materials with which to build them. On the early maps of the western part of the United States the Great Basin was labeled by different names—Mysterious Land on one of them, Unknown Land on another one. But on most of these maps there was shown a sizeable river, named Rio Santa Buenaventura. It rose in the Great Salt Lake and flowed southwest through the Great Basin, reaching the Pacific Ocean just south of San Francisco Bay. It must have been comforting to these voyagers to look forward to the pleasant last days of their journey. At the Salt Lake they would load all of their goods into the boats and float leisurely down to California. Discouraging must have been their disillusionment when they learned that there was no river, and that the most hazardous part of their journey was before them.

In fact, the members of this party had to abandon their wagons on the Salt Desert, throw away most of their provisions, mount their horses, and ride as fast as they could over this Mysterious Land lest they be overcome with thirst and starvation.

The real facts of the Unknown Land were finally to be told in the reports of Captain John C. Frémont after he had made two expeditions into it, 1843–1845. On the return from these trips he wrote a full account of the country. These reports, published by Congress, were spread by the thousands over the United States. The Clemens family kept up on the current news; they must have read how Frémont and his party toiled over the desolate reaches of the West; how his men had to walk most of the way . . . the rocks cut the feet of their horses; how, when their provisions gave out, they had to eat their dogs; how they had to abandon the little cannon, obtained in St. Louis to protect them from the Indians, in a remote cañon in the Sierra Nevada.

Frémont learned much about the Unknown Land from the Indians, found there was no Buenaventura River, dispelled the ignorance that had clouded it and warned against its dangers. He was the first American to write about the land of the Washoes—he had been guided by one of these Indians while passing through their territory. The rivers, the lakes, the mountains, and the passes in this region were named by the Great Pathfinder. They are monuments to his work.[7]

After his reports came out, hundreds of parties left the settlements along the Mississippi River, last outposts on the way to California. One of the main trails passed through Hannibal and extended directly west to St. Joseph, Missouri. Sam's knowledge of affairs at large came earlier than for most boys of the same age. Because of his father's death in 1847, he left school at the age of nine, and soon thereafter he was apprenticed as a printer to Joseph P. Ament, owner and publisher of the *Missouri Courier*. Some writers on the life of Sam Clemens regret that his formal education was cut short so early in life, but according to his own statements he was then almost a man. For hadn't he drunk his grandpappy's toddy at six weeks, and hadn't he learned to smoke cigars at nine years?

The newspaper apprenticeship gave him a finer education, in fact, than any public school in the United States could have given him. During it he had to learn spelling, reading, composition, history, current events, politics, and a lot of other things valuable to the adolescent. And in it he was thrown constantly with adult associates. He did so well at his trade that in less than a year's time he could set type, run the job press, and take charge of circulation; and in 1847, when the telegraph reached Hannibal, he was given charge of the extras that brought the news of the Mexican War. He was now a sort of subeditor. The youthful printer could not have known in reporting the stirring events of this war that not many years would go by before he would be taking an active part in the territory acquired by that war—Nevada and California were included in the Mexican Cession.

What gossip in the households of the northern towns of Missouri must have gone the rounds when the Mormons were driven from Nauvoo, Illinois, just across the river and a short distance to the north of Hannibal; when they started on their long journey to their western Zion! The thousands of saints, men, women, and children, some riding in wagons, some on horseback, many walking and pushing their worldly possessions in hand carts before them, set out to the Great Salt Lake. They, too, were filling in the West.

Soon these people would claim all of the Great Basin and ask for a separate State, Deseret. And through their perseverance they were to make the desert relax its austerity ... "Oh, the Mormon roses and the Mormon poplars! Wherever the Mormons went, they planted; wherever they have been, there roses bloom." [8] There they planted the poplar trees—symbols, it was said, of friendliness to their persecuted brothers. They were the first people to live successfully in the land of the Washoes.

People along the Mississippi were all astir in the late forties. Empire builders like John Sutter were advertising for settlers to come to California. One of the greatest migrations set out in 1846— "The Year of Decision," Bernard De Voto has called it. Along the trail that year were other Americans, boosters for Oregon and for California. Lansford W. Hastings, ambitious to be the head of some form of government in California, crossed the Great Basin to be on the trail personally and to urge the emigrants to follow his advice and to settle in "the land of milk and honey." Hastily adopting any means of recruiting his supporters, he wrote letters, placed them securely in forked sticks, and left them at intervals on the trail. One Illinois party of that year, led by Jacob Donner, listened to Hastings' advice, and followed his recommended Cut-off; for doing so, they left to posterity the tragic tale of hardships, sufferings, and deaths.

The yen to go west must have stirred in the breasts of many young people, one of whom was Sam Clemens. In his autobiography he confessed to feeling it when he saw one of his young companions start out in 1849. After he had witnessed the setting out of the party, he enviously wrote: "When he was twelve years old, he crossed the plains with his father amid the rush of the gold seekers of '49; and I still remember the departure of the cavalcade when it spurred westward. We were all there to see and to envy. And I can still see that proud little chap sailing by on a great horse, with his long locks streaming out behind. We were all on hand to gaze and envy when he returned, two years later, in unimaginable glory—for he had traveled. None of us had ever been forty miles from home. But *he* had crossed the continent. He had been in the gold mines, that fairy-land of our imagination. . . . We would have sold our souls to Satan for the privilege of trading places with him." [9]

When President Polk gave quasi-official announcement of the discovery of gold in California in his December message to Congress, thousands of excited, gullible suckers rushed to the gold fields. Among them were some intelligent people, and a few rich ones; but most of them were poor, though stout-hearted. The weak turned back, or died on the trail and were buried in unmarked graves. They jammed every discoverable route to the Pacific Coast. They crossed the Mississippi River at every point. Many pushed up the Missouri, proceeded up the Platte to its source, crossed South Pass, went on to Salt Lake City, and pushed across the difficult part of the journey—the Great Basin with its dreaded Forty-mile Desert. They clambered through every pass in the Sierra Nevada Mountains to be the first on the ground in the mad scramble for gold. Most of the routes went through the land of Washoe, incorporated in 1850 into the western part of the Territory of Utah.

The Mormons living in the western Utah valleys of Washoe, Carson, Eagle, Steamboat, and on the Truckee Meadows, were urged by their spiritual leaders to keep their heads and not to desert Zion by rushing to the gold regions, but to remain on the land, trade with the argonauts, and thereby save their souls and—incidentally—make great profits. Boasts that turnips were sold for $2 a bunch and flour for $1 a pound at the trading posts were common among the Mormon traders.

The first permanent settlement in Washoe was made by John Reese in 1851, a Mormon from Salt Lake City, on the west side of Carson Valley.[10] He set up a branch trading post known to all travelers as Mormon Station. Starting with a few loads of provisions in 1851 in a partially finished log house, he built up a trade which increased in three years to one which he sold for $23,000. Enoch Reese, the brother of John, had a large store in Salt Lake City, which, in turn, was a branch of a larger store in Brooklyn, New York. Observe that the Reeses' trading posts were the first chain stores across the United States.

Among the discoverers of gold at Sutter's Mill at Coloma was one John Bigler. He was a member of the Mormon Battalion recruited in Iowa from the migrating Mormons of 1846. They had been ordered to report to General Kearny at Fort Leavenworth and to assist him in taking Santa Fé, New Mexico. Their experiences in charting roads in the unexplored Southwest gave him a knowledge which served him well later.

Wishing to return to their families in Utah, after having been mustered out of the Army in California, the Battalion members journeyed north to Sutter's Mill. Since winter was coming on, they remained to work for Sutter. Bigler was present at the time James Marshall picked up the nuggets in the tail race of the mill.

In April the snows had melted sufficiently for the party to start over the Sierra Nevada. No road led over the mountains to Carson Valley, so Bigler directed the work of mapping out one. Hardships in clearing away the logs and boulders, and great personal suffering, attended the project; and there were attacks by Indians in which two of the party were killed.

When they finally reached Carson Valley they camped along the banks of the Carson River. About halfway down its course, they stopped at noon on a little tributary stream which flowed down a cañon from a great mountain to the west of them. Bigler decided to pan some of the dirt in the bed of the creek. He found there was gold also in the beds of the streams on the *east* side of the Sierra Nevada Mountains. Putting this gold dust in his pouch along with his gold found in California, Bigler and the party went on their way to the Great Salt Lake. They met many parties organized to go to California. To these they showed their gold and told of the new discoveries in Washoe.[11]

To this small discovery came more miners. At first only gold was found; later came the silver from which sprang the great cities of the Comstock Lode, which made many millionaires, and which betrayed many more into misery and bankruptcy. With its wealth, blocks of some of the finest buildings in San Francisco were built, and from it came many of the great enterprises of California and Nevada. It also meant that not many years were to go by before a Territory was organized and its territorial officers appointed. To that Territory came Samuel Langhorne Clemens—"only to see," he said, but actually to stay three years, and to become the greatest literary product of the mining frontier.

Other parties camped on the Carson River, and they, too, found gold. A member of the Orr party on his way west found the first nugget, a proud possession of John Orr for the rest of his life. This party named the tributary Gold Creek, and the cañon through which it flowed Gold Cañon. Prospectors and miners, like moths flitting from flame to flame, came over the mountains from California to try their luck in Gold Cañon. After 1851 there were teamsters, traders, herders, placer miners, grog-shop owners, merchants, and farmers who came regularly to the Cañon; they came in the spring and remained as long as the water flowed, returning to California for the dry months of the year.

Before long the mining regions of the Washoe district were getting notices in the California papers. Little settlements sprang up near the diggings—Chinatown (Dayton), at the mouth of Gold Cañon; Johntown, up the Cañon a short distance; Silver City, halfway up the ravine and at the forks of Gold Cañon and American Flat Ravine; Gold Hill, built on the red mound at the head of the Cañon. Over the sharp divide and at the head of Spanish Ravine, where a few miners had built their shacks and dugouts, mushroomed another little settlement, to which various names were given: Pleasant Hill, Mount Pleasant Point, Ophir, Ophir Diggings, Virginia Town. It was finally baptized Virginia City by James Fennimore, "Finney" or "Old Virginia," the real discoverer of the Comstock Lode.

In fact, so many settlers came into western Utah that some form of government was necessary. Governor Brigham Young did not heed the pleas until he learned that these people were seeking annexation by California. He acted quickly then and had the Utah Territorial Legislature create Carson County—a huge area embracing all of the Land of Washoe. Mormon Station became Genoa and was made the county seat. In order that the Zionites might outnumber the Gentiles in electing a full corps of county officers, many Mormon colonizers were sent out to Washoe. Among them were Mr. and Mrs. Alexander Cowan.[12] Mrs. Cowan, born Allison "Eilley" Orrum in the highlands of Scotland, had been converted to Mormonism when she was a young girl of sixteen years. She was sealed to Bishop Hunter, and came to America with her sister and brother-in-law, settling in Nauvoo, Illinois. When she learned of the polygamous practices of her husband, she would have none of them and straightway divorced him, later marrying Cowan.

The Cowans were among the colonizers of Carson County in 1855. When they arrived in Genoa, they were so poor that their brethren took them in. A kindly Mormon family allowed them to sleep on the floor until they could get a cabin built on the land claim they had acquired near a warm spring at the base of the mountain in Washoe Valley. Many more Mormons came to these beautiful valleys, little farmhouses were built, rose gardens planted, and the omnipresent poplar trees set out. They prospered exceedingly well.

But their peace, happiness, and religious independence were not to last long. Bigotry, prejudice, and design seized the government at Washington. The Mormons must be punished; it was reported they had defied the Federal authorities and burned their records. An army would be sent against them. Pro-Southern leaders in the nation's capital, foreseeing an impending war, coveted the great West with its gold and rich lands.

Messengers on fleet ponies came to the valleys of Carson County in late summer—all faithful Mormons must return to their holy city. It must be protected against the oncoming army. What obedience to the command of a leader! In a few days every man, woman, and child had left his farm, his crops in the fields ready to be harvested, the ripened fruit on his trees, his little home and rose garden, to go to the aid of his beloved leader. Everyone went, I say, save Eilley Orrum Cowan. Refusing to follow her husband and her people, she remained on the land claim in Washoe Valley for a while. There was nothing there that she could do to earn a living, but she could go up to Gold Cañon and wash, cook, and sew for the miners.

2

MUCHA PLATA! MUCHA PLATA![1]

SOON AFTER THE MORMONS HAD ABANDONED THEIR farms, Gentiles from California came over to the valleys and bought, leased and preëmpted the settlements. Up in Gold and Six Mile Cañons the miners worked over every inch of placer ground. As they approached the east side of Sun Mountain, from whence came the gold they washed, a bluish-gray dirt cut down the returns in their pans and their rockers. With curses they threw it away, not knowing that, in each pan of dirt, they were throwing away many dollars' worth of silver. No one knew that silver veins ribbed the great mountain save two young brothers, Ethan Allen and Hosea Ballou Grosch, sons of a Pennsylvania Universalist minister.

Of all the dramatic stories emerging from the mining rushes to the West, none can equal the pathos, the devotion, and the bravery of that of the Grosch brothers. It deserves to be immortalized. No history of early Nevada is complete without it.[2]

In the spring of 1849 while they were living with their parents in Reading, Pennsylvania, they were seized with the impulse to go to California to make a fortune. To *make* a fortune was uppermost in their minds; and they were on the brink of realizing it when Fate dealt to them one of the perverse hands that lend the true color of epic tragedy of our Western saga.

After desultory success in gold mining in California, they came to Gold Cañon in 1852. Presently they became convinced there was silver to be found in the veins in the surrounding country. Educated boys, they had a considerable library of scientific works along with their chemical apparatus and their assayer's tools. They found great comfort in each other's companionship, and did not associate with other miners working in the cañon. But a Mexican, known only as "Old Frank," told them that *"Mucha plata! Mucha plata!"* was all above them in the hills. None of the ignorant miners knew anything about assaying. However, the Grosch boys, studying their books on metallurgy, decided to test the blue stuff which was clogging the riffles of their rockers. What jubilant letters they wrote to their father, and how happy he must have been to read of his sons' good fortune!

They made two more visits to Gold Cañon, one in 1856 and another in 1857. On both trips they examined the surrounding country more thoroughly. Their investigations convinced them that they were on the road to fortune. With the aid of their Mexican guide, they located and determined the extent of the silver lodes running across Sun Mountain and extending east, west, and south. They sent diagrams of their locations to their father. The excellent teamwork of the boys kept one busy placering for gold to buy grub while the other one followed the silver experiments. Late in the summer of 1857 Allen, the older brother, wrote home that the silver assay was $3500. Undoubtedly the clergyman's family would soon be lifted to great wealth. The boys were now sure of success. Only one thing stood in their way—they had no money to work the ledges. The old Spanish proverb was surely true: "It takes a gold mine to work a silver mine."

Although the Grosch boys were reserved in disposition, they had enlisted the aid of several of their friends in the project; all of them promised money. They also knew some capitalists in San Francisco who would extend them loans. George Brown, the station-keeper at Gravelly Ford on the Humboldt, promised $600. Mrs. Laura Ellis, boarding-house keeper at Johntown, had saved $1500—she was willing to risk this hard-earned money. The boys even showed her the sharp-pointed escarpment on the north side of Sun Mountain. "There, down at the base of that point——" they said.

Near the forks of American Flat Ravine and Gold Cañon, the boys had built themselves a stone cabin. In it they had made themselves a comfortable home and workroom, with shipshape built-in bunks and a fireplace. In one corner of the cabin they built a retort for experimenting on their blue stuff; their reference books helped them work out their chemical formulas. In June, 1857, Allen wrote his father that he was confident they had struck the monster vein. "We struck the vein without difficulty, and have followed two shoots down the hill. . . . We have pounded up some of each variety of rock and set it to work by the Mexican process. . . . The rock of the vein looks beautiful . . . soft . . . violet-blue . . . indigo blue . . . blue-black . . . and greenish-black."

All summer they worked and experimented; and when their

money was about gone, Brown promised he would come at once. But on August 19, while Hosea was out prospecting, he struck his foot a blow with his pick just below the ankle. The injury, which at first seemed only a small wound, rapidly grew worse. There was no doctor closer than Placerville, more than a hundred miles away. It was with the greatest difficulty that they found the simple lotions for a poultice. Everyone helped to care for the young miner, but daily he grew worse. Bad news came to the boys when they learned that their friend Brown had been murdered by the Indians. Hosea worried over this misfortune, but he stood up well under the pain until gangrene set in and tetanus locked his jaws. Unable to say a word to Allen, who stayed constantly beside his failing brother, Hosea died on September 2, 1857.

With the help of the miners, Allen made a crude coffin, bought Hosea a new suit of clothes, and laid him to rest in a grave near the forks of the cañons. The grave was well-marked with a rock cairn. Allen was so overcome with grief and lonesomeness that he did not write his father for almost a week.

And then there were to be only two more letters ever received in that ministerial home in Pennsylvania from the remaining son. In the first, from this remote cañon in western Utah, Allen Grosch poured out his grief to his father: "In the burst of my sorrow I complained bitterly of the dispensation which deprived me of what I held most dear of all the world, and I thought it most hard that he should be called away just as we had fair hopes of realizing what we had labored for so hard so many years. But when I reflected how well an upright life had prepared him for the next, and what a debt I owed to God in blessing me for so many years with so dear a companion, I became calm and bowed my head in resignation. 'O, Father, thy will, not mine, be done.'"

In a few days he wrote the second and last: "I feel very lonely and miss Hosea very much—so much that at times I am strongly tempted to abandon everything and leave the country altogether, cowardly as such a course would be. But I shall go on, it is my duty, and I cannot bear to give anything up until I bring it to conclusion. By Hosea's death you fall heir to his share in the enterprise. We have, so far, four veins. Three of them promise much."

After Hosea's death, Allen set about to close up their affairs for the year. Bills must be paid; their books, papers, and assays had to be boxed up; and their cabin should be put into shape for the winter. By the time all of this was done, it was late in November. Just before he set out for California with his friend Richard Bucke, it was said he put Henry Tompkins Paige Comstock, a gaunt, tall Canadian, in charge of his cabin.

Packing some of his papers and some samples of the silver ore along with supplies on a burro, Allen and Bucke set out to cross the Sierra Nevada Mountains on November 20, 1857. The story of the harrowing trip was told in detail by Bucke in the daily record he kept. They followed up the Truckee River as far as Squaw Valley, where they struck out across the mountainous trail, nine thousand feet high. Soon they were overtaken by a storm which obliterated the trail and hemmed them in their solitary camp as within the walls of a prison. They debated whether to turn back or to push on; they decided it was better to go on. The delay had exhausted their provisions, and they were forced to kill their donkey for meat. They climbed from crag to crag, always waist-deep in snow, dragging themselves up by bushes and jutting rocks, struggling desperately. They reached the summit on November 29.

It was a clear but bitterly cold day. They could not see far, for the wind blew the loose snow in eddies about them. Down the other side they started. Soon another storm broke over them; again they were almost overcome with the heavy deluge of snow. They ate their scanty store of meat, but it was not sufficient to restore their strength.

At this point Allen, who had stuck to his maps and assays throughout the journey, decided to abandon them also. He tied them up securely in a piece of canvas and deposited them in the hollow of a large pine tree. The hole was quite small, and after depositing the records he cut a mark on the tree with his knife and rolled a good-sized boulder in front of the hollow. "Surely," he thought, "it won't be difficult to find the spot in the spring."

The young travelers toiled on until they came to the middle fork of the American River. If they followed this stream down its course, it must lead to some signs of life. But such was not their good fortune. It had now been two weeks since they left Gold Cañon. Hour by hour they grew weaker. On December 5, Bucke proposed that they both lie down and die; but Allen, although the weaker of the two men, urged his companion on until nightfall. Completely exhausted, they made their beds in silence and lay down to sleep. When they awakened in the morning, they were barely able to crawl on their hands and knees.

Hope was dead, but resolution enabled them to drag themselves on while they could move hand or foot. From daybreak till noon they crawled less than a mile, and their eyes were closing from overpowering faintness, when they heard the bark of a dog and saw a thin wreath of smoke in the air. The shock of knowing that they would soon be rescued was so great that they sank down with exhaustion. Grosch said he would rather die there than make any further effort. However, Bucke roused himself and went in the direction of the smoke. He discovered a party of deer hunters and, after telling them his story briefly, took them to Grosch, lying a few hundred yards away, and then sank down beside him.

The miners carried the two men to nearby Last Chance Mining Camp. They were put to bed, but they could not sleep; food was brought to them, but they could not eat. Allen was not able to speak, and never again uttered an intelligible word. The legs of both men had frozen to above the knees—they were already turning black. With a crude hunting knife, one of Bucke's legs and a part of the other foot were amputated. But Allen, comprehending what was happening, fought off the necessary operation. Bucke slowly recovered; Allen Grosch died on December 19, 1857.

In Allen's last letter to his father, he had written: "Hosea and I had lived so much together, with and for each other, that it was our earnest desire that we might pass out of this world as we had passed through it—hand in hand." This wish, at least, was granted them. United in life, in death they were not divided. When Bucke was well enough to be moved, he was taken to his old friend, Alpheus Bull, at Michigan Bar Mining Camp. The generous miners took up a collection, with which he returned to his family in Canada.

In the summer of 1865, Schuyler Colfax, later Vice-President of the United States, made an overland trip to the West. In his trunk he carried a white marble slab sent by the Reverend A. B. Grosch from Philadelphia. On June 27, Colfax participated in the exhuming of Hosea's body and its reburial in the little hillside cemetery of Silver City.[3] About two hundred people were present. Today one can visit this graveyard and read:

Hosea B., second son of Reverend A. B. Grosch
—Born at Marietta, Pa., April 23, 1826
—Died at Gold Canyon, Nev., Sept. 2, 1857

Years later Richard Bucke had a headstone erected over the grave of Allen Grosch at Last Chance, California.

During these years Sam Clemens had become a full-fledged journeyman printer. Desirous to see other parts of the United States, his restless spirit urged him to seek jobs elsewhere. From Hannibal he went to St. Louis, then on to New York, where he saw the Crystal Palace.[4] He had been working in Philadelphia a short time when he heard of an organized company that was going to South America; he resolved to join it. But this resolution was changed on his trip down the Mississippi. Sitting up in the pilot house far above the water and looking out and beyond the river's edge, he visualized himself as a river pilot. To become a first-class pilot became his burning passion.

During these same years events were rapidly shaping themselves in the Land of Washoe which were to change his life as completely as his trip down the River. The rapidly approaching Civil War was soon to bring an end to his piloting days; the rediscovery of silver in Washoe was to bring such a rush of people that a new Territory had to be created. Sam Clemens was to find his literary lodestone in the silver camps of the Territory of Nevada.

For almost two years the secret of the location of the silver lodes on Sun Mountain lay in the graves of the Grosch brothers. One day in the spring of 1858 Comstock learned of the death of Allen Grosch. Dead men tell no tales—from that moment forward Comstock claimed the Grosch cabin and everything in it. During the long winter months he had contemplated the contents of the box in which Allen had put their papers. Now this box belonged to him. He took advantage of the knowledge thus acquired, and set out to locate the ledge from which had come the ore recorded in the Grosch assays.

Comstock never revealed the source of his expert knowledge of the ledges in the vicinity of Sun Mountain. And it was further believed by men living in Gold Cañon that the Grosch brothers had not in fact trusted him with anything, nor was it likely that they had told him anything about their discoveries. After Allen left, Comstock probably went over the ground where he had seen the boys prospecting and located the likeliest places.

All during the summer and fall of 1858 the miners, now numbering a hundred or more, placered in Gold and Six Mile Cañons. Both cañons cut deep gashes on the sides of Sun Mountain. From the decomposed ledges the precious gold and silver dust ran off into the ravines below. As the miners approached the head of Gold Cañon, their returns began to increase. One day Old Virginia (James Finney) reached the red mound on the steep southern slope, half covered with snow but with some of the red dirt exposed by a gopher hole. He decided to pan some of the dirt. It literally sparkled with gold dust. Locating his claim, he let in a few of his "pals." To the red mound he gave the name of Gold Hill. Unwittingly the south end of the great ledge on Sun Mountain had been found. The news of the Gold Hill discovery reached the miners down the Cañon, even as far as Johntown.

There was an immediate rush. The horde swarmed over the Hill and up the adjacent ravines. Ever mindful of business, Nicholas ("Dutch Nick") Ambrose closed his eating house and bar in Johntown and moved up to serve the hungry and thirsty miners. Eilley Orrum Cowan, with the help of her star boarders, Lemuel S. ("Sandy") Bowers, Joseph Plato, and James Rogers, moved her boardinghouse and set it alongside that of Dutch Nick. These two houses were the first ones built in Gold Hill. Sandy Bowers acquired a good claim and called it "The Imperial." When Jim Rogers failed to pay Eilley his board bill, she jumped his claim, which adjoined that of Sandy Bowers. Sandy and Eilley beside each other in mining, why not in matrimony?

"Old Pancake," the sobriquet the miners had now given the lazy Comstock after he acquired the Grosch cabin, located a claim after Old Virginia and his three companions had staked out four claims of fifty feet apiece, the limit allowed by the Gold Hill Mining District. Comstock was exasperated. It was his ground, he said. By rights all of Washoe was his land. And ever after, he said it was his claim. In fact, he talked so much about his discovery that everyone began to refer to it as "Comstock's vein." All summer long the miners worked in Gold Cañon, cleaning up on their new discovery. Miners who were not so fortunate as to get in on the Gold Hill strike began to search in every cañon in the countryside. If there were rich placers in one of them, there must be equally rich dirt in other cañons.

Late in the spring of 1859, Patrick McLaughlin and Peter O'Riley were washing their dirt in Six Mile Cañon. As summer approached and the slender stream of water which ran off the north side of Sun Mountain grew less and less, they searched around for a larger source of water. Going up a ravine in which some Mexicans were working, they found a good spring of water. Appropriating the spring without questioning whether anyone had a previous claim on it, they set about to dig it out in order to make a larger hole in which to puddle their dirt. The ravine had been called Spanish Ravine—"Mexican" and "Spanish" being synonymous for Americans—and the placer claim in it, the Ophir Claim. With plenty of water the two Irishmen began to clean up a fortune.

Old Pancake, smarting in the conviction that he had been "done out" of the Gold Hill diggings, determined to be on the ground at any new discovery. Riding his half-blind plug over the hills, he came upon McLaughlin and O'Riley cleaning up. It was toward evening on June 12 or 13, 1859, when he saw their pile of gold dust—one day's clean-up. He could scarcely believe his eyes. It must be—*it was* —the lost Grosch ledge. There was no mistake about it this time. Jumping from his horse, he said, "You have struck it, boys! But this ground is mine and I can prove it." He fumed and raged, swore and stamped the ground.

His claim on the surrounding land was for ranch purposes. He had located one hundred and sixty acres, including the spring and the trench where McLaughlin and O'Riley were washing. They were surprised but agreed to take him in. Thoughtful of his friends, he further claimed that he and "Manny" (Manuel Penrod) had taken it up together and that he had sold one-tenth of it to "Ole Virginny." It was later believed that Comstock promised Virginny to let him in on any discovery that he might make in the future, in return for which Virginny promised to do the same for him. This assumption seems to have some basis, for Old Pancake had no sooner closed his verbal deal with the Irishman to let him in on the Ophir Claim and his agreement to let them share his spring water, than he was off to Gold Hill to see Ole Virginny. He must acquire his one-tenth share.

As usual, Ole Virginny was in his cups. Comstock offered him his mustang, $40, and a bottle of "tarantula juice," the boys' name for the brand of whiskey sold to them. Virginny had not yet learned of the strike. When he was sober enough to take a good look at his payoff, he found he had a blind mustang. So far the claims were yielding only gold. The blue stuff was still being thrown away. The Ophir continued to pay the McLaughlin and O'Riley team a thousand dollars a day. Soon the news spread to Johntown, Chinatown (Dayton), and to the valleys. Their denizens all came to see and to wonder.

Comstock told all of them that he had discovered the new strike; that it was his ground, but that he had given the boys shares in it. He was so rich that he could afford to give part of it away. Parties of men and women from Genoa came up the Cañon. To one of the women he gave a $300 pan of gold dust. If Old Pancake was possessive, he was at the same time generous. He staked off one claim on the side of the mountain and gave it to William ("Uncle Billy") Chollar. Down near a hot spring in Eagle Valley lived a man known variously as "Curry," "Abe Curry," and "Old Abe Curry." Comstock located a claim jointly for him and Alvah Gould; this bit of ground became the fabulously rich Gould & Curry Mine. L. Savage, a farmer on the Truckee, was presented with a part of the ledge. It, too, proved a bonanza. The Hale and Norcross Mine was a part of the Comstock ranch lands. Comstock was now the greatest man in all the Territory. Everyone called the ledge "The Comstock Lode." His name, not that of John Orr, nor of Hosea or Allen Grosch, nor of McLaughlin or O'Riley, was immortalized.[5]

Comstock may be the name of the ledge, but not of the town that soon began to sprawl out over the steep slope of Sun Mountain. Ole Virginny, of whom it has been said that, of all the boys in the Cañon, he had the most to do with the real discovery of the ledge, was to give his name to it. One day, shortly after the first rush to Ophir "Diggings," he stumbled over the rough ground strewn with huge boulders. In his headlong sprawl he dropped his ever-present bottle of whiskey. Teetering to his feet, he gathered himself together and declared with drunken pompousness, "I baptize this ground Virginia."

For a time the old settlers had the new diggings to themselves and were hard at work with their rockers, saving only the gold and paying no further attention to the silver than to curse it for interfering with their operations. Farmers continued to bring to the miners fresh meat, butter, eggs, and vegetables. Business was good; the boys had lots of gold dust to exchange for good grub.

One day about July 1, 1859, Augustus Harrison, a ranch worker for Stone and Gates, owners of the crossing and trading post on the Lower Truckee, came over to view the strike. Lying around on the ground near the spring was a lot of hard ledge matter. Mexican miners in the country had said that it was rich in silver. Harrison took a bagful of the specimens back with him and told J. F. Stone what he had heard about the rock. When Stone made a trip shortly thereafter to Nevada City, California, he took the specimens with him and left them at the newspaper office. The editor of the *Nevada Journal* turned them over to Judge James Walsh, who in curiosity took them to Melville Attwood in Grass Valley and to J. J. Ott in Nevada City. These men assayed the ore by the humid process; Attwood's result was $3000 to the ton.

It was agreed among the few who thus became aware that a great silver vein had been struck in Washoe that the news be kept a deep secret, at least until they could cross the mountains and locate ground for themselves. But every one of them had intimate friends who surely would not tell anyone, and these bosom friends had more friends in whom they had utmost confidence. Assayer Attwood wrote to his good friend Donald Davidson, the representative of the House of Rothschild in San Francisco, on June 30: "My assays gave from 15 to 20 per cent of silver. I am much hurried and will write you again on Walsh's return. He will bring 200 or 300 pounds of ore down with him. You may have something better than sulphurets to ship to England. In great haste."

Although Judge Walsh did not know the results of the assay until nine o'clock in the evening, the news got around Grass Valley so fast that he and his companion, Joseph Woodworth, were scarcely out of sight on their horses before half of the town was getting ready to rush to Washoe. The next day, July 1, 1859, the *Nevada Journal* published an account of the discovery; again on July 9 the same paper confirmed the report. These items were soon copied in all California papers. In a few days hundreds of miners had left their diggings in California, flocked over the mountains on horseback, on foot, with ox teams, with packed burros, or in any way that offered. They came from the wharves and from the cities.

All during the summer and late into the fall of 1859 the passes over the mountains had a continuous stream of silver miners. The little Johntown colony was soon merged into a continuous line of huts and dugouts in the sides of the Cañon which extended the entire way to Gold Hill. Up the steep slope and over the divide to Virginia Town the newcomers threw up shanties and tents, or crawled into the open pits. They came so fast that the oldtimers were strangers in a few days. By October, 1859, Dr. Henry DeGroot and Herman Camp had run a single street, supposedly on the line of the Comstock Lode. Some years later the Doctor wrote:

"On the line of this street two houses of roughly cemented stone had been built, surrounded by straggling lines of flimsy huts. Tents of dirty, ragged canvas pieced out with tattered clothes, coated with grime; hovels of pine boards roughly nailed together and pierced by bent and rusty stovepipes; heaps of broken rocks with shapeless crevices into which men crawled like lizards; shallow pits partly covered with boards and earth and embryo adits; dark, slimy holes into which the melting snow dripped with a monotonous splash, these were the winter homes of the miners in the Washoe Mining Region in 1859."

The winter of 1859 came early, too early for all of the people to get to Washoe before the passes in the mountains were closed. Impatiently they waited for the snow to melt; a few braved the winter storms and made it over safely. The Silver Rush to Washoe was on.

3

"A PEEP AT WASHOE"[1]

IT HAS BEEN SAID THAT CALIFORNIA DREW TO HER golden shores the pick of the world; Nevada, the pick of California. The mighty flood of humanity that was swept with the tide to Eldorado in 1849 backwashed to Silverado in 1859. The first trickle of this flood came from Nevada County, California. And the first from this county were Walsh and Woodworth. They had out-distanced the friends of their friends whom they had told of the great Ophir discovery. How startled must have been Old Pancake, Ole Virginny, Sandy Bowers, Dutch Nick, Eilley Orrum, and the rest of the Gold Cañon oldtimers to see these excited Californians rushing up the cañons and swarming over the hills! Where did they get the news? Newspapers seldom came to the Ophir Diggings or to Gold Cañon. Once in a great while John A. ("Snowshoe") Thompson, the giant blond Norwegian, brought papers and letters.[2]

The newcomers arrived in ever-increasing numbers; they bar-gained, they cajoled, they persuaded, and they bought. By the fall of 1859, scarcely a man who had owned "feet" on the Lode earlier that year still had one foot of his own. Walsh and his partner succeeded in making a bargain with Comstock. "In and for the consideration of $10 and $10,990 in promissory notes——" the contract ran. He sold them not only interests in his mines but also his water rights. The new owners bought all along the Lode and many miles on either side of it—even *fifty* miles from it. Comstock, Virginny, and the rest of them chuckled with glee—the Californians would soon discover they had been cheated.

A few miners along the Mother Lode on the other side of the mountains visited Washoe in the summer of 1859. Many stayed through the winter; but most of them went back home and told their friends and relatives of the silver ledges literally poking their backs out of the mountain.

In August, Comstock and Walsh took the first ore over to Cali-fornia and sold it to Donald Davidson. Shortly thereafter Davidson visited the strike and with a company of men climbed to the top of

24

Sun Mountain. When they were returning, it was suggested that the mountain be rechristened Mount Davidson, and it has gone by that name ever since. What tricks Fate does play on some people and on some places! In less than a decade and a half, the Rothschilds, Davidson's employers, brought about the downfall of the Great Lode by their influence in the demonetization of silver, better known as the "Crime of '73." [3]

This first shipment of silver ore sold for $1.50 a pound. Smelted down, it brought $112,000—all poured out in gleaming bars of white silver bullion. They were carried through the streets of San Francisco, followed by an excited throng of people, from the Mosheimer Furnace to Alsop and Company Bank. On November 1, they were shown in the bank window. People pushed and shoved one another to get to the window to see something they had never seen before in their lives. Gold—they had seen bags of it, $50 slugs of it; but silver—never before. Everyone was asking, "Where did it come from?" "Where is Washoe?" "How can one get there?"

But the elements, that so often have assumed the role of Fate in the lives of pioneering men, played havoc with their plans. The very day after the first exhibit of silver in the United States extracted from ore found in the United States was made, a storm came up worse than any experienced in all the days the Forty-Niners had been in California. It was a terrific storm. It rained torrents on the lowlands; it flooded the rivers as they had never before been flooded; and it covered the mountains and their passes with snow that was fifty to sixty feet deep in some places. The winter of 1859–1860 was the most severe in the Land of Washoe that anyone there had known. The snow fell so deep on Mount Davidson that little settlements, though only a few hundred yards apart, were isolated. Cattle, burros, and deer died from cold and hunger; Indians starved and froze to death on the Truckee Meadows. The spring was late in coming, but when it did come "it made the road from California to Washoe ten feet deep and one hundred and fifty miles long."

Nevertheless and notwithstanding, the silver-fever-stricken miners got ready and started for Washoe. Merchants shut up their shops; sailors slipped over the sides of their boats and deserted for Washoe; ministers left their prayers unsaid and joined the crowd. Gamblers, dressed in their finest, put their cards and their loaded dice in their pockets and hiked out; brothel-house keepers whispered to their scarlet ladies that there would be business in Washoe; lawyers, miners, and less well-assorted people by the hundreds went, for no better reason than since everyone else was going, so they, too, must go. "Washoe! Washoe! Glory to Washoe!"

Barnum was right. But to his calculations of the birthrate of fools he should have added: "Once a sucker, always a sucker." From the days of '49 to the days of '59 the same crowd of gullible Americans rushed to every reported strike—genuine or "salted." They followed one rush after the other. Every one of them fell for the selfsame story. They always met each other at the same rush. So frequently did this process repeat itself that it soon became a profession practiced by certain merchants, reporters, ship owners, and supply merchants to follow along behind these moon-struck fortune seekers and to fill their wants until their money was gone.

GOLD! GOLD! GOLD! That contagious, infectious, maddening, damning, alluring hope! Just let the word be shouted—or whispered, spoken, or printed—and they are off again, victims of its fascination. It brought thousands upon thousands by land and by sea to California; once in this golden land, they followed every rush until old age or death stopped them. It was always "just over the mountain," "just around the bend of the river," or "just up the next gulch." Fortune was always playing hide-and-seek.

As early as June, 1849, the first arrivals in California rushed up beyond the snow line in the Sierra Nevadas, one hundred miles north of Downieville, to Gold Lake. It was reputed to be filled, literally filled, with golden boulders. Thousands of excited fortune seekers rushed up the mountains to the Lake, endured excruciating hardships, and by thousands returned. The faker who told the story that brought on the rush disappeared overnight. Back they came, wiser for the moment—but just wait until the word "Gold!" was uttered again. It was.

This time it was on the shores of the ocean beyond the Trinity—Gold Bluff it was, in more ways than one. Three hundred miles by sea—but what did that matter when all that one had to do was to scoop up tons of the yellow stuff? They all rushed up there—spending the time en route figuring out the weight of gold they could gather up and safely return with. On arrival the bubble burst; there was no gold on the beach. Who was the humbug who had lured them up there to spend the last bit of the gold dust they had washed from the Sacramento? Never again would they be fooled. Experience was a wise teacher.

But hearken, ye suckers! Didn't you hear that gold, abundance of it, was just discovered on the Kern River? What matter if it is seven hundred miles south of Gold Bluff? Distance lends enchantment. Off again they were with their picks and pans and shovels. Surely not all of these rumors were false. Gold and lots of it had been placered from the streams along the Sacramento. Why not the Kern? Five thousand went in the spring of 1855. They always rush in the spring. And five thousand came back from Kern River. There had now been an average of one rush a year since the days of '49.

The greenhorns were given three years to get over being fooled. Year after year and from season to season they worked away on the beds of the streams of the Mother Lode. Saving, skimping, picking up every bit of gold dust there was. They were just ripe for another rush when a high shrill voice came out of the North in 1858, out of British Columbia, from the Fraser River. Hundreds of miles away— but think nothing of it! Steamers went that way. Every purser on every steamer had his pockets bulging with nuggets found on the Fraser. The papers were full of it. They headlined: "Latest news from Fraser River. Gold by the bushel baskets!" It became a disease, a fever, an epidemic.

What matter if the gold did make the round trip from San Francisco? *They* wouldn't believe it. They had to "see the elephant," too. The ships were packed to the gunwales with freight and passengers, all bound for Fraser River. Eighteen thousand went. But lo! When they arrived, the Fraser was a raging, roaring torrent. They waited and waited. Would the river *ever* drop below the flood stage? How long could the mobs remain? The placers were under the water. They couldn't wait; their money was giving out. Many of them starved to death and were buried in unmarked graves. At length California had to bring them back. What matter if it did take $30,000 to get them home! After all, these miners, these hard-working people, were the best suckers they had.

Never, *never* again would the illusive siren lure them from their homes, their little placer plots of ground, their businesses, their professions. The word "gold" was hated, cursed, despised.

But listen, boys, there's another word in the English language— one that you have never followed before. It has never done anyone harm. Cortez, Coronado, Pizarro found it, millions of dollars' worth of it! Silver! Pure silver! Virgin silver! Mountains of it, acres of it, thousands of feet of ledges of it! "Just over the mountains" in Washoe.

This plague was a new one. No one was immunized from it. Their temperatures went up, *up*, UP, when they saw the real thing in the bank window. They, too, must go and be the first on the ground. From Grass Valley, Nevada City, and Downieville they came, five thousand strong. Over the Henness Pass and the Beckwourth Pass to the Truckee River, down the river to the Lousetown Road, and over the trail to the north end of the Comstock Lode. These roads were bad enough, but they made it.

The mobs from San Francisco, from Sacramento, and from the river towns had to go over the old California emigrant trail by the way of Placerville. At this place they were stopped. The mountain passes were not yet open. It was still March, but a few hardy souls managed to cross the Sierra Nevadas in the dead of winter. They would have gone to hell for silver. It seemed, however, that that little mountain town had every mule, burro, and horse in the State of California awaiting the first break of spring.

But let J. Ross Browne,[4] a former government clerk who had a bad case of Washoe fever, tell of his delirium. He was a Forty-Niner to California; he had followed every rush from San Diego to Puget Sound. And now he was among the crowd that was in the first silver rush in the United States.

With two pairs of blankets, one spare shirt, a plug of tobacco, a notebook, and a paint-box, he set out for Placerville in April, 1860. How fortunate for posterity was that little paint-box! Browne has left the only graphic picture of the great Rush to Washoe. His book, *Crusoe's Island: A Ramble in the Footsteps of Alexander Selkirk with Sketches of Adventure in California and Washoe*, has many sketches of his fellow travelers, incidents that happened along the way, and what he found on the Comstock Lode when he arrived.

On his arrival in Placerville, Browne found the whole town in a commotion. There was not an animal in the entire community that had not been spoken for three days ahead. Every hotel and restaurant was full and overflowing; the narrow streets were blocked up with crowds of adventurers, all bound for Washoe. Goods and packages at the express office and forwarding agencies were piled high, all of them marked "Washoe, Utah Territory." How they ever got to the person to whom they were addressed is a mystery. There wasn't a post office nor an express office in all western Utah Territory; there wasn't even a town named Washoe. Washoe meant any place in a radius of fifty miles around the Comstock discovery.

Grocery stores were filling boxes and making up bags and bundles of groceries and supplies for the Washoe trade. Stables were busy packing burros, horses, and mules—starting off whole pack trains driven by Mexican vaqueros. The newspapers were full of Washoe news and advertisements for Washoe fortune seekers. Reports came in daily that enormous quantities of silver were being discovered in Washoe. Any man who wanted a fortune need only to go there and pick it up. Everybody was getting rich, hand over fist. Browne was surely glad he was at last on that road to fortune that he had been pursuing for ten years.

At once he began to look around the crowded barroom of the hotel where he was stopping for a map to lay out his route of world travel, but the only map he could find was Henry DeGroot's route from Placerville to Washoe. Overcome finally with the fatigue of his first day's journey to Washoe, he went to bed early. After several restless hours, sleep overcame him. It was a delirious sleep. Turning over for the fiftieth time, he dreamed he saw a great mountain with millions of rats climbing up its side—some were burrowing into holes, some were rolling down into bottomless pits, but all of them were labeled "Washoe." Soon the great mountain began to shake its sides with laughter, and out of a volcano on the top burst sheets of flame, through which jumped ten thousand grotesque figures in the shape of dollars with spider legs, shrieking with all their might, "Washoe! Ho! Ho! Ho! Washoe! Ho! Ho! Ho!" So vividly did he see all of these things in his dreams that he made a sketch of them for his book.

Browne was awakened early by the hurry and scurry of people getting an early start up the grade which led to Silver Land. He was among the hundreds who had to hoof it all the way to Virginia City. Joining up with four other walking silverites, each of whom had purchased supplies consisting of a tin cup, a pound of cheese, and a knife, they got off about ten in the morning. As they passed through the crowded streets of Placerville, their eyes as big as silver dollars, they were encouraged by shouts of "Go it, Washoe!"

It was one hundred and fifty miles to Washoe: up the first fifty to a nine-thousand-foot summit; down three thousand to Lake Valley, Lake Tahoe Basin; and up again to another eleven-thousand-foot summit before descending the precipitous gorge of Carson Cañon, slipping, sliding, falling, and rolling over and over down the steep trail. Once down this trail they had accomplished only half the distance. They still must go down Carson Valley to the river of the same name and then up Gold Cañon to the Lode. But come hell or high water, they must get there some way.

The first stop out from Placerville and up the trail was at a place called "Dirty Mike's," so named by the traveling public from the dirty plates, the dirty surroundings, the dirty comb tied to the common washstand and mirror, and the unkempt, unshaven, unwashed appearance of Mike himself. In the one public bedroom Browne and his companions rolled themselves up in their blankets and threw themselves on the floor with the rest of the crowd. There they slept soundly from fatigue and excitement. The next morning they resumed their trek up the trail. Trains of pack mules negotiated the climb with the greatest difficulty. Now and then a too enterprising animal, trying to keep to the edge of the road, lost his foothold, and went rolling to the bottom of the cañon hundreds of feet below. The drivers of these trains called up every malediction they possessed to urge on these struggling carriers. Browne said: "They shouted, swore, beat the mules, kicked them, pushed them, swore again; and when all these resources failed, tore their hair and resorted to prayer and meditation." A newspaper correspondent for the *Sacramento Union* noted on April 25, 1860, that he had passed in two days "1000 loaded mules, 3500 head of cattle, and from 800 to 1000 head of sheep," all bound for Washoe.

Setting out from Dirty Mike's the travelers noticed snow patches became more frequent, mountain streams larger and swifter, and the tall pine trees thicker and taller. All along the road with increasing frequency bars and taverns were in the process of erection. The oncoming crowds would find plenty of "tarantula juice" to slake their thirst and warm their blood. Board and lodging signs over tents ten feet square were common. Browne described the scene.

"An almost continuous string of Washoeites stretched like a great snake dragging its slow length as far as the eye could reach. Parties of every description and color were noted: Irishmen wheeling their worldly goods on wheelbarrows; Americans, Frenchmen, and Germans on foot leading horses heavily packed; Mexicans driving long trains of pack mules; dapper looking gentlemen riding fancy horses; women dressed in men's clothes mounted on mules or burros; Pike County specimens driving horse-drawn wagons filled with furniture and goods; organ-grinders; drovers striving desperately to get self-willed cattle up the steep grade; in short, every conceivable class was represented in this struggling pageant. Age and youth competed with one another; cripples and hunchbacks, and even sick men got up from their beds all stark mad for silver."

The second night out the Browne party reached Berry's inn, dubbed "Strawberry," it is said, by David S. Terry, former California Supreme Court justice and rabid secessionist who was hearkening the cry of Washoe. He and five of his secesh friends stopping with Berry for the night ordered good hay and beds for their horses; but when they got only straw, Terry vented his Southern temper on old Berry and gave to the inn the name it has had ever since. This place was considered the best one on the way to Washoe, but when Browne and his companions reached there, it was so crowded that they had to fight for their food and for a place to sleep on the floor. They had their dinner at the sixth setting of the table.

Tired and stiff, they set out the next morning to plod up the trail. The light rain on the way up had turned to snow, and the trail was covered to a depth of two or three feet. The pack trains had been forced to give up all hope of getting over the mountains. From three to four hundred men were trying to decide whether to continue in the snowstorm, to remain at Strawberry, or to turn back. There were eight more miles to go before they reached the summit and three more miles down the steep descent to Lake Valley near Lake Bigler (Tahoe), where the worst accommodations on the trail were said to be had, worse even than Dirty Mike's.

Browne and his friends tried to negotiate the summit—slipping, sliding, and freezing in the cold slush of the newlaid snow. When one of the men became so ill that he could not continue the journey, the party was forced to return with him to Strawberry. Starting out again the next morning, they extended themselves and made the Lake House before nightfall. Here a large party had gathered without much to eat and nothing to drink "except old fashioned tarantula juice, 'warranted to kill at forty paces.'" A third night spent in filth among an excited, swearing, scolding throng of Washoeites brought them closer to their land of Silverado. Still there was another summit to climb and still another steep descent to make. Pushing forward with all of the courage and strength they had, they finally reached the head of Hope Valley where there was one lone cabin inhabited by a trapper and his vicious dog, Diogenes. In vain they beseeched him to let them remain for the night. But, holding Diogenes by the scruff of the neck, he warned them not to approach him. There was nothing left for them to do but to trudge onward down the steep grade to Woodford's at the head of Carson Valley. There they spent the first comfortable night since they had left home.

At this place Browne set out to walk the eighteen miles to Genoa, the first settlement reached in Utah Territory. This clean, neat, prosperous Mormon settlement watched the excited crowds go by. The Mormons had not gone to California in the Gold Rush; and they were not going to Washoe in the Silver Rush. The little frame houses in Genoa were built close to the road. An old character in the village frequently wrote letters to the California newspapers. As he sat by his cabin window, he noted the crowds on their way to Washoe and wrote:

Genoa, Carson Valley
April 18, 1860

My humble habitation is built at the eastern base of the Snow Range, not far from the road which leads the fortune seeker to the promised land. This road is thronged day and night by persons plodding each way. I can sit at my window and scrutinize the features of the passers-by; here comes a fellow in a two-horse buggy, going at a 2–40 rate, leaning back in his seat and casting his eyes toward heaven, as if in thankfulness. He expects soon to be a millionaire and upon the strength of his glorious hopes has managed to get over that offensive notice posted over the livery stable door, "Positively No Credit".

Hundreds of footmen go by every day, mostly loaded down with their plunder, as if they were beasts or burden; but

"Primeval hope! Thy glittering wings explore
Earth's loneliest bounds and ocean's wildest shore!"

So upon the visages of these wayfarers, which were else a blank, a waste, a trackless desert, is depicted in most unmistakable colors the bright images of hope and anxious expectation.

Looking the other way, the Genoa observer saw coming down the road another crowd, and from the pen of this discerning reporter came the description of the pilgrims returning from their quest:

> Yonder comes a crowd from the other direction; these have "seen the elephant" and from their rueful countenances we are led to the conclusion that they are no admirers of that sagacious but unwieldy animal. However, they possess one advantage over those who have not yet paid the doorkeeper: their backs are relieved of that ponderous load with which they arrived in this country three or four weeks ago.[5]

Going on to Carson City, now almost a deserted village due to the strike in Ophir, Browne met an old friend from San Francisco, who gave him a bunk in which to sleep. He spent several days in the future capital of Nevada looking over the prospects of setting up an agency—brokerage today. Dying to "see the elephant" for himself, he took the stage for Virginia City. Upon reaching the great mining capital of Washoe, the far-famed Virginia City, he witnessed a sight which he had never before beheld. "On a slope of mountains speckled with snow, sagebushes, and mounds of upturned earth . . . frame shanties, pitched together as if by accident; tents of canvas, of blankets, of brush, of potato-sacks and old shirts, with empty whiskey-barrels for chimneys; smoky hovels of mud and stone; coyote holes in the mountain side forcibly seized and held by men; pits and shafts with smoke issuing from every crevice; piles of goods and rubbish on craggy points, in the hollows on the rocks, in the mud, in the snow, everywhere, scattered broadcast in pell-mell confusion as if the clouds had suddenly burst overhead and rained down the dregs of all the flimsy, rickety, filthy little hovels and rubbish of merchandise that had ever undergone the process of evaporation from the earth since the days of Noah."

Our writer further noted that at various intervals of space, later to emerge as city streets, human beings "rough, muddy, unkempt, and unwashed dotted the hillsides." Everyone seemed to have something to sell. "Jew clothing-men were setting out their goods and chattels in front of wretched-looking tenements. . . . Nobody had any money, yet everybody was a millionaire in silver claims. Nobody had any credit, yet everybody bought thousands of feet of glittering ore ... but not a single dime passèd hands." Every person Browne met was carrying little pieces of rock which he referred to as "cropping" and "indications" from the "Wake-Up-Jake," "Root-Hog-or-Die," "Wild Cat," "Grizzly-Hill," "Dry-Up," "Same Horse," "Let-'er-Rip," "You Bet," "Gouge-Eye," and other famous ledges and companies in which they had bought some thousands of feet.

All night long he heard through the flimsy partitions in the little box-like hotel, stuffed to suffocation with bunks, an unintelligible jargon of "cropping," "ledges," "lodes," "leads," "indications," "feet," and "strikes." "Between catnaps of oblivion" that occasionally came to him, he heard a constant babble of "fifty thousand dollars!"—"Struck it rich!"—"the Comstock Ledge!"—"the Billy Chollar!"—"Miller on the rise!"—"Mammoth!"—"Sacramento!"—"Lady Bryant!"—"a thousand feet more!"—"great bargain!"—"forty dollars a foot!" [6]

In this crowd of excited Washoeites who rushed up the mountain, who stumbled down the mountain, who raced over the Divide, and who slid down Gold and Six Mile Cañons (nothing was on the level in Washoe!) were the makers and the rulers of the West: the builders of San Francisco; the founders of colossal business enterprises; future United States senators; governors; hundreds of them; yes, ten thousand of them by the end of the first year of the Rush to Washoe. There were Yankees, secessionists, lawyers, judges, doctors, poets, editors, miners, artists, merchants, gamblers, humbug swindlers, murderers, good women, bad women, jailbirds, hurdy-gurdy entertainers, and hundreds of people—just people, unclassified—the floating scum of the Western mining towns.

No adequate description of who was in this seething mass of people can be given in generalities, but out of this crowd came the leaders of Washoe: from the little town of Downieville, California, near the northern end of the Mother Lode, came the two towering giants of the Comstock, William Morris Stewart, the greatest mining lawyer the West produced, and John W. Mackay, the richest man the Comstock made. They were friends in California; they were friends and associates on the Comstock; Stewart was Mackay's mentor, confidant, and counsel for the rest of his life.

San Francisco sent its quota of great and near-great. The secessionists, failing to swing California and its gold for the Confederacy, might get Washoe and its silver, or so thought David S. Terry, duelist for the cause, and a clever lawyer. He and his five comrades rode into Virginia City to take it for the Confederacy; Jefferson Davis had armed him with a commission to be the Governor of the new Territory of Washoe.

George Hearst heard the call of Washoe, sold out his mill in Grass Valley, invested early in the Ophir, made one of the first fortunes on the Lode, and left in June, 1860, to invest his money that was to build the foundation of the Hearst empire. Joseph Thompson Goodman, editor, printer, and all-round newspaperman, stopped in Carson City on his way to the excitement, bought out the *Territorial Enterprise*, and carted its press, type, and Chinese cook up to Virginia City to await the coming of its greatest reporter, Samuel Langhorne Clemens. Rollin M. Daggett, founder of the San Francisco *Golden Era*, rushed to Washoe, invested in real estate, became a free-lance writer, and later editor. Tom Fitch, the silver-tongued orator, writer, and would-be litterateur, came along with the throng. From over Angel's Camp way big Jim Fair, Irish-born California-trained miner who learned "to keep his eyes and ears open and his mouth shut," heard the cry and was among the first on the ground.

Dan De Quille (born William Wright), Daggett's associate on the *Golden Era*, and Clemens' co-reporter on the *Territorial Enterprise*, came to Mount Davidson with the first rush of miners. He saw the strike from the first spadeful; he knew and talked with the original discoverers; and, trusted and beloved of all who knew him, he became the Comstock's best mining reporter. A shrewd little Alsatian Jew named Adolph Sutro, tobacco-store keeper in San Francisco, followed his customers to Washoe. When in the fullness of time he drove his amazing tunnel through the Mountain, he stamped his name upon it as indelibly as Comstock had. All of these men and hundreds more of them were to be Sam Clemens' friends, associates, employers, antagonists, and victims of his satire.

When the crowds rushed helter-skelter over Washoe, looking for ledges, leads, locations, and indications of silver, they noted the rugged slopes of Mount Davidson and the irregular terrain at its base. All of these features indicated violent convulsions. In these eruptive movements the precious metal showed many ledges on the surface between which were thrown immense fragments of rock.

Every one of these ledges was located from end to end. But were these ledges part of one great lode, or was each one a separate ledge? Reduced, the question was simple: Were there many ledges on the slopes of Mount Davidson, or only one? By the consent of the miners on the Lode the original discoverers were entitled to four hundred running feet; they could put down the names of as many of their friends as they chose at two hundred feet each. Notices with dates and names had to be posted on the premises and recorded with the District Recorder. All "leads" were located with their dips, angles, and spurs—but who was to be the judge of who owned the "dips, angles, and spurs"?

The Comstock Lode was confusion worse confounded. "The Cedar Hill Company was spurring the Miller Company; the Virginia Ledge was spurring the Continuation; the Dow Company was spurring the Billy Chollar . . ." [6] and on and on *ad infinitum*. It was also a remarkable peculiarity that the great Comstock Lode was discovered to exist everywhere, however remote or divergent from the general direction. It was reported that "a gentleman discovered a continuation of the Comstock forty miles from the Ophir and at an angle of sixty degrees." The result of this confusion was two groups of protagonists—many-ledge proponents and one-ledge antagonists. A fertile field for lawyers, a tangled mess for judges, and a perfect setup for swindlers.

In the legal battle the chances for success were plainly in favor of the side with the best lawyer and the most money. But even these favorable portents had to be backed with some tangible evidence of possession. Ole Virginny had made the first location on Mount Davidson when he staked off his Ophir claim. Although drunk most of the time, he had moments of soberness. In one of these moods he wrote out his claim and carefully placed it under some rocks. When he sold his interest in this ground, the Ophir Company would not close the deal until he produced the written evidence. He maintained persistently that he had located the ground and had preserved the statement, but he was never sober long enough to produce it. Anxious to get a clear title, the new owners resorted to stratagem.

While in a drunken stupor one day, Virginny was induced by the company officials to go into a tunnel on the claim. After he was safely in it, they shut and locked an iron gate at its entrance. There they left him for the night. On the following morning the captive was sober, but a roaring, raging animal. On Virginny's promise that he would lead them to the spot where the location was buried, in return for which they promised they would bring him his daily quota of whiskey, he took them to the spot where the most precious piece of paper on the Comstock lay buried. Although the paper was two years old—yellow and covered with dust and moth eggs—the writing was still legible, and clearly laid claim to the main ledge "with all its dips, spurs, and angles."

The first rush to Washoe in 1860 dropped off rapidly; California newspapers gleefully reported that "the Comstock is all washed up." A depression followed. The values of "feet" fell rapidly. This first depression was made worse by the Piute Indian Wars of May and June. Many people fled back to California; women and children were sent out of the country or put into fortified houses; the army came, and so did many would-be Indian fighters.

But this setback was only temporary. New strikes, new ledges, new suckers rushed in, and this time twenty thousand people were on the Mountain. From the time the Mormons left in 1857, the Gentiles had besought and petitioned Congress to separate Washoe from Utah and to create a new territory. Washoe Territory it was to be, but bungling in Washington made it Nevada Territory on March 2, 1861.

It was not long before Sam and his elder brother, Orion, were on their way to Washoe—the former to make his start to literary fame, the latter to take up his new post of Territorial Secretary.

BOOK II

MATRICULATION

4

THE BROTHERS—SAM AND ORION

"IT IS PROBABLY NOT EXAGGERATION TO SAY THAT the greatest single influence in Mark Twain's life was his older brother——" * [1] From childhood through the publication of *Roughing It,* the lives of the two brothers, for better or worse, were closely interknit. Even at that, the many years in which their paths were parallel are not more revealing than the scattered periods in which they were divergent. Born of poor but proud parents, both of them had to get out early in life to learn a trade.

Both of these Clemens boys were apprenticed as printers in the same town, Hannibal, Missouri—Orion at fifteen years, Sam at eleven years. It took about the same time, two years, for each of them to become a good journeyman printer.

In 1842, seventeen-year-old Orion went down to St. Louis [2] to work at his trade, at which his accomplishment was soon recognized. Soon after he had obtained a job, he formed an acquaintance with Judge Edward Bates, a successful lawyer. Orion's father had early instilled in him the idea that he should follow a profession, particularly a legal one. His acquaintance with Judge Bates was one on which he could capitalize in that direction

Although Orion Clemens had curious dispositions in his make-up, he possessed many good characteristics. His illustrious brother gives the reader an analysis of his character in several places in his writings. He tells us that one of his most conspicuous characteristics was "eagerness." It was so all-consuming that Sam said: "He awakened every morning with a new one. It consumed him all day; it perished in the night and he was on fire with a fresh and new interest next morning before he could get his clothes on." [3]

Mr. Bates was a patient person, and he allowed Orion to bring to him each new project, from which he usually tried to dissuade him;

* Reprinted from *Mark Twain, Son of Missouri,* by Minnie M. Brashear, by permission of The University of North Carolina Press. Copyright, 1934, by The University of North Carolina Press.

but soon he found that it was not necessary to use argument or logic. The eagerness died the day it was born.

Mr. Bates did, nevertheless, encourage Orion to study law in his office. This enthusiasm lasted for an entire week. Orion then thought he wanted to be an orator; Mr. Bates gave him lessons in this new pursuit. Walking the floor and reading aloud from an English book and translating rapidly from English into French was an exercise that he recommended to Orion. But since Orion knew no French, it was therefore necessary for him to study this language. He worked at his French for several days—then he gave it up.

While he was in St. Louis, he became religious-minded: he joined a church, found that he didn't like it, and joined another. The sampling of the various churches in St. Louis for one to his liking went on until he had joined a number of them. In some of them he taught Sunday school; and every time he changed his religion, he likewise changed his teaching viewpoint and philosophy. He was the same way about his politics. But in spite of the vagaries of his mind, he was always sincere about his efforts. In business and in financial matters he was honest and steadfast in his principles.

After the boys' father died, Orion came back to Hannibal and took over the *Hannibal Journal*, a struggling village paper, with the profits from which he hoped to support his mother and himself. His two employees, Sam, and Henry, the youngest boy in the family and likewise a printer, were worked hard to make the paper pay. But Orion was impractical and visionary in business matters; he could not make a go of it financially. First he changed the name of the paper and "advanced the price—two blunders." Then he was compelled to reduce the subscription price as well as the advertising rates. "Finally as a last resort he adopted a descending scale of charges and expenditures to keep pace with his declining circulation. . . ."

Trying desperately hard to make the paper pay, without success, he sought other means for more income. Leaving Sam in charge of the paper, he made a trip to Tennessee to see if something could be realized on the large tract of land that their father had left them. It was the luckiest break Sam Clemens ever had. For the first time in his life he was in complete charge of a newspaper.[4]

It seemed to him the *Hannibal Journal* had been entirely too dull. It might be a paying proposition if it could be livened up a bit. At least he would try it. His plan was to lampoon the editor of the rival paper in the town. The satire was effective—the *Journal* perked up, and the belabored editor left town, never to be heard from again. Sam learned that this method brought attention to a paper—he used it many times in his Western journalism.

When Orion returned, unsuccessful in his land venture, he reduced Sam to the ranks and assumed the management again— a mistake he soon realized and later regretted. But for Sam it had been a great opportunity. "He got his first taste of print and he liked it." After six years of hard work, Orion sold the paper for just what he had paid for it. Sam had little or nothing for his work other than the experience in journalism and the close association with his brother. He had learned for the first time that Orion was impractical and incompetent in business matters.

There was nothing in Hannibal to keep Sam. Since he was restless to see the world, he set out to practice his trade. Jobs in St. Louis, New York, and Philadelphia, and a visit to Washington, engaged him for more than a year. However, homesickness overcame him; he wanted to see his family again. He always clung closely to his relatives. If he went on a trip or took a job, he did not keep it for a great length of time. He seemed to feel the need of his mother or his brother—someone to give focus to his efforts.

After Orion's failure in Hannibal, he left Missouri and went some distance up the River to Muscatine, Iowa, where he tried once more to publish a newspaper. There he bought a part interest in the *Muscatine Journal*.

On Sam's return to the West in 1854, he went up to Muscatine to see his mother and brothers. Just how long Sam remained in Iowa this time is not known, but it is on record that Orion tried to get him to stay and work on his paper, to which Sam replied that he was unable to "afford that luxury." Instead he returned to St. Louis to work as a compositor. His sister Pamela had married William A. Moffett, a well-to-do merchant in that city.

While in Muscatine, Orion fell in love with Mary Ellen (Mollie) Stotts, and married her on December 19, 1854. A deliciously humorous story is told about Orion's absent-mindedness when he took his bride on their wedding trip from Muscatine to Keokuk, Iowa. The River being closed with ice, the trip had to be taken by stage. When he stepped into the stagecoach after having carefully arranged the baggage, he wrapped the buffalo robe around him and leaned back with composure, awaiting the departure of the conveyance. A gentleman standing near by said to the dismayed bride, "Miss, do you go by this stage?" Orion heard the remark, sprang out, and, helping her in, exclaimed, "Oh, I forgot!" A wife was a new kind of possession to which he had not yet become accustomed.[5]

History does not tell us what became of Orion's business venture in Muscatine, but it is known that it could not have lasted long, for in June, 1855, Orion and Mollie moved to Keokuk to live. There he bought the Ben Franklin Book and Job Office, and there on September 14 their little Jane, called "Jennie," named for mother Clemens, was born.

The print shop got some business, but it did not pay enough for the little family to live on. To keep going they moved in with Mollie's father and mother. In the fall of this year Sam again got lonesome for his family and paid them a visit. Orion offered him a job in the printing office for five dollars a week, a salary far too high for the office to afford. To save himself embarrassment when he could not meet his weekly payroll, Orion took Sam in as a partner. This elevation in rank was for Sam a sadly unsatisfactory substitute for more material remuneration.

Nevertheless the junior partner of the Ben Franklin Book and Job Office was not particularly disturbed. The needs of living cared for, he had little use for money. And he did have a good time with some of the friends he had made there.

A new impulse, however, was seizing him. Reading about the fortunes to be made from gathering cocoa on the Amazon River, he resolved to take a boat to New Orleans and from that city sail to South America. Driven to raising some money for taking the trip, he agreed to write some travel letters for the *Saturday Post,* a Keokuk weekly paper. Unlike his brother Orion, Sam never underestimated his ability—the price for the first letter was five dollars; for the second, seven dollars and fifty cents. Emboldened—and perhaps a little surprised—by the meekness with which his demands were met, he raised the fee for the third to ten dollars, which was the publisher's limit. These letters, signed "Snodgrass," were the first of his writings for which he used a *nom de plume*.

When Sam went down the Mississippi River on the *Paul Jones* en route to South America, he fell in love with piloting. Horace

Bixby, one of the pilots of the *Paul Jones*, allowed him to do some steering in the daylight watches. When the adventurer reached New Orleans, and found not only that there was no boat leaving for the South American continent, but also that there "probably wouldn't be any that century," he proposed that Bixby make a pilot out of him. After consideration, Bixby set a value on his tuition of five hundred dollars, a sum which Sam did not have. However, his successful brother-in-law William Moffett, in St. Louis, let him have the fee. Within eighteen months Sam Clemens had mastered the River. He was licensed as a river pilot on September 9, 1858.

Apparently Sam set about to learn the River as thoroughly as he had learned the printer's trade. For in a comparatively short time he had accomplished the stupendous task of learning by heart the twelve hundred miles between St. Louis and New Orleans—"of knowing it as unfailingly, even in the dark, as one knows the way to his own features." He became not merely a good pilot, but admittedly one of the best and most careful pilots on the difficult run. He had charge of some of the largest and most valuable boats on the River.

During the years Sam Clemens spent as a pilot, he learned both life and men. The same variety of people traveled then as today. Of them he observed:

> I got personally and familiarly acquainted with about all the different types of the human nature that are to be found in fiction, biography, or history . . . the feature of it I value most is the zest which that early experience has given to my later reading. When I find a well-drawn character in fiction or biography, I generally take a warm personal interest in him, for the reason that I have met him before—met him on the river.

On the River, for the first time in his life, he was able to express himself with little or no restraint. He fraternized with men of all walks of life, ate with them, drank with them, and observed them under complex circumstances and in all their vagaries. He developed a tenacious memory from the rigid training in memorizing the River; and while he sat high up in the pilothouse, monarch of a river boat, he did a lot of reading, a heap of philosophizing, and some scribbling. He learned that people liked to hear him talk; he got a reputation for telling a good story. And during these years he heard the oft-repeated but none the less comforting call from the leadsman below: "Mark twain!"

A Mississippi River pilot was a man of considerable distinction, not merely because of the exacting training needed to qualify one, but also because he commanded respect and earned a good salary. In those days it meant a fortune—it would even today—for a young man of twenty-one to make $250 a month. It also meant that Sam Clemens was the head of his family—its financier and its counselor.

Just how long Sam might have continued on the River, barring Fate, is problematic. The oncoming Civil War brought an end to his piloting.

Other events also were shaping a different destiny for him. One was forecast by Madame Caprell, the famous clairvoyant of New Orleans; she played a curious part. In the reading she gave him, she described Orion, and urged Sam to tell him "to devote himself to his business and politics with all his might, for he must hold offices under the Government . . ." He had been practicing law, first at Alexandria and later at Memphis, Missouri, and he was soon to "hold offices under the Government."

By early spring of the eventful year of 1860, the issue between the North and the South was fast approaching a crisis. It was reached when the National Republican Nominating Convention, meeting in the Wigwam in Chicago in May of that year, nominated Abraham Lincoln for President of the United States. That convention had far-reaching influence, not only on Orion and Sam Clemens, but also on the lawless, excited, ungoverned people in the Land of Washoe.

William H. Seward, a former Governor of New York, a United States Senator from that State, and an antislavery leader, was believed by the political wiseacres to have the Republican nomination "in the bag." So, too, believed campaign manager, James W. Nye, a skillful and clever politician from New York City. Nye had collected a large campaign fund, and with it a big crowd of supporters looking forward to Federal appointments. These men accompanied Seward to Chicago, where elaborate preparations were made by which to impress the delegates to the Convention: there were illuminated banners; and a magnificent band, brilliantly uniformed with epaulets on their shoulders and white and scarlet feathers waving from their caps, marched every session from Seward's headquarters in the Richmond House to the convention hall. They were about a thousand strong, under orders of campaign-manager Nye. And although they made a wonderful showing the first day, many of the delegates from the frontier States were unpleasantly awed at the spectacle. It was the first time in convention history that any candidate had put on such a "show." The plain people were somewhat doubtful of the sincerity of a man who could spend such a sum of money to get himself nominated.

Edward C. Bates, Orion's old friend and mentor, distinguished lawyer from St. Louis and former Congressman from Missouri, was another potential candidate, but he withdrew his name early in the convention proceedings in favor of Lincoln. The contest was then between Lincoln and Seward.

The third ballot came on the second day of the Convention. Unfortunately, on that day the march of the Seward supporters led by Nye was delayed too long, and what with the hall already packed with Lincoln supporters, they could not get in to scream and to toot when Seward's name was mentioned. Abraham Lincoln was nominated with great enthusiasm. The Seward backers, ashamed and embittered, were terribly stricken down.

After Lincoln was elected, he set about to select his Cabinet members. To William Seward went the number-one position, Secretary of State; to Edward Bates, the office of Attorney General.[6]

Not long after it was known that Abraham Lincoln was to be the next President of the United States, the Governor of South Carolina called a meeting of the State legislature. On his recommendation it dissolved the bonds that joined it as a State to the Union. Other States of the South followed one by one, and soon the Southern Confederacy was formed. The fall of Fort Sumter on April 14, 1861, opened the Civil War—it closed piloting days for Sam Clemens, who happened at that moment to be in New Orleans.

On the way up the River, he saw preparations for war everywhere: he saw troops drilling; he barely escaped the blockade at Memphis, Tennessee. Stopped by cannon boom at St. Louis, and narrowly missing actual bombardment, the boat on which he was traveling was finally examined and passed. It was the last boat to make the trip from New Orleans to St. Louis before the River was closed.

After spending a few days in St. Louis, Sam went up the River to Hannibal to visit his old friends. When he arrived he found a number of military companies being formed: some were for the Union, others for the Confederacy, and at least one was being formed by young fellows out for a lark. Sam joined a group of his old friends who were forming the Marion Rangers. They were espousing the Confederate cause. After formally organizing themselves into a fighting unit by electing their own officers—Sam got a second lieutenancy—there were just three privates left.

Rain, a stubborn mule, and a severely sprained ankle which laid him up for several weeks ended his military career. He humorously told the story in *The Campaign That Failed*.

His lieutenancy in the Confederate army had lasted two weeks, during which time he narrowly missed the distinction of being captured by Ulysses S. Grant. When he resigned from the army, he explained that he had become "incapacitated by fatigue through persistent retreating." He had had enough of war; so he went up to Keokuk to visit Orion, now an enthusiastic Union supporter.

Orion had been practicing law in Memphis, Missouri, a small town in the northern part of the State, when Lincoln was nominated. A vigorous supporter of Lincoln's candidacy and the platform of the Republican Party, he closed his office and stumped this part of the State for his party. Taking such an active part in the campaign meant a political job, "an office under the Government."

In January 1861, Orion went down to St. Louis to pay his old friend Judge Bates a visit—and to see if Bates could get him an office.[7] The new Attorney General promised him a job, but at that time there was no indication what it was to be. Although the bill to create the Territory of Nevada had passed on March 2, President Buchanan had done nothing about organizing the new Territory or filling the offices for it.

In the course of time, Lincoln appointed the officials for Nevada Territory. To Seward as Secretary of State went the privilege of appointing the Governor of the Territory. This plum went to his old campaign-manager Nye, and from him Bates secured the privilege of appointing Orion Clemens as Territorial Secretary. Orion received the notice that he was appointed on March 27, 1861; his commission and the "Book of Instructions" arrived on April 20. Soon thereafter he took Mollie and Jennie to live with Mollie's parents. She had worked hard to get Orion ready for his new position. Books—an unabridged Webster's Dictionary, Iowa statutes, assorted rules of order—were packed in a large portmanteau, along with formal clothes, tobacco, pipes and other administrative impedimenta.

In the meantime Sam had gone back to St. Louis. It was better, perhaps, for a late lieutenant of the Confederacy to be in more friendly territory! As usual, Orion was out of money. Where to get the necessary stage fare to Nevada was a problem. There were two possibilities—brother Sam and brother-in-law William A. Moffett. It was Sam who agreed to put up $300 for their fares, if he, in turn, could have a job in the new Territory. Orion should have *some* patronage; and besides—he would *need* a private secretary!

The brothers were together again. For the next four years they were not separated for longer than a few months; and during a lot of this time Sam lived in Orion's home in Nevada—Carson City.

The story of their departure; the experiences on the overland trip to Nevada; the descriptions of the country, the people, the government, and the industries of the Territory of Nevada are vividly told by Sam Clemens in *Roughing It*. Because two-thirds of this book gives the world an unforgettable picture of early Nevada, the reader should know why it was written, who helped Sam Clemens write it, and how it was regarded when it was published.

Let the author first tell why he wrote it: "This book is merely a personal narrative and not a pretentious history . . . there is information in this volume . . . concerning an interesting episode in the history of the Far West, about which no books have been written by persons who were on the ground in person, and saw the happenings of the time with their own eyes. I allude to the rise, growth, and culmination of the silver-mining fever in Nevada—a curious episode, in some respects; the only one, indeed, that is likely to occur in it."

Indeed it is the only book, even at this late date, that deals adequately with the character and the manners of the primitive civilization of early Nevada. It was written in that informal, spontaneous manner which today the old hard-rock miner uses to spin his yarns to his listeners. *Roughing It* may seem to the uninformed to be a loosely written, anecdotal narrative. But such is not the case. When the history of the era is known, the continuity of the book is obvious. This volume is intended primarily to offer the background; Mark Twain's stories, in *Roughing It* and other writings, supply an astute and amazing running commentary on the scene.

Roughing It was written almost ten years after Sam and Orion Clemens set out for Nevada. It was begun September, 1870; it was published in February, 1872. In writing it, Sam was aided by Joseph Thompson Goodman, William Dean Howells, and the notes Orion kept when he was in Nevada. Goodman refreshed his memory and encouraged him. "You are doing a great book," exclaimed Goodman after reading the manuscript.

It was the review by Howells, however, that presented it favorably to the reading public:

> The grotesque exaggeration and broad irony with which he described the life are conjecturably the truest colors that could have been used, for all existence they must have looked like an extravagant joke, the humor of which was only deepened by its netherside of tragedy ... everything far-fetched or near at hand is interwoven, and yet the complex is a sort of "harmony of colors" which is not less than triumphant . . . the work of a human being, it is not unbrokenly nor infallibly funny; nor is it to be praised for all the literary virtues; but it is singularly entertaining, and its humor is always amiable, manly, and generous.

Roughing It is a classic every Nevadan loves. He reads it more often than he does the Bible; with which, as Mark once said at the risk of slight irreverence, it sells right along! Indeed it is to be found in practically every home in the State, humble and pretentious. It is undoubtedly quoted more often than even the Holy Book by legislators, by presidents of chambers of commerce, by members of the bar, by the press and industrial agents. Every old prospector tells and retells the same old tales he once heard from his older pards. The attachés of every meeting of the State's legislature today commemorate the "Third House" by holding a mock session, after the manner of the first notable one of which Mark Twain was the uproarious and tyrannical "Governor."

5

WITHOUT THE LAW

DURING THE TIME THAT SAM CLEMENS WAS PILOTING on the River and Orion Clemens was trying to cope with the arithmetic of life, exciting events were transpiring in the Land of Washoe. When the general exodus of the Faithful was called by Brigham Young, President to the Mormons, Governor Young to the Gentiles, there were only a few people left in the valleys of western Utah—and precious little government! All but one of the officers of Carson County had been Mormons, and when they left for Salt Lake City they took the county records, the books, and all other official documents with them.

The exodus of the Mormons was noted in many Western papers. It was not long before the abandoned Mormon farms were bought up, leased, or preëmpted, chiefly by Californians. Also, it was not long before the highwayman, the bandit, the swindler, the horse thief, and the outlaw learned that there was little or no law in Carson County. From Honey Lake Valley in the north to Carson Valley in the south, the law-abiding citizens were terrorized by every form of lawlessness. When conditions became intolerable, the citizens took affairs into their own hands. Frontier law was crude but effective. It was not written, codified, or bound around by limitations. The punishment was made to fit the crime.

The most notorious and self-licensed individual in western Utah was William B. ("Lucky Bill") Thorington. He was far worse than a cattle thief, claim jumper, or highway robber. Lucky Bill, a sort of "wolf in sheep's clothing," pretended to be a law-abiding citizen. To a few unregenerates he was a picaresque ideal, but to most of the upright settlers he was the personification of Satan himself. At length Bill carried his satanic exploits a little too far; and for his transgressions he was arrested, tried, and condemned to be hanged by a self-constituted citizens' court.

Lucky Bill, so named because he never was the loser in anything whatsoever he went into, came west from the State of New York with the rush of '49. He made a comfortable fortune gambling in the mining camps along the Mother Lode, and then came over to Carson Valley in 1853. In this year he bought out Israel Mott's Carson Cañon Toll Road establishment, now Fredericksburg, in the upper end of Carson Valley. Every traveler had to stop at his place and pay toll for himself, his wagons, and his animals. Many of these travelers stayed overnight with him at his wayside inn, before making the long pull over the summit of the mountains; and almost everyone who did tarry for a while lived to regret his stay.

Bill dealt faro, not out of the usual box, but by hand; and he also had his own little "thimblerig game." He never lost at any of his games. He sometimes won everything an emigrant had—wagons, horses, and provisions. When all was gone, Bill would loan the poor victim some money to go on his way—then gamble even that away from him. But in justice it must be recorded that Bill always took the part of the underdog in a fight; and it was said that he was good to widows and children, and gave heavily to all charitable causes.

By 1855 he had acquired sufficient money to pay $23,000 to John Reese for a large share in the Old Mormon Trading Station at Genoa and for Reese's Eagle Valley Ranch. Oldtimers in Carson Valley today talk at great length about the good and bad points of Bill's character. He must have been notorious, for these now-old men and women who never saw him can describe for you in detail everything about him. They will tell you that he was over six feet tall; that he had jet-black curly hair which he wore quite long; that he weighed over two hundred pounds; that his eyes were cold and steel gray and looked out from under heavy, projecting brows; and that he had little or no education. To children he was an ogre, whose dread name their mothers invoked to frighten them into obedience.

It was said that there were many people in Carson Valley who had some score they wanted to settle with Lucky Bill. There were no officers, no court, no jail—in fact, no one to curb his unbridled offenses. But there were so many "strikes against him" that, when retribution caught up with him, he didn't have a Chinaman's chance. The offended ones had their opportunity in 1858. Lucky Bill had made the grave mistake of giving protection to Bill Edwards, a murderer for whose crimes an innocent man had been hanged in Honey Lake Valley. When it was learned that Edwards was the real murderer, and that he himself had directed suspicion to the unfortunate sufferer for the crime, he fled the valley. The Honey Lake citizens located Edwards in Carson Valley.

The irate mob obtained Edwards' arrest and put him in irons on June 14. With the people of Carson Valley, they formed a vigilantes committee to try him. But Edwards, aided by Lucky Bill Thorington and his young son Jerome, made his escape.

It was said that young Thorington knew of Edwards' hideout, and that he carried food and other things to him. Learning that Edwards was still in the country, the committee promised Jerome immunity for his father and himself if he would tell them of Edwards' whereabouts. Acting in good faith, Jerome betrayed his father and the murderer into the hands of the vigilantes. The citizens promptly arrested Lucky Bill as well as the murderer.

The trial took place on June 17 in a barn on a ranch near Clear Creek. One man was a self-appointed sheriff, another the judge, and eighteen more constituted the jury. The evidence was carefully taken down by a clerk. Both prisoners were found guilty and condemned to be hanged: Edwards for the murder he had committed in Honey Lake Valley, and Lucky Bill for being an "accessory to the murder after the fact."

Three hours after the verdict was given, Lucky Bill was hanging dead from the limb of a cottonwood tree. Tradition states that he aided his executioners in adjusting the noose around his neck and that, as he swung free from the wagon driven out from under him, he was singing "The Last Rose of Summer" as loud as he could.[1]

Edwards was taken back to Honey Lake for his execution. Whether or not he was hanged remains a mystery to this day. It is certain that there was no public hanging for him. He was led off with some of the vigilantes who had constructed a crude pine box in which to bury him. He was never seen again, nor was his body ever exhibited. It was known that he had cached a large sum of money on the other side of the mountains, and it is believed that he promised to show his executioners where it was if they would let him go. After the money was located, it is thought that they told him to keep on going and never come back again.

One of the commonest of practices where there was no law was cattle rustling. Food was scarce, particularly after the first rush to Washoe, and consequently cattle brought a good price. Two men, George Ruspas and David Reese, had been stealing cattle for some time, and one of them had already been punished for this offense. In August they stole some cattle at Chinatown, now Dayton. They drove them over to Washoe Valley and offered them at such a low price that it was suspected that they were stolen animals. The men were arrested, and an informal jury was summoned. The trial was held under a big pine tree near the western shore of Washoe Lake. After the evidence had been introduced, the jury pronounced the men guilty. Their punishment was to have their left ears cut off, after which they were to be banished from the country. Jim Sturtevant, an old rancher in the Valley, was appointed official "ear marker." Jim obtained a big knife, and after he had ascertained its sharpness—not finding it to his liking, he gave it several rakes against a rock—he walked up to Reese, pushed back his hair, took a firm grip on the upper part of his left ear, and shaved it off close in a single slash. He then tossed it over to the jury, which was still sitting under the pine tree.

As Sturtevant approached Ruspas to carry out the mandate of the jury, he observed him to be greatly amused over something. Surely he could not be smiling over his partner's loss of an ear, nor because he was about to lose one of his own! As the "ear marker" pulled aside Ruspas' long hair, which hung about his shoulders frontier-fashion, he saw that there was no ear left! It had been taken off to pay for some previous crime. The executioner was in a dilemma.

The joke was so good that Ruspas could not refrain from looking Sturtevant straight in the eye and giving forth a hearty laugh. The problem was now squarely up to the jury. The men again went into a juridic huddle and reconsidered their sentence. It was decided that, rather than disappoint anyone, the right ear should be taken off. When the thief heard the reconsidered sentence, his smile faded. Sturtevant looked for the right ear, found it still there, took a firm hold, and with a vigorous slash severed it. After doing so, he tossed it over to the jury, saying that now they had "mates—a right and a left ear." The sentences carried out, the two men were forcefully directed to take the road that led west and never return to that country.

Out of every group of people, Nature for her own recondite purposes selects a man with something compelling and fatal about him, a man who knows how to make others follow him. Such a man was William M. ("Bill") Stewart. He stopped in Genoa on his way to Washoe and practiced law there for a short time, but he, too, could see that Carson City was to be the leading town. There he went; there he built one of the first homes in the city; and there he brought his family to live.

Bill Stewart, Yale-educated and a California Argonaut, became a lawyer and a politician before he rushed to Washoe. He was a giant in intellect. However, brains were not sufficient to carry one through successfully on the frontier. One had to have brawn, too. Stewart had both. Six feet two inches tall, weighing two hundred pounds, red-headed and hot-tempered, he could fight the best of them. His reputation as a lawyer and a fighter in California followed him to Washoe, and soon he was the counsel for the leading mines on the Lode.

Bill made himself respected by everyone soon after he arrived, when he worsted desperate Sam Brown in a criminal suit in Genoa. Sam Brown had come to Washoe with a reputation for having killed thirteen men in Texas and California. In the summer of 1859, he was keeping a station on the Humboldt River Trail. An agent for the express called at Sam's station and asked for something to eat. Brown pointed to a strip of bacon hanging on the wall. The agent, not having anything with which to cut it, asked Brown for the loan of his knife. With a sinister smile Brown pulled out his big sheath-knife and then put it back into his bootleg, saying: "I'm superstitious about using a knife to cut bacon that has killed five men." The visitor was likewise scrupulous and left the station without his meal.

One of Brown's first exploits, with which he impressed Washoe desperadoes and terrified lesser luminaries of the bandit world, was the murder of an underwitted barroom lounger, whose weak discretion was made weaker with liquor. In his stupor one day he staggered up to Brown in a saloon and made a witless remark, at which Brown took offense. Without a word, the giant wound his big arm around his victim and, thus holding him, pulled out his sheath-knife and drove it twice into the quivering body, turning it "Maltese fashion." Then, flinging the bleeding body on the floor, he strolled over to a billiard table, lay down, and went to sleep. Nothing was *ever* done to Brown for this outrageous act.

In this way Sam Brown built up quite a reputation in Washoe as a man-killer. One day he heard that one of his pals, who had killed an innocent man, had been arrested and was to be taken before Judge Cradlebaugh in Genoa. Brown couldn't allow one of his gang to be bullied by anything like a judge. He must handle this case himself. He braided his long red whiskers, tied them under his chin, buckled on his spurs, mounted his mustang, and rode over to help out his friend. Brown did not know that big Bill Stewart had been employed to assist the district attorney in the prosecution.

It was said that, when the gangster from Virginia City rode into that little courtroom in Genoa, some of the jurymen dived out of the window and many of the spectators hid behind benches for safety. Brown's usual procedure when he entered a place was to open fire and shoot up the joint. Stewart, who was well informed of Brown's tactics, was not at all impressed by the entrance of the bad man. Before Brown could draw, Stewart had him covered with two derringers, one in each of his hands. He shouted, "Throw up your arms!"

Brown was so startled at this new and unprecedented reception in a court of law that he raised his arms. Then Stewart ordered the officers to disarm him and to swear him in as a witness. On the stand Brown was made to admit some things that he did not want to: he confessed that his accused friend had a bad reputation, that he himself not only knew nothing of the case but was also under indictment in Plumas County, California, for assault with a deadly weapon. His pal was convicted, and Brown's reputation badly injured. However, he pretended to be a good sport about the matter and invited the crowd to come with him to the nearest bar, where the drinks would be on him.

After the affair was all over and Brown was alone, he began to brood over the way that he had been worsted. He knew that his prestige had suffered by his defeat. Disgruntled, he rode down the road to Henry Van Sickle's station. The innkeeper greeted him as he entered the house. But Brown was stewing in his fury; instead of replying, he resorted to his usual means of restoring his badly mangled self-respect. Drawing his gun, he shouted: "I have come to kill you. You G— d— sonofa b—!" Not being armed, Van Sickle rushed back into his dining room with Brown roaring at his heels. When Brown saw some twenty men eating there, he experienced a sudden change of heart, left the inn, mounted his horse, and rode away. Van Sickle secured his gun, got on his horse, and at once started after Brown. Dark was coming on, and Brown, not being acquainted with the country, lost his way. Van Sickle knew the country so well that he took a cutoff and arrived at a point on the trail before Brown could reach it. There he awaited the coming of the desperado.

Van Sickle took good aim as Brown came riding down the road; and, when the latter was at close range, yelled out to him the same greeting he had earlier received: "You G— d— sonofa b— I have you now." Then he neatly fired seven shots through the center of Brown's body. Thus ended the career of one of the frontier's worst characters.

Van Sickle then rode back to his ranch, told everyone what he had done, and with the help of the men at the station went back and brought in Brown's body. As soon as it was possible, Van Sickle saw that Brown was well buried at his expense; then he demanded a complete investigation of the whole affair. When the jury viewed the perforated remains, the verdict was, "It served him right." [2]

Anarchy and confusion continued to reign in western Utah for the remainder of 1860. In this year many mining corporations were formed in Washoe, and soon the entire district, with few exceptions, was owned by stock companies. The inevitable litigation arose over the geological character of the district and the extent of each company's claims. In the attempt to restore some kind of order in Carson County, President Buchanan, answering the pleas of the law-abiding citizens, appointed John Cradlebaugh, a pioneer lawyer, to the bench of the Second Judicial District, Utah Territory.

Judge Cradlebaugh opened court in the only available space in the town, a badly lighted room over a livery stable, at Genoa, Carson Valley, on September 3, 1860, to determine the legal titles to mines worth millions of dollars. It was said that the town was full of "lawyers, litigants, witnesses, and jurors. A bundle of straw in a barn was eagerly sought as a bed, and the judge slept contentedly between rival attorneys while the humbler attendants spread their blankets on the sagebrush." A number of cases were heard at this session of court. Bribery was openly admitted by some of the jurors after the verdicts were returned. Rival companies therefore moved for new trials.

The companies that had lost their suits appealed to the President to remove Judge Cradlebaugh. To add to the confusion, the President listened to their stories, removed the Judge, and appointed his old friend R. P. Flenniken, a former United States Minister to The Hague. Judge Flenniken really thought that he had been assigned to a court of considerable dignity. What a picture he must have made in his high silk hat and long frock coat, the first ever to be worn in Washoe, as he came before the heavily bearded, high-top-booted, slouch-hatted, and roughly clothed miners and their lawyers! Judge Cradlebaugh steadfastly refused to recognize the authority by which he was removed! It was established, he believed, that Federal judges could be removed only by impeachment by the House of Representatives and conviction by the Senate; and therefore he did not intend to resign until March 4, 1861.

Now Judge Flenniken was a pompous old fellow, and carried himself as though he were being presented at the royal court of Holland rather than to a group of determined frontiersmen. His arrogancy immediately made him disliked by everyone. Bill Stewart, who favored Judge Cradlebaugh's decisions, encouraged the latter to hold his ground. David S. Terry, the rival lawyer in most of the suits, supported Judge Flenniken. The different mining companies fortified the law with armed guards protected by hastily-thrown-up forts on the mining claims in dispute. Appeals were made to the Supreme Court of Utah Territory to determine the jurisdiction of the two judges. On February 15, the Pony Express brought the report. The decision was in favor of Cradlebaugh, and Flenniken announced that he would submit to the decision. Stewart and *his* judge had clearly won out over Flenniken and the President of the United States. Believing that there would be no further trouble, Stewart went to bed that night. Early the next morning he was awakened by his associate counsel with the news that Flenniken had had a change of heart during the night and would hold the fort against all comers.

Stewart dressed hurriedly and went out on the street, where he soon found Flenniken standing in front of a saloon. He demanded the latter's resigation at once. As he spoke, he seized Flenniken by the shoulders, giving him a sudden jerk which almost threw the Judge to his knees. Again he insisted that Flenniken resign. The Judge resisted as best he could, but seeing that Stewart meant what he said, he followed the lawyer to the telegraph office, where Stewart dictated messages to the sheriff, the marshal, and the President. He then ordered the telegraph operator to stay away from his machine for a few hours.[3]

Judge Cradlebaugh thus held his seat undisputed, but as the validity of his appointment was doubtful, legal actions were at an end until Abraham Lincoln was inaugurated.

Terrorism and lawlessness cannot last long in Anglo-Saxon communities without something's being done about the situation. Since there were no county officers to enforce the law, since Governor Young was too involved in the Utah war to do anything for his distracted people five hundred miles away, and since appeals to the national government went unheeded, the people had to act for their protection. To correct unbearable conditions, Isaac Roop, a leading citizen of Susanville in Honey Lake Valley—which was considered at that time to be under the jurisdiction of the Utah Territory— inaugurated a movement in 1858 to form a separate Territory.

On August 8, 1857, even before all of the Zionites had set out for the Mormon capital, a mass meeting was called in Genoa for the purpose of considering secession from Utah Territory. One of the most prominent movers in this direction was Major William S. Ormsby, formerly of Sacramento and later agent for the Pioneer Stage Company. At this meeting resolutions were drawn, Congress was memorialized, and the new Territory was dubbed "Columbus" —the name went well with Genoa. A long report was written about this movement, of which the "Columbians" wanted the world to know. Copies of it were sent to the leading Eastern and Western papers.

Frontier organizations are always informal and free from conventions. The greatest perplexity of this group was the question of how to get their grievances before Congress. Not one member of the Convention thought himself capable of presenting them.

Chance offered a way out of the dilemma. James M. Crane, a prominent journalist and native Virginian who had gone to California in the Gold Rush days, happened to be in Washoe collecting material for a series of geological lectures. One day a member of the Convention casually asked Crane to come over and give them a talk. His address was so well-received, and he made such a good impression on them, that he was selected at once as the Congressional delegate to go to Washington and to plead the cause of the

"Territory of Columbus." A collection was taken up, and he was sent on his way.

A short time after Crane arrived in the nation's capital, a bill to create the Territory of Columbus was introduced. The Committee on Territories disliked the name "Columbus" and changed it to "Nevada." Although Crane's bill received considerable encouragement—it easily passed the lower House—it was dropped in the Senate.

Crane returned to Carson County and urged the seceders to try again. Although Brigham Young sought to revive Carson County, the Gentiles were determined to live no longer under Mormon tyranny. It would be better, perhaps, if a new and different seat of government were located. Acting on this assumption, Major Ormsby and Abraham V. Z. Curry went down to Eagle Valley, selected a town-site, and laid out Carson City, Carson County, Territory of Utah.

Curry erected a large stone house from a quarry near some hot springs on the old California trail, and Ormsby built a small hotel opposite a four-acre plaza on the Carson City townsite about a mile to the west of Curry's establishment. With good water, pleasant surroundings, and vigorous boosting, Carson City soon became a populous community. With the new "Capital" well on its way, a second convention was called in June, 1859. A constitution was prepared, and another delegate was selected to go back to Washington. A governor and a full corps of officers were selected for the people to vote on. Isaac Roop of Susanville, in Honey Lake Valley, was elected Governor. Everyone was allowed to vote—even the traveling public was stopped and urged to cast ballots for the favorite candidates.

While these determined people were pushing their efforts for a new Territory, the California papers were publishing the news of the discovery of Washoe. Crowds began rushing over the mountains. They passed through Genoa, and on through Carson City to the Comstock Lode. Many of the new arrivals liked Carson City. Thinking it a good place to which to bring their families, they stopped, opened offices, built homes, and started industries.

But the provisional government was swept away by the flood of the oncoming silver-mad horde. All through the winter of 1859–1860 they came, wave after wave of hungry, weary fortune-seekers. And wave after wave, they went back over the same route. As they passed down the trail, fires from the tops of mountains and along the streams were burning. The smoke from these fires was the signal to faraway Indians that white men were coming to take possession of their lands. The palefaces were cutting down their pine-nut trees and were driving off their game. Soon they would starve to death. Too, the white men mistreated their young squaws.

At last vengeance broke out in a fury. The Indians sneaked up on Williams Station on the California Trail by the side of the Carson River, burned it, and killed five men. When the Pony Express brought this news to Carson City and Virginia City, the settlers were frightened into a panic. Many women and children were loaded into wagons and rushed to California while many more were herded into improvised forts. A volunteer army was enlisted to pursue and punish the Indians.

Unorganized and undisciplined, over one hundred men set out to drive the Indians from the country. The army traced the red men to their camp on the lower Truckee River, near Pyramid Lake. As they rode along the river trail, they did not see a single Indian. The canny redskins were watching from behind rocks and sage-brush. Swift young Indian runners kept Chief Winnemucca constantly informed of the white army's movements. About fourteen miles from the big bend of the Truckee, at what is now Wadsworth, the army pulled away from the trail and rode down to a plain covered heavily with high sagebrush, so high that a man lying prone could not be seen.

Slowly the army rode down into this valley, where the Indians thus hidden ambushed them. The volunteers had ridden into a trap. They were outnumbered, outmaneuvered, and outfought.

For three days frantic wives and friends awaited news of the Indian fighters. On the fourth day an excited, dust-covered horse-man rode furiously back to Virginia City. He was one of the few who had survived the battle. More than two-thirds were left dying on the trail, each man pierced by many arrows. Among them was Major Ormsby, who, wounded by a poisoned arrow, toppled from his horse and, when found dying by an Indian, was shot in the head to put him out of his misery; brave young Henry Meredith had fallen from his horse and was killed.

Washoe was in a terrific panic when the few living stragglers crawled back to the settlements and related the story of their terrible defeat. Martial law was declared, forts were hastily thrown up, and appeals for men and arms were sent to the Governor of California. Another army was organized to avenge the deaths of the brave men who had just been killed; the Indians must be subdued or driven out. Colonel "Jack" Hayes, an old Indian fighter, Major Daniel E. Hungerford and Captain Edward F. Storey, fighters in the Mexican War, and Captain Jasper M. Stewart of the Regular Army stationed at San Francisco commanded this new army. With such a well-disciplined force there could be only one outcome. The Indians were defeated and put to rout, but brave Captain Storey was among the few who fell in this last engagement with the redmen.

When the fighting was over, the bodies of the men who had lost their lives in the first battle were packed on their horses and brought back for burial. Captain Stewart was ordered to built Fort Churchill, and for this purpose he selected a high knoll on the Carson River which overlooked the trail.[5]

It was into this state of confusion that the new Territorial officers of Nevada came.

6

GOVERNOR NYE AND HIS BRIGADE

THERE WAS GREAT REJOICING IN THE LAND OF Washoe on the night of March 29, 1861. In Carson City bonfires were lighted, large fireballs were thrown through the air, and all manner of firearms were shot off. For on that day, twenty-seven days after the passing of the Act, the fleet messenger of the Pony Express had brought the news that the Territory of Nevada was born. By the time the Territory itself was informed of its existence, the Governor of the Territory had been appointed and a full corps of officers selected. Such was the great distance the news had to travel in those days! [1]

In a letter to William Seward, Secretary of State, written on December 8, 1860, President Lincoln had advised him about the patronage policy: "In regard to the patronage sought with so much eagerness and jealousy, I have prescribed for myself the maxim, 'Justice to all,' and I earnestly beseech your cooperation in keeping the maxim good." However, Seward was so busy in Washington trying to make his office as great as that of the President that he did not bother with selecting all of the officers for the Territory of Nevada. He gave that patronage, with the exception of the appointment of the Secretary of the Territory, to the newly appointed Governor, James W. Nye.

Now Mr. Nye had been a politician in the State of New York for a long time, and he had a devil of a lot of political debts to pay. How better could they be paid off than by promising his supporters jobs out in Nevada? It was a wonderful way of rewarding the party workers, the ward-heelers, and the rest of the avid office-seekers! It was also a splendid way for the party to clean house after a national election.

Not only did Nye pay off his own debts, but he also let some of his appointees pay off their debts. His official family and its appointees came from New York, New Hampshire, Ohio, Missouri, Minnesota, Michigan, and California. It was never thought that there might be one or two persons in the new Territory who could qualify for some of the offices. Anyway, not one was selected from Nevada. It was Sam Clemens who gave this motley crowd of "carpetbaggers" its name, "The Irish Brigade." [2]

Not only did Nye and his appointees set out for Nevada, but some of them brought their relatives as well. Last, but emphatically not the least of the train was Mrs. "Bridget" M. Murphy, to whom in *Roughing It* Sam Clemens refers as "Mrs. O'Flannigan." This motherly, talented, and energetic Irish woman had been a boarding-house keeper in New York City, and the new Governor imported her, and as many as possible of her beloved pots and pans, to keep house in the new Territory for "The Brigade." Most of Nevada's official family accompanied the Governor on the steamer *Ariel* via the Isthmus of Panama. What a celebration there must have been before the party embarked on the voyage! All of the members got aboard, but not all of the baggage. Some of the bags were left on the dock when the ship sailed. In fact, the most important ones were left—those of the Governor containing his official papers for organizing his Territory.

On June 26, Nye and his party arrived in San Francisco. There they had to wait until the next steamer brought the lost bags. During their stay in California they enjoyed themselves immensely. The Governor made himself popular—the local newspapers referred to him as "one of the jolliest orators that ever stumped a state. When he was a Democrat, all of the Whigs went to hear him, and when he was a Republican, you couldn't hire a Democrat to stay away." He was a striking-looking politician with long white hair, "a friendly face, and deep lustrous dark eyes that could talk a native language, the tongue of every feeling, every passion, every emotion. His eyes could out-talk his tongue, and this is saying a good deal, for he was a very remarkable talker, both in private and on the stump. He was a shrewd man. He generally saw through surfaces and perceived what might be going on inside without being suspected of having an eye on the matter." Such was the estimate Sam Clemens made of the first Governor of Nevada in *Mark Twain's Autobiography*. Sam and the Governor were good friends and often cruised around together.

Nye, who had come from good New York stock, had spent his youth working on the towpath of the Erie Canal. Through his own efforts and without benefit of a college education, he had become a

OPHIR MINE, ORIGINAL DISCOVERY ON THE COMSTOCK LODE

MR. AND MRS. WILLIAM MORRIS STEWART

JAMES W. NYE
Territorial Governor of Nevada, 1861–1864

ORION CLEMENS
Secretary of Territory of Nevada

lawyer, later going into politics. When the metropolitan police force of New York City was created, he was a member of the commission; he was later chosen president of it during the troubles which preceded the establishment of the police force on an efficient basis.

During the ten days Governor Nye was forced to spend in San Francisco, he made many friends. Indeed, he enjoyed himself so thoroughly that he later spent more of his time there than he did in Nevada. Anxious to make a favorable impression on Californians, he accepted an invitation to give a lecture at the Music Hall on the night of his arrival. The hall was jammed with people, many of whom had to remain standing during the speech. With his persuasive voice and his ready wit he captured the hearts of San Franciscans:

> Hail California! The youngest and brightest star in the constellation of her sisterhood of States! Wonder of the world, whose history finds no parallel in the history of states or nations! Rich beyond computation; rich in her minerals, rich in her agricultural productions, rich in her commerce, but richer still in her lion-hearted citizens. . . .
>
> Hail San Francisco! Magical city that has sprung up like a gourd in the night, and stands waving her golden helmet to the older cities of the East.
>
> Magical city . . . but still more magical than all your history, in the power and the enterprise of your people. . . .

The audience loved the speech and, when he had said his final words, it leaped to its feet and, "after long applause, gave him three tremendous cheers." [3]

While he was still in San Francisco, several prominent Nevadans went down to meet the new Governor. Among them was William ("Bill") Stewart of Carson City. A number of Nevada towns were bidding strongly for the honor of being the capital of the new Territory. Not the least of them was Carson City. It seemed that the capital was to be located at a place to be designated by the Governor. Stewart's gift of persuasion is apparent in the fact that the Governor announced, before having even set foot in the country, that the capital would be at Carson City. Stewart invited the Governor to be his house guest until he got settled.

The coming of the Governor was impatiently awaited. As a Nevada correspondent wrote to the *Daily Alta*: "The non-arrival of Governor Nye is placing everything in a very awkward fix. Without law, we are in a state of confusion most confounded. . . . Not an official, not a man in power to advise and act. A pretty state of things truly. This state might secede, and what then?" But the Governor's delay in arriving *did* give the people of Washoe a chance to make elaborate preparations to receive him. He arrived in Carson City Thursday evening, July 8. His reception was a royal one. A delegation of prominent citizens went out and met him five miles from the city with decorated carriages and a cavalcade of horsemen to accompany him. As he entered the main street, a cannon (Frémont's twelve pounder) announced his approach. The entire populace lined the street to cheer him. After a brief rest at the Stewart home, he made a short address to the people:

> With the most heartfelt emotion I greet you. . . . Allow me to assure you that not one star shall be permitted to be removed from the old (34). Twenty-five million freemen will not permit it. And I have come here to this distant country with the hope of adding one more—a bright and glorious star—Nevada.[4]

Not to be outdone by Carson City, the Comstockers, too, made great preparations to greet the Governor, and two days later he entered Virginia City escorted by a brass band, the city trustees, and the Virginia Union Guards, a civilian military organization. As the party proceeded down C Street, the band boomed out "Hail to the Chief," the Guards presented arms, and the trustees rose in their carriage and uncovered their heads. At the intersection of Union and C streets the Governor passed under a floral arch of desert flowers made by the ladies of the city. Here the procession halted, the mayor welcomed the Governor officially, and the Governor made a fitting reply. After this ceremony the party went into the International Hotel where the day's festivities ended with an elaborate banquet. Champagne flowed freely as toast after toast was drunk to the Governor and to the Territory of Nevada. Nevada may have been a little pond, but, by this time, "the frog was almost as big as a bull."[5]

A series of proclamations were issued by the Governor and the wheels of the machinery for the Territory began to turn slowly. But still another delay prevented them from running at full speed. There was no Territorial Secretary with his "Book of Instructions" to record the official acts. Nye appointed one of the Brigade, J. C. Gallagher of the New York *Daily News*, to fill this position temporarily until the official Secretary arrived.

While Nye was getting along the best way he could without a Secretary, Orion and Sam Clemens were traveling to Carson City by steamboat and Overland Mail stagecoach.[6] Orion was extremely modest in his patronage: he promised Sam only that he could be his assistant secretary. In return, as will be recalled, Sam agreed to advance the stage fares for both of them. The Clemens brothers left St. Louis July 18 on the river steamer *Sioux City* for St. Joseph, Missouri. It took the boat six days to walk over the snags, to butt the reefs, and to get off the sand bars. "In fact," Sam says, "the boat might almost as well have gone to St. Joe by land, for she was walking most of the time. . . ."

As soon as the boys reached St. Joe, they hastened over to the office to learn when the next stage left for Carson City. The Overland Mail stage by the central route had been operating only since July 19 of that year. When Sam purchased their tickets, he learned that each of them was allowed only twenty-five pounds of baggage. Before they had left St. Louis, they had packed heavy traveling trunks with a great variety of things. It now became a difficult task to select the articles so as to reduce the weight, and still prepare themselves to travel over hot dusty plains and across the high mountain plateaus where the temperature dropped to freezing. They finally decided in favor of Orion's Colt revolver, Sam's "pitiful little Smith and Wesson seven shooter," two or three blankets, their pipes with five pounds of smoking tobacco, two large canteens in which to carry water, a "shot bag of silver coins," also Sam's capital of some eight hundred dollars, a Webster's Unabridged Dictionary, and some United States statutes. Their long-tailed coats, white kid gloves, and patent-leather boots were sent back home in their trunks.

The heavy bag of silver was a nuisance, as was also the Unabridged Dictionary: "It weighed about a thousand pounds, and was a ruinous expense, because the stagecoach company charged for extra baggage by the ounce. We could have kept a family for a time on what that dictionary cost in the way of extra freight—and it wasn't a good dictionary anyway—didn't have any modern words in it—only obsolete ones that they used to use when Noah Webster was a child."

The route of the Overland Mail Company lay largely over the historic trail of the explorers, trappers, traders, and Argonauts. It cut across northeastern Kansas, and into the Nebraska Territory to the Platte, which it followed to the crossing at Julesburg; then on to Fort Laramie, where the fleet horses of the plains were exchanged for mules to pull the passengers up the Rocky Mountain slope to South Pass. Beyond this point the road turned southwest to Fort Bridger and on down through Echo Canyon. Late in the afternoon on the twelfth day out from St. Joe, they reached Salt Lake City.

Although these days were tedious ones cramped inside a stage-coach half filled with mail and their own possessions, they were fascinating ones. Every ten or twelve miles the driver changed horses, at which time travelers could get out and stretch their legs. At certain division points where more mail and more passengers could be taken on, meals, such as they were, were served. Sleeping would not have been so difficult had they been able to put the dictionary somewhere. Especially was this indispensable book (which they could have bought in San Francisco, only one day from Carson City, had they known it) disturbing to their slumbers. On the steep banks of the streams everything inside the stage, which was slung on thorough-braces somewhat as a baby carriage is, got mixed up.

"Every time we avalanched from one end of the stage to the other, the Unabridged Dictionary would come too; and every time it came, it damaged somebody. One trip it barked the Secretary's elbow; the next trip it hurt me in the stomach; and the third it tilted Bemis's [a fellow traveler] nose up till he could look down his nostrils—he said. The pistols and coin soon settled to the bottom, but the pipes, pipestems, tobacco, and canteens clattered and floundered after the Dictionary every time it made an assault on us, and aided and abetted the book by spilling tobacco in our eyes, and water down our backs."

In *Roughing It*, Sam makes careful note of the arrangements of the stage company. He describes the stations, the station keepers, and the hostelers; comments on the conductors and the importance of the drivers; relates the stories that he heard them tell of brushes with the Indians and the badmen on the trail; and, with his inimitable lucidity, tells how interested and anxious they all were in watching for the Pony Express rider. The route for the ponies lay along the same one that they were taking; only the pony made it in eight days. All along the way they looked for him, but somehow or other he passed them in the night. Finally near the end of the journey, the driver exclaimed: *"Here he comes!"*

"Every neck is stretched further, and every eye strained wider. Away across the endless dead level of the prairie a black speck appears against the sky, and it is plain that it moves. Well, I should think so! In a second or two it becomes a horse and rider, rising and falling, rising and falling—sweeping toward us, nearer and nearer—growing more and more distinct, more and more sharply defined—nearer and still nearer, and the flutter of the hoofs comes faintly to the ear—another instant, a whoop and a hurrah from our upper deck, a wave of the rider's hand, but no reply, and man and horse burst past our excited faces, and go swinging away like a belated fragment of a storm!"

When the Clemens brothers arrived in Salt Lake City, they went to a hotel and unpacked their baggage. After a good supper, they walked about the streets, looking in the shop and store windows. The city and its people fascinated them. Sam was particularly interested in the housekeeping arrangements of a Mormon family and gaped in at every open dwelling-house door he passed. Bemis, their fellow passenger, roamed off by himself and took on too much "valley tan," the Mormon whiskey. He came into Sam's and Orion's room late in the evening "full of cheerfulness, and talking loosely, disjointedly, and indiscriminately, and every now and then tugging out a ragged word by the roots that had more hiccups than syllables in it. This, together with his hanging his coat on the floor on one side of a chair, and his vest on the floor on the other side, and piling his pants on the floor just in front of the chair, and then contemplating the general result with superstitious awe, and finally pronouncing it too many for him, and going to bed with his boots on, led us to fear that something that he had eaten had not agreed with him."

For two days they took in the sights, met a lot of people, and learned a great deal about the Zionites and their religion. Orion made the acquaintance of some prominent Utah Territorial officers; this was to serve him well when he took up his own official duties.

After this brief sojourn in the Mormon capital, the brothers started the last lap of their trip. The three-day stretch across the Great Salt Desert and the long sagebrush and sandy wastes of Nevada on hot August days was fatiguing. At Reese River Station (now Austin, Nevada), they found that the telegraph constructors had stretched their wires that far. Orion wired Governor Nye that he would arrive in Carson City the next day.

When the stage reached Ragtown on the Carson River, they were on the western edge of the Great Basin. Ten miles out from this settlement they found a poor wanderer who had lain down to die. He had walked as long as he could, but hunger and fatigue had overcome him. Touched with pity, they paid his fare to Carson City, and took him aboard. By chafing him and pouring whiskey between his lips, they revived him. When he was able to utter a few sounds, he said: "I take it you are strangers to this great thoroughfare, but I am entirely familiar with it. In this connection I can tell you a most laughable thing indeed, if you would like to listen to it. Horace Greeley . . ."

Sam warned the stranger to proceed at his peril, saying that he himself had heard the anecdote so many times that either his mind or his self-control would snap at another repetition of it. The invalid did not tell the anecdote, but trying to retain it in his system so strained him that he died in their arms.

The first time they had been told of the Horace Greeley story was just after they had left Julesburg, Colorado; two days later a Denver man they picked up at the crossroads remarked, "I can tell you a most laughable thing indeed, if you would like to listen to it. Horace Greeley . . . etc." At Fort Bridger a cavalry sergeant told them the same story; a Mormon preacher eight hours out from Salt Lake City related it to them also. Drivers told it to them, as did conductors, landlords, passengers, Chinamen, and even the Indians. Sam had to listen to it "four hundred and eighty-one or eighty-two times" in the thirteen times he crossed and recrossed the Sierra Nevada Mountains by stage during the six years he was in the West.

The occasion for this bromidical story was a speaking tour of the West which Horace Greeley made in the summer of 1859.[7] The stage on which he rode from Carson City to Placerville was driven by Henry ("Hank") Monk, dean of "whips" in the West. Horace told Hank at the outset that he had a speaking engagement in Placer-

"Keep your seat, Horace, I'll get you there."

From *Roughing It*

ville and that he was anxious to get there on time for it. Hank took the box, and cracked his whip furiously, which caused the horses to jump, giving the stage occupants a sudden jerk. Passengers who were familiar with stagecoaching thought nothing of these antics. But Horace was a newcomer.

"The coach bounced up and down in such a terrific way that it jolted the buttons all off of Horace's coat, and finally shot his head clean through the roof of the stage, and then he yelled at Hank Monk and begged him to go easier—said he wasn't in as much of a hurry as he was a while ago. But Hank Monk said, 'Keep your seat, Horace, and I'll get you there on time'—and you bet he did, too, what was left of him."

Of course, Sam Clemens' version of the story is somewhat exaggerated. There were ten other passengers on the stage at the time, and one of them told his version of it. Hank, too, had his interpretation of the ride and of Greeley's fright at the excessive speed with which he drove the stage. He often related it to entertain his passengers.

The passengers enjoyed it so much that they decided to immortalize the ride in the form of a gift to Hank of a handsome gold watch. It was ornate, heavily chased, and elaborately decorated with repoussé figures and scenes, and was three inches in diameter. It cost $1500. It was said that the gift idea originated with and was promoted by George R. Hearst, father of William Randolph Hearst and himself a passenger on the stage. The inscription inside the front case reads:

Presented to

Hank Monk

as a testimonial of appreciation of his friends for his skill and carefulness as a "whip".

W. Thompson, Jr.	Alex O'Neil
Joe Clark	John S. Henning
H. P. Wakelee	W. M. Lent
J. O. Earle	Geo. Hearst
W. W. Stowe	H. H. Raymond

"Keep your seat, Mr. Greeley, I'll have you there."
Dec. 1, 1863 [8]

HORACE GREELEY
WENT WEST IN 1859

HANK MONK, DEAN OF WHIPS
"Keep your seat, Mr. Greeley, I'll have
you there."

ORMSBY HOUSE, MARK TWAIN'S FAVORITE LOAFING CORNER

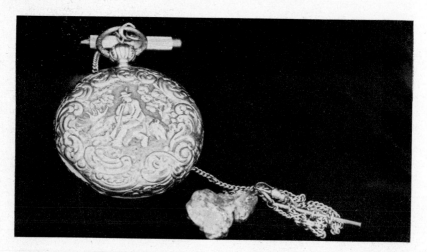

WATCH PRESENTED TO HANK MONK IN MEMORY OF RIDE WITH HORACE GREELEY

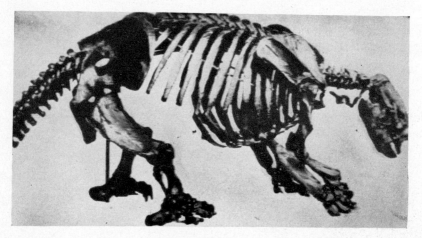

ONE OF THE ANIMALS THAT MADE THE CARSON FOOTPRINTS

The drivers of the stages of the frontier days did somewhat as the conductors of our modern trains do today. That is, the watch was held in the hand until the appointed minute of departure had come. Then the driver jumped to his seat and off he went. How proud Hank Monk must have been thereafter as he held that beautiful timepiece in one hand and his whip in the other, awaiting the departure of his stage!

On the morning of the twentieth day out from St. Joe, the Overland Stage rolled into Carson City. The regular stage stop was the Ormsby House, a two-story brick rooming house situated on the corner of Carson and Second streets, directly opposite the plaza. The site of Carson City, selected by Major William Ormsby and A. V. Z. Curry was a broad, sandy plain at the immediate eastern base of the towering, majestic Sierra Nevada Mountains. Carson Street, the main avenue running north and south and parallel with the mountains, had four or five blocks of little white frame buildings and a few brick ones, all ranged along the western side of the street. These buildings were "too high to sit down on, but not too high for various other purposes. . . ." Scattered among the sagebrush where mythical streets ran were a few dwelling houses. The plaza (the present capitol building stands on one of these acres) was a "large, unfenced, level vacancy, with a liberty pole in it." It was here that public auctions were held; horse traders here exhibited their animals and made their bargains; mass meetings gathered in this area to rally around the flag during the Civil War; and the traveling public and teamsters used the ground for camping purposes.

After Sam Clemens had been in the territory a few weeks he observed in a letter home to his mother: "The country is fabulously rich in gold, silver, copper, lead, coal, iron, quicksilver, marble, granite, chalk, plaster of Paris (gypsum), thieves, murderers, desperadoes, ladies, children, lawyers, Christians, Indians, Chinamen, Spaniards, gamblers, sharpers, coyotes (pronounced Ki-yo-ties), poets, preachers, and jackass rabbits."

There was no celebration for the new Secretary and his brother when they arrived. After their baggage was unloaded, they decided to take up their lodging in a downstairs front bedroom in the Ormsby House; and "when they had got their bed, a small table, two chairs, the Government fire-proof safe, and the Unabridged

Dictionary into it, there was still room enough left for a visitor—maybe two, but not without straining the walls." This room was sleeping room at night and Orion's office by day. And what with a "carpet . . . a genuine queen's ware washbowl . . . and a painted oilcloth window-curtain," the Secretary and Sam were aristocratically settled. However, Sam soon moved upstairs and joined the "untitled plebeians," Nye's Irish Brigade, in a fourteen-bed dormitory.[9]

The first step taken by Orion and Sam was to pay an official visit to the Territorial chief. They found the Governor elaborately domiciled in a one-story, two-roomed white-frame palace. "It compelled respect of the citizen and inspired the Indians with awe." The other members of the official roster were settled around the town in private homes; they had their offices in their bedrooms, too. Since most of them ate at Mrs. Bridget Murphy's boardinghouse, Orion and Sam did likewise. The boys named it "the ranch." Her rates were exceedingly low—ten dollars a week—especially when paid in depreciated currency. They were, in fact, too low to permit her to extend credit to any of them on the frail expectation that he was going to get a political job.

Since Governor Nye had permitted, even encouraged, many of Bridget's "ranchers" to come out to Nevada with him, she therefore held Nye morally responsible for their board bills. With Irish persistency she urged the Governor to find employment for them until the legislature could meet. After some cogitation and contemplation, the resourceful chief decided on a plan. Since there were few roads in his Territory—and most of them were toll roads—and no railroads at all, it might be well to have a route for a railroad surveyed. He promised: "When the legislature meets, I will have the necessary bill passed and the remuneration arranged"—he had proclaimed the opening of the first Territorial legislature for October 1. With this assurance in mind, Mrs. Murphy carried her boarders along for a few months.

And so it was that the would-be Territorial officers from New York, New Hampshire, Ohio, and elsewhere were converted into "surveyors, chain bearers, and so on."

The railroad, the Governor thought, ought to be surveyed westward over the Sierra Nevadas.

"What! A railroad over the Sierra Nevada Mountains?" queried one workman.

"Well, then, survey it eastward to a certain point."

In this direction the surveyors could go on indefinitely, "lugging their chains through sand and sagebrush." They did their work well, surveying slowly, deliberately, and carefully. Every night for a week they returned to the ranch, "dusty, foot-sore, and hungry but very jolly." After the first week they were so far from Carson City that they had to set up camp in the field. They were naturally interested in where that "certain point" was for an eastern terminus. To a particularly importune inquiry from one of the party of "How far eastward?" the Governor wired back:

"To the Atlantic Ocean, blast you! And then bridge it and go on!" This reply brought the entire party back to town. The Governor finally admitted that he meant to stall until they had surveyed into Utah Territory—and then to telegraph to Brigham Young to hang them for trespass!

But Nye did not get rid of his retainers so easily. They hung around Carson City until after the legislature had met and the Territorial and county governments had been set up. Some of the "carpetbaggers" did get offices, a few turned to mining, and still others went over to California or returned to their homes.

These fellows were, for the most part, young and adventuresome. They had to be to want to leave their families, their homes, and settled communities to come out to the frontier.

In addition to the financial hazards and the physical hardships they experienced, there were certain annoyances peculiar to this desert country. In the summertime the desert is infested with snakes, scorpions, and tarantulas. These latter are prodigious, black, hairy-legged, yellow-stomached spiders with a wicked sting, delivered from beneath when infuriated. Goaded into fury, they can jump knee-high, turn over quickly, and give a bite which makes their victims desperately sick. (No person has ever been known to die from a tarantula bite.)

The surveying gang became fascinated with these desert denizens. They observed how they ambled along in search of food. They noticed that at the opening of their holes they wove a trapdoor web with a double purpose: to keep out intruders and to catch and hold the trespasser until the occupant returned. From time to time the boys brought in ten to twelve of these spiders. Their usual method of keeping a tarantula for observation was to place it under a heavy glass tumbler.

The Brigade arranged the glass prisons on the shelves back of their cots. On the night that the surveyors returned permanently from their expedition, a "Washoe zephyr" came up. These wicked down-drafts that swirl from over the Sierras and twist and turn have a tremendous force behind them. The green lumber with which most of the first buildings were constructed had dried out in the hot summer months, thus loosening the boards which were not too securely nailed down. About midnight the roof of an adjoining building blew off and a corner of it crashed through one side of the dormitory. The terrific noise it made awakened the sleepers, who tumbled or sprawled out of bed into the narrow passageways between the cots. Bob Howland, Governor Nye's nephew, awakening from a deep sleep, sprang up quickly, knocking down the shelf with his head. Collecting his thoughts from the blow, he remembered the hairy prisoners under the tumblers and shouted: "Turn out, boys, the tarantulas are loose!"

"No warning ever sounded so dreadful. . . . Every man groped for a trunk or a bed and jumped on it. Then followed the strangest silence . . . waiting, expecting, fear. It was as dark as pitch, and one had to imagine the spectacle of those fourteen scant-clad men roosting gingerly on trunks and beds for not a thing could be seen. . . . Only a frightened ejaculation located a sufferer. 'Ow!' followed by a sudden thump was the only way one could tell that positions had been changed from bed to floor. Silence again—a gasping voice hissed, 'S-s-omething's crawling up the back of my neck!'

"Every now and then you could hear a little subdued scramble and a sorrowful 'Oh Lord!' and then you would know that somebody was getting away from something he took for a tarantula, and not losing any time about it, either. Directly a voice in the corner rang out wild and clear:

" 'I've got him! I've got him!' (Pause, and probable change of circumstance.) 'No, he's got me! Oh, ain't they *never* going to fetch a lantern.' "

The tumultuous crash and the frightened shouts of Mrs. Murphy's boarders awakened her, too. In due time she fetched the lantern to ascertain the damage to her dormitory. The Brigade presented a very grotesque and serious-faced appearance, perched as they were on boxes, beds, and trunks. Although the boys took candles and looked high and low for the spiders, none was ever seen again. However, they didn't go back to bed again that night. Instead they "sat up the rest of the night playing cribbage and keeping a sharp lookout for the enemy." Ten years later, when writing *Roughing It*, Sam said, "I know I am not capable of suffering more than I did during those few minutes of suspense in the dark, surrounded by those creeping, bloody-minded tarantulas. . . . I had rather go to war than live that episode over again."

The few months Sam spent playing around with the Brigade and living in that dormitory were equivalent to the same time spent in a college fraternity house. From among these boys he found his future companions in play, in work, and in adventure. From the prattle that he listened to, over Mrs. Murphy's boardinghouse table, he became quite well acquainted with the political setup of Nevada's burgeoning government. He had a chance to take the measurement of these egotistical politicians, some of which were to be the butt of his writings.

While the Brigade was out surveying, Sam and Orion were reading in the Book of Instructions, one chapter every morning and two of them in Sunday school, trying to find out about Orion's duties as Secretary of State, Treasurer, Comptroller, and Acting Governor in the Governor's absence.

So far there was no place for Sam as a private secretary. But Sam took his anticipated job seriously, if one is to believe the Nevada Directory of 1861. In it one reads:

> ORION CLEMENS, Secretary of State.
> SAM'L L. CLEMENS, Assistant Secretary of State.

Compared to the other members of the "political emigrant party" Sam was a plutocrat. He had $800 in capital, which would go a long way with board and room at only $10 a week. He loafed around Carson City, spending considerable time in just seeing things and hearing street talk. Observers noticed this gimlet-eyed, ramshackle character as he leaned for hours at a time against the hotel corner. The Ormsby House was the center of the village's activity. It was the only hotel, and as such it was the regular stop for stages and the Pony Express rider. As it was directly opposite the Plaza, Sam was able to see the covered wagons roll in and camp, the California auctioneers unload their wares and sell them, and the ever-present California Mexican cowboy exhibit his horsemanship.

Soon after Sam had arrived in Carson City, he "went Western," changing to "wearing a damaged slouch hat, blue woolen shirt, and pants crammed into boot-tops, and gloried in the absence of coat, vest, and braces." It made him feel "rowdyish and bully. . . . It seemed to me nothing could be so fine and romantic."

The "ranch" boys had been about the country in the few weeks that they had been in the Territory. They were "oldtimers" by now and thoroughly Westernized. Since the Territory was not yet organized and therefore none of them had a job, some of them had gone prospecting while others had laid the foundation for a future fortune by going up to the mountains bordering Lake Bigler (Tahoe) and taking up timber claims.

Captain Thomas C. Nye, brother of Governor Nye, who had gone to California in the Gold Rush days, came over to Nevada when his brother was appointed Governor. The Captain and several companions had already taken up timber claims and had established a camp on the Lake. Food had been cached and a boat acquired. Sam heard so much about the claims, the Lake, and its possibilities that he wanted to go, too. He and John Kinney, one of Judge George Turner's retainers from Cincinnati, Ohio, set out for the Lake.

Sam's resolve to stay a short time had been changed. "In two or three weeks I had grown wonderfully fascinated with the curious new country and concluded to put off my return to the States a while." With blankets and an ax apiece, Johnny and Sam started out to hike the eleven miles to the Lake. Eleven miles on level ground was not much of a hike, but to take a stiff climb over rough mountain terrain, crossing not one but several summits, each higher than the preceding one, was fatiguing.

They "toiled laboriously up a mountain about a thousand miles high" (Sam confused miles with feet) "and looked over. No Lake there." They "descended on the other side, crossed a valley, and toiled up another mountain three or four thousand miles high, apparently, and looked again. No Lake yet." They sat down "tired and perspiring" and "hired a couple of Chinamen to curse those people" who had intrigued their curiosity about the Lake. Sam Clemens always did have trouble with his bronchial tubes.

Refreshed, they went on for two or three hours. At last the Lake burst upon them, "a noble sheet of blue water lifted six thousand three hundred feet above the level of the sea, and walled in by a rim of snow-clad mountain peaks that towered aloft full three thousand feet higher still. . . . As it lay there with the shadows of the mountains brilliantly photographed upon its still surface, I thought it must surely be the fairest picture the whole earth affords." How fortunate Sam Clemens was to have seen that aristocratic wilderness in all of its pristine loveliness! Without the virgin forest —most of it now in the mines of Virginia City or burned up in the mills—and with the present "hot-dog" stands, service stations, and other aspects of modern civilization moved in, it can still "lay Como in the shade."

The boys found the skiff, the food, and a place in which they made their own camp. They slept rolled up in their blankets, cooked their food in the open, and breathed the same pure, fine air "the angels breathe" for four days and nights. Skirting along the shore one day about three miles from the Nye camp, they took up three hundred acres of choice yellow-pine timberland. The simple rule governing the holding of their claim was to fence it and to build a house, but since cutting three trees apiece was all the physical labor they could stand, they decided to rest their claim on that work. The next day they were going to complete the required work of building a house. However, after one log was cut, this work also seemed too elaborate; they compromised on one built of saplings. But pine saplings were a job to cut, too, so they decided on a brush house to satisfy the law.

Their work now completed, they fished, slept, smoked their pipes, played faro, bathed in the lake, and read some wornout novels. One evening when Johnny was bringing in a fresh supply of food, Sam lighted a fire and then went back to the boat to get the frying pan. While he was doing this, he heard a shout from Johnny and, looking up, he saw that his fire had spread to the dry pine needles and was galloping all over the premises! "In a minute and a half the fire seized upon a dense growth of dry manzanita chaparral six or eight feet high, and then the roaring and popping and cracking was something terrific."

For four hours they watched their timber claim go up in smoke and flame. Their food gone and their house destroyed, they lay down on the sandy beach to sleep.

The next morning they started back to the Nye camp. While they were rowing along the shore, a terrible storm came up on the Lake. Battling the waves for some time, they decided then that it would be better to beach the boat "than go down in a hundred fathoms of water." As they were trying to do so, "a wave came over the stern that washed crew and cargo ashore. . . ." The boys were so starved by that time that they ate the rest of the Brigade's provisions and set out for home to tell of their experiences and to get forgiveness. The latter was "accorded upon the payment of damages." [10]

Sam Clemens was to make many more trips to Lake Tahoe. A large number of his future descriptions of scenery compared other places to this lake.

From the time Sam Clemens arrived in the Territory of Nevada in the middle of August, 1861, until December of that year, he was a member of the Brigade. The Territorial legislature met on October 1, and Sam probably waited around Carson City to see if there were any possible appropriations for an Assistant Territorial Secretary or if there were any other grave State position that he might receive. All of the time he was in the Territory he was interested in its politics and its politicians, and enjoyed reporting the meetings of the legislature and the first State Constitutional Convention. Indeed, it was during this period that he made the keen observations of Nevada's first politicians, whom he was to lampoon in his writings and to burlesque when he was "The Governor of the Third House," an honorary title which he bore for the remainder of the time he spent in Nevada.

7

THE SHIP IS LAUNCHED

AS SOON AS ORION AND SAM WERE COMPLETELY
settled at Mrs. Murphy's boardinghouse, the Secretary plunged
into his official duties. He soon found that they expanded into
Treasurer, Comptroller, Secretary of State, and Acting Governor in
the absence of Governor Nye. The book of instructions which he
had sworn to obey faithfully outlined in general what he was supposed to do. However, it was one thing for the Secretary of State at
Washington, D. C., to write out these instructions and an entirely
different thing for a Territorial Secretary three thousand miles away
to carry them out. Documents prepared in Washington have ever
been famous for their ambiguity, but this one seemed to be more
obscure than most of them.

Governor Nye had proclaimed the Territorial legislature to meet
on October 1, 1861; it was now the latter part of August. To get a
ruling or a clarification of an instruction was practically impossible:
a round-trip reply from the national capital took at least six weeks.
Orion had to do the best he could to carry out his orders. Although
Sam Clemens learned soon after his arrival in Carson City that
there was no provision for a salary for an Assistant Secretary of the
Territory, he remained with Orion and helped him.

The Congress had appropriated $20,000 a year to pay the salaries
of the Territorial officers and the legislators, to buy material for their
use, to rent a place for the meetings of the legislature, and to pay
for anything else connected with the organization of the new
government.

And, mind you, this money was not advanced to the Secretary.
Oh, no—everything he purchased had to be on credit and the
proper voucher issued for it. The voucher must then be forwarded
to Washington, where that distant government decided whether the
Congressional appropriation could be drawn on for the amount
or not.

Conscientious Orion Clemens had to ask for credit or advance
the money himself in getting the ship launched. Nevada business-

men were apprehensive and even suspicious of these "emigrants." (The rank and file had other names for these newcomers. The usual reference to them was either "tenderfoot" or "stinkfoot.") They had come from other parts of these United States to set up their government. How could the merchants, hotel- and barkeepers know whether or not the credit of the Territory of Nevada was good? It wasn't even in existence yet.

There was another thing that the "Secretary, Treasurer, Comptroller, and Acting Governor" had to take into consideration: the relative value of specie and greenbacks. The people of Nevada always had contempt for currency—especially so when it was worth only forty cents on the dollar! Most transactions in those days were made in the raw gold dust itself. But the Congress had legislated that one hundred cents of one kind of money was equal to any other kind, and due to this law Secretary Clemens had many embarrassing situations to meet.

The first and hardest nut Orion had to crack was to find a meeting place for the Territorial legislature. Since Governor Nye had proclaimed Carson City the capital, *some* place in this village had to be found for the capitol. In 1861, Carson was a one-story town with very few buildings. It was at about this time that Sam wrote home to his mother that it was "situated in a flat sandy desert . . . surrounded on all sides by such prodigious mountains, that when you gaze at them awhile—and begin to conceive of their grandeur— and next to feel their vastness expanding your soul—and ultimately find yourself growing and swelling and spreading into a giant— I say when this point is reached you look disdainfully down upon the insignificant village of Carson and in that instant you are seized with the burning desire to stretch forth your hand, put the city in your pocket, and walk off with it."

"There is something solemnly funny about the struggles of a new-born territorial government to get a start in this world. Ours had a trying time of it." It was an easy thing to get legislators at three dollars a day. What difference did it make if board and room were four-fifty a day? Think of the prestige and distinction that went with being a legislator, and one of the first ones at that! But *where* to find a place to meet—just floor space large enough to crowd in twenty-four legislators and rooms for the privacy of the committees?

All of these details were left to the Secretary. His chief, the Governor, had gone over to California, so there was no one with whom he could confer about these grave matters of state except his brother Sam. Nevada always did bore Governor Nye. He had come out to Nevada for bigger and better things for himself. It seems that he spent as little time there as he could. Shortly after Orion arrived and the Governor saw what a fine Secretary he had, one who *could* act in his absence, he hiked out for more pleasant climes than Carson City in August.

At this time the Governor announced that he was going down to Sacramento to do a little research in the ways of government—his friends said that it was to get away from his heavy gubernatorial responsibilities. Governor Nye could always find a partner in fun, and in Governor John G. Downey he found one after his own heart. While Nye was in the California capital, Downey invited Nye to go to the Marysville fair with him. The highlight of this festivity was a ball on Friday night. The two governors had a "helluva" good time. "They never missed a dance except for one little hour shortly after midnight spent with a few good friends in a retired room of the Pavel comparing relative merits of French and California champagne," Governor Nye's favorite drink.

The room at the hotel where this discussion took place had an awkward entrance: the door was neither more nor less than a window with a low but clumsy flight of steps at either side. After several rounds of the cup that cheers, the Governors started back to the dance. Approaching the door-window, Downey urged Nye to go first, but Nye urged that Downey should precede him. This Alphonse-and-Gaston act went on for some time. Finally Nye could stand it no longer, and in his best champagne manner exclaimed:

> "Governor Downey, you're a real Governor, you are; you're a legitimate Governor, elected to this office by a great and generous people, you are. I'm but, I am, an appointed Governor, I am, appointed Governor of Nevada Territory by the Administration, I am; and any blasted fool can get an appointment." [1]

This irresistible appeal was too much for Downey—he bowed graciously and went first.

After Orion and Sam had made a thorough canvass of Carson City for a legislative hall and had found no place for it to lay its young head, "Curry, Old Curry, Old Abe Curry" came forward, unaided and alone, and shouldered the Ship of State over the bar and got her afloat again. But for him the legislature should have been obliged to sit in the desert. He offered the huge barnlike second story of his Warm Springs Hotel, two miles from Carson City, rent-free.

Abram V. Z. Curry was an enterprising frontiersman who had come over from California and settled in Genoa. There he met another American, Major Ormsby, equally as enthusiastic as himself. While the delegates of the Gentiles of Carson County, Territory of Utah, were trying to get recognition for their Provisional Government in 1858, the people of Carson Valley were looking forward to setting up the new capital of Washoe in Genoa. Town lots and property went sky-high, too high for Ormsby and Curry. They had other ideas about the location of a capital—one which would bring them financial returns.

Why couldn't they, themselves, lay out a town over in the next valley and boom it for the capital? No sooner thought of than done. These two men acquired a considerable stretch of land, from the mountains on the west to some warm springs on the east side of Eagle Valley where the old California trail crossed it.

Alongside of these springs that came out from under the low hills was a fine sandstone deposit, ideal for building purposes. From this rock, Curry cut blocks and built a two-story hotel and a bath house. Part of the lower floor was used by the Curry family for living quarters (he had a wife and five daughters); another part was set off for a bar and a public dining room. Space in the upper story was rented to the traveling public. There it could unroll its blankets and bunk on the floor.

The best part of Curry's establishment, outside of the fine liquor he served at the bar and the equally fine table he set, was the bath house. In its soft warm water, travelers could get their first bath to soak off the layers of alkali and sweat of many weeks' accumulation.

About two miles from the "Hotel de Curry," as the legislators later dubbed it, Ormsby laid out a modern town. The future capital of Nevada was planned with broad streets and large city blocks running north and south and east and west of a four-acre plaza. The main street, Carson Street, ran along the west side of this open space, a characteristic of most Western towns. Here, they decided, was the ideal site for the capitol building.

Directly opposite the center of the plaza, Major Ormsby built a two-story hotel, called the Ormsby House, the first hotel in the city and the center of all activities. This little community flourished, other business buildings sprang up, the Overland Stages came this way, and the Pony Express paused to leave and to pick up the mail and to change horses. Little shacks sprang up out in the sage-brush around the plaza. Emigrants camped in the plaza, and Mexican cowboys tied their broncos to the fence Ormsby built around it.[2]

In fact, everything was going splendidly until that fateful day of May 9, 1860, when Major Ormsby rode off at the head of the unor-ganized posse from Carson City, Virginia City, and other Washoe communities to punish the depredations of the Pyramid Lake Indi-ans who had burned Williams Station and killed four men. A week later Ormsby's arrow-filled body was found by his brother near the battlefield on the lower Truckee River. His death was generally mourned, but Abe Curry carried on for Carson City.

It was in this same year that William Morris Stewart came over from Downieville to make Carson City his home.[3] He and Curry became good friends. Stewart, too, believed that Carson City should be the capital. In fact, he took the task of seeing that it *was* the head and the permanent seat of the government of Nevada. This friend-ship became more binding as the years went by and was commemo-rated in a stepping-stone which Abe had cut out from his quarry. On one side is the inscription, "From A. Curry to W. M. Stewart," and on the other side is cut, "May our friendship be as lasting as this stone." Although these far-sighted conspirators made no public pronouncement of their plans at the time, there is evidence that they were forming plans to use Warm Springs for some State insti-tution. Stewart repeatedly promised Curry that when the State government should materialize, the capital would remain in Carson City.

The road to the temporary capitol building—and the stone quarry —lay over deep sand in summer and a muddy quagmire in winter. To carry the heavy loads of stone over it, Curry had to improve it. This he did by laying scantlings edgewise. The rolling stock for the "Eagle Valley Railroad" was described by one of the reporters of the

Sacramento Daily Union who was sent up to report the proceedings: "It runs or rather trots from Carson City across the Eagle Valley a distance of a mile and three-quarters (more or less) to Curry's Hot Springs Hotel, that is to say, to the Provisional Capital of Nevada Territory. The rolling stock consists of a platform car, which carries freight from Curry's stone quarry to Carson, and a windowless passenger car of primitive construction. Two mules act in the capacity of locomotives. Into this car the assembled wisdom of the legislature is transported to Curry's Hotel and at night to be carted back again. The car has no springs, and the members think their daily rides afford excellent exercise for the dyspeptic." [4] Every legislator had a free pass on the railroad. At least it was free for this session, but the Territory was later to pay handsomely for these privileges.

Orion and Sam had to make many trips over this railroad in getting everything in readiness for the session. They also became very good friends with the Curry family—a friendship which continued through the years. Together they planned the layout for Nevada's first legislative hall. The large upstairs room, which Curry gave rent-free, was divided into four sections, separated by canvas partitions. Orion bought the cloth and paid $3.40 for it. When he sent in the voucher for this sum, he was reminded that although the instructions permitted a liberal *rent* for a legislative hall, the United States Government was not *paying* for the *dividing of rooms*. The fact that an appreciable sum of money was being saved the country by Mr. Curry did not alter the matter. The upshot was that this sum was subtracted from the Secretary's $1800-a-year salary.

The room at the west end was assigned to the House of Representatives; the Territorial Council met in the room at the east end. The space between the two houses was divided into two small rooms for committee meetings. Orion had plain pine desks and wooden benches made for the legislators—there was but one furniture store in Carson City where chairs could be purchased and Orion could not obtain credit there for the Territory, so there was nothing else that he could provide for them to sit on. And he could not give them secrecy—neither locks nor keys could be bought. He did get from some source two large American flags, which he draped on the wall back of the desk of the presiding officers. The floors were uncarpeted, and when the legislators moved about with their hobnailed boots the noise was so great that little could be heard. Curry corrected this annoyance by having fresh sawdust spread over the floor. It served two purposes: it softened the noise and it took the place of spittoons. The Council did boast of a fine clock—nobody has stated whence it came.[5]

Orion had another experience with the Comptroller of the United States Government that he lived to regret. The instructions told him to purchase penknives, envelopes, pens, and writing paper for the legislators. For these things he received credit in San Francisco. After he had distributed the articles to all of the legislators, he found that he had one extra penknife. He gave the extra one—the penknives cost three dollars apiece—to the Clerk of the House. The Secretary, who was expected to account for the distribution of all supplies, honestly reported the gift. The Comptroller replied that the Clerk was not a member of the legislature—hence, the cost of the penknife must be deducted from Orion's suffering salary! Commenting on these proceedings, Sam wrathfully declared: "Nothing in this world is palled in such impenetrable obscurity as a United States Treasury Comptroller's understanding."

Two more incidents should be cited to console the present generation in its dealing with national ambiguity. The first concerned the matter of printing the proceedings of the legislature, wherein Orion ran into a snag. The Instructions ordered him to have the Journals of both houses printed; they further stipulated the exact sum that he was to pay for having the printing done. Orion had to figure everything in greenbacks when making out the voucher, but he had to figure in gold when having the work done.

Nevada's first legislators were garrulous. In fact, it cost so much to get their verbosity on record that Orion discontinued the printing of it after a short while. When he wrote the Comptroller what he had done, enclosing a copy of the current market report of prices in the West—and calling his special attention to the cost of hay at $250 a ton—he was not only sternly rebuked, but also warned to correct his ways: the printing had to be done, and he was reminded that there was "nothing in his instructions requiring him to purchase hay."

The second matter in which the Secretary had some difficulties with the stupidity of Washington officials was the problem of getting wood sawed. Orion had much ado to get heat for the legislative hall. There were no heating stoves in Carson City—and even had there been, they could not have been obtained on credit; stoves were a great luxury in that frontier town. However, Orion found a way out of this difficulty. He borrowed stoves from the government of the Territory of Utah, over in Salt Lake City. He had met several of the officials of that Territory on his way out to Nevada. Evidently he had impressed them as being an honest man. So heating stoves were loaned to Nevada by Utah—what difference did it make if freight on them had to be paid for five hundred miles?

White men's wages in Carson were $3 to $4 a load for sawing up stove wood, a sum which Orion and Sam knew was too exorbitant for the United States to allow. They hired a lowly Indian who worked for half the wages of a white man. When the red man had finished his job, Orion made out the usual voucher and sent it in to be allowed. To it he signed no name but instead explained that, although the Indian could not write his name, he had done his work well. Again Orion was "stuck" for the amount, which was taken out of his salary. "The United States was too accustomed to employing dollar and a half thieves" to believe the Secretary's explanation.

The next time that wood had to be sawed to provide for the legislative warmth, Sam took charge of the contract. He employed the same Indian and taught him to make a cross.[6] When the work was finished, and the voucher made out, the Indian affixed an "X" that "looked like it had been drunk a year." Here is the signature, as it was witnessed by Sam:

Satisfactory Voucher
From *Roughing It*

The voucher went through. Sam later said that he was sorry he hadn't had the Indian cut a thousand loads of wood!

At half-past noon on October 1, 1861, Orion Clemens called together the first meeting of the Territorial legislature of Nevada. Mr. George Turner, appointed Chief Justice of the Territorial Supreme Court, administered the oath to the legislators. Turner, a young fellow from Ohio and a Nye appointee, was a small man, but what he lacked in height he made up in oratorical vim and egotistical demeanor. Sam took his measure and had plenty to say about him in his reportorial days.

The House organized quickly, and got off to a respectable start by employing the services of a clergyman, the Reverend F. A. White of Carson City. For $1.50 a day he opened each session with a prayer. The members of the Council didn't feel that such a decorous procedure was necessary for them. However, after the Council had been in session for several prayerless weeks, one of the members had a change of heart on the subject and introduced a resolution suggesting that the Council have the same preacher that the House had. The President of the Council, J. L. Van Bokkelen, opposed it vigorously. Stepping aside from the presidential chair, he remarked that "he did not think it was necessary to go to an expense of a dollar and a half a day for a short and concise prayer in the morning by a Chaplain; it would hardly prove a paying investment." He added that "he had sat under prayers costing ten thousand dollars a year and did not know that they did him much good. Moreover, members of the Council would hardly be likely to preserve a due and decorous gravity during prayer time." [7] In later years Sam Clemens said that this man needed prayers more than any other man he knew.

This prayer discussion amused the California reporters no end; they made considerable mention of it in their newspaper columns. They followed all the talk on the subject and noted that several days later another suggestion was made in the Council. This one proposed that the two houses take turn-about—one chamber employing the Reverend to give prayers in it one day, the other on the following day.

After this kind of prattle had gone on for some time, one of the Councilmen recalled that there was a preacher in the Council itself: the Right Reverend Henry Smeathman, Rector of the Episcopal Church in Carson City. This revelation closed the discussion. A resolution was introduced and adopted that this clergyman offer the prayers for the Council. President Van Bokkelen, who had at first opposed the prayers, now approved the idea, commenting that "he was in favor of domestic manufacture and consequently approved of home-made prayers."

Several years later Sam Clemens visited the Territorial legislature of Hawaii, meeting in Honolulu. He observed the decorum of that body, the members of which attended it barefooted, and concluded that "Legislative etiquette is a low grade everywhere. . . . I find no exception to the rule. I am ashamed to say their etiquette [the Hawaiian] is a shade superior to that of the early Washoe Legislature. 'Horse' Williams was a member of them, and he used to always prop his vast feet upon his desk and get behind them and eat a raw turnip during prayer by the Chaplain." [8]

Soon after the legislature was in working order, many of the ladies of Carson City came out to observe its proceedings. When they noted that venerable men had only wooden benches upon which to sit, they were moved to do something about it. Through the efforts of Mrs. Ormsby, widow of the Major, and Miss Hannah Clapp, principal of the Sierra Seminary, a private school in Carson, chairs were procured—some from their friends, and some from their own homes. Resolutions of thanks were spread on the Journals of both houses, expressing heartfelt appreciation to these women, and when they later visited the legislature, they were invited inside the railings and given seats of honor.

With all of the difficulties, delays, and obstructions Orion Clemens had, he managed, with the aid of his brother Sam and of Abe Curry, to get the legislature launched. However, there was still one thing that he had to do by himself. There was no Territorial seal. He designed one. It showed a rugged miner in the foreground holding an American flag in his right hand and a miner's pick in the left one. At his feet a miner's pan was placed. In the background details of the mining industry were depicted: an overshot wheel of a mill turned by a stream gushing from a mountain, a man running an ore car out of a tunnel, and the open door of a five-stamp quartz mill in action. Around the outer rim of the seal was printed "TERRITORY OF NEVADA, U. S. A." The motto selected and printed on a scroll at the bottom read "Volens et Potens." The Clemens imprint was already being left permanently on Nevada.[9] (See page 92.)

Although Sam stood manfully by his brother in all of his Secre-

Needs Praying For

From *Roughing It*

tarial duties, sometimes giving advice, other times rebuking him for his actions, he received not a cent for his work. It may be supposed that he hoped for even the smallest crumb, for some menial job at the legislature; but all of the clerkships or reportorial jobs had been promised to the Brigade or had been given as patronage to members of the two houses. He got, however, something more valuable than money could buy from these experiences: he learned to know these politicians, their conceit and chicanery, egotism and incompetency. It was humorous articles written about these would-be political "big shots" that obtained for him his first job on the *Territorial Enterprise*.

Territorial Seal of Nevada
Designed by Orion Clemens

Besides Curry and Stewart, mention must be made of William H. Barstow, Assistant Secretary of the Council. He was one of the attachés from Virginia City; later he went on the *Territorial Enterprise* as financial secretary. He was later influential in obtaining Sam a position on this newspaper. Then there was Clement T. Rice who reported the first legislature; Sam and he cruised around together at a later session when Sam gave him the nickname of

"The Unreliable." Samuel Youngs, Bob Howland and Horatio Phillips: they were to be pals of Sam's in Aurora. William Claggett, Sam's old friend from Iowa, and A. J. Simmons, the two men with whom Sam had his picture taken at a meeting of the legislature of 1863, were also among those present.

While Sam was loafing around the Ormsby House with little or nothing to do but go out and watch the legislature, he resolved to buy a horse. At any time of day he could see the California Mexican cowboy exhibit his horsemanship up and down the streets. Means of transportation were so scarce in those days that practically everyone had to have a horse if he expected to go anywhere. Admiring the ease and speed with which those cowboys rode their horses, he was desirous of owning one, too. The Mexicans, generally from California, had gone out on the range, lassoed the wild cayuses, brought them in and half-broken them to the halter and the saddle. But only an expert could handle them. Good money could be made by auctioning them off; the chief stand for this business was on the plaza, where the biggest crowd could be congregated. While acquisitive notions were passing through Sam's mind, an "auctioneer came scurrying through the plaza on a black beast that had as many humps and corners on him as a dromedary— Going, going, at twenty-two! Horse, saddle and bridle at twenty-two dollars, gentlemen," shouted the auctioneer. A "come-on" bystander, who turned out to be the auctioneer's brother, boosted the sale by remarking that the Spanish saddle alone was worth the price—just note the great *"tapidaros"*!

Sam began to look interested. The booster could see *that* at a glance, and confided to him that he knew that horse, "knew him well. He is, without a shadow of a doubt, a Genuine Mexican Plug!" Surely that must be some kind of a thoroughbred with which he was not familiar. Inquiring if he had any other advantages, he was told that the horse could outbuck anything in America. Sam now knew for sure that he was going to own a Genuine Mexican Plug, or die. However, during this contemplative delay, the auction price had advanced to twenty-four dollars and a half.

"Twenty-seven!" Sam shouted.

"And sold!" said the auctioneer, and passed over the Genuine Mexican Plug to Sam. Sam was so pleased with his purchase that he could scarcely contain himself. After paying the price, he put his

Plug in a livery stable, and went to get something to eat and rest himself from his exhilarating excitement.

In the afternoon Sam brought his newly bought prize back into the plaza to try him out. He got some citizens to hold the beast by the head, and others to steady him by the tail, while he mounted his Genuine Mexican Plug. When they let go, the bronco "placed all his feet together, lowered his back, and then suddenly arched it upward, and shot me straight into the air a matter of three or four feet! I came as straight down again, lit in the saddle, went instantly up again, came down almost on the high pommel, shot up again, and came down on the horse's neck, all in the space of three or four seconds. Then he rose and stood almost straight up on his hind feet, and I, clasping his lean neck desperately, slid back into the saddle, and held on. He came down, and immediately hoisted his heels into the air, delivering a vicious kick at the sky, and stood on his fore-feet." (What else did he expect—wasn't the horse guaranteed to outbuck anything in America?)

When Sam went up the third time, he heard a stranger say, "Oh, *don't* he buck, though!" At that moment a bystander gave the Plug a thwack with a leathern strap, and when Sam "arrived again the Genuine Mexican Plug was not there."

A California bronco-buster chased the horse up, and asked Sam if he might ride him. Sam gave his consent with pleasure. When the expert mounted, he made the mistake of applying his spurs, and "the horse darted away like a telegram. He soared over three fences like a bird, and disappeared down the road toward the Washoe Valley."

Sam sat down on a stone to take inventory of his anatomy: "By a natural impulse one of my hands sought my forehead, and the other the base of my stomach. I believe I never appreciated the poverty of the human machinery. Pen cannot describe how I was jolted up. Imagination cannot conceive how disjointed I was—how internally, externally, and universally I was unsettled, mixed up, and ruptured."

A crowd gathered around him to commiserate with him. Among the sympathizers was "Old Curry, Abe Curry, Old Abe Curry." He told Sam he had "been taken in . . . he is a simon-pure, out-and-out, genuine d——d Mexican plug, and an uncommon mean one at that, too, . . . you turnip, . . . there's chances to buy an *American* horse

The Genuine Mexican Plug elevates Sam

From *Roughing It*

for mighty little more than you paid for that bloody foreign relic." Sam said little about it at the time, but he resolved that "if the auctioneer's brother's funeral took place while he was in the territory he would postpone all other recreations and attend it."

Although the California cowboy did sixteen miles in his trip to Washoe Valley on the plug, they came tearing back to town and, after a "final skip over a wheelbarrow and a Chinaman, cast anchor in front of the 'ranch,'" Mrs. Murphy's boardinghouse. Old Genuine showed by his panting and blowing that he had been on a swift trip somewhere—but *could* he be controlled? Miles Mitchell, Speaker of the House, thought that he could, and requested transportation to take him down to the "Capitol." When "his Lordship" mounted him, Old Genuine cleared "a pile of telegraph poles as high as a church . . . and his time to the Capitol—one mile and three-quarters—remains unbeaten to this day." But the plug took an advantage: "he left out the mile, and only did the three-quarters . . ." cutting across lots, jumping fences and ditches instead of following the road, and "when the Speaker got to the Capitol, he said he had been in the air so much he felt as if he had made the trip on a comet."

After the session was over, Speaker Mitchell "came home afoot for exercise, and got the Genuine towed back behind a quartz wagon." The following day Sam loaned him to the Clerk of the House to go down to a silver mine six miles away. The Clerk walked back, too, and got the horse towed back. Sam kept on loaning him, hoping that something would happen to Genuine on one of these trips that would justify him in collecting damages. "But nothing ever happened to him."

Finally Sam turned him over to an auctioneer for sale. For four days the horse went up and down the streets, "dispersing the populace, interrupting business, and destroying children," without so much as a bid, except one for eighteen dollars which Sam hired a "bum" to make. When the auctioneer brought in his bill, Sam withdrew Genuine from the market and tried to trade him off privately, "offering him at a sacrifice for second-hand tombstones, old iron, temperance tracts, any kind of property." But Sam could find no takers, and "retired him from the market again."

Although Sam never rode Genuine again, he had to do something with him. The horse was eating his head off at the stable.

When the livery-stable owner brought in his bill for keeping the animal six weeks, Sam found that he was charged fifteen dollars for the stall and two hundred and fifty dollars for hay. Sam paid. In desperation he tried to give the plug away. The only answer to his proffered gift was the remark that "earthquakes were handy on the Pacific Coast—they did not wish to own one." Sam offered him to Governor Nye for the use of the Brigade. At first the Governor thought well of the idea, but on second reflection "he said the thing would be too palpable." At long last, Sam succeeded in giving him to an Arkansas emigrant who was passing through Carson City.

The Genuine must have been quite a horse, for years later a correspondent from Austin, Nevada, writing to the *San Francisco Post,* compared his horse with Sam's by stating that it was "a cross representative of Don Quixote's Rosinante and Mark Twain's quadruped that used to indulge in the vain endeavor to kick a fly off his forehead with one of his hind feet." [10]

Sam *did* ride other horses while he was in Washoe—but they were not Genuine Mexican Plugs!

BOOK III

UNDERGRADUATE DAYS

8

LEGISLATIVE FOOTPRINTS

"NEVADA'S FIRST LEGISLATURE WAS AN INTERESTING menagerie . . . a fine collection of sovereigns. . . . They levied taxes to the amount of thirty or forty thousand dollars and ordered expenditures to the extent of about a million."[1] So said Sam Clemens after he had observed the deliberations of the Territorial delegates. The members sat sixty days and passed all kinds of legislation necessary for the organization of a new Territory. They had their moments of economy and their fits of reckless expenditures; they acted on all manner of subjects, to regulate morals, elections, notaries, duels, crimes and misdemeanors. They granted licenses and franchises, created counties, set up county seats, and established the permanent capital of the Territory.

Speaking of franchises: fortunes were made from the privilege of collecting tolls for passing over a road or bridge. In fact, big money could be made in a thousand different ways in a new mining country, other than working ledges. Since all of Washoe was either uphill or downgrade, there was a great need for roads to carry the stupendous amount of freight necessary to build the mine shafts, the mills, the homes, and the business houses. To most parts of this country there were only animal or Indian trails. Men not inclined to mining, but not averse to making fortunes from serving money-mad men, rushed right in behind them, rolled away the boulders, scooped out a few shovelfuls of dirt to form hazardous paths around precipitous mountainsides. Only very sure-footed animals could pull the heavily laden wagons over them. The builders of these roads set up stations at the most advantageous places on them to collect tolls from persons on foot, drivers of livestock, and single, double and multiple-numbered teams. As soon as the first Territorial legislature met, these enterprising men applied for the legal and exclusive right to do business at their stands. Hundreds of private franchises were granted by this legislative body and by succeeding legislatures. (There is one toll road left in Nevada today.)

When the legislature adjourned, Sam Clemens said "it was estimated that every citizen owned about three franchises, and it was believed that, unless Congress gave the Territory another degree of longitude, there would not be room enough to accommodate the toll roads. The ends of them were hanging over the boundary line everywhere like a fringe." [2] The real fact was that the freighting business had grown to such proportions that there was nearly as much excitement over a suddenly acquired toll-road fortune as over the ownership of a newly-discovered silver ledge. Indeed, the fortune was much more certain.

The climax of this first session was the fight over the site of the capital. To be sure, the townsite owners of Carson City had given the Territory four acres in the center of the business district for this purpose, but this gift meant nothing to the other cities—large, small, one-horse, and synthetic—that wanted the prize also. After some time the fight narrowed to Virginia City and Carson City: the former because it had almost fifty per cent of the delegates and the largest population in Washoe; the latter because Governor Nye had proclaimed *it* to be the Capital of the Territory.

This question eclipsed all others. Virginia City led off by announcing early in the session that that city was after the honor of being the capital. By strategy and artifice the Virginia City delegates won from the Carson City delegates the presiding chairs of both houses of the legislature. Two strikes to their score, and if they could only win over the Governor, the victory was as good as in the bag.

A plan to influence and persuade the Governor was made. Rufe Arick, the mayor of Virginia City, and Joe Goodman, the editor of the *Territorial Enterprise* (at that time the only newspaper in the Territory and published in Virginia City), arranged a great demonstration for him. Hiring a hack, these two men drove down from the Lode to Carson City, and invited Nye to accompany them back to their city where an entertainment and a banquet awaited him.

The show was held in the Golden Age Dance Hall; there Emma Pastor sang and danced for them. Twenty-dollar gold pieces rained approval of her performance. After the show about one hundred of the leading citizenry of Virginia City sat down to an elaborate banquet at Chauvel's restaurant, a banquet of foods and liquor imported from San Francisco especially for the occasion. Champagne flowed freely. The hosts and the guest of honor provided the entertainment. The Governor, always brilliant and charming from the sparkle that produces good fellowship, arose and sang "The Battle Cry of Freedom."

Mayor Arick,[3] sober and designing, selected the moment supreme to say his piece. In a flowery speech in which he used the most complimentary words he could assemble, he presented to his Excellency, the Governor of Nevada, an expensive and handsome silver service. A clever Mayor *he* was to take on this expense without consulting the brand-new City Board of Trustees or finding out the financial condition of the city treasury!

Although the mines of Virginia City were producing millions of dollars' worth of silver bullion, the city treasury of the newly incorporated town was as bare as Old Mother Hubbard's cupboard. The city's credit was not good with the silversmith nor with the restaurant keeper. The way out of this financial difficulty was the issuance of city scrip paying four, five, and even six per cent interest per month. Before Virginia City finally attained solvency, after its bid for the capital, it had to redeem pledges for the banquet, the entertainment and the gift, amounting to $12,000.[4]

The great city of the Comstock Lode may have had a cordial mayor, a big-hearted board of trustees, and a scant majority of votes in the legislature, but it did not have the best politician in the Territory. That advantage went to Carson City in the person of its leading citizen, Bill Stewart, Councilman from that town. He had had ten years of experience in frontier politics in California before he came to Washoe, and he knew how to capture the prize. He was master of the entire session—he introduced and had passed more bills than all the rest of the members put together. Stewart also knew that he had been elected by the people of Carson City to swing the capital for them.

Making a point of meeting every delegate to the legislature as he came to Carson City, Stewart asked each what he wanted out of the session. The almost inevitable reply was "a county seat for the community from which I come." Hence, in the course of the legislative proceedings, Councilman Stewart introduced a bill dividing the Territory into counties and setting up their county seats. He attached to it a rider providing that the capital should be Carson City!

The bill was the most hotly debated one of all those introduced during the entire session. One evening, while the bill was still being debated, many of the legislators were in the bar at the Ormsby House, awaiting the arrival of the Overland Stage. J. L. Van Bokkelen, delegate from Virginia City and the President of the Council, made some disparaging remarks about the bill, which reflected on the Carson City delegation. Among other things, he accused them of selling out at a very cheap price. John Winters, delegate from Carson City, took exception to the remarks and demanded an immediate retraction. At first Van Bokkelen was inclined to grant Winters' demand, but he later restated his accusations. Winters again became angry over the statements, and made a gesture of taking off his coat to fight. Van Bokkelen, not to be outdone in these dramatics, said that he preferred pistols, and challenged Winters to a duel. Hot words flew thick and fast. Friends of both parties saw that the situation was rapidly getting out of hand and tried to step between the two men.

By this time Winters had worked himself into a high temper. Crowded into a corner of the bar near a box of stove wood, he grabbed from it a robust spar and, shouting that he would hit his best friend if he interfered, struck Van Bokkelen over the head, felling him to the floor; after which he kicked the prostrate man many times with his heavy boots before the crowd could stop him.

The senseless man was carried from the room. Two doctors worked over him for some time before animation could be restored to him. The attack was so severe that it prevented his presiding over the Council for several days. While he was *hors de combat,* the vote on the county-capital bill came up, and by the slender margin of one vote Carson City became the capital of the Territory of Nevada.[5]

The first Territorial legislature created a State Board of Prison Commissioners and shortly afterwards appointed "Old Curry, Abe Curry, Old Abe Curry" the first warden of the Territorial penitentiary. At the same time it entered into a contract with Curry to rent cell space and to board the prisoners at his Warm Springs Hotel. (This historic old inn was the seat of the first Territorial legislature of Nevada and its first temporary prison. In 1864 the legislature bought the hotel from Curry, who took $75,000 in Territorial bonds in exchange. Since then the State of Nevada has enlarged the buildings and added many improvements to the grounds.)

Curry continued to operate his hotel and to cut stone from the quarry for Carson City buildings. When the surface dirt had been stripped away and the stone cut back into the hill, the stone masons in 1864 came upon some strange imprints of prehistoric birds and animals—some of which resembled the footprints of a giant primeval man. The report of this primigenial discovery created a great sensation in the Land of Washoe; the account of the find was copied in the Pacific Coast papers; and it finally reached the leading scientific journals of the United States. Thus was precipitated one of the most hotly debated questions in the annals of the scientific world.

The geologic truth about the tracks fixed them as having been made about eighty million years ago in the Quaternary period. A dinosaur with big feet had walked across a stretch of thin shale-like muck made by a rapidly shifting lake or river. There never was any controversy about the mastodon, saurian, or bird tracks. They were too self-evident to admit of any question over which even scientists could quarrel; besides, the mastodon was considerate enough to leave his bones, which rendered his identity indisputable. He had been killed by some natural enemy or had become stuck in the mud and, being unable to extricate himself, died in that spot.

However, the creature whose tracks resembled human footprints was the one that made the debate a blisteringly hot one. Were they made by a gigantic man or a huge sloth?

So important did this question become that several of the leading scientists were induced to go to Carson City to view these fossil footprints. Among them were Joseph LeConte, Professor of Geology and Natural History at the University of California; Dr. Albert Harkness, American classical scholar and founder of the American School of Classical Studies at Athens; and Professor O. C. Marsh, American paleontologist and professor at Yale University. Casts of the prints were made, reproduced on canvas, and later published in the *Journal of the Academy of Scientists*.

Dr. Harkness unhesitatingly expressed his belief that the tracks were those of a human being. Professor LeConte, on the other hand, was not so positive—with his sensitive religious conscience, he straddled any question where science and religion conflicted. The discussion reached astonishing proportions: it even threatened to split the California Academy of Sciences into two opposing factions. From California the war spread until there was scarcely a scientific man of any prominence in the United States, or, for that matter, in the world, who did not advance his opinion on the subject. The arguments used in favor of the human origin of the footprints were just as sound and conclusive as those put forward to prove that they were made by a sloth.

When the polemics were raging hottest, Sam Clemens could restrain himself no longer. He always took a fiendish delight in exploding the egotism of a person who was impressed with himself. And his article on the "Carson Footprints," published in 1885, was double-barreled: one shot taken at the scientists who were working themselves into such a dither over the origin of the fossil remains, and the other at the members of the first Territorial legislature. It will be remembered that they could have given Sam a job. He was not above making them rue their neglect!

"It may be all very well for Professor Marsh and Professor Harkness to talk about the Carson footprints, and try to saddle them onto primeval man, the Irish elk, and others who are gone and cannot defend themselves . . . but it is not *moral*. For I know the cold facts about the footprints, and I know they were not made by the primeval man . . . they were made by the first Nevada Territorial Legislature, and I was there when it was done. It was done at the time of the *sine die* adjournment. It had rained all the evening outside, and it had rained whiskey all the evening inside—inside the fence, I mean, for there were no buildings in that early day—and neither you nor a much older man could have told on which side of the fence the weather was the most inclement. I was on both sides of it, and sometimes on it, for a brief uncertain season, and I couldn't tell.

"The footprint quarry, where that Legislature sat—stood, while they could, I mean—was a dry alkali flat with a fence around it, when the rain began; just a dry alkali flat, containing a fence full of dry alkalied flats from all over the Territory; and in three hours that first-mentioned flat was absolutely soaked to a depth of three inches; and the others all the way through. I make no exceptions; I mean all. I was there, and I know. So the place was just become a regular marsh, full of irregular marshes, so to speak—meaning the Legislature. Meaning the Legislature, but intending no disrespect. And when the weather moderated so that one could venture outside —outside the fence—these latterly adjourned.

"They adjourned in the usual form—form used by Territorial Legislatures of that day—the Speaker bringing down his gavel on the head of the member mistaken by these scientists for the Irish elk—which he, the Speaker, mistook for a fence post—and thus, as you see, is the gloom and sorrow of a double error spread over the mouldering historic incident—and said—common time, four beats to the measure, that is to say, four hiccoughs to the sentence—: 'The modder having weatherated,' and so on, in a similar train, till he got through. I remember it as if it were but yesterday. Thus dissolved they departed thence."

The legislature did adjourn during a most rainy and stormy day, November 29. Tradition has preserved a most hilarious story of this historic legislature. Old Curry, host of the bar at his Warm Springs Hotel, had laid in a special stock of liquors for the parting legislators. Undoubtedly Sam Clemens, Governor Nye, Bob Howland, and many others of the boys had a goodly share of the drinks —on the house and on one another.

Anyway, Sam says: "It was then they made the tracks. They couldn't help making them; for the place was a marsh, as I was telling you. I saw it done, for I was there. I was there, and I shall now cast light upon this pale dim void of scientific conjecture the lurid glare of history. I was there and I saw them march. The primeval man was absent; the Irish elk did not arrive; the cave bear responded not to the summons; the old Silurian ass got left. The *menagerie* was entirely local. Part of it I *saw,* and the rest of it I was. This is history; this is cold history, and history cannot lie.

"The Speaker went first. He made large tracks—the ones that are eight inches broad and eighteen inches long, and resemble the footprint of a champagne basket. He was a prime man in two or three ways, and evil in forty; but he was not the primeval man, just the same; reflect upon this. I was there; I was all the time; and I knew him well. He made the large tracks. And he did it without an effort. He could have done it with one hand tied behind him. He said so himself, he didn't tell me so, but he told others so, though I knew him well. His name was Welsh; either Welsh or Sanders, I don't remember which, but it was a name that sounded like those.

"He was a rancher, kept a ranch, cattle ranch; and did not wear shoes, such not being his custom. . . . And always when he went forth ranching with his might into the pasture amongst the cattle, there was much hay and straw lying scattered about, and with it much other material and the straw did of a truth and by custom combine and form unto him incrusted sandals, as you may say—incrusted because not projected by volition nor wrought by dirt—nay, they were but the cumulative achievement of time—that is to say, time and patient neglect.

"And as the prosperous years rolled on, his sandals waxed, and gathered grace and style, and also magnitude and majesty; insomuch that the footprint of him was like to the footprint of a hogshead which is up-ended in the snow. And he became a legislator and also Speaker. But there was a jealousy because of the splendor of his attainments in the field, there was rancor because of the sublimity of his sandals And, besides, there was not room; for the alkali flat was circumscribed in area, and he unjustly occupied space proper and sufficient for the representation of several counties; also he trod upon the feet of distant members. Those near at hand could see the danger and avoid it; but those who were further removed, having no warning, his step being noiseless, like to that of the stealthy and cushioned cat, suffered. Yet his intentions were pure; he did these things inadvertently—usually while absorbed in thought concerning the national debt.

"So charges were brought against him and he was indicted, tried, and condemned as an obstructionist. The verdict was confirmed by the Appellate Courts in succession, etc., and this latter condemned him to cut his sandals down to eight inches broad and eighteen inches long, with costs; and thus it was with these reduced powers, these diminished capacities, that he made the now world-renowned footprints for the primeval man. . . ."

Having disposed of the theory that primeval man had made the tracks, Sam proceeds, by trial and error, or by the process of elimination, to dispose of several other theories. He says: "The Irish are a comparatively recent formation. They belong in the old blue grindstone Tertiary, and are there confined to the stratified rocks of the post-Pliocene alluvium and upper Pentamerus limestone. The assertion of Hugh Miller and other early observers, that traces of them are discoverable in the Jurassic deposits of the Carboniferous chalks, between the median layer of old basaltic gneiss and the marsupial crinoids of the Paleozoic conglomerate, was regarded with suspicion at the time and is now known to have been wholly bituminous. Now, then, we come to the point.

"If these footprints belong to the old red sandstone period, what becomes of your Irish elk? What was he doing there when there weren't any Irish yet? Answer me that. Crack me *that* nut, Messieurs Marsh and Harkness—and pray let us have no scientific folderol about it. Let us have a square deal about it. Let us have a square deal just this once. The case is simple; I see your geological blunder, and go you a geological *fact* better—now call me if you can. Then we'll draw three apiece and double the not. I think nobody can offer fairer than that. . . .

"Now we come to the cave bear. What is his period? He belongs among the talcose hornblendes of the post-Tertiary Devonian along with the codontsaurians, crytogramous batrachians, and other gold-bearing rocks of the Asoic age; and there isn't a trace of him to be found anywhere else for money. . . . And another thing: the cave bear couldn't have lived in Nevada anyway, for there isn't a cave in it, from one end of it to the other except the comparatively recent ones in the mines and perhaps here and there in the mining stocks. . . .

"Now then—enough of that. Let conjecture stand aside, and history go to the bat. For I was there myself, and I know. The tracks . . . were made by an Irish bricklayer named Stephen McGinness. Member of the Legislature. I knew him perfectly well. . . . These are truths, these are facts; in a word—history. For I was there.

"Little remains to be said. Only this: The cave bear tracks were made by Mr. R. M. Daggett, now grown honorably famous in other walks of life, but still depositing the same identical track to this day, let us freely believe, when he goeth unshod—as was the sternly simple custom of the pioneer legislator of the Territory of Nevada in a day when virtuous endeavor was held above the comfort of the body and godliness above meretricious gauds of fashion.

"The tracks attributed to the old Silurian ass were not made by the old Silurian ass. I made them myself. I made them myself, and I am not an old Silurian ass. I may be some *kind* of an ass and some observers have held the theory that I *was and am*; but I am *not* an old Silurian ass. I made those tracks; and I make the same tracks now; and it appears that even an expert cannot tell it from an *old* Silurian ass' track, and neither can I, for that matter; but it is *not* an old Silurian ass' track, just the same, any more than I am an old Silurian ass, by reason that I made that track. And it *must* not be repeated.

"For I have feelings, as well as another, and the man that *calls me* an old Silurian ass, and *proves* it, shall not go out of this world alive. I have said it. The language may not be intemperate, but the provocation is great. These scientists are in an ill-concealed sweat because they cannot tell *why* there are so many tracks, and all going one way, all going north. It was a large legislature, dear sirs, and the saloon was north. This is history, not conjecture. For I was there—in person.

"And they cannot divine why the primeval man took such short steps, yet with so little lateral spread. Think of the feet he carried; also remember his condition, of course a person could not spread laterally in his condition, as deftly as he could formerly, but not latterly, the conditions being reversed, you see. This seems simple. Also unanswerable.

"And they are perturbed because they cannot tell why the tracks are so confused, and move in such subtle sinuous curves. Listen then: I will explain this also. It is a law of Nature that whiskey cannot be conveyed in straight lines by a legislature, except in buckets. A legislature never uses buckets, man.

"I am done.

"Such is history. Such are the Carson footprints. They are not fossiliferous; they are legislative; they are uniform, they are identical with the tracks deposited by all adjourning legislatures. In the West, I mean. Let us have peace." [6]

9

CONFEDERATE, "SECESH," AND "CHIV"

MANIFEST DESTINY SWEPT THE UNITED STATES TO the Pacific Coast and with it thousands of pro-slavery Southerners —backers of the expansionist program of America. They were looking for adventure, fortune, and political emolument. Fortunate indeed it was that gold was discovered in California that same January, 1848, and that the Treaty of Guadalupe was signed, transferring the Mexican Cession to the possession of the United States. To the gold fields rushed thousands of Northerners—balancing the Confederates, the Chivalry—"Chiv" for short—, and the Secessionists— derisively called "Secesh."

The leaders in the movement to swing California into the slave-holding columns included old and distinguished Southern names: William E. Gwin, Tennessee-born, who went to California in 1848 and who openly announced upon arrival his intention of assuming political control of that Territory; Henry S. Foote, former Governor and United States Senator from Mississippi; Dr. Selden A. Mc-Means, Colonel David S. Terry, and General William Walker, all three Tennessee-born; and Major Daniel E. Hungerford, a distinguished officer of the Mexican War.

In the California Constitutional Convention of 1849 Gwin, through political manipulation, tried to secure the adoption of a proposal to include most of the Mexican Cession in the State of California. California would then have extended from the Pacific Ocean to the Rocky Mountains. He would thereby provide for the extension of slavery if and when this area were divided into smaller States. In this plan he was vigorously opposed by another group advocating a smaller State extending to the summit of the Sierra Nevada Mountains. Neither proponent succeeded in its plan—a compromise line settled this question. Had the large State party's plan succeeded, it would have meant the triumph of the Southerners, fixing once and for all the institution of slavery in the West.

Not all of the Southerners were agreed upon the union of California with the rest of the States. Many of them would have liked to have a separate republic established, for then there would be no interference by the Federal (or any other) government in its political decisions. Actually two different movements in this direction gained some momentum, in the premature Bear Flag Revolt, and the setting up of the Pacific Republic. Flags for both of these fiasco governments flew over parts of California. These republics, supported by Southern leaders, could cooperate with the pro-slavery States and divert the much-needed gold to the Confederacy. As California went, so would all of the country west of the Rocky Mountains go!

But the Compromise of 1850 put a momentary end to these abortive activities. Instead, the free State of California was admitted to the Union, and the squatter sovereign territories of Utah and New Mexico were established. (The western part of these two territories was made the Territory and later the State of Nevada.) Although the Compromise was hailed as settling the slave question, the fight for Southern control of California continued until Lee surrendered to Grant in 1865.

Secret Southern organizations flourished in California cities and mining camps. Gwin, elected the first United States Senator from California, kept his affiliates informed of the national policy. He aided and abetted these organizations through his political patronage. J. Ross Browne—mentioned in an earlier chapter as the first historian of Nevada—sent to California as an inspector of Internal Revenue accounts, was in reality a part of the espionage system to report on appointees who did not favor Gwin and his party.

Two schemes to effect control of the West and California in particular—in case war broke out between the pros and the cons, or in case the region were made a part of the Secessionist Republic —were resorted to: the purchase of a number of camels and the ineffectual Mormon War. Both of these plans had a direct influence on the Land of Washoe.

Jefferson Davis, West Point graduate, Secretary of War under President Pierce from 1853 to 1857, and later the President of the Confederacy, had great ideas about linking California to the South. Since there were no military wagon roads or railroads to the West, there had to be some means of transportation for the large amount of supplies necessary for supporting an army. Hence in 1855 Secretary Davis induced the Congress to appropriate $30,000 to purchase and to import camels from Egypt. The first of two herds, consisting of thirty-five animals, arrived in Texas with their Arabian trainers in 1856; the following year a second drove of forty-one camels came. Most of these animals were taken to southern California to be tried out on the desert and mountain trails. However, they proved unsatisfactory and were soon replaced by the old reliable army mules. At last the camels were sent to the Benicia Barracks on Carquinez Straits, and from there to San Francisco, where they were auctioned off on the streets.

Nevada mine operators needed some way to get large quantities of salt carried from the salt deposits, one hundred and fifty miles away, to the mills. Many of the camels were brought up to Virginia City and were useful for this purpose until salt was found closer to the Lode.

The second intrigue, reaching almost Machiavellian proportions, was a diabolical plan to send the greater part of the United States Army to the West to hold by force the rapidly developing western empire. Carefully concealing the real reason for sending troops out West by magnifying the insubordination of the officers of the Mormon Church in Salt Lake City to Federal authority, the Secretary of War gave the orders. At that period of history, many newspapers and periodicals carried articles about the Latter Day Saints, articles which were more or less acrid and unfair. However, this propaganda *did* furnish an excuse for the expedition.

The story of this ill-starred scheme is a long one—too long to be told here—but there are certain features in the narrative necessary to show the extremes to which sympathizers with the South went in preparing for the impending War between the States. This premeditated stratagem called for six thousand trained men, about one-third of the United States Army, to be sent to Utah in the summer of 1857. These soldiers, mobilized at Fort Leavenworth, Kansas, proceeded westward over the old Oregon Trail as far as South Pass where they turned southwest toward the Salt Lake Valley. The troops did not know where they were being sent, why they were being sent, nor what good they could do in being removed to the most sparsely settled part of the United States. They were well equipped, and the quantity of their supplies was stupendous: two thousand head of beef cattle were driven along with the men, and millions of pounds of food were transported—in reality, sufficient for an army of ten thousand men.

Brigham Young, president of the Mormon Church and Governor of the Territory of Utah, was not disturbed particularly over the news of the approaching army. Driven westward, ever westward from New York State to the banks of the Jordan River in the Utah Territory, he had learned steadfastness. He advised that the Saints stand and fight. Preparations were hastily made—fast messengers were sent to all Mormon settlements in the United States, including Carson Valley and western Utah, and even foreign countries, calling upon all the faithful members to return to help defend their Church headquarters. Most of them obeyed their Leader. Young Mormon men were sent out along the trail to burn the grass, to destroy baggage and supply wagons, to stampede the cattle, and to build fortifications. Warning was sent to the commanding officers of the army *not* to enter the Salt Lake Valley. They heeded the warning and spent a devastatingly cold winter at Fort Bridger. Deprived of some of their most-needed supplies, dozens of men died of cold and exposure in the winter of 1858-1859.

By the latter year "Buchanan's War" was a national joke: the army was not yet in Salt Lake Valley, no shots had been fired, no lives had been lost in fighting, and so far the war had cost the United States $15,000,000. In the spring of 1859, the subtle reason for sending the troops West came out. In its March issue, the *Atlantic Monthly* made the statement that "Buchanan's idea in ordering the Utah expedition was to gag the North and induce her to forget that she had been robbed of her birthright by forcing on the attention of the country other questions of absorbing interest."

The way out of the *impasse* between Governor Young's defiance and the position of the army locked up in the cold, uninhabited region of the Rocky Mountains was furnished by the mission of Colonel Thomas Kane, emissary plenipotentiary of President Buchanan. Kane, traveling with terms of peace, via the Isthmus of Panama and horseback from Los Angeles to Salt Lake City, arrived in the Utah capital. Conversations between the church president and his apostles, and a private conversation between Young and Kane, the contents of which have never been made public, opened a way for the Army and the Saints to arrange a *modus vivendi*.

The unarmed troops commanded by General Albert Sidney Johnston, a devoted and loyal follower of the Confederate cause, were permitted to come into Salt Lake City for a few days before a site was selected for a permanent army fort in Utah. (Fort Douglas was planned at this time.) Albert C. Cumming, another Southerner from Georgia, came with the army as the newly appointed Governor of Utah Territory. After a few months some of the soldiers were sent to Arizona, but the greater part of them were ordered to the Presidio at San Francisco, still under the command of General Johnston. In the meantime the great Comstock Lode had been discovered. Now the quantities of silver from Washoe and the gold from California could be seized and conveyed to the Southern cause by the Army.[2]

Between 1860 and 1861, in the West as elsewhere in the United States, events were transpiring which were to change the course of history. In California, United States Senator Gwin was opposed by David C. Broderick, junior Senator from that State. Both men were Democrats, Gwin from the South, Broderick trained in the Tammany school. In a quarrel over the division of Federal patronage, David S. Terry, a stanch supporter of Gwin and Justice of the Supreme Court of California, was charged by Broderick with working against him. Terry, angered over this accusation, challenged Broderick to a duel.

Resigning his position as Justice, Terry met Broderick on September 13, 1859, in Marin County, across the bay from San Francisco. The weapons were duelling pistols, the distance thirty paces. Both men were good shots. Broderick thought that he had a charmed life since he had escaped death in two previous duels. In one he had not been hit, and in the other the bullet had struck his gold watch. However, Broderick had a peculiar muscular defect in his trigger finger. He had sought to overcome it by taking lessons from an expert duellist, but when his failing persisted, he had been advised by his instructor not to fight a duel with a hair-trigger pistol. His refusal to heed this advice cost him his life. His shot entered the ground at least ten feet from Terry, but Terry's bullet entered Broderick's body, inflicting a mortal wound. Terry decided to leave California.

Gwin, dispenser of Confederate government patronage as well as of Union jobs, gave Terry a commission to be the Governor of the Territory of Nevada, the bill for the creation of which was then before the Congress.

Terry, with five well-mounted and well-armed Secesh body-guards, took part in the rush to Washoe in March, 1860. Arriving in Virginia City, Terry, taking up his headquarters in Johnny Newman's saloon—then the only stone building in the town, and Johnny himself a Secesh—selected three strategic positions around Mount Davidson on which to erect forts. As soon as he had arrived on the Lode, he had announced that whoever held these forts when the war opened would likewise hold the mines. One fort was near Gold Hill on the south, another was built on Ophir ground to the east, and the third was on a hill near the opening of Devil's Gate. More Secesh recruits were added to his following, and with them he manned his fortifications. These guards, on duty night and day, watched the crowds come up the Cañon, saw the bullion go out of the mills, and kept Terry informed of everything.

The Paiute Indian War of 1860 brought hundreds more pro-slavery men to Washoe. They came armed to fight the Indians; they remained to try to turn Nevada for the Confederacy. Indeed it looked as though nothing could prevent the rich Comstock Lode from falling into the hands of the Secesh. Bad it appeared until Bill Stewart took charge of things. He arrived in the Territory a few days after Terry did. In the litigation which arose over the legal ownership of the Comstock claims, Terry, an excellent lawyer, was employed by the locators who advocated that the Lode was made up of many ledges, while Stewart, an equally fine barrister, was hired by the parties holding that there was but one ledge.

In this test case there was a great deal more at stake than the mere settling of a geological dispute: Stewart, an ardent Union man, knew that if Terry won the suit, Washoe was in the ranks of the South. In this case Stewart outmaneuvered, outargued, and out-witted Terry, and finally won the court decision. These were the proceedings mentioned earlier, in which Judge Flenniken, imported for the purpose of giving the Southern man the decision, was forced by Stewart to resign; and the intrepid high sheriff, John L. Black-burn, and his deputies served the injunctions on the guards on Terry's forts, forcing them to evacuate their positions. Terry ad-mitted defeat and soon afterwards left for the South, where he entered the army and fought on that side during the Civil War.

As soon as Abraham Lincoln was elected President and it became evident that a war was inevitable, many of the Secesh left Washoe. However, some demonstrations in behalf of the Confederacy were made: Johnny Newman flew the Confederate flag over his saloon until he was shown that it would be better for his health to haul it down; and attempts were also made to break up Union recruiting meetings. Large caches of Secesh arms were discovered and promptly confiscated.

There was one serious danger still left on the Pacific Coast: the headquarters of the Army of the West in San Francisco were as yet commanded by General Johnston. The seriousness of this position was sensed by James McClatchy, editor of a Sacramento newspaper. He explained the precarious situation in a letter to President Lincoln and dispatched it over the Pony Express. Lincoln sent General Edwin Vose Sumner, via the Isthmus of Panama, to San Francisco. The first news that General Johnston had of his removal was when Sumner appeared at the Presidio to take over the command of the Army of the Pacific. From that time on secession was doomed in the West. General Johnston resigned from the Union army, joined the Confederate forces, and in 1862 was killed at the Battle of Shiloh.[3]

Perhaps the last outburst of secession sympathy in the West occurred in Carson City on November 29, 1861. Many members of California Secesh and "Chiv" guerrilla bands, formed to seize property to take over offices, and to assume control of the mines, came over to Washoe in the rush. They carried on their clandestine operations in this territory, watching the proceedings of the first legislature. Among these outlaws was William ("Bill") Mayfield, a professional gambler. He made many friends and even fell in love with a Carson City girl.

A "Chiv" in the person of Henry Plummer, who had directed the operations of road agents and murderers that terrorized the mining regions of California, fled to Carson City, a fugitive from an arrest for murder. A requisition to arrest him had preceded him, and the Nevada officers were on the alert. Knowing that Plummer was a Confederate and that Mayfield was one of their leaders, the officers believed that sooner or later Plummer would make a contact with Mayfield. William L. Blackburn, a loyal Northerner and formerly United States Marshal for western Utah, who was then the newly appointed Sheriff for Ormsby County (of which Carson City is the county seat), had made a good guess, but he was too late to catch the crook.

Blackburn, a dangerous man and a reckless lawbreaker, had an unbridled temper when he was drunk, which was often. No one could escape his fury. In fact, some of the most respectable citizens of Washoe had barely saved their lives from his ungovernable passion. It was hoped by many a person that someone would "get Blackburn."

One story will suffice to illustrate this brutal officer's gory pugnacity. One day he went out to arrest a witless drunk and take him to jail. Before locking him up, Blackburn stopped at a saloon to get a drink for himself. The drunk, in a very happy mood, persisted in singing at the top of his voice. Blackburn told him several times to stop making so much noise, but the orders meant nothing to the half-conscious singer. At last, the enraged Sheriff whipped out his pistol and shot his prisoner dead, remarking, "Now I guess you'll be quiet!"

Mayfield knew that the officer would probably come to his cabin in search of Plummer; so he had him transferred to that of another member of the Secesh gang. In Jack Harris' home a more secret hiding place was made by cutting through the lining of the ceiling, placing a bed, provisions, and other necessities of life upon the girders, and then closing and concealing the aperture. In this hideout Plummer remained until he was ready to make another escape.

Blackburn, going to Mayfield's cabin and accusing him of harboring a fugitive, was told that Plummer was no longer there, although he had been. The thought of having been foiled in his attempt to arrest Plummer threw Blackburn into a fury of frustration. Whenever he was irate, he always went to the nearest saloon and filled up on whiskey. Thus fortified, he started out to find Mayfield. The latter had avoided Blackburn, but in the evening the two men met in the St. Nicholas saloon. As soon as Blackburn saw his adversary, he staggered up to him and screamed out: "I'll arrest Plummer and no one can prevent it. I can arrest anybody. I can arrest you, Bill Mayfield, if I wish to."

"You can arrest me if you have a warrant for my arrest, but you can't without," Mayfield coolly replied.

Again Blackburn came forth with epithets: "I tell you I can arrest you or anyone else and —— ——, I'll arrest you anyhow!" Blackburn made a movement as if to draw his gun, but John Winters and other friends seized him. They tried to force him into another room, but he broke loose from his restrainers and made a lunge at Mayfield. Quick as a flash, the latter pulled his bowie knife from his boot, plunging it into his assailant's breast—not once, but half a dozen times. Blackburn, now a raging, frenzied animal, tried to close with his assassin but it was too late. With blood spurting from his many wounds, he fell limp to the floor and died in a few minutes.

In the confusion over the stabbing of an officer, Mayfield escaped from the saloon, fled to the place of one of his Secesh friends, and was secreted in the hogpen for the night. The next day some of his cohorts found a more savory hiding place for him. All of Washoe was shocked, and Governor Nye was frightened lest there be a general uprising against the Union men on the part of the Confederates, Secesh, and Chivs.

As the news spread from person to person, the short main street was filled with an angry, swearing, drinking mob of men. Blackburn may have been a killer himself, but he was a Unionist and a —— —— —— —— Secesh had killed him. Rewards began to be offered for Mayfield, dead or alive. The following day the legislature in its closing session offered a large reward. The Ormsby County commissioners increased it. It rose and rose until $3000 was posted for the assassin.

So incensed were patriotic Americans over the incident that the minister who preached Blackburn's funeral sermon made it the subject of his eulogy. In it he urged everyone to join a posse to hunt out the enemies of the United States, and he said that he would lead the searchers himself. The reward was high enough for everyone to go on the manhunt.

Finally the murderer was found, placed under arrest, put in chains, and held in the small log jail on Carson City's main street. To hold the prisoners securely in the jail, they were fastened to a heavy log which ran the full length of the jail.

As soon as the news that Mayfield had been found got around on that evening of November 21, the jail was surrounded by an angry mob. Threats of lynching were heard; secessionist sympathizers, gamblers, and people looking for excitement began arriving from all of the near-by communities. The Secesh were determined to rescue Bill; the Unionists were just as bent on hanging him. On the night that he was arrested, Governor Nye did not go to bed—twice he visited the jail to see if the prisoner were still chained up. One of the hastily appointed guards whose loyalty was questioned was disarmed. It looked as though the Battle of Bull Run would be fought again in Washoe and, judging from the Secesh numbers, the result would be the same.

To make life safe, the Governor telegraphed to the commanding officer at Fort Churchill to send troops at once. In the dead of darkness on that winter night, the rapid approach of the mounted guards was a welcome sound to Washoe. With trained men on duty, commanded by a Lieutenant, the Secesh found their retreats safer than the streets of Carson City.

The Chivs quieted down, but they at once commenced to collect a purse to employ counsel for Mayfield. John R. McConnell, leading California secessionist, was his chief defender, but after a trial Bill was convicted and sentenced to be hanged on February 28, 1862. McConnell asked for a retrial on the grounds that there were only Unionists on the jury. He failed on this point, but he did get a stay of execution. Since a parole or pardon was impossible, it was about the only thing that could be given the condemned. Because the hanging date was now uncertain and the soldiers were needed elsewhere to quell Indian depredations, the military guard was withdrawn.

During the legislative session a State Prison Board had been created, and after this Blackburn-Mayfield affair the need for a Territorial penitentiary became imperative. The only stone building available was Curry's Warm Springs Hotel. The Board appointed "Curry, Abe Curry, Old Abe Curry" warden on January 1, 1862. At the same time it contracted with him to board and guard the Territorial prisoners. Mayfield was then transferred to what was thought a more secure prison. Curry was also permitted to keep his hotel and bar open to the traveling public; so Bill's friends found it easy to get tools for him to cut himself free from his irons.

By working cautiously, so as not to attract the attention of the guard who was in the adjoining room, Mayfield was able to make his getaway about nine o'clock on the night of March 15. Stealthily he crawled out of the prison building, beyond which he was met by a Secesh friend. His sympathizers had collected a purse of $1000 and had secured a fast horse for him to flee the country.

On the night of his escape he had ridden as far as Peavine Valley, about ten miles west of the present site of Reno, when he remembered his sweetheart whom he had left in Carson City. Torn between love and freedom, he chose love, and turned back to retrace his course. In the Truckee meadows he stopped at the ranch of Daniel Huffaker, a loyal Secesh. With this protection he made known his whereabouts to the girl he had left behind. For two weeks it was said that he had regular rendezvous with her.

Soon it became known that Bill Mayfield was back in the country, and not far from Carson City at that. Again feeling flared up, and a search was started for him. Sheriff Gasherie, Blackburn's successor, was sent out to search the Huffaker house for him. The officer was allowed to go all over the large stone home, but not before Mrs. Huffaker had hidden the fugitive in a closet among her dresses where his legs and feet were plainly visible below the skirts. Gasherie made a superficial search, returned to Carson, and reported that "he could see him all of the time but could not find him."

It was circulated around the country that Gasherie was admittedly afraid of Mayfield and his followers; besides, he was grateful to the man who had made a vacancy for him. When mobocracy again began to take hold of affairs in Washoe, Mayfield was warned to get out of that Territory and "pretty *damned* quick." Heeding this advice, he skipped for the wilds of Idaho, where, a few years later, he was killed in a quarrel over a card game.

The humor of this Civil War flare-up in Nevada was furnished by Mayfield himself in an article he wrote which was published in the *Territorial Enterprise*. He was so happy over cheating the gallows and his ultimate triumph in outwitting the Unionist officers that he had to gloat over it. The most amusing part of the story was the way that he eluded Curry:

"The guard was walking back and forth in the wardroom, while Old Man Curry was sitting playing poker with some of the workhands about ten feet from my cell. I got down on my hands and knees, and, watching the old man's eyes, started for the door. As I got to it I saw the old man raising the hand that had just been dealt him, and as his eyes were directed toward me, I thought I would wait until he got a big hand, for, being an old gambler myself, I knew it would always excite an unsophisticated gambler to have a high hand dealt to him. A few minutes afterwards a big Irishman who was playing in the game got a big hand, queens and sevens, before the draw. He bet 'twenty beans.' The old man saw it, and they took one card each. The old man drew a king, making him a king full; the Irishman drew a queen, making him a queen full. They bet and bet until they had about two hundred beans in the pot. All this time I was fixing to go, and I came to the conclusion that if I couldn't go out on that hand I never could, and so I went."

When Governor Nye arrived in Nevada July, 1861, he assured the people of this Territory that "not one star shall be permitted to be removed from the old thirty-four." All of the appointed officers of Nevada Territory were chosen for their loyalty to the Union. Orion Clemens, a stanch member of the Union Party, had stumped the northern part of the State of Missouri for Lincoln. After Sam Clemens had had his experience in the Marion Rangers, he was through with fighting. His association with Orion and other loyal Northerners convinced him that the cause of the Union was right.

No one can doubt the loyalty of Sam after one reads his tribute to the flag. The occasion for this patriotic piece of writing was the effect of an unusual electric storm which came up in July, 1863. Late in the afternoon there was a heavy rainstorm, lasting some five or ten minutes. Because it seldom rains in Nevada in summer, the people were stricken with something like awe at the sudden blackness which obscured the heavens. They huddled, talking nervously. The Great Mountain put on a funereal appearance, and all eyes in Virginia City looked up to the top to see if Old Glory were still in sight. All of a sudden an ear-splitting thunderbolt parted the clouds, and "a little tongue of rich golden flame was seen waving and quivering in the heart of the midnight, away up on the extreme summit! In a few minutes the streets were packed with people, gazing with hardly an uttered word, at the one brilliant note in the brooding world of darkness. It flickered like a candle-flame, and looked no larger; but with such a background it was wonderfully bright, small as it was. It was the flag!—though no one suspected it at first, it seemed so like a supernatural visitor of some kind—a mysterious messenger of good tidings, some were fain to believe. It was the nation's emblem transfigured by the departing rays of a sun that was entirely palled from view; *and on no other object did the glory fall*, in all the broad panorama of mountain ranges and deserts. Not even upon the staff of the flag—for that, a needle in the distance at any time, was now untouched by the light and indistinguishable in the gloom."

Sam Clemens' observations of this dramatic sight impelled him to describe it: "For a whole hour the weird visitor winked and burned in its lofty solitude, and still the thousands of uplifted eyes watched it with fascinated interest. How the people were wrought up! The superstition grew apace that this was a mystic courier come with great news from the war—the poetry of the idea excusing and commending it—and on it spread, from heart to heart, from lip to lip, and from street to street, till there was a general impulse to have out the military and welcome the bright waif with a salvo of artillery!"

And there was but "one sorely tried man, the telegraph operator sworn to official secrecy, who had to lock his lips and chain his tongue with a silence that was like to rend them; for *he,* and *he* only, of all the speculating multitude, knew the great things this sinking sun had seen that day in the East—Vicksburg fallen, and the Union armies victorious at Gettysburg!" The reason for the secrecy was the way that transcontinental news was relayed to Nevada: it was first telegraphed to San Francisco and then sold back to the inland papers. Had the "glorified flag on Mount Davidson" been able to speak and tell of its joyous news, it would have been "saluted and resaluted . . . as long as there was a charge of powder to thunder with; the city would have been illuminated; and every man that had any respect for himself would have got drunk. . . ."[4]

The legislative loyalty of Nevada was expressed by the wording which the first Territorial legislature used in sending the *first* telegram across the continent over the newly completed transcontinental telegraph line to President Lincoln on October 23, 1861:

Greetings:
  Nevada for the Union, ever true and loyal! The last born of the nation will be the last to desert the flag! Our aid, to the extent of our ability, can be relied upon to crush the rebellion.[5]

10

"GO IT, WASHOE!"

"HO, WASHOE!" "GO IT, WASHOE!" "HURRAH FOR Washoe!" were the cries that rent the Sierra Nevadas in the spring of 1860. A year later Mother Clemens wrote, "Tell everything as it is— no better, no worse," to which her son Sam replied, "Well, 'Gold Hill' sells at $5,000 per foot, cash down; 'Wild Cat' isn't worth ten cents." [1] So much were the prices of stocks on his mind that he could think of nothing else to tell her. In fact, everyone was talking about these extraordinary mines. Ask a man how his grandmother was and he began to quote the stock market from top to bottom. Go into a bar in Washoe and everyone was drinking a toast to the latest discovery. Children, horses, cats, dogs, everything was named after "the big ones." Everyone was going Washoe, and Sam Clemens had gone too.

On every corner Sam heard the talk: "Tom So-and-so sold out to the 'Amanda Smith' for $40,000—hadn't a cent when he 'took up' the ledge six months ago." "John Jones sold half his interest in the 'Bald Eagle and Mary Ann' for $65,000, gold coin, and went to the States for his family." "The Widow Brewster struck it rich in the 'Golden Fleece' and sold ten feet for $18,000—hadn't enough money to buy a crape bonnet when Sing Sing Tommy killed her husband at Baldy Johnson's wake last spring."

"The 'Last Chance' had found a 'clay casing' and knew they were 'right on the edge'; consequence, 'feet' that went begging yesterday were worth a brick house apiece today, and seedy owners who could not get trusted for a drink at any bar . . . were roaring drunk on champagne today. . . . Johnny Morgan, a common loafer, had gone to sleep in the gutter and waked up worth a hundred thousand dollars . . . and so on—day in and day out. . . ." [2]

Mining and lumber mills went up daily—forty strong on the Carson River alone. Bars of gold and silver bullion loaded on hay wagons were pulled through the streets daily en route to the San Francisco mint. Who wouldn't go Washoe?

Every day Sam and Orion Clemens heard the talk at "The

Ranch," Mrs. Murphy's boardinghouse. Look through the *Carson City Directory* for 1861 and note the professions of the boarders: Patrick Doyle, speculator; James Neary, speculator—real names they were, with many more listed as brokers. Talk of feet, big dividends, free milling, decomposed quartz, and the like was heard at every meal—the favorite vegetable. Sam Clemens would have been an odd person indeed if he too had not succumbed to the fever.

However, feet on the rich Gold Hill ledge or the Comstock Lode were selling far too high for Sam's capital. He had to get in on the ground floor of some new discovery. After all, his total bankroll was only $800 when he arrived in Washoe, and with that sum he had had to keep himself and Orion. (The national government paid its officers quarterly.) Please remember also that Sam had bought a Genuine Mexican Plug, to get rid of which had cost him considerably. Then he had taken a trip to Lake Tahoe, and had skipped down to Aurora "to take a look-see."

That Sam Clemens got the "get-rich-quick" fever only *after* several months in Washoe was all nonsense. He had it when he arrived. It was in his blood—a congenital trait. Weren't Father Clemens' dying words to his family an inflationary admonition? "Cling to the land (in Tennessee). Cling to the land and wait. Let nothing beguile it away from you." Sam could see the same kind of a fortune in laying timber claims at Lake Tahoe—virgin forests in this magnificent wilderness—a few days after his arrival in Carson City. "And if we succeed in getting one Mr. Jones to move his sawmill up there, Mr. Moffett can just consider that claim better than bank stock." [3]

These expansive ideas were written home to his sister Pamela on October 25, just a few weeks after he had arrived in Washoe. In the very same letter he said that he had "got about 1,650 feet of mining ground—and also had made a trip to the Esmeralda" mining district where a young fellow had given him fifty feet in the "Black Warrior" claim. The rest of this letter was filled with speculative dreams beneficial to the entire Clemens family. For Orion and himself, he had plans to get rich which couldn't possibly fail. He acknowledged, however, that neither of them was yet a financier. But Uncle Jim Lampton must be persuaded to come out to Nevada. "I don't believe it would take him six months to make $100,000 here. . . ."

Late in the summer of 1861, the Esmeralda and the Humboldt mining districts were enjoying the spotlight.[4] Which one to go to first was Sam Clemens' greatest problem! He had acquired feet in both districts. By this time he "had grown well accustomed to wearing a damaged slouch hat, blue woolen shirt, and pants crammed into boot-tops. . . ." His decision was made when he learned that William H. ("Billy") Claggett,[5] an old friend of his when he lived in Keokuk, Iowa, was making preparations to go to Humboldt. He joined this party, which consisted of Billy and himself, A. W. ("Gus") Oliver [6] and Mr. Ballou, a sixty-year-old blacksmith. Sam and Gus provided the horses—Sam's contribution being "Bunker," a horse named for Benjamin B. Bunker,[7] Attorney General of the Territory of Nevada. Sam had become well acquainted with both the Attorney General and the horse on a short prospecting trip; and in describing the horse to his mother, he had said that he felt that it was a relative of their family—its infernal laziness being the common characteristic. He wondered, however, if there wasn't some significance in the similarities between the slow mental process of the Territorial lawyer and of the horse.

This prospecting party did not leave until after the tenth of December. This delay was caused by the fight in the legislature over the county-capital bill. Humboldt County was being set up in that bill; and Unionville, the destination of the party, was planned as the county seat. Gus Oliver had been promised the position of Probate Judge in the county by the Governor; while Billy Claggett, also a lawyer, wanted one of the profitable Notary Public commissions. So he too had to wait for the passing of the bill creating these offices before he could leave.

All set, the party of four men, two horses, and Ballou's dog Curney, "a little mean, white, curly, grinning whelp, no bigger than a cat—with a wretched, envious, snappish, selfish disposition, and a tail like an all-wool capital O, curled immodestly over his back," left Carson City on a cold December afternoon. The route to Humboldt, some two hundred miles northeast of Carson, followed down the Carson River to Ragtown, cut across the Forty-Mile Desert to the Humboldt Meadows, where the road turned eastward toward the Humboldt Mountains for twenty miles or more.

The wagon filled with their supplies, "ten pounds of Killikinick,

14 decks of cards, a cribbage board, one small keg of lager beer, Watt's Hymns, and the *Carminia sacrae*," weighed eighteen hundred pounds including the provisions. It was far too heavy a load for their team to haul through the deep sand, over rocky stretches, and up steep grades. At first Billy Claggett drove, and the other three men got behind the wagon and pushed—all on account of Bunker, the "near horse on the larboard side. . . . Whenever he came to a hard piece of road, that poor, lean, infatuated cuss could fall in a deep reverie about something or other, and stop perfectly still, and it would generally take a vast amount of blacksnaking and shoving and profanity to get him started up again. . . ."

On the way down the river the party camped near Chinatown, a few miles below Dayton. Here Billy and Sam borrowed a pup from a Chinaman without his permission. They named him Tom, and fussed a great deal over him when he made life miserable for Curney.

All the way down the river they passed the burned Pony Express and Overland Stage stations—such depredations!—they cost the companies $75,000 to replace in Nevada alone. The newly made graves of the Indians' victims impressed the travelers fearfully. The road down the river had been bad enough; but could they have known what difficulties lay ahead of them, they might not have had the courage to go on.

Five days out they came to Ragtown, the last settlement on the Carson River before entering the dread Forty-Mile Desert—Ragtown, so named by the Forty-Niners who had come this way on their mad quest for gold. Struggling through that vast solitude of sand and rock, with no drop of water for man or beast in the entire distance, they had cast off their rags when they reached water, trees, and a frontier-shack station. For miles around, the sagebrush and ground were strewn with the rags of months of toil and endurance. Across this stretch of endless sand man pitted his wits and guts against its resistance.

When the Clemens-Claggett-Oliver-Ballou party crossed this desert in one terrifying drive of twenty-three hours without stopping for so much as a bite to eat, a drink of water, or a minute's rest, they could still see the skeletons and carcasses of animals, abandoned by the emigrants passing this way for a decade or more. Thousands of dollars' worth of furniture, harness, books, wagons, wagon parts, clothes, boxes, and guns had been thrown out to lighten the load. This *jornada,* once successfully passed, had taken so much out of the party that it rested two days on the north side of the desert at the Humboldt Sink. Man and beast had given every ounce of strength to get through.

Had anyone in the party been given to philosophizing, he might have quoted the following passage from Ralph Waldo Emerson:

> Every sweet hath its sorrow; every evil its good. In nature nothing can be given; all things are sold. For things of great value the price is high; while worthless things are cheaply gained. Gold is the emblem of material worth, and the price of gold is correspondingly great. Men search for it not in the meadows or beneath the shade of beneficent trees, but in the sterile and inaccessible places of the earth. Could anything of lesser value tempt men to live in desert wastes where water is not, and where the aggregate cruelties of nature combine to destroy?

But Sam Clemens said:

"It was a hard, wearing, toilsome journey, but it had its bright side; for after each day was done and our wolfish hunger appeased with hot supper of fried bacon, bread, molasses, and black coffee, the pipe-smoking, song-singing, and yarn-spinning around the evening campfire in the still solitudes of the desert was a happy, care-free sort of recreation that seemed the very summit and culmination of earthly luxury. It is a kind of life that has a potent charm for all men, whether city or country bred."

Utterly exhausted, the party ate heartily and then lay down to sleep. Soon they were aroused by the war whoops of a band of Paiutes. They jumped to their feet in an instant—pictures of the burned cabins and stations and the unmarked graves of the red-men's victims rushed before their eyes. It was Sam Clemens who first pulled himself together and, after putting his hand to his head to make sure that he still had his scalp, drawled: "Boys, they have left us our scalps. Let's give them all the flour and sugar they ask for."

On the fifteenth day out from Carson City the silver-mine prospectors pulled into Unionville, Humboldt Mining District, in a blinding snowstorm. This community, one of six smaller mining

A. J. SIMMONS, SAMUEL CLEMENS, BILLY CLAGGETT

UNIONVILLE, HUMBOLDT MINING DISTRICT, NEVADA

MARK TWAIN'S CABIN, UNIONVILLE, NEVADA

communities scattered over thirty miles of high mountain slopes, was discovered in the spring of 1860 when four Paiute Indians led two white men to Star Cañon on the west side of the Humboldt Mountain Range, a cold, bleak, cheerless and treeless area. The men prospected the range and found that there were many ledges of promising value; the news soon got out; a rush followed. Over a region of many miles men scattered in all directions. When Horace Greeley came that way, he heard about the discovery and was reported to have said: "It is good—good for nothing."

The following year, Captain Hugo Pfersdorff, aided by Indians, went into the district and laid out a town, giving it the name of Buena Vista. However, this fat-headed Prussian charged so much for his lots that nobody would buy them. Especially not when, a short time later, Chris Lark went a mile farther down the cañon and laid out another townsite. To entice the crowd down there Chris either gave away the lots or sold them ridiculously cheap. To this town the name "Dixie," the choice of the Secesh in that district who were proud of the Confederate victories of 1861, was given.

After a few months the Union men began to outnumber the Chivs. So on July 14 a mass meeting was called for the purpose of changing the name. Angry discussions followed and hard feelings were aroused, but when the vote was taken, "Unionville" was the choice for the renamed town; and a large flagpole was erected in the center of the town from which the biggest American flag obtainable was flown.

When Sam Clemens and his party arrived in Unionville, there were eleven cabins, arranged six on one side, five on the other. The party built a three-sided one against the hillside, using the sharp slope of the hill as a fourth side. The roof was a piece of canvas, which covered the top except for a small opening for a chimney. There was no flooring in the cabin. Here these four men camped during the latter part of December, 1861, and the first part of January, 1862.

The rush to most of the newly discovered mining camps in California and Nevada was brought about by letters written to newspapers, often from correspondents which the papers sent to the new districts. A good article could send the public scampering off in any direction. It was an article in the *Territorial Enterprise* that influenced Sam and his companion to go to Humboldt. Who wouldn't get excited? Just read these delirious words:

> But what about our mines? I shall be candid with you. I shall express an honest opinion, based upon a thorough examination. Humboldt County is the richest mineral region upon God's footstool. Each mountain range is gorged with the precious ores. . . .
>
> The other day an assay of mere out croppings yielded four thousand dollars to the ton. . . . A week or two ago an assay of just such surface developments made returns of seven thousand dollars to the ton. . . . The intestines of our mountains are gorged with precious ore to plethora. . . . Such fecundity throws the Gould and Curry, the Ophir, and the Mexican, of our neighborhood, in the darkest shadow. . . .

No wonder that Sam Clemens later naïvely confessed that he expected to find masses of silver lying all about the ground: "I expected to see it glittering in the sun on the mountain summit." However, having a secret suspicion that these extravagant ideas were exaggerated, and not wanting to bring derision unnecessarily on himself, he "sauntered carelessly away from the cabin, keeping an eye on the other boys, and stopping" every now and then to look up at the sky when he thought he was being watched. As soon as he was safely out of sight he dashed away in search of his fortune.

Feverishly he crawled about on the ground, grabbing at every likely-looking piece of rock, blowing away the dust and rubbing it on his clothes just as he had seen the old prospectors do. Soon he found "a bright fragment" and his heart fairly bounded. Hiding behind a large boulder, he polished it furiously, then scrutinized it anxiously. The closer he examined his specimen, the more convinced he was that he "had found the door to fortune."

He marked the spot where he made his discovery and went on searching "up and down the rugged mountainside. Of all the experiences of my life, this *secret* search among the hidden treasures of silver-land was the nearest to unmarred ecstasy. It was delirious revel."

As Sam dashed about in riotous glee, he came to a shallow rivulet where he found some "shining yellow scales" and breath almost left him. *"A gold mine!* and in my simplicity I had been content with vulgar silver! I was so excited that I half believed my over-wrought imagination was deceiving me." Fearing lest someone might be observing him and sense his discovery, he made a circuit of the place. Ascending a small knoll, he reconnoitered to see if anyone were around. Satisfied that he was alone, he returned to his gold discovery.

Excitedly he scooped out his golden treasure for an hour or more, following down the course of the little stream until the sun set. While he was returning to the cabin, he could scarcely suppress his ironic laughter at being so excited over discovering silver, when gold was staring him in the face. So full was he of exultation over his riches that he had to restrain himself from bursting out with the news to his friends. Resolving, however, to be calm and serene about it, he waited until after their evening meal was over and they had moved into their usual pipe-smoking reveries.

Breaking the news slowly and leading up to his climax gradually, he asked a lot of misleading questions about ledges and feet, directing most of them to Ballou, the old and seasoned prospector. Cagily he led up to the information he wanted to draw out from the old miner by remarking that "just for the sake of argument, suppose—in a kind of general way—suppose some person were to tell you that two-thousand-dollar ledges were simply contemptible—contemptible, *understand*—and that right yonder in sight of this very cabin there were piles of pure gold and pure silver— oceans of it—enough to make you all rich in twenty-four hours!"

"I should say he was crazy as a loon!" said old Ballou, but wild with excitement nevertheless.

Preparing himself for the most dramatic act of his life, he excitedly announced: "Gentlemen . . . I haven't been around . . . and of course don't know anything . . . but all I ask of you is to cast your eyes on that!" tossing the specimen before his companions. Ballou took a good look at it and exclaimed: "Think of it? I think it is . . . nothing but a lot of granite rubbish and nasty glittering mica that isn't worth ten cents an acre!"

Sam's castles-in-the-air vanished, his hopes were dashed, and he was left stricken and forlorn. Moralizing over his innocence, he said: "All that glitters is not gold," to which Ballou added that "nothing that glitters *is* gold." Sam was through with prospecting by himself. From this time on he would go out with his partners.

They climbed the mountains, scrambled over rocks, straddled sagebrush through the snow and bitter winds of January high up in the rugged terrain of the Humboldt Mountains. Day after day they continued their search, returning each night to their cheerless and cold cabin shelter completely exhausted. Still they found neither silver nor gold ledges such as the correspondent in the *Enterprise* had led them to expect. The younger men "grew sicker and still sicker of the promiseless toil."

Once they were terribly excited over Mr. Ballou's judgment on a piece of quartz he knocked off a ledge. He said that there were indications of silver in it—then he gave the inexperienced mining men a long harangue on the tedious process that must follow to get the silver from the rock. They located a claim and named it "Monarch of the Mountains"—for which name poetic Gus Oliver probably was responsible. They started work on their discovery promptly. After a week of trying to sink a shaft and run a tunnel in the flintlike granite, only twelve feet of work had been done. Sam quit and resigned; Gus and Billy did the same. They all agreed that what they wanted was a developed ledge, and since there were none in the county, they dropped the Monarch.

Hundreds of other excited people had read the same articles that the Clemens party had, and they too arrived in camp to seek their fortune. Clemens and his companions thought that what they needed was more feet; so they went about acquiring them until they had an interest in fifty or more mines and owned *thirty thousand* feet! The speculators and brokers arrived, and they too acquired feet; not to work, however, but to sell to the suckers. Each and every one of them had feet to sell in "the richest mine on earth," and they had proof of it—*just* look at the assays!

The young silver miners resolved never again to touch their tunnel or shaft; they had learned (so Sam thought) the real success of silver mining, and that was never to mine themselves "by the sweat of our brows and the labor of our hands, but to *sell* the ledges. . . ." [8] But had he had enough of mining to abandon the quest then?

Some time before he left for Humboldt, he and Orion had acquired feet in the Esmeralda Mining District along with Robert ("Bob") Howland and Horatio G. Phillips. These two men had come down from Aurora on August 24, 1861, as delegates from the Esmeralda Union Club, a large patriotic association of Aurora, to support Governor Nye in his proclamation for loyalty to the Union. They attended the Union Convention which recommended a candidate for Territorial delegate to Congress. These two young fellows ate at Mrs. Murphy's boardinghouse. Sam became well acquainted with them and became partners with them in some claims in Aurora.

After the convention Bob and "Raish" Phillips had gone back to Aurora, the largest community in the Esmeralda Mining District, to work and to look after their mining investments. To keep Bob and Raish in grub and mining materials, Orion and Sam had to send them assessment money. Leaving his Humboldt interests, only temporarily (at least, that was what he implied in a letter to his mother), he decided to return to Carson to make ready for his trip to Aurora.

Sam, Ballou, and Captain Pfersdorff set out for Carson City some time near the middle of January, 1862. Sam bought another horse for this trip home. He had turned old Bunker out to feed for life. The last time he saw him, he was grazing high up on the slopes of Star Peak, where, perhaps, he became the antecedent of the many wild bands of horses that roam those hills today. Gus and Billy stuck with the camp to make their name and fortune in less arduous ways than mining: Gus Oliver, now called "Judge" by everyone, was elected and re-elected judge for this county, and Billy Claggett laid his foundation right there in Unionville for a legislative career. Elected three times to the Territorial legislature of Nevada and also to the first Constitutional Convention of the State, he gained experience which later took him to Congress from Montana. However, Sam and Billy were to see a great deal of each other before they both left Nevada.

The Clemens-Ballou-Pfersdorff party left Unionville in a blinding snowstorm; but, all being mounted, they made fast progress, reaching Honey Lake Smith's Ranch on the Carson River, over one hundred miles, in two days. This station, on the edge of the Twenty-six Mile Desert, was the only one for miles in either direction. It was the Overland Mail station and had been a home station for the Pony Express. A two-story building of logs served as the hotel, while an adobe brick structure was used for the large stables.

When the Clemens party arrived, they found the inn crowded with teamsters, stage drivers, vagabonds, and the traveling public.

After supper the Carson-bound travelers went out for a walk, as the weather had cleared. They soon came upon an Indian camp, where they found the redmen in a terrific hurry about something, packing everything they had in preparation for a quick getaway. When they asked questions, an old buck answered, "By'm by, heap water!" That ought to mean that a big flood was coming down the Carson River. But taking a look first at the clear skies and then at the foot-deep, sickly river, they were of the opinion that the Indians must have something else besides a flood on their minds.[9]

Later in the evening the travelers retired for the night, with their clothes on and all three in the same bed—even the chairs and all available space on the floor were used for sleeping the guests. They were no sooner asleep than a great commotion outside awakened them. By picking their way among the snoring sleepers on the floor, they reached the window of the long upstairs room. In the bright moonlight they could see the river running bankfull. The rushing water was beginning to sweep madly around the twists and bends of its course, carrying big logs, brush, and debris in its speed.

The commotion outside had been caused by the teamsters working feverishly to bring their wagons, horses, and hay to high ground around the station house. The travelers' horses had been tied up in a small log stable near the old river bed; and seeing that their horses, too, were in danger, they "joined the crowd of excited men and animals." Wading knee-deep into the stable to unfasten their horses, they had to walk waist-deep to get them out, so fast was the river rising. By eleven o'clock that same night only the roof of the log stable was visible above the water. Water was everywhere filling the depressions around the inn until nothing but water could be seen in every direction. By this time everyone in the house was up and no one slept the rest of the night. How could the Indians have known that the flood was coming?

The water continued to rise. There were no longer hopes that man or beast could get away until the waters subsided. For eight days and nights these men were marooned at Smith's station, with a motley crowd of drinking, swearing, fighting hoodlums, and amid the most undescribable filth and vermin. Two men in the mob irritated Sam Clemens: a young Swede about twenty-five years old, who knew but one song and who was forever singing it; and a quarrelsome traveler from Arkansas. The Swede's monotonous song, always heard above the "profanity, whisky-guzzling, 'old sledge,' and quarreling," was bad enough, but the constant badgering of Smith by the great big ruffian "Arkansas" gave Clemens an opportunity to immortalize the way these swaggerers pick a fight.

Arkansas tried in every conceivable way to get someone to insult him so that he could shoot one of his two pistols which he kept on his hips, or could pull the ever-present bowie knife from his boot-top. He bullyragged Smith and some of the other guests day after day to say something that would give him an excuse to fire, but he was not successful. They would always appease him with another drink, or give him an apology. At last he got the landlord where he wanted him and, picking up a trivial remark about something to the effect that there were too many people at the inn, Arkansas worked himself into a rage.

"So *that's* what's ranklin' in your heart, is it? You want us to leave, do you? There's too many of us. You want us to pack up and swim. Is that it? Come!"

"Please be reasonable, Arkansas. Now *you* know that I ain't the man to——"

"Are you a-threatenin' me? Are you? By George, the man don't live that can skeer me! Don't you try to come that game, my chicken—cuz I can stand a good deal, but I won't stand that. Come out from behind that bar till I clean you! You want to drive us out, do you, you sneakin' underhanded hound! Come out from behind that bar! *I'll* learn you to bully and badger and browbeat a gentleman that's forever trying to befriend you and keep you out of trouble!"

"Please, Arkansas, please don't shoot! If there's got to be bloodshed——"

". . . It's me you're goin' to murder, is it? But you can't do it 'thout I get one chance first, you thievin' black-hearted white-livered son of a nigger! Draw your weapon!"

With this deliverance, Arkansas began to shoot, and Smith to clamber over benches, and the rest of the men in the bar to dive behind or under anything available for protection. In Smith's haste to dodge the fire he crashed through a glass door, and as Arkansas charged after him, the latter was met by Smith's enraged wife. With all the fury of a woman defending her man, she advanced on Arkansas with her scissors. Backing him away from her husband to the center of the room, she held him at bay while she gave him such a tongue-lashing that she drew a rousing cheer from the crowd. Arkansas was completely subdued for the duration of the flood.

Although the waters were still too high for safe departure on the eighth day, life at Smith's station had become so unbearable that come hell or high water Clemens and party were resolved to try an escape. It had started to snow again, and although visibility was scarcely one hundred yards ahead of them, they set out. Putting their saddles in a canoe and towing their horses behind, they started to paddle across the lake of water surrounding the station. Pfersdorff was paddling in the bow, Ballou in the middle, and Sam sat in the stern holding the three horses. Warning the Prussian to be careful lest they be swept into the main current of the river when the farther bank was reached, they started to the other side. As soon as the canoe touched the bank, Pfersdorff gave a leap which turned the canoe upside down, throwing Sam and Ballou out. The captain saved himself by grabbing hold of sagebrush to pull himself ashore, but Sam and the old blacksmith almost lost their lives swimming out with their overcoats on. Of course they lost their saddles; but after tying the horses to bushes and getting the canoe righted, they were able to paddle back to the station for more saddles, get themselves dried out, and ferry back some hay for the horses. This incident delayed them another twenty-four hours. It was still snowing.

Again they started in such blinding snow that they could not see a hundred yards ahead. Had they been able to see, the mountain ranges would have guided them toward Carson City. However, the fat-headed captain declared that his instinct was perfect and that he could guide them to their destination in a straight line. He said as well that "if he were to straggle a single point out of the true line, his instinct would assail him like an outraged conscience." Convinced that the German could be relied upon, they jogged along for half an hour or so, when they came upon some fresh horse tracks. The captain was so proud of his "bee-line" accuracy that he urged his companions to hurry along and join the party ahead of them.

At the end of another hour's traveling time "the tracks looked

Clemens, Ballou, and Pfersdorff leave the Stage Station at high
waters of the Carson River

From *Roughing It*

still newer and fresher—but what surprised us was that the number of travelers in advance of us seemed to steadily increase." Knowing that Fort Churchill was a short distance up the river, one of the party suggested that a company of soldiers was being moved, but presently the tracks increased so rapidly that the company soon expanded into a regiment.

It was old Ballou who became interested in the movement of so many troops. Dismounting from his horse, he made an examination of the tracks. When he had traced them for a distance he found that the tracks were their own, and that they had been "circussing round and round" and were still in sight of Smith's Station which they had left several hours before. Such a cussing out as Ballou gave the captain!

Saved at last by the Overland Stage on its first trip to Carson City in more than a week, the party got behind it and knew they could follow in its wheel tracks. Soon the stage outdistanced them and the fast-falling snow covered all traces of it. Night came on and the travelers could see nothing. "Plainly the situation was desperate. We were cold and stiff and the horses were tired." Knowing that it was futile to try to go on or to go back to Smith's, they resolved to build a sagebrush fire and to remain on the desert for the night. After picking sage twigs and piling them up, they tried the pistol method of lighting it; but when the shot was fired, it only "blew the pile clear out of the county." Sam held the horses' bridles while this process was going on, but in his complete absorption he had loosed his grasp of the bridles and the horses had wandered off. There wasn't the slightest chance of finding them that night.

At the most critical moment of their plight Ballou fished out four matches from one of his pockets. One by one he lighted them. The first three burst into a flash and died out. Tillou then concentrated on the fourth one, and so did the rest of them, ". . . as Mr. Ballou scratched our last hope on his leg. It lit, burned blue and sickly, and then budded into a robust flame. Shading it with his hands, the old gentleman bent gradually down and every heart went with him—everybody, too, for that matter—and blood and breath stood still. The flame touched the sticks at last, took gradual hold upon them, hesitated, took a stronger hold, hesitated again, held its breath five heartbreaking seconds, then gave a sort of human gasp, and went out.

Clemens resumes his smoking, Ballou his card-playing, and
Pfersdorff his drinking

From *Roughing It*

"Nobody said a word for several minutes——" Finally Pfersdorff broke the silence: "Brothers, let us die together." Beginning first to unburden his soul for death purification, he confessed that he had no hard feelings toward his companions. His speech was so soulful that he broke down and tears came; Sam began to cry, and so did old Ballou. Each one prepared himself for imminent death. Freeing themselves of their vices, the Prussian threw away his bottle of whisky and swore never to drink a drop again; Ballou tossed out his playing cards; and Sam threw away his beloved pipe. Putting their arms around one another's necks, they sat down and "awaited the warning drowsiness that precedes death by freezing." It came presently, and they bade each other "a last farewell."

How long they remained in oblivion was not known, but finally "the gray dawn" came and aroused them from their sleepiness. To their amazement and chagrin, they found themselves within fifteen paces of the station at Buckland's Ranch, where their horses were standing bridled and saddled, entirely sheltered from the storm, under a shed. Unsaddling the horses, they sought shelter and food in the station.

This story can readily be believed if one has traveled over this route in a blinding snowstorm. The papers of this date told of five persons who were drowned in trying to cross the Carson River; every mill and bridge on its course went out; and no stage came through for over a week. Many communities were completely isolated, and flour went to a dollar a pound in some towns.

Sam Clemens said in all sincerity that "I have scarcely exaggerated a detail of this curious and absurd adventure. It occurred almost exactly as I have stated it." Each man, sure now that he was going to live, resumed his simple vice, and the party set out to complete the last part of their journey, arriving in Carson City on January 29.

Although Sam had been through two months, more or less, of bitter and disappointing efforts to find a fortune in silver or gold mining, he had not yet "seen the elephant." He still had faith in Humboldt. In a letter written to his mother on January 30, he told her that he had left his two partners in Humboldt "making preparations for a prospecting tour; and before I can go to Esmeralda and get back to Humboldt, they will have laid, with the certainty of fate, the foundation of their fortunes. It's a great country, Ma." [10]

GOVERNOR NYE AND
SAM CLEMENS

WHEN SAM CLEMENS RETURNED TO CARSON CITY IN
January, 1862, from his Humboldt trip, he found Orion and Governor Nye in serious political disagreement. These two men, appointed the chief directors of the affairs of the Territory of Nevada,
had had diametrically opposite training in the ways of politics.
The elder Clemens had been reared on the frontier in an orthodox
Presbyterian home. He was naïvely honest, and he had always to be
at peace with his inward monitor. His sole political experience had
been his association with Judge Bates in St. Louis and the part he
had taken in giving President Lincoln support in a speaking campaign in 1860. He had not had direct contact with the national
government before coming to Nevada.

On the other hand, James W. Nye, already a man over sixty
years of age, had been schooled in the devious and subtle ways of
political machines through his association with Tammany Hall.
For many years he had taken an active part in New York State and
City politics; he had been a close and personal friend of William
Seward; and he had participated in many local and national campaigns. These experiences classify him as a professional politician.
He knew politics as a game to be played, and he had learned how
to play it successfully.

Since Orion had taken his oath to follow his Instructions faithfully, he tried to do so with religious devotion. A man might sway
his point of view on a question, might convert him to a new and
different religion, might convince him that he should change his
politics, but no one could divert him from the straight and narrow
path of honesty. Never a financial success himself and forced always to follow the most rigid economy, he knew no different way
of conducting Territorial affairs than his own parsimonious training
had afforded him.

However, Governor Nye knew that official Washington could

not and would not be bothered with trivialities of an insignificant Territorial government three thousand miles away. It was he who would have to make the adjustments of the discrepancies which arose in the expenditures of funds allotted for the maintenance of the Territory. Orion could not be brought to the Governor's point of view in handling "special bills and accounts." And the government at Washington could not appreciate the insistent frugalities which Orion tried to effect in the use of Territorial funds.

In the two months of Sam's absence, relations between the Governor and Orion had become severely strained. And Nye's "stand in" at the national capital might easily jeopardize Orion's position. A serious point of controversy was the price paid for renting office space in Carson City. Nye had set himself up in proper gubernatorial style by renting the best place obtainable on the main street, while Orion had his office in a shack out in the "sticks." The Instructions allowed a liberal rent for both offices. Nye had learned that the Federal government was not interested in economy, but Orion had not. Consequently, his meager salary was continually drained by expenses which his superior met painlessly by the customary juggling of accounts to take care of "necessary adjustments."

When Sam heard Orion's version of the disagreements and noted that his brother's integrity was attacked, he was righteously indignant. With all of the wrath which the situation warranted, Sam delivered himself of his feelings by "telling off" the Governor in no uncertain terms. As one old pioneer said, "Sam gave the Governor merry h——!" And A. B. Paine, Sam's biographer, said, "We may regret that no stenographic report was made of the interview. It would be priceless now."[1]

Sam's undertaking to handle the situation was entirely satisfactory. Not only did the Governor leave Orion alone in the performance of his duties, but Sam gained the Governor's admiration. In fact, this little episode increased their companionship. As for Orion, he never again made an important decision in matters of state without consulting Sam. Since Nye was out of the Territory for long periods, during which time Orion was Acting Governor, it is not extravagant to say that Sam Clemens had an important influence on the politics of the Territory of Nevada. Sam was exceedingly proud by nature, and he wished Orion to live up to the importance of his office.

Apparently some of this official wrangling had been written home, for in one of her letters to Sam his mother declared: "It looks like a man can't hold office and be honest." In answer to which remark Sam ironically wrote:

Why certainly not, Madam. A man *can't* hold public office and be honest. Lord bless you, it is common practice with Orion to go about town stealing little things that happen to be lying around loose. And I don't remember having heard him speak the truth since we have been in Nevada. He even tries to prevail upon *me* to do these things, Ma, but I wasn't brought up that way, you know. You showed the public what *you* could do in that line when you raised me, Madam. But then you ought to have raised me first, so that Orion could have had the benefit of my example. Do you know that he stole all the stamps out of an 8-stamp quartz mill one night, and brought them home under his over-coat and hid them in the back room?[2] [One stamp in a quartz mill weighs about six hundred pounds.]

A good story illustrating the handling of funds appropriated for the Indians in Nevada was going the rounds at that time. It concerned the $75,000 appropriated by the Congress with which to build a sawmill for the Indians. Nye was, by virtue of his office, Commissioner of Indian Affairs. The poor Indians, subdued by the United States Army, had been herded onto reservations but recently set up. In the absence of adequate building material, they had thrown up rude tepees so thin and fragile that during the hard winter of 1860–1861 a number of their inhabitants had frozen to death. Nye selected a spot on the lower Truckee River where the water could be dammed for the mill, but the mill never materialized. When the mill was not put up, the joke was that "Nye had a dam by a mill site but no mill by a damn sight."

While Sam was waiting for the weather to clear before setting out for Aurora, he had the pleasure of being present at the trial of "The Great Landslide case of Hyde vs. Morgan." This joke, as old as the very hills of Nevada, has been told and retold, sometimes in one way, sometimes in another. The Sam Clemens version of it will live longest. Today it goes by the title of "The Story of Slide Mountain."

It is highly probable that nowhere else have people enjoyed playing jokes on one another as much as on our frontiers. It was common practice in California in the days of '49; these selfsame people carried the sport to Nevada. In the absence of organized amusement, they had to make their own fun, and particularly did they enjoy horseplay.

If any man conducted himself in a fashion to invite persecution, his life was made miserable by these jokesters. Sufferer of this particular mockery of justice was Benjamin B. Bunker—"General Buncombe" Sam Clemens called him—who was Attorney General for Nevada. "He was shipped out to Nevada in the invoice of Territorial officers" from Thornton, New Hampshire. Although "he considered himself a lawyer of parts and very much wanted an opportunity to manifest it . . ." he was regarded by other lawyers as one of the most thick-headed men in the country. Besides, Bunker's meager salary needed to be increased by taking such private business as came his way. Sam had evidently sized up the legal officer some time before the events of "The Great Landslide Case." In a letter home in October, 1861, he had told of being on a prospecting trip with him; following which he had named his slow-thinking horse, that he bought for the Humboldt trip, Bunker.

The strange natural phenomenon which gave rise to the joke was in Washoe Valley some ten miles north of Carson City, where the mountains west of the valley rise to prodigious heights—in some places to eleven thousand feet. At the base of these peaks many early settlers preëmpted the fertile lands and had developed beautiful and valuable farms. One of these peaks, Slide Mountain, was said to have been formed by a glacier and was, therefore, "rotten ground." The south side of this peak appeared to have been neatly sliced off by some giant from the land of Brobdingnag, the missing face having slipped down to the valley below.

The jokesters planned to "frame" the bumptious Attorney General in a suit to determine the ownership of a fictitious farm that had been entirely covered up by the landslide. On the day prescribed, Dick Hyde,[3] an early settler in the valley, rode excitedly up to the office of Bunker in Carson City and asked him to conduct a suit for him. He offered the opportunistic attorney a fee of five hundred dollars for a successful prosecution. He then told his counsel the grounds for his grief.

Directly on the mountainside above Hyde's ranch another farmer, Tom Morgan (Tom Rust in reality), had settled. But one of the frequent landslides in Washoe Valley had "come and slid Morgan's ranch, fences, cabins, cattle, barns, and everything down on the top of *his* ranch property, to a depth of about thirty-eight feet."

Through his sobs, Hyde described the awful scene when he heard the racket and looked up at the hill and "the whole world was a-ripping and a-tearing down the mountainside—splinters and cord-wood, thunder and lightning, hail and snow, odds and ends of haystacks, and awful clouds of dust!—trees going end over end in the air, rocks as big as a house jumping 'bout a thousand feet high and busting into ten million pieces, cattle turned inside out and a-coming head on with their tails hanging out between their teeth!—and in the midst of all that wreck and destruction sat that cussed Morgan on his gate-post, a-wondering why I didn't *stay and hold possession*! Laws bless me, I just took one glimpse, General, and lit out'n the country in three jumps exactly."

The worst insult of all, said the weeping Hyde, was Morgan's refusal to vacate the premises. He insisted that he liked it better than when he was higher up the hill, and declared "he was occupying his own cabin and not interfering with anybody else's and said the cabin was standing on the same dirt and same ranch it had always stood on, and he would like to see anybody make him vacate." At this remark, Hyde said he had become so insane with rage that "For two days I couldn't find my way to town—been wandering around in the brush in a starving condition—got anything here to drink, General?"

After General Bunker had heard his client's story, he, too, was outraged, and said that "he had never heard of such high-handed conduct in all his life as this Morgan's." He vowed, moreover, that there was no need to go to law over it: in his opinion, there wasn't a lawyer who would take Morgan's case. Bunker was, of course, ignorant of the fact that Morgan had already employed a lawyer, and "a very smart lawyer" at that.

Hyde went on to explain further that, the courts being in recess, it had been arranged to have "ex-Governor" Isaac Roop hear the case as referee; that a large public hall near the Ormsby Hotel had been hired; and that Referee Roop would open court that afternoon at two o'clock. The General was surprised to learn that the case was to be heard, but "he had suspected all the time that the people of Nevada Territory were fools and now he knew it." He told Hyde to stop his weeping, besought him to rest easy, for victory was certain, and instructed him to go out and get his witnesses. Hyde left, but instead of doing as he had been advised he went out on the street and told everyone that Bunker was to be the object of a huge joke that afternoon!

At the appointed hour Roop opened court surrounded by sheriffs, witnesses, and spectators. (Sam Clemens was among them.) However, Roop was playing his part so well and with such solemn demeanor that "some of his fellow-conspirators had misgivings that maybe he had not comprehended, after all, that this was merely a joke" on General Bunker. When court opened, Lawyer "Buncombe" pushed his way through the crowd, laden with law books. As soon as Roop saw the dignitary coming up to the bar of justice, he, as the judge, ordered the crowd to make "way for the United States Attorney!" Such recognition increased the latter's already inflated head.

Witnesses were called: "legislators, high government officers, ranchmen, miners, Indians, Chinamen, Negroes," most of whom were called by defendant Morgan; "but no matter, their testimony invariably went in favor of the plaintiff Hyde." The hand-picked witnesses only strengthened Hyde's case that a man could not lay claim "to own another man's property because his farm had slid down on top of it." Then Morgan's lawyers made their speeches, singularly weak ones.

When the General, now feeling dead sure of his victory, rose to give his closing arguments, "he pounded the table, he banged the lawbooks, he shouted, and roared, and howled, he quoted from anything and everybody, poetry, sarcasm, statistics, history, pathos, bathos, blasphemy, and wound up with a grand war-whoop for free speech, freedom of the press, free schools, the Glorious Bird of America, and the principles of eternal justice!" The audience applauded approval; the General felt that his speech would bring victory if nothing else would.

Roop, playing his part well, "leaned his head upon his hand for some minutes, thinking"; "the audience was silent"; then he "got up and stood erect," still with bowed head, and thought again.

"Then he walked the floor with long, deliberate strides, his chin in his hand, and still the audience waited." At last the decision came:

> "Gentlemen, I feel the great responsibility that rests upon me this day. . . . Gentlemen, I have listened attentively to the evidence . . . to the remarks of the counsel . . . and I commend the masterly and irrefutable logic of the distinguished gentleman who represents the plaintiff. But, gentlemen, let us beware how we allow mere human testimony, human ingenuity in argument, and human ideas of equity, to influence us at a moment so solemn as this. Gentlemen, it ill becomes us, worms as we are, to meddle with the decrees of Heaven. . . . It is plain to me that Heaven, in its inscrutable wisdom, has seen fit to move this defendant's ranch for a purpose. . . . If Heaven has chosen to favor the defendant Morgan in this marked and wonderful manner . . . it ill becomes us, insects as we are, to question the legality of the act or inquire into the reasons that prompted it. No, Heaven created the ranches, and it is Heaven's prerogative to rearrange them, to experiment with them, to shift them around at its pleasure . . . Gentlemen, it is the verdict of this court that the plaintiff Richard Hyde has been deprived of his ranch by the visitation of God! And from this decision there is no appeal."

The General, not perceiving the joke to be on him, was wild with wrath and indignation. He said that Roop was a "miraculous fool, an inspired idiot." Not wishing to lose the fee if he won the case, he sought out Roop that night and "implored him to walk the floor and think for half an hour, and see if he could not figure out some sort of modification of the verdict." Roop accommodated the General and thought for *two hours and a half* and finally told him that "it had occurred to him that the ranch beneath the new Morgan ranch still belonged to Hyde, that his title to the ground was just as good as it had ever been, and therefore he was of the opinion that Hyde had a right to dig it out from under there and . . ." [4]

General Bunker never waited for the end of Roop's argument. For two months he took the sly laughter and the open baiting that were the penalty of his loss of face. It is not known nor recorded

when General Bunker finally saw the light of day, but it is
known that he resigned and returned to New Hampshire.

Having been successful in ensnaring the Attorney General of
the Territory in a joke, these same wags went out for bigger game.
On several occasions they had tried to score one on Nye, but he
had been successful in outwitting them; he just "went on smiling his pleasant smile as if nothing had happened." However, the
perpetrators of these jests did not take defeat easily. Ringleaders
from Carson City and Virginia City conspired to unite their efforts
in getting a laugh on the Governor—a design that he was well
aware of. Disguising their purpose, "they banded themselves together to the number of ten and invited the Governor" to a banquet
of "pickled-oyster stew and champagne," luxuries for Nevadans in
those days.

The Governor, wanting a companion in fun for the occasion,
took Sam Clemens along with him. Quite aware that something
was afoot before they went, he said to Sam, "It's a poor invention.
It doesn't deceive. Their idea is to get me drunk and leave me
under the table, and from their standpoint this will be very funny.
But they don't know me. I am familiar with champagne and have
no prejudices against it."

The consummation of this little joke was not reached until two
o'clock in the morning. "At that hour the last joker joined his
comrades under the table, drunk to the last perfection." Governor
Nye was "serene, genial, comfortable, contented, happy, and sober—,
although he was so full he couldn't laugh without shedding champagne tears." When the Governor and Sam were the last ones left
above the table, Nye nonchalantly remarked: "This is a dry place,
Sam. Let's go and get something to drink and go to bed." Tradition does not relate a successful joke's being played on Nye, but it
does tell us of many which were played on Sam Clemens.[5]

The ten days of delay in getting off to Aurora were full ones
for Sam Clemens, what with getting himself ready for the journey,
getting Orion's affairs straightened out so that they should run
smoothly in his absence, and taking part in jokes. The weather was
still bad; and reports came in constantly of drownings in the swollen
rivers, of mills and bridges being taken out, and of trails made im-
passable by great drifts of snow. Besides, Sam's "sore-back horse"
had to get better before he could take a hard ride.

All of the members of the Aurora party are not known. The papers for February, 1862, mentioned that Bob Howland was in Carson City, and since he and Sam were partners, it is reasonable to believe that he was in it. Sam speaks only of Bob's uncle, the Governor's brother, Captain Thomas C. Nye (John Nye in *Roughing It*). The Captain, who had come out to California in the Gold Rush, was well and favorably known in many of the California camps. When his brother was appointed Governor of the Territory of Nevada, he came over to Washoe to look for a political job. He was Clerk of the first legislature and for a short time secretary to his brother.

Both of the Nye men loved to talk; and from all accounts of persons who knew them well, they were successful in making impressions with their persiflage. However, a persistent talker, one who was boastful and who never let another person get a word in edgewise, always irked Sam Clemens. Old friends of his on the Lode said that *he* liked to do the talking, and that anyone who usurped his prerogative in this capacity came in for a castigation. Anyway, Captain Nye came in for his punishment for talking too much on this trip to Aurora. Sam said that the Captain had "a good memory, and a tongue hung in the middle," in which there was not a dull moment in the one-hundred-and-twenty-mile journey.

On this three-day trip on horseback, Captain Nye told the party among other things that he could "lay out a railroad, organize a political party, sew on buttons, shoe a horse, set a broken leg or a hen." Another characteristic which he had was "a spirit of accommodation that prompted him to take the needs, difficulties, and perplexities of anybody and everybody upon his shoulders at any and all times, and dispose of them with admirable facility and alacrity." Since the stations along the way were crowded with people en route to Aurora, he had plenty of opportunity to display his gifts.

Arriving at a little station on the second day out, the party was told that there was no room for them and no hay or barley for the horses, and that they must go on. But Captain Nye would not have it that way. Although the rest of the party were all for pushing on to the next stop before nightfall, he insisted on staying around for a while. When the party entered the inn, no welcoming smile greeted them; but "within twenty minutes" the Captain had "found old acquaintances in three teamsters; discovered he used to go to school with the landlord's mother; recognized his wife as a lady whose life he had saved once in California, by stopping her runaway horse; mended a child's broken toy and won the favor of its mother, a guest in the Inn; helped the hostler bleed a horse and prescribed for another horse that had the 'heaves'; treated the entire party three times at the landlord's bar; produced a later paper than anybody had seen for a week and sat himself down to read the news to a deeply interested audience."

The party was indeed grateful for Captain Nye's blandishments. The innkeeper found feed for their horses, got them a trout supper, good beds in which to sleep, and "a surprising breakfast in the morning. . . ." Thus refreshed and sustained, the party tackled the short day's ride to Aurora, Esmeralda Mining District.

The discovery of this mining district was made on August 25, 1860, by three men from California, J. M. Corey, James M. Braley, and E. R. Hicks, who had come over to Nevada in the rush to Washoe. Unable to obtain any interests on the Comstock, they decided to prospect elsewhere. Since they were not successful in the vicinity of Virginia City, they decided to go south and prospect the eastern base of the Sierra Nevada Mountains, as far as old Mexico if necessary. Having traveled some hundred miles without finding any promising ledges, they concluded that they had better climb high up on the Wassuck Range to map out a course southward. (One can see a hundred miles or more in the thin, clear mountain air.)

Having made camp for a few days by a spring in a narrow cañon surrounded by rugged and steep cliffs, Hicks started out to do some hunting. Passing over the crags to the west of the camp, he noticed the peculiar formation of a number of quartz ledges. He broke off a number of samples from the several outcroppings and took them back to camp for examination by his partners, who were better miners than he. They gave the samples simple tests and found them to be rich in silver.

All intentions of going farther south were abandoned, and a thorough examination of the countryside was made. It seemed literally to be ribbed with narrow quartz veins. Excitedly they staked out the seven best claims for themselves before they made their discovery known to the world. Believing their discovery to be in California, they decided to go down to Monoville, the nearest settlement, which was twenty-five miles away.

On August 30, twenty men returned with the discoverers to lay out claims for themselves and to help organize the Esmeralda Mining District, an area ten miles square. At the suggestion of Corey, the immediate area around the spring, which faced the east and caught the first rays of the morning sun, was named "Aurora." The two mountain peaks to the west of the community were named Mount Braley and Mount Hicks after the discoverers. (Many a girl born in this town received the name Aurora Esmeralda.)

Selected samples of quartz from the Old Winnemucca ledge, the first one discovered, were sent to Virginia City. The assay on them went as high as $10,000 to the ton. Excited word-of-mouth spread the result of the assay over the other mining districts. Before winter set in, men began swarming to Aurora by stage, fast freight, horseback, and on foot. Stations sprang up all along the routes: the road of about one hundred and twenty miles and the trail of over ninety miles. The nearest station was a ranch on the narrow bend in the East Walker River, which was known as the Elbow Ranch.

In spite of the heavy winter of 1860–1861, building material and supplies were rushed to Aurora, and cabins, brick saloons, mills and other constructions went up. Express companies began to carry valuable mail and packages to the town; political clubs were formed; fire companies were organized; and "feet" were taken up for miles around. By 1862, it was said that there were five thousand people in Aurora.

The uncertainty of the exact location of the Nevada-California boundary line kept Aurora in a state of political vagueness. The latter State, believing that it was in California, organized Mono County and made Aurora the county seat on March 24, 1861. A large courthouse, three stories on one side and two on the other, was erected; county officers were elected; and the California State laws were enforced. When Governor Nye arrived in Nevada in July of the same year, he thought that Aurora was in *his* territory. So he proceeded to organize for his jurisdiction: officers were appointed and elections were held there for delegates to the first Territorial legislature of Nevada. Esmeralda County, Territory of Nevada, was created November 25, and Aurora was made the county seat. It was not until July, 1863, that it was finally determined that

Nevada had jurisdiction over this area, for Aurora was found to be six miles from the California State line. The courthouse Mono County had built was sold and converted into a hotel.

There are no letters extant from Sam Clemens during the first few months of 1862 that he was in Aurora. This hiatus may be accounted for by the storms of that spring. In a letter by another commentator, printed in the San Francisco *Daily Evening Bulletin* and written from Monoville on February 1, a few days before Sam Clemens and his party arrived in Aurora, it was stated that "as late as January 17, the storms were quite severe over that entire region. Prior to that date it rained for eighty hours and the rain falling on a body of snow from one to five feet deep caused a flood surpassing anything ever before seen in those parts by the white residents and judging from the water-marks, greater than any that had occurred of late years."

The letter went on to say that the toll road leading to Carson City was washed away, and Marsh's House at the crossing of the East Walker was swept away as was the toll house at the Elbow Ranch. Mr. Osborn, the constable at Aurora, was drowned in the Walker River. It was this same rain that had caused the flood on the Carson River when the Clemens party was marooned at Smith's station. This same paper reported as late as April 10 that the weather was still disagreeable, and the stock of flour was almost exhausted at Aurora. Snow lay on the ground that year until late in the summer—as it frequently does. It is a common statement in that country that "the breaking-up of one winter is celebrated by the coming of the next one."

Sam Clemens became interested in feet in Aurora some time prior to October 25, 1861; for in a letter to his sister of that date he told her that he had been given fifty feet in the Black Warrior, an unprospected claim, by a young fellow whose name he did not mention. He went on to say in the same letter that he had gone down eight feet on the ledge, and found it eight feet thick "and pretty good rock, too." He said he could "take out rock *now* if there were a mill to crush it—but the mills are all engaged (there are only four of them) so, if I were willing, he would suspend work until Spring. I wrote him to let it alone at present because, you see, in the Spring I can go down myself and help him look after it. There will be twenty mills there."

Sam must have made a hurried trip to Aurora at some earlier date, for in another letter, which he wrote to his mother and sister on February 8, 1862, he said that "one of my old Esmeralda friends, Bob Howland, arrived here, and I have had a talk with him."

Bob had been appointed Town Marshal when Governor Nye organized Esmeralda County. Sam and Bob had become good friends; they were to bunk together part of the time when Sam went up there to look after his interests. In this same letter he said that he owned feet with Bob "in the 'Horatio and Derby' ledge," and that the tunnel on this property was in fifty-two feet, and a small stream of water had been struck "which bids fair to become a 'big thing' by the time the ledge" was reached—"sufficient to supply a mill. Now, if you knew anything of the value of water here, you would perceive at a glance that if the water should amount to fifty or a hundred inches, *we* wouldn't care whether school kept or not. If the ledge should prove to be worthless, we'd *sell the water* for money enough to give us quite a life. But you see, the ledge *will not* prove to be worthless. We have located, near by, a fine site for a mill; and when we strike the ledge, you know, we'll have a mill-site, water power, and pay-rock, all handy. *Then* we shan't care whether we have capital or not. Mill-folks will build us a mill, and wait for their pay. If nothing goes wrong, we'll strike the ledge in June—and if we do, I'll be home in July, you know."

Some of the reasons why Sam went into detail about the tunnel, mine, and mill were the invitations which he had extended to different members of his family to come out to Nevada. His sister Pamela, probably because Sam had given her the notion, wanted to come West very much, and when she pressed the point, he had to tell her that "it's all talk and no cider so far." Although he was morally certain that his Esmeralda mining interests were going to prove successful, he had to tell her that he "had only *talked,* as yet, but proved nothing" . . . that he had "expended money in this country but have made none myself" . . . and that he had "never held in my hands a gold or silver bar that belonged to me." Sam admitted that he had exaggerated the picture "with 40-horse microscopic power."

In this same letter he regretted that he didn't have more money to put into his mine: "By George, if I *just* had a thousand dollars, I'd be all right! Now there's the 'Horatio,' for instance. There are five or six shareholders in it, and I *know* I could buy half of their interests at, say $20 per foot, now that flour is worth $50 per barrel and they are pressed for money. But I am hard up myself, and can't buy—and in June they'll strike the ledge and then 'goodbye, canary.' I can't get it for love or money. Twenty dollars a foot! Think of it. For ground that is *proven* to be rich. Twenty dollars, Madam, and we wouldn't part with a foot of our seventy-five for five times the sum." [6]

Thus for the last time Sam set out in his quest for a fortune in mining. This search for gold had begun when as a young boy he and his playmates had romantically staked out claims near the Tom Sawyer caves on the bank of the Mississippi River. There in 1849, when the goldseekers were rushing through Hannibal on their way to California, the boys pretended to dig gold and to pan it out "half a dollar a day at first; two or three times as much, later, and by and by whole fortunes, as our imaginations became inured to the work." The imagination was just the same fifteen years later, and the results of their efforts were no more rewarding.

12

SAM SEES THE ELEPHANT[1]

WITH SOME DAYS FILLED WITH HIGH HOPES AND others replete with disappointments, Sam Clemens spent over six months in the Esmeralda Mining District. Absolutely certain that fortune was coming to him and Orion from the interests they had obtained there, he entered into the development of these claims with a zeal unparalleled in his life. From his letters home to his sister and his mother, and from his correspondence with Orion, emerges the story of his last mining adventure and his delirious faith in its success.

All during the months of March and April of 1862, it snowed, rained, and blew in the high Sierras. Snow lay deep on the mountainside—some of the claims in which Sam had feet, he wrote were "still under the snow." He had never seen them. Even when he was on the ground, he did not know what they were like. During these months Aurora was so isolated that flour went to $100 a sack, and for a time there was none at all. "For one month the people lived on barley beans and beef. . . ."

Naturally it cost a good deal to live—even on short rations. Sam was already out of money. He had to depend on what Orion sent him out of his salary to buy grub and supplies with which to mine. Orion didn't have any too much money to spend. He had to keep himself in Carson City, and he had to send money to support his family in the East.

For the first few months in Esmeralda, Sam lived with Horatio ("Raish") Phillips and Bob Howland. Bob was able to get along nicely: his uncle, the Governor, had appointed him Town Marshal. On the other hand, Raish and Sam had to get along as best they could. Shortly after these three men arrived in the mining camp, they acquired a ten-by-twelve cabin situated down by the "China gardens." Wishing their cabin to be in a better part of the town, they resolved to move it up the cañon. (Here it remained until it was moved to Reno in 1924.)

Bob Howland said, in later years, while "reminiscing" about the months he lived with Sam and Raish, that fifteen or twenty of the boys stood in to help do the moving. When they went through the main street and got as far as the Exchange Saloon, they put the cabin down to go in and have a drink. As they ranged themselves at the bar, Bob and Sam were "awful jolly and happy to think how quickly and how cheaply they were getting the cabin moved." But soon the crowd began to pour into the bar, "each man showing how and where he had blistered his hands while assisting to move the cabin," and "it dawned upon them that at two bits a drink it would have been almost as cheap to buy a new one with a mansard roof and an observatory." It was said that two hundred and fifty men, at least, drank on that moving job. Bob Howland said that if he "had not put in a demurrer, they would have been drinking until now." [2]

After Sam had been in Aurora a month or more, it became necessary for him to make a trip to Carson City to look after renting office space for Orion. On April 2, he wrote his mother from that city that he was "waiting here, trying to rent a better office for Orion." He added that he had obtained "the refusal after next week of a room 16x50 on first floor of a fire-proof brick—rent eighteen hundred a year." [3]

Governor Nye had spent most of this hard winter and long cold spring in San Francisco; and while he was away, Orion had to look after the Governor's work as well as his own. An Acting Governor ought, Sam thought, to have a fine office, a well-furnished office. In this same letter to his mother he told her that he hoped he was "wearing the last white shirt that will embellish my person for many a day—for I do hope that I shall be out of Carson long before this reaches you."

And before the letter could get back to his mother, he *was* back in Aurora—Sam always said Esmeralda, California [4]—and was writing Orion about their mining investments and his office room. Sam was so anxious that Orion set himself up as befitted his position that he talked the matter over with Colonel Samuel Youngs, representative to the Territorial legislature from Esmeralda County. The Colonel told Sam that Orion "must rent Kinkead's room by all means—the Government would rather pay $150 a month for your office than $75 for [Attorney] General North's. Says you are playing your hand very badly, for either the Government's good opinion or anybody else, in keeping your office in a shanty. Says put Governor Nye in your place and he would have a stylish office, and no objections would ever be made, either. When old Colonel Youngs talks this way, I think it time to get a fine office. I wish you would take that office, and fit it up handsomely, so that I can omit telling people that by this time you are handsomely located, when I know it is no such thing."⁵ To Sam, the proud member of the family, keeping up appearances was uppermost in mind.

After Sam went to Esmeralda, there was a serious Owens River Indian outbreak in the California region to the south of the camp. Fearful lest it spread to the Indians in Nevada, aid was sought from Nevada Territory. Orion, anxious to know the details, had asked Sam to write him about them. In his April 13 letter Sam answered: "[Warren] Wasson got here night before last 'from the wars.' Tell Lockhart he is not wounded and not killed—is altogether unhurt. He says the whites left their stone fort before he and Lieutenant Noble got there. A large amount of provisions and ammunition, which they left behind them, fell into the hands of the Indians."

A number of cattlemen and prospectors around Aurora, and as far south of this section as Owens Lake, had been killed, and the farmers' livestock driven off. On March 28, the cattlemen fortified themselves in a stone fort above Owens Lake and then sent to Visalia, California, and to Carson City for help. Acting Governor Clemens had communicated this request to the commanding officer of Fort Churchill, the military headquarters of Nevada, from which post Lieutenant H. Noble with fifty regulars went to the aid of the settlers. At Aurora, Noble was joined by eighteen men under Sheriff N. F. Scott. An informal army from California, under the command of Colonels Evans and Mayfield, joined forces with the Nevada delegation.

This army engaged the Indians in a badly managed campaign in which a number of whites were killed, including the sheriff, Sergeant Gillespie, and both of the California colonels. The livestock were recovered from the Indians, but the redmen continued to terrify the countryside with their murders and depredations. However, Sam was too full of mining to give Orion a fuller report, dismissing the account by saying: "And, as Cousin Sally Dillard says, this is all I know about the fight." [6]

In his first letter to Orion describing their Esmeralda interests, Sam was impatient, irritated, but excited and hopeful. No work was begun on the "Horatio and Derby" because he hadn't seen it. "It is still in the snow." He thought they could begin work in three or four weeks and that the ledge would be struck in July. "*Why* didn't you send me the 'Live Yankee' deed—the very one I wanted? . . . Send me $40 or $50—by mail—immediately. The 'Red Bird' is probably good—can't work on the tunnel on account of snow. The 'Pugh' I have thrown away—shan't relocate it. It is nothing but bed-rock croppings—too much work to find the ledge, if there is one. Shan't record the 'Farnum' until I know more about it—perhaps not at all. 'Governor' under the snow. 'Douglas' and 'Red Bird' are both recorded. . . ."

Short of money, always short of money, he besought Orion a second time in the same letter: "Stir yourself as much as possible, and lay up $100 or $150, subject to my call. I go to work tomorrow, with pick and shovel. Something's got to come, by G——, before I let go, here. . . . Don't buy *anything* while I am here—but save up some money for me. Don't send any money home. I shall have your next quarter's salary spent before you get it, I think. I mean to make or break here within the next two or three months."

And Sam Clemens did go to work with a pick and shovel in one of the quartz mills for $10 a week and his board. He didn't last long. What with his slight figure, graceful hands, and not too sturdy constitution, he could not hold up under the strain. It took bone, muscle, and stamina to handle one of the long-handled shovels. He never could learn to swing it right. "As often as any other way, the sand didn't reach the screen at all, but went over my head and down my back, inside my clothes." There were two reasons why "this palatial life, this gross and luxurious life, had to come to an end. . . . On my side, I could not endure the heavy labor and on the company's side, they did not feel justified in paying me to shovel sand down my back; so I was discharged just at the moment that I was going to resign."

In describing this work in a quartz mill in later years, he said that it was:

"A nice place, truly, for the proprietor of a hundred silver mines. But I was glad to get that berth. But I didn't know how to keep it. They did not want me. I didn't know why. I was the most careful workman they had ever had. They said so. I took more pains with my work. I was shoveling sand. The technical term is 'tailing.' The silver rock is ground over once or twice, and they clean it up and work it over again. Whenever I had a lot of that sand to shovel, I was so particular that I would sit down an hour and a half and think about the best way to shovel that sand. And if I could not cipher it out in my mind just so, I would not go shoveling it around needless. I would leave it alone until next day.

"Many a time, when I would be carrying a bucket full of sand from one pile to another, thirty or forty feet off, right in the middle, suddenly a new idea would strike me, and I would carry that sand back, and sit down and think about it, and like enough get so wrought up and absorbed in it that I would go to sleep. Why, I always knew there must be some tip-top, first-rate way to move that sand.

"At last I discovered it. I went to the boss and told him that I had got just the thing, the very best and quickest way to get that sand from one pile to the other. And he says, 'I'm awful, awful glad to hear it.' You never saw a man so uplifted as he was. It appeared to take a load off his breast, a load of sand, I suppose. And I said, 'What you want now is a cast iron pipe about thirteen or fourteen feet in diameter, and, say forty feet long. And you want to prop up one end of that pipe about thirty-five or forty feet off the ground. And then you want a revolving belt—just work it with the waste steam from the engine—a revolving belt with a revolving chair in it. I am to sit in that chair and have a Chinaman down there to fill up the bucket with sand and pass it up and as I come around, I am just to soar up there and tilt it into that pipe, and there you are. It is as easy as rolling off a log.' . . .[7]

Although Sam lasted but one week at the pick-and-shovel job, he was still hopeful that one of his silver ledges would pay a dividend. On May 11 he wrote Orion that "I have 'got my d——d satisfy' at last. Two years' time will make us capitalists, in spite of anything. Therefore, we need fret and fume and worry and doubt no more, but just lie still and put up with privations for six months. Perhaps three months will 'let us out.' " [8]

Dividends may have been only three months away, but in the same letter Sam said: 'R. and I are strapped and we haven't three days' rations in the house. Raish is looking anxiously for money and so am I. Send me whatever you can spare conveniently—I want it to work the 'Flyaway' with." Rations were short inside their cabin, but Sam didn't want the world to know it. So far as he was concerned, he wanted the public to think that plutocrats lived there. To convey this impression he came home one evening with a couple of barley sacks full of tin cans and champagne and wine bottles. These he dumped out near the cabin—the manner, in mining camps, of disposing of rubbish.

Preparing for the day when they could live like capitalists, Sam advised Orion to rent "the corner upstairs office . . . provided it has one fine, large front room superbly carpeted, for the safe and a $150 desk, or such a matter—one handsomely gotten up, perhaps, for records and consultations, and one good-sized bedroom and adjoining it a kitchen, neither of which latter can be entered by *anybody* but yourself—and finally, when one of the ledges begins to pay, the whole to be kept in parlor order by two likely contra-bands at big wages . . . make them fix for you *before* the 1st of July—for maybe you might want to 'come out strong' on the 4th, you know." [9]

So surely could Sam visualize himself—sitting in the "handsome room amidships" with two black Negroes to wait on him, and help-ing Orion steer the Territory. All he would have to do would be to collect the dividends. In every letter that he wrote to Orion he told of the wonderful prospects of their mine investments; from time to time he sent specimens from them. Once he sent some from the "Flyaway," the "Antelope," and "My Darling Monitor" which he called "choice—any d——d fool would. . . . If I had anything more to say, I have forgotten what it was, unless, perhaps, that I want a sum of money—anywhere from $20 to $150, as soon as possible."

It was still May when Sam wrote his brother again. In the mean-time Orion had become excited, too, about acquiring ledges. Al-

AURORA, ESMERALDA MINING DISTRICT, NEVADA

MARK TWAIN'S CABIN, AURORA, NEVADA

VIEW TO THE EAST FROM VIRGINIA CITY

In the center foreground Six Mile Cañon and Sugar Loaf

THE GREAT MOUNTAIN

MOUNT DAVIDSON AND VIRGINIA CITY

though Sam approved of the specimen which Orion sent him, he admonished him "to touch it lightly as far as money is concerned, though, for it is well to reserve the code of justice in the matter of quartz ledges—that is, consider them all (and their owners) guilty (of 'shenanigans') until they are proved innocent." Sam did not heed this advice that he gave his brother but went right on buying more claims and begging Orion for more money. "If you can spare $100 conveniently, let me have it or $50, anyhow, considering that I own *one-fourth* of this ['Flyaway']. . . ." The money went fast to keep Sam in grub, tools, and black powder.

His hope of gaining a fortune in finding a "ready made ledge" began to waver. The young miner concluded that "The pick and shovel are the only claims I have any confidence in now. . . . My back is sore, and my hands are blistered with handling them today." However, finding a rich ledge this way was doubtful, for he wrote that "the work went slowly, very slowly. But—if we strike it rich—I've lost my guess, that's all." Dissatisfaction with conditions slows up enthusiasm: "Couldn't go on the hill today. It snowed. It always snows here, I expect." There are only two seasons in these parts of the high Sierras—"the breaking-up of one winter and the beginning of the next." That is a truth for which anyone who has lived in this section of Nevada will vouch. Sam Clemens said that "as a general thing when a man calls for a brandy toddy there, the bar-keeper chops it off with a hatchet and wraps it up in a paper, like maple sugar." And it was "further reported that the old soakers haven't any teeth—wore them out eating gin cocktails and brandy punches." [10]

The lonesomeness that accompanies vanished hope came in the letter to Orion in which he asked: "Don't you suppose they have pretty much quit writing at home?" Sam was surely seeing the elephant. Still determined, however, to make or break himself in Aurora, he declared, "I have struck my tent in Esmeralda, and I care for no mines but those which I can superintend myself."

One of the first disasters that befell the Clemens' investments in Esmeralda was the loss of the "Darling Monitor." "Two or three men of the old 'Salina' company entered our hole on the 'Monitor' yesterday morning, before our men got there, and took possession, armed with revolvers. And according to the d——d laws of this forever d——d country, nothing but the District Court (and there ain't any) can touch the matter. . . . The Clemens' Company—all of us—hate to resort to arms in this matter, and it will not be done until it becomes a forced hand—but I think that will be the end of it, nevertheless." [11]

After midsummer Horatio Phillips was not mentioned again in any of Sam Clemens' letters to his brother. Instead Sam took on another "pardner," Calvin H. Higbie, a man of great stature, who "was muscled like a giant. He could handle a long-handled shovel like an emperor, and he could work patiently and contentedly twelve hours on a stretch without ever hastening his pulse or his breath." Cal, who was a hard-rock practical miner, gave Sam the benefit of his mining experience, as Ballou had done on the Humboldt trip.

In the wake of vanishing hope of success, Sam had one more outburst of distrust and disgust with Orion's attempt to invest in mines. Sam had little or no confidence in him in most matters and practically none in mining affairs. When Orion had the poor judgment to write Sam about it, Sam fairly exploded: "You have *promised* me that you would leave all mining matters, and everything involving an outlay of money, in my hands. Sending a man fooling around the country after *ledges,* for God's sake!—when there are hundreds of feet of them under my nose here, begging for owners, free of charge. I *don't want* any more feet, and I won't *touch* another foot . . ." [12] which he could not examine himself.

Most of the mining camps of the West were resurgent. As soon as any kind of strike was made in a region and the excited crowd rushed to it, the less fortunate ones began to fan out in all directions looking for more ledges. One of the excited reports that came to Aurora was the discovery of a rich cement mine near Mono Lake, some thirty-five miles to the southwest of Aurora. This mine, belonging to a Mr. Whiteman, was supposed to be fabulously rich—gold nuggets were mixed throughout the cement, like raisins in a fruit cake. When Mr. Whiteman, who naturally did not want anyone to know where his mine was located, came to Aurora for supplies, he was watched carefully by the curious ones in this town.

Whenever it was reported that Whiteman had passed "stealthily through Esmeralda at dead of night, in disguise," everyone went wild with excitement. "In less than three hours after daylight all the horses and mules and donkeys in the vicinity were bought, hired, or stolen, and half the community were off for the mountains in the wake of Whiteman." Whiteman took different and devious paths, purposely wandering through· gorges for days, until the provisions of his followers ran out and they had to return to the settlements.

If no one else knew where this cement mine was, it was not morally certain that Whiteman himself knew its location. It seemed that he was given the map and a specimen of the gold-filled cement by one of three surviving German boys who had gone to California many years before. Cal knew Whiteman by sight; and a Mr. Van Dorn, a friend of Sam's and Cal's, knew him well. Van Dorn said that he had Whiteman's promise that "he should have a private hint in time to enable him to join the next cement expedition," and Van Dorn had promised to extend the promise to Sam and Cal.

One evening Cal came into the cabin in great excitement to announce that he was certain that he had seen Whiteman up town in a "pretended state of intoxication." A few minutes later Van Dorn entered to corroborate Cal's suspicions. Whiteman had told Van Dorn he was going out to the cement mine in his usual misleading manner and that he could follow in his wake. Immediately Sam, Cal, and Van Dorn decided to go to the cement diggings. Making the arrangements as quietly as possible, they concluded that they would leave town at midnight in three separate parties, the three to meet on the divide overlooking Mono Lake. They were confident that they were the only persons in Aurora who knew that Whiteman had been in town. After packing their animals, they set out about midnight to pass up the narrow road which led out of the camp.

Sam, riding in the rear, leading the pack-horse with all of the provisions, allowed his companions to get so far ahead of him that they were soon out of sight. He "coaxed and bullied the pack-horse" till he got him into a trot; but at such speed the rattle of the tin cups and the pans frightened him so that he broke into a fast run. Sam, who had his *riata* wound around the pommel of his saddle, was pulled from his own mount, and the two animals went on without him. As the pack-horse ran, he tumbled all of the cargo off him to the ground. This noise awakened the occupants of one of the last cabins on the edge of town. One miner appeared—then another one. "Hello!" they shouted—Sam lay down and kept still. The two miners walked toward him, and stopped within ten steps of him. "Ssh, listen." He heard them sit down on a boulder, he thought, though he could not distinctly see them. One of them said: "I heard a noise, as plain as I ever heard anything. It seemed to be about there . . ."

One of the miners, to test his calculations, picked up a stone and threw it. It whizzed by Sam's head—he "flattened himself out in the dust like a postage stamp, and thought" that if his assailant corrected his aim a little, "he would probably hear another noise." Sam promised himself that if the Sierra Nevada Mountains were ribbed with cement mines, this one would be his last. Sam heard one of the awakened miners say that a friend had told him he saw White-man in town that day. Believing that the noise Sam had made was Whiteman going out to his mine, the miner declared he was going to town at once to tell his friend that Whiteman had passed that way. Soon the miners left for town, and when it was safe to reload the cargo, Sam was off again to overtake his party.

Just as the sun was coming up, the Clemens party passed over the divide where they could see the Lake. Descending to the valley below and, believing that they had eluded everyone, they stopped to cook breakfast and to rest. But to their dismay the miners had spread the word around that Whiteman had passed their way to his mine. Like wildfire the rumor spread. Hundreds of Aurora miners were soon on their way to the Whiteman cement mine. Sam observed: "Three hours later the rest of the population filed over the 'divide' in a long procession, and drifted off out of sight around the borders of the Lake!" in the direction of what was believed to be the cement mine.

Sam and party held a conference as to what was the best way out of their unfortunate predicament. Since they knew that under the circumstances Whiteman would never show them the way to his mine on this trip, they decided to stay a week or more and camp around Mono Lake. In *Roughing It* Sam Clemens gives an accurate description of this lake, its peculiarities of formation, and the brackish qualities of its water. He and Cal had an exciting time exploring it. At the end of a week they went farther into the Sierra Mountains on a fishing trip. It took them as far as Castle Peak, that picturesque mountain area on the far eastern boundary of

Yosemite National Park. Fishing at an altitude of ten thousand feet in one of the many lakes in this section was successful, "cooling ourselves during the hot August noons by sitting on snowbanks ten feet deep . . . and at night entertaining ourselves by almost freezing to death." Returning to Mono Lake, they found that the cement-mine rush was over, and they joined the last of the stragglers who were going back to Aurora.[13]

There they found another excitement about to break. Along in the summer of 1862, Aurora was thrown into a frenzy by a report that the "Wide West" mine had struck it rich. Some development work had been done on the claims, but up until the summer of 1862 nothing unusual had been found.

Every mining camp had at least one delirious spree when everyone fought to get an interest in a strike, legitimate or faked. Everyone went to take a look, and "for some days there was such a crowd of people about the 'Wide West' shaft that a stranger would have supposed there was a mass-meeting in session." (There were about five thousand people in Aurora at this time.) Every visitor to the shaft was given a sample of the rich ore, a common practice among market-rigging speculators. Every new owner of a sample ground it up and washed it out to prove to himself that it *was a real strike*. Calvin Higbie brought a sample of it to their cabin and, "when he had washed it out, his amazement was beyond description."

The mine promoters got the local newspaper, the *Esmeralda Star,* of May 31 to give the mine a good write-up along with a general description of the mineral wealth of the district. In this article the "Wide West" was boosted sky-high:

"The next which demands our attention is the 'Wide West' and here we must pause, for it deserves our especial care in observation, and the startling truths we are compelled to mention in connection with this ledge are astounding. We were kindly permitted by Mr. [A. D.] Allen who is working the ledge to enter the shaft which inclines and reaches the bottom at about seventy-five feet in depth; here we saw two men at work picking the decomposed quartz which lay in abundance, and by holding a lighted candle to the sides of the shaft, the gold glistened all over it, and it was difficult to tell which was in the greater quantity, gold or the decomposed quartz; two ounces of which yielded $1.75. Mr. Allen gave us about a pound to take away with us. . . . We have been in California since the spring of '49, visited many of the mines, but never saw anything to compare in richness with the ledge of the 'Wide West,' we have only spoken of the gold which could be seen and we were told that it was equally as rich in silver."

With such articles as this one appearing in the local paper and copied in many of the California papers, the stock shot up rapidly on the Exchange, and the owners of the "Wide West" were offered "a thousand dollars a foot."

So many visitors came to the mine that the owners put a stop to giving ore specimens away. At the same time the foreman was ordered to forbid any person, except their own workmen, to enter the mine for any purpose. Now Cal Higbie may have been a big-muscled, hard-working miner with little education, but he did have a tolerable lot of practical mining experience. He did a heap of puzzling over the "Wide West" sample, "examined it with a glass, inspected it in different lights and from different points of view" and after each and every turn, he muttered the selfsame opinion:

"It is *not* 'Wide West' rock!"

Determined to satisfy himself that he was right, Cal resolved, even at the risk of his life, to have a look down in the "Wide West" shaft. After several attempts to enter the hole, he finally succeeded, broke off some of the ledge matter, and returned to their cabin to announce "with smothered excitement" that it was "a blind lead." Everything was there—"hanging wall, foot wall, clay casings, everything complete!" In this district's mining rules and regulations anyone could locate a blind lead—that is, one that does not show on the surface of the claim. Since the "Wide West" Company did not know of the blind lead down in the shaft, it was public property, and therefore Cal and Sam could locate it for their own.

When Cal pronounced it to be a blind lead, Sam was overjoyed that at last the riches which he had been seeking for almost a year were in his grasp. His mind went through spasms of excitement: "doubt—conviction—doubt again—exultation—hope, amazement, belief, unbelief—every emotion imaginable swept in wild procession through my heart and brain, and I could not speak a word." In his

Sam and Cal rejoice over the "Blind lead"

From *Roughing It*

flash of excitement he did not know how to express his joy. At first he shouted, "Cal, let's—let's burn the house—or kill somebody. Let's get out where there's room to hurrah! . . . It is a hundred times too good to be true." Cal took off his hat and swung it around, giving three cheers, and Sam chimed in: "For I was worth a million dollars, and did not care 'whether school kept or not.' " [14]

When the two miners collected their wits, they decided to locate the blind lead. It was thought well to have a friend in on the deal, and that friend had better be none other than the foreman of the "Wide West," Mr. Allen himself. Cal left and secured him and brought him to their cabin. After he was told the story, he agreed to be the third partner. (What else could he do?) "The notice was put up that night, and duly spread upon the recorder's books before ten o'clock," where "the evidence of many witnesses, and likewise that of the official records of Esmeralda District, is easily obtainable in proof that it is true history." Also, according to the rules of this district, locators of claims must do a fair and reasonable amount of work on their claims within ten days after the date of the location. If this work was not done, the property was forfeited and any person could "jump the claim."

The night, after Cal and Sam had their blind lead securely recorded, was spent lying in their bunks in their cheerless, floorless, drab cabin, building castles in the air; taking trips to Europe, building mansions, and spending their fortune recklessly. Suddenly Sam recalled that they owed the butcher six dollars. Cal replied, "Hang the butcher!" to which exclamation Sam echoed, "Amen."

It was useless for the millionaires to try to sleep that night. By three o'clock they found themselves up and about. They "played cribbage and smoked their pipes until sunrise," at which time they decided to stay up.

The recorder's books were noted daily by most of the people of the camp, and soon the news was around. Sam, enjoying his new status, walked around the town "serene and happy." Cal remarked that "the foreman had been offered two hundred thousand dollars for his third of the mine." But Sam's price was a *million*.

In mid-afternoon of the following day, when Sam was coming out of the post office, he met M. C. Gardiner, owner of the Elbow Ranch, sometimes known as the "Nine Mile Ranch." Gardner told him that Captain Thomas Nye was "lying dangerously ill," at his ranch and that he and his wife could not give him the care that he needed. Feeling a responsibility toward the old Captain, Sam resolved to go with Gardiner and help care for the sick man. Before leaving, however, he recalled that the work on the blind lead must be done in ten days to hold it. He rushed over to the cabin. When he found Cal was not there, he wrote him a note and left it on the table. In a short time Sam was on his way to his sick friend.

Captain Nye was very ill indeed with "spasmodic rheumatism." Newspapers in the Territory and in California where he had lived reported his illness and wished him a speedy recovery. The ill man was in such great pain that he was difficult to care for and often swore at Sam—"So much so, indeed, that I determined to go back to Esmeralda." After eating his supper one night, he waited for the moon to rise (it would be folly to travel in the dark with so many open shafts and in such rough terrain) and then started back on foot to cover nine miles.

Just as he was coming up the hill overlooking the town, he glanced over "at the hill beyond the cañon and in the bright moonlight saw what appeared to be about half the population of the village massed on and around the 'Wide West' croppings." There must be, he thought, another exciting strike at the mine. Not reaching the cabin until after one o'clock, "tired but jolly, the dingy light of a tallow candle revealed Higbie, sitting by the pine table gazing stupidly at my note, which he held in his fingers, and looking pale, old, and haggard. I halted, and looked at him. He looked at me, stolidly. I said:

" 'Higbie, what—what is it?"

" 'We're ruined—we didn't do the work—*the blind lead's relocated!'* "

Sam was "sick, grieved, broken-hearted." Soon there were mutual explanations: Sam had depended on Cal and Cal had depended on Sam. Each of them had written the other one a note, but Cal had never gone inside to leave his message; he had ridden by on horseback and thrown it in through a broken pane of the window. Sam had thought that reliable Cal would do the work on the blind lead, but Cal had again succumbed to the cement-mine secret when the man Whiteman had passed through Aurora and had told Cal that he would "find it this time." Worried lest Sam had not done the assessment work, Cal came back from the cement mine by one road, while Sam returned to town by another one. At midnight of the tenth day, fourteen men, duly armed and ready to back their proceedings, put up their notice and proclaimed their ownership of the blind lead under the new name of the "Johnson." [15]

On July 23, Sam wrote Orion: "No, I don't own a foot in the 'Johnson' ledge—I will tell the story some day in a more intelligible way than Tom [Nye] has told it. I own twenty-five feet (1-16) of the east extension on it—and Johnson himself has contracted to find the ledge for one hundred feet. . . . An eighteenth of the 'Ophir' was a fortune to John D. Winters—and the 'Ophir' can't beat the 'Johnson' any. . . ." Although in a preceding letter he was getting skeptical of the "Horatio and Derby," he was still pinning his faith on this extension.[16]

Sam was blue. He was out of money and had no job. Cal was discouraged, too, because he could find nothing to do. In "an outburst of pathetic longing" he expressed a wish that he would like a job at the Pioneer Mill at $5 a day. Sam told him that that was easy if he would only follow his "infallible scheme for finding work for the unemployed." Then Sam went on to explain to Cal that he was to go to the foreman of the mill and tell him "that you want work as a laborer, that you are tired of being idle; that you are not used to being idle, and can't stand it; that you just merely want the refreshment of work and require nothing in return." Not even board.

Cal followed Sam's instructions, got the job, and for a while received no wages. However, just as Sam had told him, the foreman broke down and offered him a job with pay. After that Sam "led an easy life, with nothing to do . . . and so during many succeeding weeks I was a gentleman of leisure, with books and newspapers to read and stewed dried apples every day for dinner the same as Sunday, and I wanted no better career than this in this life. Higbie supported me handsomely, never once complained of it, never once suggested that I go out and try for a job at no wages and keep myself." [17]

All of this time Sam's debts were piling up so fast that he didn't know "how in h—l I am going to live on something over $100 until October or November. . . . The fact is, I must have something to do, and that shortly, too. . . ." It was not possible to expect very much from Orion's salary during this quarter for he had sent money to Mollie and Jennie to come out to Nevada.[18] Sam said that he had bought $25 worth of clothing, had grubstaked Cal to $25 in the cement diggings, owed about $45 or $50, and had $45 in his pocket. Complete disillusionment in gaining a fortune at mining was setting in.

Sam had had little or no money when he went to Aurora. He had lived and mined almost entirely on what money Orion could send him. That he had tried to make some money or get a job was evident in his letters. He and Raish Phillips were in the same financial predicament, and during the first few days when they were living together, they both did some writing. He was in one of those rising tides of energy which came and went throughout his life. Every mining camp had correspondents from the Territorial newspapers as well as from the leading ones on the Coast. Cooped up in their cheerless cabin in March and April, they had written together. In Sam's letter to Orion on April 13, he asked him to send Raish "one of those black portfolios . . . and put a couple of pen-holders and a dozen steel pens in it." A month later he said that he or Raish would "drop a line to the [Carson City Daily] 'Age' occasionally. I suppose you saw my letters in the [Virginia City Territorial] 'Enterprise.'"[19] It was said that one of these early articles written for the *Enterprise* was about an old "Rackabones" of a horse. He may have had in mind the poor old nag with the saddle sores that he rode out to Aurora. No money had been received for these articles, but the fact that they had been printed gave Sam considerable encouragement. He applied for a job as a compositor on the *Esmeralda Star,* but there was no place for him.

When times were getting hard in late June or early July, Sam tried to get an appointment as Deputy Sheriff. He wrote Orion to "ask Gasherie why the devil he don't send along my commission. . . . The fact of my being in California, and out of his country, wouldn't amount to a d——n with *me,* in the performance of my official duties." It was thought at that time that Aurora was in California. That State had organized it and made it the county seat of Mono County, and as such it had elected representatives to go down to Sacramento. Governor Nye, believing it to be in *his* Territory, had organized Esmeralda County and set up Aurora as the county seat. Delegates went down to Carson City to represent this district in

Nevada. Amazingly enough, one of the representatives who went to the California capital became speaker of its lower house; and one of the delegates sent to the Nevada legislature was elected to the same position in its Assembly.

In the same letter Sam asked Orion: "How do the Records pay?" Perhaps there would be a job from this source. The "Records" meant the recording of the mining corporations, of which there were so many that Orion soon had to have help for this work. "And if I can't move the bowels of those hills this fall, I will come up and clerk for you until I get money enough to go over the mountains for the winter."

He also wrote Orion and asked him to "write the Sacramento *Union* folks, or to [A. J.] Marsh, and tell them I'll write as many letters a week as they want, for $10 a week—my board must be paid. Tell them I have corresponded with the *New Orleans Crescent,* and other papers, and the *Enterprise.* California is full of people who have interests here, and it's d——d seldom they hear from this country. . . . If they want letters from here, who'll run from morning till night collecting materials cheaper? I'll write a short letter twice a week, for the present, for the *'Age,'* for $5 per week." [20]

The sketches which Sam Clemens had sent to the *Enterprise* and signed "Josh" were attracting considerable attention. Orion, always proud of Sam's accomplishments, began telling around that they were written by Sam. The later articles were satirical in nature and were believed to be pointed at some members of the Brigade. The full text of the "Josh" letters is not extant, but one, "Professor Personal Pronoun," was a burlesque of an egotistical speaker whose lecture could not be printed in full because the printer had run out of capital "I's."

The satirical gem which landed Sam his berth on the *Enterprise* was the paraphrase of a speech supposed to have been delivered on the Fourth of July near Owens Lake. Its opening line was immense: "I WAS SIRED BY THE GREAT AMERICAN EAGLE AND FOALED BY A CONTINENTAL DAM!" All through the speech "Josh" used phrases which everyone recognized as those which Judge Turner always included in his speeches. Sam had heard them so often—during the opening of the first Territorial legislature, and on other occasions—that he didn't have to attend the celebration. [21]

William Barstow was the financial secretary of the *Enterprise.*

He and Sam had become good friends during the days of the organization of the Territory. Barstow liked Sam's articles and had called them to the attention of Joseph Thompson Goodman, the twenty-four-year-old proprietor of the *Enterprise*. The paper was about to lose one of its local reporters—Dan De Quille was leaving soon for the States to visit his family in Iowa—and the paper needed a man to take his place while he was gone. On August 7, Sam wrote Orion, saying that "Barstow wrote that if I wanted the place, I could have it. I wrote him I guessed I would take it, and asked how long before I must come up there. I have not heard from him since."[22]

Before he heard from Barstow, he planned a walking trip of "sixty or seventy miles through a totally uninhabited country, and it is barely possible that mail facilities may prove infernally slow during the few weeks I expect to spend out there. But do you write Barstow that I have left here for a week or so, and in case he should want me he must write me here, or let me know through you."

There is no record of where Sam Clemens went for this week. It is reasonable to think that he went out to see Cal Higbie. Sam's conscience would not have let him leave Aurora without making it right with his "pardner." Cal had stood by him through thick and thin. Together they had prospected, mined, and bunked; together they had starved; and together they had shared each other's joys and sorrows. Indeed, Cal had supported Sam when the former had a job and Sam was down and out. He probably would have gone much farther than sixty or seventy miles to square everything with Cal.

It may be that he owed Cal some money, for in the letter in which he told Orion that he was going to take this walk, he mentioned that he would have paid a fee of $1.50 for Judge Turner "but I want money now as I leave town tonight." Since there were no communities in those days in any direction, except a few prospectors here and there, the money must have been for the payment of some bill he owed. When he added in the same letter that "I may want some when I get back . . ." that suggested that what money he had when he started out on the walk would be gone when he got back to Aurora.

Through the years this association with Cal Higbie kept a sentimental prominence in his memory, and when he published *Roughing It,* he dedicated it:

To

CALVIN H. HIGBIE OF CALIFORNIA, AN HONEST MAN, A GENIAL
COMRADE, AND A STEADFAST FRIEND, THIS BOOK IS INSCRIBED BY
THE AUTHOR IN MEMORY OF THE CURIOUS TIME WHEN WE TWO
WERE MILLIONAIRES FOR TEN DAYS

Sam was back in Aurora by the middle of August, at which time
he wrote his sister that he was cabining with Dan Twing and Dan's
dog, and "will continue to do so a while—until I leave for——" [23]
The sentence was not completed.

In a few days Sam was off on another long hike from Aurora
to Virginia City, too broke, it was said, to go by stage. He does not
state whether he took the trail or the wagon road—probably the
former. Although a distance of ninety miles, it was thirty miles
shorter than the wagon road. In the hot days of August, when the
sun's rays come down in a vertical shaft of heat, walking was done
by moonlight. Sleeping in haystacks on the ranches along the
Walker and Carson rivers, he arrived in Virginia City a veritable
hayseed.

BOOK IV

WASHOE SCHOOL OF
JOURNALISM

13

MARK TWAIN'S NEVADA

"THE LIFE OF THE COMSTOCK IN THE OLD DAYS never has been written so that those who did not share it can understand; it never can be so written, for to be like it, all would have to be set down, and that's a feat beyond mortal pen. Many have tried, and all have failed. Mark Twain has come the nearest to the reality—not so much in what he has told, but in the spirit of his work. It was there that Mark got his point of view—that shrewd, graceless, good-humored, cynical way of looking at things as they in fact are—unbullied and indifferent to traditions—which has made the world laugh." So wrote Arthur McEwen, newspaper contemporary, one-time business manager, and friend of Mark Twain.[1]

Impossible as it may be to comprehend the life of the Lode when the great humorist was being forged from this crucible, certain pictures of the times stand out in bold relief. Washoe burst like a meteor on the world. For a time, from 1860 to 1864, all eyes were turned toward this lodestone; its name was on the tongue of everyone. The Comstock Lode was the center of Washoe, Virginia City the center of the Lode. Beginning high up on the steep pouter-pigeoned breast of Mount Davidson, the city stretched down around its flanks. A single street, C by name, surveyed by Dr. Henry De Groot in 1860, became the avenue of first importance.

Let Mark Twain describe the view from this position:

"From Virginia's airy station one could look over a vast, far-reaching panorama of mountain ranges and deserts; and whether the sun was rising or setting or flaming in the zenith, or whether night and the moon held sway, the spectacle was always impressive and beautiful. Over your head Mount Davidson lifted its gray dome, and before and below you a rugged canon clove the battlemented hills, making a somber gateway through which a soft-tinted desert was glimpsed, with the silver thread of a river winding through it, bordered with trees which many miles of distance diminished to a delicate fringe; and still further away

the snowy mountains rose up and stretched their long barrier
to the filmy horizon—far enough beyond a lake that burned
in the desert like a fallen sun, though that, itself, lay fifty miles
removed. Look from your window where you would, there was
fascination in the picture." [2]

Virginia City is singularly uneven in its uprisings and down-
fallings. "Nothing was on the level, figuratively and literally"—so
said the tenderfoot who lost all of his money gambling in the saloon
or in Comstock shares. At first it was difficult for the visitor in the
early days of the camp to figure out just how the city was laid out.
Browne said that when a man saw the town in 1861, "His impression
is that it never was laid out at all, but followed the dips, spurs, and
angles of the immortal Comstock. Some of the streets run straight
enough; others seem to dodge about at acute angles in search of an
open space, as miners explore the subterranean regions in search
of a lead. The cross streets must have been forgotten in the original
plan—if ever there was a plan about this eccentric city. Sometimes
they happen accidentally at the most unexpected points; and sometimes they don't happen at all where you are sure to require them.
A man in a hurry to get from the upper slope of the town to any
opposite point below must try it underground or over the roofs of
the houses, or take the customary circuit of half a mile. Everybody
seems to have built wherever he could secure a lot."

The Comstock is famous for more things than its production of
gold and silver. Its weather is notorious, its wind villainous. Everyone talked about it, Mark Twain wrote about it, but no one did anything about it. "The Washoe Zephyr," Mark called it. "It was a
peculiar institution," he said, and scriptural because "no man know-
eth whence it cometh." Actually it comes from over the tops of the
western Sierran crest. There is a down draft from this direction
which blows in terrific gusts. Mark also added that "its office
hours were from two in the afternoon till two the next morning." [3]

When J. Ross Browne visited the Lode in 1860, he was forced
to write about these zephyrs, which came "from the four quarters
of the compass, tearing away signs, capsizing tents, scattering the
grit from the gravel-banks with blinding force in everybody's eyes,
and sweeping furiously around every crook and corner in search of

A Washoe Zephyr

From *Roughing It*

some sinner to smite. Never was there such a wind as this—so scathing, so searching, so given to penetrating the very core of suffering humanity; disdaining overcoats, and utterly scornful of shawls and blankets. It actually seemed to double up, twist, pull, push, and screw the unfortunate biped till his muscles cracked and his bones rattled—following him wherever he sought refuge, pursuing him down the back of the neck, up the coat-sleeves, through the legs of his pantaloons, into his boots—in short, it was the most villainous and persecuting wind that ever blew, and I boldly protest that it did nobody good." [4]

The Washoe Zephyr always provoked a writer to express his opinion about it. Dan De Quille, who was on the Divide one day when this institution opened for business, declared that "the air is filled with dust, rags, tin cans, empty packing cases, old cooking stoves, all manner of second-hand furniture, crowbars, log-chains, lamp-posts, and similar rubbish. Hats! More hats are lost during the prevalence of a single zephyr than in any city in the Union on any election held in the last twenty years. These hats all go down the side of the mountain and land in a deep gulch known as Six-mile Cañon. . . .

"After a very severe zephyr, it is said, drifts of hats fully fifteen feet in depth, are to be seen in the bed of the cañon just named. All these hats are found and appropriated by the Piute Indians, who always go down to the cañon the next morning after a rousing fruitful gale to gather in the hat crop. When the innocent and guileless children of the desert come back to town, they are all loaded down to the guards with hats. Each head is decorated with at least a dozen hats of all kinds and colors—braves, squaws, and papooses are walking pyramids of hats."

It was said in the early days of the camp, when hats were hard to buy, the Indian made money selling back to the owner the hat he had recovered from down the cañon. As the Indian walked through the street with his head piled high with the hats, the citizen examined the headgear in search of his own hat or one he could wear.

C Street was, for a time, the most famous avenue in the United States; and Union and C streets was the most frequented spot in Virginia City. On the northeast corner of the junction of these streets, the International Hotel, one of the finest in the West, was

A supply of brandy, gin, and whiskey on its way to Washoe

From Browne's *A Peep at Washoe*

built. In and out of its doors passed the great and near-great who
visited the Comstock Lode. Near this corner the leading saloons, the
"Sazerac" dispensing the famous Pisco Punch, the "Sawdust Corner," the "Bucket of Blood," and many lesser ones, with enormous
mirrors, costly pictures over the bars, and crystal of the finest Euro-
pean glass, dispensed "the staple Washoe beverage of whiskey to
their insatiable patrons."

Towns in Nevada during this time, and for that matter any
mining town in the West, were rated by their saloons and the cost
of the drinks in them. A two-bit town was a first-class one, but a ten-
cent town rated low. "Forty-rod" was the name given to the plain,
raw, fiery brand of bar whiskey—just plain American whiskey. A
regular guy was supposed to drink it down without a chaser; and if
one was a native and not a tenderfoot, he could navigate at least forty
rods without passing out completely. The size of this drink was
generally four fingers.

At all hours of the day and night "the movement in and out of
these saloons and along the principal streets was like the flow of a
twisting stream over a rocky bed, apparently seeking an outlet at
every point, but turning back into its source again and again." Money
flowed as freely as did whiskey. Seldom was there a coin that passed
for any commodity less than "two-bits," twenty-five cents. Regardless
of how much or how little a person had in his pocket, he spent his
money like a prince. If he had enough, he entertained lavishly, drank
deeply, played for high stakes, and became for his brief day a spectacular figure in a delirious city. Such an orgy lasted as long as his
money did; then he passed off the stage to make way for the seem-
ingly endless line of other spendthrifts.

Across the street from the International Hotel, Mark and Dan
went in and out of the *Territorial Enterprise* office. During the days
when they were local reporters together, they saw (in Browne's
description) "store-keepers rolling their merchandise in and out
along the wayside; fruit venders are peddling their fruits; wagoners
are tumbling out and piling in their freights of dry goods and ore;
saloons are glittering with their gaudy bars and fancy glasses, and
many-colored liquors, and thirsty men are swilling the burning
poison; auctioneers, surrounded by eager and gaping crowds of speculators, are shouting off the stocks of delinquent stockholders; organ
grinders are grinding their organs and torturing consumptive

monkeys; hurdy-gurdy girls are singing bacchanalian songs in bacchanalian dens; Jew clothiers are selling off prodigious assortments of worthless garments at ruinous prices; bill stickers are sticking up bills of auctions, theatres, and new saloons; newsboys are crying the city papers with the latest telegraphic news; stages are dashing off with passengers for "Reese' [Austin], 'Frisco.' . . ."

All was excitement, avarice, lust, deviltry, and enterprise. A strange city, indeed, truly abounding in strange exhibitions and startling combinations of the human passions. Where on this earth was there ever such another place as Virginia City?

On C Street purveyors to every human want paid exorbitant prices for fifty-foot frontages—in 1864 as high as $20,000. Fine brick and wooden buildings with overhanging balconies or covered porches lined this street, where wooden planks or sidewalks covered the ledges beneath. Like other streets of the city, it was graded with ore, hauled from the mine dumps—paved literally with unrefined gold and silver. C Street had no beginning—it had no end. Extending southwest over the high Divide, it wound around down through "Slippery Gulch," which formed the principal street of Gold Hill. It passed through this ten-cent town, down the narrow road through Gold Cañon, and westward to the great highway which led to California. Northward, C Street clung close to the side of the great mountain, until it joined the Geiger Grade; then it wound around and around the mountains, and down a tortuous grade to the Truckee Meadows.

Hacking out Gargantuan steps around the mountain, other streets running somewhat parallel to C Street were arranged. From the steep ascents of the lower slopes of the mountain to the uppermost parts, several avenues were graded for well-marked blocks. So steep are these streets that buildings are one-story on the uphill side and three-story on the downhill slope. Arranged along these streets were the houses, churches, schools, mine offices, county and city buildings.

No community ever segregated its residents in such well-defined sections as did the great city of the Lode. Its several quarters were separated from one another by sharp lines of discrimination. On the upper streets above C Street, mining superintendents, leading merchants, brokers, lawyers, and people of quality, aristocracy, and wealth built their homes. Bill Stewart's home cost $40,000. And it will be remembered that Mark and Dan lived at 1 North B Street—one street above C Street.

Just east of C Street, and one street below where most of the shafts were situated, cheap, cheerless wooden cabins and bunk-houses accommodated the homeless miners when they came off shift. Near by was another distinctive quarter marked out by municipal and moral law for the residences of the frail sisterhood—"two rows of white cabins with gaudily furnished rooms at whose uncurtained windows the inmates sat, spider-like, waiting for flies." Ruby-colored lighted lamps directed the traffic this way by night.

Still farther down the hill, the "sickly odor of burning opium" came from the Chinese quarters. Hundreds of the celestials, forbidden to mine, toiled "sixteen hours in twenty-four over washtubs or cook stoves." These useful workers were "snubbed and scorned by everybody, Indians not excepted, and were only tolerated in the town because it was practically impossible to fill their places with white servants." This quarter was a world apart from the rest of the city. It had its own stores dispensing Oriental foods, trinkets, and clothing imported directly from China. There was a joss-house where the penitent could swing the prayer wheel for a coin and be forgiven. In their crude huts, bunks built one above the other shipshape, the Chinaman slept his quota of hours between shifts, or enjoyed unreal fantasies through the fumes of opium smoke. Slumming in Virginia City in the 1860's meant visiting Chinatown. And far down the mountainside, and also down the town's social ladder, a few ragged huts and wickiups scantily sheltered the Paiute and Washoe Indian families. These poor vagabonds—once lords of the soil, who had been the proud possessors of all the mountain—were now forced to live on the refuse of the human strata above them, or to wander among the back alleys in search of rotten food thrown out by the markets. To complete the picture, on the mountain itself and on its adjoining ridges, and in the intervening cañons, great wooden buildings, covering blocks of ground, housed the mining shafts and milling machinery.

Washoe was a man's country—thousands of men, many from foreign countries, flocked to the mines. There were Cornishmen, Canadians, Irishmen, and Germans—young men and giants of strength. The lives of these homeless men were generally barren of culture and refinement. Their lives were constantly fraught with dangers in the mines from scalding water, fires, sliding ground, or explosions. Gambling and drinking were their staple amusements. "Duels at the hurdy-gurdy houses and bar-room wrangles were the natural consequences." Once in a while their daily routine was varied with cockfights, bear fights and prize fights. Speaking of the last-named sport, Comstockers witnessed on September 23, 1863, "two bleeding and gasping fools" fight fourteen rounds. When "the referee ruled that a foul blow had been struck," the decision instantly excited a furious dispute, culminated in a fusillade of pistol shots, a wild stampede of terrified horses, and a hand-to-hand fight of the maddened crowd."

The place assigned to women in this region was an inconspicuous one. The mining frontier drew sharp distinctions in women. Not only the wives and daughters of the mining barons, but the female relatives of the humble mucker as well, were assumed to be of charming purity; they were gay, beautiful and often witty, and their virtue was quite probable because it was practically enforced in the stubborn adherence to a chivalric pattern. Some of their social functions had unusual charm and formality, but in general they were maintained on the simplest scale. "The fallen woman," on the other hand, was present in the hundreds. Every town had its full quota, but her existence was publicly ignored.

To serve the forty thousand Washoeites living in or near Virginia City, and to supply the hundreds of mines and mills on the Lode, stupendous quantities of freight arrived daily from California. Browne revisited Washoe in 1864. He could not believe it was the same place he had seen in 1860. "The hammering of the stamps, the hissing of steam, the whirling clouds of smoke from the tall chimneys, and the crowds of people presented the appearance of a great manufacturing city." When he reached Gold Cañon he observed its six-mile length to be "a continuous line of quartz mills, tunnels, dumps, sluices, water-wheels, frame shanties and grog shops."

People who saw Virginia City at this time wondered if the scene were real. It seemed as though an eternal battle was being waged between man and earth. "Myriads of swarthy, bearded, dust-covered men are piercing into the grim old mountains, ripping them open, thrusting murderous holes through their naked bodies; piling up engines to cut their vital arteries; stamping and crushing up with infernal machines their disemboweled fragments, and holding fiendish revels amid the chaos of destruction; while the mighty earth, blasted barren, and scarred by the tempests of ages, fiercely affronts the foe—smiting him with disease and death; scoffing at his puny assaults with a grim scorn; ever grand in his desolation, ever dominant in the infinity of his endurance."

To bring the immense quantities of freight to the Comstock, conveyances known as Washoe wagons were made in Placerville by John Studebaker, later of automobile fame. Teams of horses, mules, or oxen, numbering from eight to sixteen animals to each wagon, made terrific efforts to drag these land schooners with their ponderous wheels and axles over the bad roads and steep grades. It was told what a pitiable sight it was to see these animals "smoking hot, reeking with sweat, dripping with liquefied dust," pull, jerk, groan, fall back, and dash forward, tumble down, kick, plunge, and bite; then buckle to it again, under the galling lash of the driver's whip.

The teamsters who drove these struggling labor-worn beasts along their way were a class by themselves. They were brawny, coarse-bearded fellows whose faces were so ingrained with the dust and grit of earth, and tanned to such an uncertain color by the burning sun and the dry winds that "they resembled Hindus more than Aryans." With their leather-thonged whips and equally long oaths they urged on the dumb beasts so long as there was life in them.

No word picture of this time when Mark Twain was in Nevada is complete without describing that fantastic scheme of freighting with camels. The reader will recall that this idea originated in the fertile brain of Jeff Davis when, as Secretary of War, he bought them to aid the Confederacy in its pre-Civil War scheme of setting up an independent government. But when the war broke out, the War Department decided it did not want the camels. They were then at Benicia Barracks, California. In 1861, they were auctioned on the streets of San Francisco, where enterprising businessmen bought them. Nine of these Bactrian beasts were brought to Washoe in 1863 to carry salt from the salt beds, situated at the forks of the Walker River, to Virginia City. Great quantities of salt were used to separate the gold from its base associates.[5]

The life of these poor animals in this work was a deplorable

Washoe ore wagons

one—the sharp rocks cut their feet, the heavy loads opened great sores on their backs, and the alkali dust galled their wounds. Despised by other animals, they had to be brought into the city over an unused trail after midnight when the horses and oxen were bedded down or were locked safely behind corral gates. They were seldom permitted on the main streets but were rather forced to camp down with the Indians in the lower part of the hill. Horses and mules that could scent their malodorous breaths a mile away bolted and ran in terror lest they be spewed with their rotten cud.

Two members, Old Brigham, the patriarch, and Old Tule, the matriarch, watched over this herd, which soon increased to forty. Old Brigham, when relieved of his heavy packs, liked to climb to the highest point on the Divide and sniff the fresh breezes which always blew over this ridge. His four-foot mane was the envy of all the cowboys who preferred hair lariats to hempen ones. One day W. T. ("Joggles") Wright, superintendent of the Sierra Mine, who thought himself a cowboy of parts, decided he was going to have some of Old Brigham's hair for a rope. Riding down to where the camel herd fed near the Carson Sink one day, he urged his pony as near Brigham as he could, then let go his lasso. He made a good throw and caught the camel by the throat. Then he began slowly to tighten his rope. As Brigham felt the noose binding his neck, he started after Joggles. With ears laid low, and hissing and spewing, he came on at a terrific pace. Joggles put spurs to his horse, with Brigham in hot pursuit, still attached by his lariat to the pommel of his saddle. Only by cutting his prized rope—always a heartbreaking necessity to a cowhand—could Joggles save his skin.[6]

A continuous string of stagecoaches rolled into the Comstock day and night. They shuttled back and forth between Washoe and San Francisco and wayside cities. There were many special coaches and conveyances carrying nabobs looking after their interests in Nevada. Many hundreds of men in less fortunate circumstances walked in and out of the city all of the time. These poor dregs of humanity, too stupid or too lazy to work, hung around the bars and other dens of iniquity and begged for food and their daily swigs of whiskey.

When these men became intoxicated they were insolent—cursing everyone and everything. They were generally armed, and fired their ordnance pieces at the least provocation. "A man for breakfast" was a steady diet in most of the towns of Washoe for many years. In a letter Mark wrote home to his mother he postscripted it: "I have just heard five pistol shots down street—as such things are in my line, I will go and see about it." In a second note to the same letter written at five o'clock the same morning he added, "The pistol did its work well—one man—a Jackson County Missourian, shot two of my friends (police officers) through the heart—both died within three minutes. Murderer's name is John Campbell." [7]

Life was cheap on the frontier; the officers took little or no trouble to apprehend the man-killers. If indictments and trials had followed every murder, the Territory would have been put to immense expense—it was better to let men kill each other than for the State to have to hang them. The indifference to these murders can well be illustrated by the story of a man who was shot between the eyes in a billiard saloon in Virginia City in 1863, meeting his death about four o'clock in the morning. Just as it fell, his body lay prostrate half under one of the billiard tables until nearly noon. The Coroner had not gotten around to holding the inquest. The billiard games went on, however, as if nothing had happened; the players were at times obliged to make their shots with one foot each side of the dead man. [8]

At last the newspapers became so outraged at the condition of things that they lashed out at the officers of the law. The Virginia *Evening Bulletin* of October 29, 1863, wrote:

> The drawing, and exhibition, and use of deadly weapons in the streets, places of amusement, and saloons of our city has of late become of such frequent occurence that they create not the least excitement in the community when they happen. A man may be shot down in the streets like a vicious cur, and not one in ten of the passers by will stay ten minutes to inquire into the cause of the murder or the name of the murderer! And when our police officers, at the peril of their lives, arrest one of the ruffians that have brought about this disgraceful state of things by their almost daily practice of shooting or exhibiting their weapons in the public streets, they are invariably let off by those entrusted with the administration of the law on the plea of justification, as if any cause could justify a respectable man in converting the public streets of a populous city into a

shooting gallery, to the imminent danger of the lives of the public, much less a ruffian who has been before arrested for a similar crime.

Is it no violation of law for a man of notoriously bad character to fire a loaded pistol among the throng of people that must of necessity pass through the public thoroughfare? If there is no existing law to punish such a dangerous practice, we trust that the legislature when they assemble will *immediately* adopt one, that shall be stringent enough to curb, if not control, the crowd of ruffians that infest our city much to its disgrace and injury; a law that shall make it dangerous for those entrusted with its administration to abuse its power; a law that shall not be used solely to screen ruffianism, and to enrich a miserable horde of shystering attorneys, who would sell their souls, their country and their very God to obtain whiskey money. It is time that this state of things were put a stop to, if Virginia is ever to become free from this disgraceful state of things that is ruining her interests and her reputation.

There was a great deal of quarreling and lawlessness, not only among the mobs, but also among the mine locators. The simple, crude, and ill-defined early notices of mining locations brought about claim-jumping, blackmailing, perjury, and corruption of the courts. All of the mines of any value were involved in many suits— mine companies had 369 cases on their hands from 1862 to 1863.

The "carpet-bag" Territorial judges appointed by President Lincoln and paid only $1800 a year were untrained in the fine points of the law in general. No wonder they were incapable of ruling on special points of the law. In practically every suit they were called upon to pass on questions involving millions of dollars. It was the lawyers who reaped the harvest of fees in such litigation. And Bill Stewart got the biggest fees of all of them because he always won his suits. "He was a big, high-handed domineering man accustomed to driving his cases through the courts. . . ."

He met his match in a suit in 1862, in his first trial against A. W. ("Sandy") Baldwin, one of the ablest lawyers in California, who had come to Washoe in the fall of that year. Sandy was not afraid of Bill and came back at him as hard as he sent, in his arguments before the court. Once when Sandy won several objections to

Stewart's bullyragging methods used before the court, Stewart turned savagely on Baldwin and said: "You little shrimp, if you interrupt me again I'll eat you!" To which remark Sandy quietly replied: "If you do, you'll have more brains in your belly than you have in your head."

Stewart liked that kind of backtalk. If Baldwin could argue that way, he wanted him for his law partner. The resultant firm of Stewart and Baldwin was the best in the West in mining suits.

From 1860 to 1864 it was one orgy of litigation, "when judges were corrupted, the verdicts of juries were purchased and troublesome witnesses were killed or spirited out of the Territory. . . ." The greatest trouble the lawyers had with the judges was to keep them bought. They all agreed that "an honest judge is a son of a gun that will stay bought." There was no coyness or modesty on the part of the judges. They sent out their brokers and demanded a specific price for a favorable decision. The mine owners had little objection to that procedure. It was straightforward and businesslike. The biggest howl came when a mining company, after squarely meeting the judicial demands, encountered an adverse decision— and discovered too late that their opponents had made a higher bid for the court's favor!

Volumes can be written on the corruption of Washoe judges. The most frequent difficulty faced by the mining companies was to keep the judges "bought" long enough to secure an agreement as to whether there was one ledge on the mountain or many ledges. In this dereliction of justice, as in all cases of human frailties, there is one classic illustration. It was the Chollar-Potosi suit, in which Bill Stewart was the lawyer for the Chollar Company. After four years of litigation, the case remained undecided. During these years, one of the judges was paid to resign, so that another man, known to favor a certain decision, could be appointed to take his place. At long last, the companies ended a hopeless impasse by merging.[9]

In 1863, the open flagrancy of bought opinions reached a disgraceful state of affairs. Judge John N. North, whose appointment was said to have been obtained for a fee of $25,000 for a Potosi decision, and Chief Justice Turner, whose egotism Sam Clemens made famous by his lampoons (he signed his name on hotel registers as "CHIEF JUSTICE OF THE UNITED STATES, U.S.A.") favored the Chollar outfit. The third judge, Powhatan B. Locke, of whom Bill

Stewart said that he was the most ignorant man who ever came to Washoe, was torn between the two companies.[10] At first he favored the Potosi. Then Chollar partisans labored with him all one night— plied him with whiskey, with threats, and with promises. When morning came, he made a complete *volte face* and wrote an addendum to his Potosi opinion. Chollar had won!

But the battle had not ended. Potosi henchmen, in turn, took control of Locke and carried him over in the same manner. Another addendum to the former one—and Potosi had won again!

The Chollar partisans had the *Enterprise* on their side. Joe Goodman and his local reporters had a great time following these judges around, watching who visited them and what they did during their absence from the courtroom. "Poor P. B. Locke! From Virginia to Tahoe, from Tahoe to Carson, from Carson to Washoe, he was carted about, harried, flattered, bullied, again plied with whiskey. Was ever justice so bedevilled!"

The most shameful story told in the matter was the one about the bribe paid to Judge Turner late one night at the Ormsby House in Carson City. The litigant doing the bribing was told by the Judge's broker that $10,000 had to be paid before court convened the following morning. It was already night. There wasn't that much gold coin in the capital city. So the briber had himself driven hurriedly to Virginia City, and there borrowed the sum from the saloons and gambling tables. He returned to Carson and knocked at the Judge's hotel-room door. Mrs. Turner, who opened it, told the caller the Judge was asleep. When the business at hand was explained hurriedly to her, she undertook to receive the money. She spread out her voluminous nightgown, and the sack of gold was emptied into it. The weight proved too heavy for the garment. It was torn completely from her body, leaving Mrs. Turner as naked as a worm, with hundreds of twenty-dollar gold pieces at her feet![11]

This disgraceful state of affairs aroused the citizens on the Comstock to circulate petitions demanding the resignations of the entire Territorial judiciary. Three thousand names were published in *The Enterprise,* comprising nine-tenths of the voting population. When the Supreme Court convened in August, 1864, the judges were notified that the lawyers of the district, as a body, refused to practice before them unless they vindicated themselves of the pub-

BACTRIAN CAMELS BOUND FOR WASHOE
"Old Brigham" in the background

CUT STONE MANSION OF LEMUEL
S. "SANDY" AND ALLISON "EILLEY"
ORRUM BOWERS, BUILT IN FRANK-
TOWN, NEVADA, 1863

JOSEPH THOMPSON GOODMAN
Discoverer of Mark Twain

lished charges against them. Judge North resigned first. "Personal-pronoun" Turner attempted, with much bluster, to hold out. But when Bill Stewart faced him with endorsed checks of certain mining companies, he too sent in his resignation. Then Bill asked them both down to Pete Hopkins' Magnolia Saloon for a round of drinks.

There was one man missing—Judge P. B. Locke. Soon he was found and brought into the saloon to face the angry lawyers. Looking straight at the spokesman, Locke said: "Mr. Stewart, what do you think I ought to do?"

"Do!" exclaimed Bill. "Resign, and resign now." [12]

In the course of a few hours President Lincoln had three telegrams of resignation, and Washoe had no judges. When the President attempted to appoint more judges, he received another wire telling him that Washoe wanted no more of his judges. They would elect their own officers as soon as Nevada became a State.

Not only were the stockholders of the mining companies assessed for bribing corrupt judges; they were also taxed to provide funds for useless experiments with secret and humbug processes to reduce the ore. To be sure, the Washoe mills were technical schools for these experimentations. Many times, however, the formulae were absurd concoctions matching the broth brewed by the three weird sisters. All sorts of mixtures were used in them—even the bark from the cedar trees and the native sagebrush were tried out.

And more money probably was wasted on unwise and unsuitable mechanical devices to mill the ore than on the allopathic doses to physic the silver and gold from the rock. Mills were built and furnished with expensive machinery which many times failed to perform the work for which they had been built. When it was found inadequate, the machinery was discarded, and more constructed—just as though there was an inexhaustible treasury from which to draw. The Ophir Mill, built in Washoe Valley in 1861 twelve miles from the mine, was one of the early examples of prodigal extravagance. Built on *hacienda* proportions, it looked like a miniature city with its large and costly structures, pasture lands, grain fields, and vegetable gardens. Two thousand acres of magnificent timber land to the west of the Ophir Mill belonged to this establishment.

There were dozens of mills built in Washoe—largely at the expense of the stockholders. Not one of these institutions excelled in extravagance and fantasy the one built in 1863 by the Gould & Curry Company at the junction of Six and Seven Mile Cañons. It was "the most conspicuous monument of inexperience and extravagance ever erected in a mining district." On a rocky point an artificial plateau was made on which to erect this mill. The design resembled a Greek cross 250 feet long, with 75-foot arms 50 feet in width. The lower story and foundation were built of massive stone blocks supporting the heavy frame structure of polished wood. All around broad verandas, painted inside and out, enhanced the beauty of design. Smooth paths were cut and blasted out of the hillside to provide easy approaches. Arched sewers built of hewn stone, and graded terraces reached by flights of broad stone steps, surrounded the mill. That there be a lawn and flowers around the grounds, a reservoir was hewn from solid stone above the mill, from which iron pipes conducted water to hydrants on the terraces below. Further to heighten the artistry of its appearance, and to counteract the necessarily offensive and disagreeable aspects of milling, there was built a fifty-by-thirty-foot water basin. In the center of this pool "three water nymphs supported a rock shell whereon floated a white swan that with upturned head spouted a jet of water high in the air."

Nearly a million dollars were spent by the end of the year. After this mill was given a thorough trial, it was found to be unsatisfactory. An addition was recommended to correct the deficiencies. The only objection raised by the artistic superintendent was its injury to the original design. A new superintendent, appointed in 1864, discarded most of the original machinery and rebuilt it at a cost of another $500,000.[13] These whimsical experiments of Washoe Mill superintendents "were simply in keeping with the prodigal ideas of the time." It was the duty of Dan and Mark to write up all of the new edifices which were built in the vicinity of Virginia City, but none of the copies of the *Enterprise* of this period is extant.

In every town in the United States, the country store was the important meeting place. In the Western mining camps the leading saloon supplanted this store. In Washoe there were two important places where almost everything in the Territory was settled—the Magnolia Saloon, kept by Peter Hopkins in Carson City where

Mark Twain laid the scene of part of his "Empire City Massacre," and The Sazerac Saloon on South C Street in Virginia City, owned by Thomas Peaseley.

The Magnolia was the rendezvous of the Territorial politicians; it was the fount and origin of the village gossip. Men met there, just as men meet some place today, to talk over things in general. Pete Hopkins was on every official welcoming committee the capital ever had, and many times he was the chairman for important affairs. His name was always included on such programs right along with the Governor's, the mayor's, and those of the leading businessmen and the ministers.

The Sazerac was the headquarters for everything that went on in Virginia City. Tom Peaseley, thirty-two years old when he came to Nevada in 1861, was originally from New York City, from which place he migrated to San Francisco. He was a giant of a man, with a pantherlike tread and prodigious strength. He never engaged in mining—he would rather be privy to the secrets of men over his bar.

He was a born leader. Had Tom had a good education, he would have been a figure among Virginia's potentates; without it, he had to be content with lesser honors. He was elected foreman of the Virginia Engine Company No. 1; and later, when all of the fire companies merged into one, he was elected the fire chief of Virginia City. The most powerful men on the Lode were in Tom's company. They had to be giants to keep up with their chief. He ruled them with an iron hand. Tom's surplus of strength often led him to commit excesses not expected of most men. So huge and powerful were his hands that he often knocked over an acquaintance with a playful slap on the back. A locked door meant nothing to him. He smacked in the panel with one blow. To prove his superiority over other so-called chiefs of the lawless element, he bashed the head of Langford Peel against the wall of the International Hotel—not because he had any particular grudge against him, but simply to show his mastery in strength! What a "bouncer" Tom would make today!

Every public occasion found Tom Peaseley on the committee of arrangements. It was on a national fête day that he had Julie Bulette crowned queen of the fire boys, and placed her in the parade, dressed in firemen's clothes, holding a spanner filled with roses. And when

Adah Menken came to the Comstock Lode, Tom showed her the town, danced with her at the Melodeon, rode horseback with her, bucked the tiger with her, and met her after each performance for a midnight supper. Between 1862 and 1864 he was sheriff of Storey County.

Among the swaggering young fellows in Virginia City at this time was "a tall wax-faced, loose-jointed young fellow" by the name of "Sugar-foot Jack." He wanted to be a desperado, but he had none of the qualifications except the will to be. Late in 1863 Pease-ley, in one of his excesses of rough playfulness, knocked Sugar-foot down at a masquerade ball. The would-be bad man did not show his affront at the moment, but after he left the ballroom he mut-tered threats against Tom. He went around the town uttering bloody intentions. Some of Tom's friends told him that Sugar-foot was "gunning" for him. Tom, who couldn't have his prestige in-jured in that manner, armed himself and went out on a manhunt. Soon he found Sugar-foot hiding behind an awning post, cringing at the sight of his adversary. Peasley drew his gun and riddled him with bullets.

He was not held for the murder—the threats and actions of the victim made a plain case of self-defense. But the incident had a very bad effect on Tom's conscience. From that time on, he was a different man in many ways. The old braggadocio was gone, and in its place there was a restrained and gentle manner, a general soften-ing in his entire make-up. He got out of the saloon business and engaged in the management of theatrical productions. In 1865, he was sergeant-at-arms of the Nevada State Senate.

While he was in Carson City at that time, an incident occurred which led to his death a year later. Standing at a bar with a party of friends one evening, he misunderstood a remark, which he avenged by knocking down an innocent bystander, Barnhart by name. Although Tom apologized profusely for his mistake in the person, and offered to make any reparation for the error, the aggrieved victim refused to be placated. In the following summer Tom and Barnhart met at Glenbrook House, Lake Tahoe. Barnhart wanted to fight Tom then, but the latter refused—he wanted to drop the matter.

The next winter Tom went down from the Lode to Carson City

to meet some of the friends he had known in the preceding legislature. While he was playing billiards in a saloon early in the evening,
he saw Barnhart come in and drink at the bar several times.
Tom took little notice of him.

About two o'clock in the morning, Tom went to his hotel, the
Ormsby House, and sat down by the stove to finish a cigar. A
number of other men were sitting around the stove also. Presently
Barnhart and two companions came in and approached Tom.

"Why didn't you fight me last summer at the Glenbrook
House?" was Barnhart's query.

"I don't know," came the hesitating reply. "Are you always on
the fight?"

"Yes," replied Barnhart, spitting vile epithets and pulling his
pistol.

"You don't mean to murder me, do you?" exclaimed Tom.
The answer was two bullets fired in quick succession into the region
of Peaseley's heart. As he started to rise, Barnhart caught him by
the shoulders and beat him over the head with the barrel of the
pistol, breaking his skull. Peaseley in his helplessness called out:
"Don't let him murder me! What are you all doing?"

Barnhart broke his pistol by the repeated blows; the barrel fell
to the floor. One of the bystanders wrenched the stock from his
hand, saying: "There, that will do; you've beaten him enough."

By this time Tom had staggered to his feet and had drawn his
pistol. Seeing the action, Barnhart made a rush for an adjoining
card-room, shouting: "Don't let him shoot me!"

Peaseley pursued him, and fired once through the frosted glass
door as it closed behind the fugitive, then threw it open and aimed
a deadly shot at his cowering antagonist. Before he could fire again,
he reeled and fell full length on the floor.

"My God!" he exclaimed. "I'm shot through and through!"

It was thought by everyone that he was now dead, but his
great strength sustained him. Motioning to one of his friends to
come close to him, he requested that his brother, Andy, be sent for.
He also inquired about Barnhart. When told that he was dead, he
smiled grimly. Then came Tom's final request:

"Take off my boots!" [14]

And in this manner did Tom Peaseley leave this world as he

had wanted. (No respectable man in those days wanted to die with his boots on; it implied that he must be buried in that part of the cemetery called "Boot Hill.")

Mark Twain had known Tom well on the Lode. He had frequented his saloon. In *Roughing It* Mark described Tom's ("Buck-Fanshaw's") funeral in the chapter "Scotty Briggs and the Parson." Mark's friend, the Reverend Franklin S. Rising, "the fragile, gentle, spiritual new fledgling from an Eastern theological seminary," was the person who preached Tom's funeral sermon.

"The obsequies were all that 'the boys' could desire. Such a marvel of funeral pomp had never been seen in Virginia. The plumed hearse, the dirge-breathing brass-bands, the closed marts of business, the flags drooping at half-mast, the long plodding military battalions and fire companies, draped engines, carriages of officials, and citizens in vehicles and on foot, attracted multitudes of spectators to the sidewalks, roofs, and windows; and for years afterward, the degree of grandeur attained by any civic display in Virginia was determined by comparison with Buck Fanshaw's funeral." How pleased and proud Tom Peaseley would have been had he known how he was regarded in death!

Countless more stories and anecdotes can be related of the time when Mark Twain lived in Nevada. He has told many of them himself in his writings, especially in *Roughing It*, a true and sincere account of the days when he was the "wild humorist from the Sagebrush State."

Wander over the slopes of Mount Davidson today. Picture in your mind this excited mob of humanity, digging, boring, picking, and shoveling. Some of the scars are too deep for nature to heal. Other spots have been reclaimed, and sagebrush again grows on the site where miners once hoped to dig out a fortune. As one looks over the panorama, he is reminded of the Scriptural verse:

"Then shall the dust return to the earth as it was: and the spirit shall return unto God who gave it."

No description of Nevada at this time can be complete without including the sudden rise to wealth of Sandy and Eilley Orrum Bowers—Mark Twain called Sandy "John Smith," in *Roughing It*.[15] In 1860 Eilley, a convert to Mormonism in her native Scotland,

married and divorced twice after she came to America, in Gold
Hill, Nevada, met Lemuel S. ("Sandy") Bowers, an "honest, kind-
hearted soul, born and reared in the lower ranks of life, and miracu-
lously ignorant," and married him. Fortune smiled on them by
dropping a rich deposit of gold ore on their adjoining claims, making them Nevada's first millionaires. When riches came to them so
fast that they could not spend it in Nevada, they decided to go to
Europe. Before leaving Virginia City, they planned a $400,000
mansion to be built on land Eilley had been granted by the court
in her second divorce. This land, situated on the west side of Washoe
Lake near some hot springs, was in an isolated spot at that time—
so remote, in fact, that Mark Twain said, "The Indians killed the
architect when he went over there to plan the house."

Sandy and Eilley skipped San Francisco, took only a fleeting
glance at New York, and headed straight for Paris, where they
went on a wild spending spree. While they were in Europe they
bought ornate Victorian furniture, Italian marble fireplaces, superb
jewels, and magnificent clothes. The French mirrors specially made
for them had to be cut into two parts when they arrived at the
Bowers' mansion; they were too large to be carried through the
doors. The final extravagance was the order for the manufacture
of innumerable silver pieces made from the bullion taken from
their mine.

Before Sandy and Eilley set out for Europe they were told by
some of their friends that the proper thing to do was to give their
friends a banquet. "Banquet goes," said Sandy, and the International
Hotel was engaged for the affair. Every obtainable luxury of the
market in Virginia City or San Francisco was served. Champagne
flowed like water. Toasts were drunk, to which Sandy replied in his
inimitable Irish manner:

> "I've been in this yer country amongst the fust that come
> here. I've had powerful good luck, and I've got money to throw
> at the birds. Thar ain't no chance for a gentleman to spend his
> coin in this country, and thar ain't nothin' to see, so me and
> Mrs. Bowers is a goin' to Yoorop to take in the sights. One of
> the great men of this country was in this region a while back.
> That was Horace Greeley. I saw him and he didn't look like
> no great shakes. Outside of him the only great men I've seen in

14

WASHOE—LITERARY FRONTIER

"MY STARBOARD LEG SEEMS TO BE UNSHIPPED. I'D like about one hundred yards of line." In such a way did Sam Clemens introduce himself to Dennis McCarthy as he entered the *Territorial Enterprise* office on North C Street, Virginia City. "I want to see Mr. Barstow or Mr. Goodman. My name is Clemens, and I've come to write for the paper." [1]

With disheveled hair, an unshaven face, wrinkled clothes, and hay literally still clinging to him, he presented himself for the job which had been offered to him. With him came to the frontier a new kind of literature—one which the masses could understand. It was human, middle-class; it met the approval of the country-store, to-bacco-spitting, gossiping crowd.

Before the rush to Washoe there had been precious little writing done in western Utah. In the bucolic days of the little Mormon settlements there was one feeble attempt to bring some literature to the farmers and village dwellers in Genoa. Stephen A. Kinsey, a county recorder and one of the first settlers, started a manuscript newspaper in January, 1857. No copy of this paper, called *The Scorpion,* is now believed to be extant, but a copy of the July issue of that year was placed on display in the *Enterprise* office on April 12, 1871. A full description of it was given: "It had twelve columns of illustrations with many pleasing articles. The editorial column contained the following notice: '*The Scorpion* is published monthly at Genoa, in Carson Valley, and edited by S. A. K. [Stephen A. Kinsey]. It will contain a full and extensive digest of all the current news and discussions of the day. It will be more especially made up to suit Carson Valley, containing a great variety of matter, particularly interesting to our patrons, and nothing which can interest the general reader will be omitted.'"

This little community lived up to its Mormon tenets. In the second column two profiles were sketched: one of them was a man who joined the Sons of Temperance, and the other, one who did not. Although isolated from all communication with the outside world, the people were not forgetting that July 4 was near. A celebration in the form of a dance was to be given at "Lucky Bill" Thorington's hotel. The biggest event in the lives of these people was the arrival of a pack train. The paper announced that two outfits were soon to arrive with a large stock of goods. The most singular item, and one which cast aside all doubt about the presence of Chinese in this part of the country, announced that a number of the Celestials had been brought in and were commencing work in Gold Cañon.

There was a poetry column in *The Scorpion*. A contributor who signed himself "George" wrote a lovesick quatrain:

> I sat me down in thought profound,
> This maxim wise I drew:
> It's easier to like a girl
> Than make a girl like you.

The comic column offered the following: "Rumor says there is a man in this town whose nose is so long that he is unable to hear himself sneeze." Besides advertisements of stage and express lines, the paper announced that this one was the sixth number, and that the "next issue will contain articles from Henry Ward Beecher, Fanny Fern, Charles Dickens, Longfellow, Dow Jr., etc., etc."

Up in Gold Cañon, thirty miles from Genoa, another effort to report the news in manuscript form was made in a paper called *The Gold Canyon Switch*. It was said that this paper contained news of the miners in the cañons leading up to Sun Mountain and of the settlers in Chinatown (Dayton) and Johntown. There is no copy known to exist today.

For over a year there was no literary effort put forth in Washoe. When the Mormons left Carson Valley in September, 1857, their ranches and business firms were preëmpted, bought, or leased by Californians who came over from the mining towns on the western slope of the mountains. A new character was given to society in this region and likewise a new type of literature was introduced.

At once enterprising Californians, ever eager to be in on the ground floor of every movement, flocked to Genoa. Among these people came W. L. Jernegan and Alfred James from Placerville to set up the first press in Nevada, the *Territorial Enterprise*. These men bought an old Washington hand press, moved it over to Genoa, and set it up in the second story of Thomas J. Singleton's store. The type, some badly battered bourgeois which had been used in printing the *San Francisco News,* arrived in Genoa so· badly "pied" that there was great difficulty and delay in getting out the first issue. The paper on which to print the news was brought over from Placerville by Lew Doran on snowshoes. It took him four weeks to make the trip. Paper for the following issues was carried from the same town by "Snowshoe" Thompson. He also brought the exchanges and news from the other side of the mountains. This little weekly paper, the first number of which came out December 18, 1858, had a struggle to exist. There were not more than two hundred people in Genoa—and the miners in Dogtown, Chinatown, Johntown, and Gold Cañon did not much exceed twice that number.

The *Enterprise* press was used for something else beside running off the paper. The Mormons were law-abiding people, but what with the law gone and the valleys a good refuge for the horse and cattle thief, the settlers had to form their own Vigilantes committee. Not having a jail in which to keep the prisoners, they were chained to the press of the *Enterprise*. Then when the paper had to be run off, a self-appointed officer stood guard over them until they could be chained up again.

Shortly after the Mormons left western Utah in 1857, a correspondent from Genoa, W. G. Atkinson by name, wrote a number of letters to the San Francisco *Herald*. He signed them "Old Tennessee." In these letters he kept the world informed of the news of this small isolated community. He was particularly critical of the Mormon rule. When the crowds were pouring through Genoa on their way to the Ophir strike on Sun Mountain he wrote amusingly in Letter No. 69, entitled "The Emigration," of the hopeful look on the faces of the men en route to their fortunes. In the same letter he described the disillusioned countenances of the men who had paid "to see the elephant."

Soon after the rush to Washoe, other men began to write letters describing the new camp. One of the first to report on the development of Washoe mines was Almarin B. Paul of Gold Hill, himself the builder of the first steam quartz mill in the district. Writing under the pseudonym of "Cosmos," he told of the rapid progress in Washoe mining and milling.

During 1860 and the years immediately following, a flock of writers sprang up. Every paper in California carried Washoe items. Most of these articles were signed with some *nom de plume.* "Veritas" wrote for the San Francisco *Daily Evening Bulletin.* Articles signed "Wyoming" came from Santa Clara, Humboldt County. While Sam Clemens was living in Aurora, several correspondents wrote for California Coast and Valley papers. "Vox Populi," "Diomed," and "Ante Poste" sent articles to the Sacramento *Daily Union.* Sam and Raish Phillips were among the men who wrote mining notes from this camp to Nevada and California papers in 1862. It is known that Sam signed his articles "Josh," but there is no record of what name Raish wrote under.

The first great writer of Washoe was described by Wells Drury, an editor of the *Territorial Enterprise,* who in later years said, "Of all the men I knew on the Comstock I consider William Wright— Dan De Quille—the most thoroughly characteristic of the camp and its inhabitants." De Quille was a Quaker, born in Ohio and reared in Iowa. Migrating to California in the early 1850's, he wandered over the State prospecting and writing. During this period he wrote under the names of "Ebenezer Queerkut" and "Picaroon Pax."

When Dan arrived in Washoe in 1860 he settled first in Silver City, where he continued to write and also to acquire firsthand knowledge of the geology of Washoe. He was one of the few men to have seen the stone cabin of the Grosch brothers and their little smelting furnaces. (He has described it in his book, *History of the Big Bonanza,* published by Mark Twain's press in 1876.) In the spring of 1862 Joe Goodman gave him a job on the *Enterprise.* He remained on this paper for thirty years, filling its columns with news, scientific mining articles, and fantastic stories which Dan called his "quaints." When he decided to take a trip back to Iowa to see his family in the summer of 1862, Goodman asked Sam Clemens to come down from Aurora to take Dan's place on the paper.

The owners of the *Territorial Enterprise* were alert to business. When Abe Curry and Major William Ormsby set up Carson City as a rival candidate for the capital of the new "State of Washoe," they induced the owners of this paper, to the extent of giving them financial backing, to move the press to Carson City in November,

1859. There were so few buildings in Carson at that time that Ormsby allowed the paper to set up its press in the second story of his adobe building on the plaza. The paper was soon purchased by old Colonel Jonathan Williams and I. B. Wollard.

There is one existing description of the *Enterprise* while it was in Carson. It is given by J. Ross Browne, who will be recalled as having been in that excited crowd which rushed to Washoe in the spring of 1860.

> Chief among the curiosities of Carson City is the *Territorial Enterprise*—a newspaper of an origin anterior to the mining excitement. I was introduced to "the Colonel," who presides over the editorial department, and found him uncommonly strong in the ultimate destiny of Carson. His office was located in a dirty frame shanty, and general rubbish of dark and literary aspect; there those astounding editorials which now and then arouse the public mind are concocted. The Colonel and his compositors live in a sort of family fashion, entirely free from the rigorous etiquette of such establishments in New York. They cook their own food in the composition room (which is also the editorial and press room), and being, as a general thing, short of plates, use the frying-pan in common for that purpose. In cases of great festivity and rejoicing, when a subscriber has settled up arrearages or the cash is paid down for a good job of hand-bills, the Colonel purchases the best tenderloin steak to be had in market, and cooks it with one hand, while with the other he writes a letter of thanks to the subscriber, or a puff on the hand-bill.

Browne, an inveterate wanderer from the time that he left Dublin, Ireland, at eleven years of age, until he settled down to spend his last years in Oakland, California, was sent out to California ostensibly as a Collector of Internal Revenue, but really as an informant to Southern leaders. He had acquired a knowledge of shorthand, and painting was his hobby. After he came to California, he was "stung" with the gold fever and followed every rush from San Diego to Vancouver. A keen observer of social practices and of scientific processes, he combined his talents to write a number of books on mining and travel.

Of Browne it may be said that he gave Washoe its first national notice when he wrote "A Peep at Washoe." This article appeared in the December, 1860, issue of *Harper's Monthly*. He had gone to Washoe in the spring of 1860 with the purpose of setting up a mining agency—brokerage—in either Carson or Virginia City. He stayed only a little over a month, but during this time he made sketches and took notes which he used in several later articles. What an agent he would have been! Read his account of the rumors that were abroad in San Francisco before he set out for Washoe: " 'Sir,' said my informant to me, in strict confidence, no later than this morning, 'you may rely on it, for I am personally acquainted with a brother of the gentleman whose most intimate friend saw the man whose partner had just come over the mountains, and he says there never was the like on the face of the earth! The ledges are ten thousand feet deep—solid masses of silver.' "

When he arrived in Virginia City and looked over the way that people were living there, he was moved to write with characteristic Irish good humor that it was "a mud-hole; climate, hurricanes and snow; water, a dilution of arsenic, plumbago, and copperas; wood, none at all except sagebrush; no title to property and no property worth having. . . . The Washoe mines are nothing more than squirrel-holes on a large scale, the difference being that the squirrels burrow in the ground because they live there, and men because they want to live somewhere else."

Browne was as enthusiastic about the beauty and exhilarating qualities of Lake Tahoe as was Sam Clemens after he had visited the "lake of the sky." Browne recommended it: "To dyspeptics, consumptives, and broken-down stock brokers. . . . If you want your digestive apparatus put in complete order so that brickbats will stick to your ribs without inconvenience, spend a month at Lake Tahoe; if your bronchial tubes distress you, swallow a few gallons of Lake Tahoe air, and you can blow bellow blasts from your lungs forever after; if your nervous system is deranged by bad speculation in stocks, bowl ninepins and row a boat on Lake Tahoe for six weeks, and I venture to affirm stocks will rise a thousand per cent."

"A Peep at Washoe" anticipated *Roughing It* by several years. Sam Clemens read it—he was sufficiently impressed with the article to recommend it to his sister to read.

The rush to Washoe left Genoa and Carson City far behind. Everyone flocked to Sun Mountain; Virginia City, Silver City, and Gold Hill became sizable towns in the summer of 1860. Saloon-keepers, gamblers, speculators, merchants, and all other sorts of people went to the Lode, and so did the *Territorial Enterprise*. Able to obtain only a small frame shanty on the corner of A Street near Sutton Avenue, the owners of the press moved it there, and the first issue to come out in Virginia City appeared on November 12, 1860. Colonel Williams, an erratic old fellow of whom it was said that he "wrote strong, but in villainous English, and was given a great deal to his cups," employed two smart young typesetters—Joseph Thompson Goodman and Dennis E. McCarthy. Both had been trained on the San Francisco *Golden Era*.

On March 2, 1861, Goodman and McCarthy became partners of Williams. At this time William Wright—Dan De Quille, as he signed himself—was employed to write the local and mining news. As Virginia City grew in population and wealth, the *Enterprise* advanced with it. Soon it became one of the biggest money-making establishments on the Lode. Goodman and McCarthy knew how to spend money better than they knew how to save it. The paper was in need of a good business manager. He was found in Jerry Driscoll, an old Sacramento printer and a man of fine business capacity. Driscoll bought Williams' interest and took entire charge of the management of the paper.

The Goodman-McCarthy-Driscoll-De Quille team worked well together. Goodman wrote the editorials, while McCarthy was the foreman, Driscoll the bookkeeper, and De Quille the local news-gatherer and mining editor. The paper was a money-maker from the start in Virginia City, at $2 a year for subscription and anything it chose to charge for advertisements.

While the paper was being published on A Street, the press and all hands connected with it were housed in the one-story frame shanty with a lean-to shed addition on the north side. In the main structure, the cases of the compositors, the table at which all of the writing, local and editorial, was done; the bookkeeper's desk, and the press were all crowded in together. The shed was used as a combination kitchen, dining room, and bunkhouse. The sleeping accommodations were bunks built up along the side of the room, one above the other in ship fashion. Here all hands ate and slept. Here, too, "Old Joe," the Chinese cook, prepared the food and waited on the boarders seated at one long table.

Old Joe was considered the best cook on the Lode. In those days, cooks were rated by their ability to put food on the table attractively, if not appetizingly. His skill in molding lions, tigers, dragons, and other Chinese motifs in the butter rated him high in his profession. So highly praised was he for his artistry that he spent too much of his time in this work and neglected to keep his food free from mice, fleas, and bugs that infested the kitchen. Soon mouse hairs began to be found in the biscuits. The office force could stand it no longer. A committee of some of the boarders was appointed to investigate the premises. In their search two or three dead mice were found in Joe's lard keg. He was accustomed to pour the hot fat back into the keg without discovering the mice that had been trapped in it. After this find and others of a similar nature were made, Joe was fired; and other Chinese cooks were employed, none of whom proved any better than Joe. All hands then scattered out and found their own boarding houses.[2]

While the *Enterprise* kitchen was in operation, the favorite joke of the boarders was to invite some friend or acquaintance to a meal to determine how strong his stomach was. By prearrangement, when everyone was settled down to the good dinner and enjoying his food, someone of the boarders would begin to relate incidents calculated to test the strength of the guest's stomach. It was said that more than one person was known to leave the table with gastronomic regrets, amid the laughter of the case-hardened boarders. Such was the idea of humor on the Comstock.

When the weather reached its greatest extreme in the winter, the thermometer often dropped below zero. The icy winds from the west blew gales on the slopes of the mountain. Snow fell as deep as ten feet some winters. In this shack the editors had to pull their table, and the compositors their cases, nearer to the stove. It is said that the printers stood at their cases with old barley sacks lashed around their feet with pieces of baling rope. Their fingers became so stiff from the cold that they frequently had to go to the stove to thaw them out.

When the snow on the roof began to melt, the office leaked like a sieve. To divert the water from their work tables, the printers fastened strings against the roof where the leaks were at their worst. These strings, swung outward to the sides of the building, carried the water over and beyond the tables and cases. At times there were so many strings that the ceiling of the office resembled a huge cobweb.

When the main business district was moved from B Street to C Street, the *Enterprise* acquired a large brick building on North C Street. It was to this building that Sam Clemens came to write for the paper in late August, 1862.

There was an abundance of exciting news for the reporters in those early days. All early Western mining camps were the rendez-vous of desperate characters—early editions of modern gangsters. They blackmailed, extorted, fought, stole, ran crooked games, and, when in a tight place, fought it out. So common were the battles of rival gangs or fights in the saloons or hurdy-gurdy houses that men who were engaged in a good poker game or were busy at their work never bothered to look up to see what had happened. There were so many of these affairs that the local editor had to pick one out to write up. Sometimes, while he was busy getting down the data on one shooting affray, another one took place.

At the time when the articles that "Josh" (Sam Clemens) sent in to the *Enterprise* attracted the attention of the editors, the paper was in need of a man to take the place of Dan De Quille. Dan planned to leave sometime during the fall of 1862 to visit his family in West Liberty, Iowa. However, "Josh" and Dan had three months together before the latter left on his eastern trip in December. At this time there was begun between these two men a friendship the like of which is seldom found. They made a magnificent local team. Humorously, they spoke the same language, but in every other respect they differed. Dan was the careful, methodical, honest, hard-working reporter. He strove always to give an accurate description of the latest mining strike or the latest development in milling methods. He took the most meticulous care to see that every detail was represented just as it was. As a result, his readers had implicit trust in everything he wrote. "Josh," on the other hand, was careless, carefree, and sketchy about his writing.

Once in a while, however, Dan launched a hoax for his own amusement. Then, because people were accustomed to believe him, there was the devil to pay. The public felt that he could not and must not write anything to fool his readers. Such was the feeling of the *Enterprise* readers when Dan published his story of "The Traveling Stones of Pahranagat Valley." This tale was a pseudo-erudite account, given in minute scientific detail, of the peculiar activities of stones in this valley in southern Nevada.

By some mysterious power they were drawn together, and then by the same and equally unexplained force they were scattered wide apart, only to be returned in moving, quivering masses to what appeared to be the magnetic center of the valley. In observing these actions of the stones, Dan propounded a new theory concerning electrical propulsion and repulsion. Dan's vivid and scientific description was so convincing that it was copied in many newspapers in the United States. When the story reached Germany, it threw the scientists into a great state of excitement. A group of learned gentlemen in that country were studying, at that moment, electro-magnetic currents. The secretary of this group wrote to Dan and demanded further details from him. His reply to them that there was no truth in his story only evoked censure from them. The denial was treated as an unprofessional attempt to keep his brother scientists in ignorance of the truth. They were very sure that he had made a startling discovery concerning natural laws, the effect of which, they were convinced, had been "first observed and recorded by Herr Dan De Quille, the eminent physicist of Virginiastadt, Nevada."

Even Phineas Taylor Barnum, the great American showman and circus proprietor, sent Dan an offer of $10,000 if he could make the magnetized stones perform under a canvas tent in the manner he described in his article!

One of Dan's "quaints" completely deceived a prominent engineering journal. This periodical took up, and even endorsed as entirely feasible, his proposition to produce perpetual motion in pumping machinery by causing a windmill to hoist loose sand, in addition to the usual load of water, during the hours when the wind blew; this sand, then allowed to fall, would operate turbine wheels, and thus keep on pumping after the wind had died down. Dan's description of such an apparatus, which he said was invented by Colonel W. E. Townsend of Mono Lake, was so convincing that an engineer in Boston actually figured out the exact horsepower to be produced by the machinery in question.

There were many of these "quaints" [3]—Dan always wrote one when news was scarce. One more of them will convince the reader that, when two humorists like Dan and "Josh" got together, there was no telling what might result. This story he called "Solar Armor": The excruciating heat of the desert in the neighborhood of Death Valley stirred Dan's mind to invent a helmet. It was fitted up inside with an ammonia tank; when the ammonia evaporated, it furnished cold air to neutralize the heat.

One torrid July day when the thermometer was reaching its highest point, the inventor put on his helmet and started out to cross the desert. When no word was received from him for several days, a relief expedition was sent out to search for him. They found him sitting on a boulder in the middle of the desert, covered with icicles and frozen stiff to the blistering sand. Dan explained that he had loaded the apparatus with too much ammonia and that before he could get his helmet off, refrigeration had congealed him. When the Coast papers mildly scolded Dan for writing such extravagant stuff, he only laughed and resolved never to do it again. Washoe, however, knew Dan, and could tell what was humor and what was truth.

Sam Clemens was a natural for Washoe. He caught the spirit of recklessness which was everywhere. Getting exact facts and details irked him, but he perceived at once what delighted his readers. Dan had pleased them, and now that he was going away, the *Enterprise* had a writer who could fit perfectly into his place.

Sam had been on the paper a little over a month when he wrote his first hoax. Unlike Dan, who duped his readers with scientific treatises, Sam lambasted some politician or small-town officeholder, or exposed some miscarriage of justice that he thought needed correction. Especially did he delight to ridicule a person who had offended him. In one such burlesque, which he called "The Petrified Man," published in the *Enterprise* on October 12, 1862, he selected Judge G. T. Sewall, Justice of the Peace and ex-officio Coroner for the Humboldt Mining District, "to give a workover." In some unknown way the Judge had offended Sam. It rankled in him. Here was his chance to get even, a pastime in which he often indulged.

At this particular time in California and Nevada, unusual petrified objects and other natural wonders were being described in the papers. In fact, the news was full of them—a mania approaching the ridiculous. Combining the desire "to touch up" the Judge and "to kill the mania with a delicate, a very delicate satire," "Josh" wrote up the tale of finding a petrified man at Gravelly Ford, an old emigrant crossing on the Humboldt River, and some one hundred and twenty miles beyond the jurisdiction of the Judge. "There wasn't a living creature within fifty miles of there, except a few straying Indians, some crippled grasshoppers, and four or five buzzards out of meat and too feeble to get away." (It may be noted here that Dan and Sam often laid the locale of their hoaxes at some place well known, but devoid of people.)

This satire on justice and petrifications declared that learned men had pronounced the stone man as having been in this state for ten generations. As soon as the Judge "heard the news, he summoned a jury, mounted his mule, and posted off, with noble reverence for official duty, on that awful five days' journey, through alkali, sagebrush, peril of body, and imminent starvation, *to hold an inquest* on this man that had been dead and turned to everlasting stone for more than three hundred years!" When the jury reviewed the remains, it returned "the verdict that the deceased came to his death from *protracted exposure.*"

The hoax maker then moved on to "higher flights of imagination" and related how the members of the jury wanted to give the man a "Christian burial." They discovered that the limestone sediment that had run down from the crags above and under him had cemented him fast to the bedrock. "The jury (they were all silver miners)" examined their difficulty, "got out their powder and fuse," and commenced drilling a hole under him "to blast him from his position." The Judge, observing all of these things, objected. And "with that delicacy so characteristic of him, forbade them, observing it would be little less than sacrilege to do such a thing."

Sam used a literary device in this story which he employed in some of his other frontier absurdities: he purposely scrambled his description. First he described the sitting position of his petrified man; then he told of the position of one foot; next he related how "his right thumb was against the side of his nose"; he then came back to the other foot; and then went up to the fingers of the right hand, which he described as being "spread apart." To confuse the reader, he discussed the position of the head before telling how the left thumb was hooked into the right little finger; he then rambled off about something else; and when all was satisfactorily obscure, he drifted back again to describe "the fingers of the left hand" as being spread like those of the right one.

Sam was bitterly disappointed when the article was first published: many of the papers "received it in innocent good faith." Not so, however, the San Francisco *Bulletin*. On October 15, this paper republished the story, calling it "A Washoe Joke," and went on to say that "the interior journals seem to be copying [it] in good faith." One of these "interior journals" was the Placer *Weekly Courier* of October 18, a copy of which is now extant. This paper summarized the story, and commented on it with complete conviction. The "stone man" took his place along with the other "genuine marvels our Nevada has produced. . . ." When the satire was copied in many papers and the exchanges came into the *Enterprise* office, Sam "began to feel a soothing secret satisfaction. . . ." He said in later years, "I hated . . . in those days, and these things pacified and pleased me. I could not have gotten more real comfort out of him without killing him."

And he was more than gratified when he saw that "The Petrified Man" had "penetrated territory after territory, State after State, and land after land till he swept the great globe and culminated in sublime and unimpeachable legitimacy in the august *London Lancet*. To add insult to injury, every time an exchange came into the office, Sam marked the story of the hoax "with a prominent belt of ink" and sent it to the Judge.

Washoe humor, the kind J. Ross Browne inaugurated, was carried on by Sam Clemens. It was robust, virile, salty, coarse. The readers of the papers in the mining towns liked it—the *Enterprise* was getting a reputation, and the smart young reporter on it was getting one, too. It gave him confidence, and it revealed to him the tremendous license he could assume in his burlesques—so long as they were amusing.

Many another person was handled roughly in the *Territorial Enterprise* by Sam Clemens. Joe Goodman did not care. When Sam joined the staff of the paper, the only admonition he received from his boss was, "Never say, 'We learn' so-and-so, or 'It is reported,' or 'It is rumored,' or 'We understand' so-and-so, but go to headquarters and get the absolute facts, and then speak out and say 'It is' so-and-so. Otherwise people will not put confidence in your news."

Joseph Goodman, handsome, charming, *bon-vivant* bohemian, third member of the *Enterprise* literary trio, was a true product of the *Golden Era*. He never became the writer of Comstock witticisms. He loved to write poetry—not short verse, but long poems. Whenever there was a national holiday, a commemorative event, or an obituary, Joe Goodman was called upon to write something for it. Many of his poems have vanished. But Nevadans remember him best for the poem which he wrote in later years in nostalgic reverence of the days he spent on the Comstock:

VIRGINIA CITY

In youth when I did love, did love
(To quote the sexton's homely ditty),
I lived six thousand feet above
Sea-level, in Virginia City;
The site was bleak, the houses small,
The narrow streets unpaved and slanting,
But now it seems to me of all
The spots on earth the most enchanting.

Let Art with all its cunning strive,
Let Nature lavish all her splendor,
One touch of sentiment will give
A charm more beautiful and tender;
And so that town, howe'er uncouth
To others who have chanced to go there,
Enshrines the ashes of my youth,
And there is Fairyland, or nowhere.

Who tends its marts, who tread its ways,
Are mysteries beyond my guessing;
To me the forms of other days
Are still about its centers pressing:
I know that loving lips are cold,
And true hearts stilled—ah, more the pity!
But in my fancy they yet hold
Their empire in Virginia City.

Unhallowed flames have swept away
The structures in which I delighted,
The streets are grass-grown, and decay
Has left the sunny slopes benighted—
But not for me: to my dimmed sight
The town is always like the Olden,
As to the captive Israelite
Shone aye Jerusalem the Golden.

I would not wish to see it now,
I choose to know it as I then did,
With glorious light upon its brow
And all its features bright and splendid;
Nor would I like that it should see
Me, gray and stooped, a mark for pity
And learn that time had dealt with me
As hard as with Virginia City.

Besides Joe Goodman there was another rhyme weaver on the Comstock, whose name was Rollin M. Daggett.[4] There was considerable rivalry between these two poets over their productions. Daggett, who at first wrote occasional editorials, later became a regular editor. These two men were the best of friends in everything but verse-making. About once a week a poem written by Daggett or Goodman would appear in the *Enterprise*. Each effort drew forth its quantum of praise or criticism and each of the poets had his army of followers.

Little Steve Gillis was a pronounced Daggett man while Dennis McCarthy was a Goodman supporter. It was said that it was an amusing sight to see Steve Gillis, well filled with Joe Mallon's whiskey,[5] delivering a barroom lecture on the excellence of Daggett's verse. "This is the real stuff!" he would shout, waving the *Enterprise* in the air. "This has the true ring. Hear this, everybody," and in a loud voice he would roll out the strong passages of Daggett's verse and point out their beauties to the admiring crowd. Then the crowd would empty tankards of foaming beer to Daggett, the Comstock bard and the glory of the town.[6]

A few evenings later Dennis McCarthy would expound the beauties of Goodman's verse. "Talk about poetry! This is the only true music ever written on the ledge. Here's a line, gentlemen, that strikes the heart like a soft beam of moonlight falling from a cloud. I tell you it's the divine fire from Olympus. Where is the man that says Daggett can write poetry? That man can't write mottoes for a first-class candy factory." Then Goodman would be elevated to a pedestal of poetic fame.

The war, however, was carried beyond the smoky, sawdusted barrooms. The followers of each of the poetic rivals schemed in every possible way to have his idol chosen the poet of the day. Goodman was generally chosen for Decoration Day, the Fourth of July, and Pioneer Celebrations. Soon these duties became very unpleasant, and whenever Sam Clemens found Joe shut up in his office writing a poem for some public occasion, he described his employer as "being chained in a cell on a fish-and-water diet, wrestling with the Muses."

One night the *Enterprise* poets had a contest writing against time. A subject was set, and twenty minutes by the watch was allowed. Joe easily won, with a half column of verse; Daggett in the same length of time had produced only a few lines. The title of "Boss Poet of the Comstock" was conferred on Joe Goodman by common consent.

No book was published in the Territory during the time that Sam Clemens lived there.[7] The only attempt was the writing of a serial novel, inaugurated by Tom Fitch when he started the *Weekly Occidental* in September, 1863. Tom's wife, Anna M. Fitch, was to write the first chapter, followed by Mr. Dawson, "a dark and bloody editor of [one of] the dailies," the *Enterprise*. Mr. Fitch followed the third week. About this time a dissolute stranger arrived in Virginia City looking for literary work, and Mr. Fitch engaged him to help write the novel. After he had looked over the efforts of the chain writers, he proceeded to mess up the affair so badly that Fitch fired him. Although he had delayed the next appearance of the paper, no one could rewrite the chapter in time, and so the paper was published without the novel. Sam Clemens' chapter was to come next, but the "absence of the novel probably shook the public confidence; at any rate, before the first side of the next issue went to press, the *Weekly Occidental* died as peaceful as an infant." Sam has made humorous reference to this literary effort in *Roughing It*. He was proud, however, to have been connected with the magazine.

He had written some rhymes for it, but it had died before they were printed. He therefore put into *Roughing It* the poem, "The Aged Pilot Man," which was on the "first side" of the issue that never went to press.[8]

But the greatest literary triumph for Washoe was its first newspaper. The *Territorial Enterprise* was not only the first newspaper published in Nevada, but it was also the best paper published there. A two-year start before another paper entered the field gave it a leadership that was never disputed. Late in 1860, the Carson City *Silver Age* was launched to take the place of the *Enterprise,* which had been moved to Virginia City that year. (It will be remembered that Raish Phillips and Sam Clemens sent articles to the *Age* when they were in Aurora.) J. L. Laird, part owner of it, and his associates moved their press to Virginia City in the fall of 1862 and started publication under the name of the Virginia City *Daily Union* on November 4, 1862. It was with the editors of this paper that Sam Clemens had his editorial difficulties in the spring of 1864.

Two more newspapers sprang up in Washoe in 1862: the *Esmeralda Star* on May 10, 1862, and the Washoe *Times* on October 18 of the same year. Both papers were weeklies—the former one of three papers ever to be published in Esmeralda, and the latter the only editorial voice of Washoe City. It will be remembered that in the summer of 1862, Sam Clemens tried to obtain a job as compositor on the *Star*. The other organ had the doubtful distinction of changing its name once a year for the next three years: the *Old Pah Utah,* the Washoe *Weekly Star,* and the Washoe *Weekly Times*.[9]

Posterity has evaluated the *Enterprise* school and its productions. The literary movement of the West began with this paper. It wound itself around the hearts of the people of Washoe; it was always filled with stirring pictures, strong editorials, strange and weird stories, sweet and sentimental poems, and the best and finest reports on the mines. George Dunlap Lyman, indigenous writer of Comstock life, has said that it was "The nerve center of Washoe, the brainiest sheet on the Coast. It was privy to all the Mountain's secrets, both above and below the earth's crust. It had acquired enormous prestige. It could make any man in the Territory. It was honest and fearless. It might fear God—but no puny man. It was the mouthpiece of Sun Mountain—her final tribunal—

her judge and advocate. It could be loved; it could be feared like the plague. When it got angry, it had claws like those of a mountain cat. It was Comstock to the core—the mirror of her astounding personality—the sounding-board of her buoyant, virile young life." [10]

Men on Sun Mountain had to match its greatness. There never had been in any other place in the world such a rich spot as the Comstock Lode. There never had been an Ophir, a Gould & Curry. Nowhere in all the length and breadth of the land had the mettle and spirit of mankind been tested as on the Lode. Cruel Nature cast the weak aside—only the strong could endure the colossal demands. The *Enterprise* rose to this responsibility in full measure. Its literary personnel was the greatest of any paper in the Territory; Samuel Langhorne Clemens was the greatest of these writers.

15

1863—YEAR OF FULFILLMENT

THE MYSTERY OF WHY JAMES W. NYE EVER CON-
sented to leave the great State of New York and to come out to
Nevada to become the Governor of the Territory was solved. "He
had gone out there to become a United States Senator. All that
was necessary now was to turn the Territory into a State. He did
it without any difficulty." [1] His friendship with President Lincoln,
his influence with Secretary Seward, and his own political astute-
ness assured the accomplishment of the necessary legislation.

In 1862 the people of Nevada voted overwhelmingly to take on
statehood. There wasn't anything they wouldn't tackle! Nye left at
once for New York and the national capital. It would take strategy
to handle the Congress.

The year 1863 was to witness the greatest change ever to come to
the Sagebrush State. The Comstock boom reached its height. Never
again were there to be such feverish excitement, such boisterous
orgies, or such naïve anticipation of getting rich. In September of
1862, the San Francisco Stock and Exchange Board, the first mining
exchange in the United States, was organized. The members of the
Exchange centered their attention on Comstock mines. This intensi-
fied the speculative spirit of an already supercharged public. The
boom of 1863 got off to a wonderful start when the Gould & Curry
discovered the largest and richest body of ore yet to be found on the
Lode. Other mines also brought in paying ore bodies. This news
sent stocks up to a spectacular height. Ophir jumped from $1225 a
foot to $3800 in six months; Gould & Curry went from $500 to $2500
during the same period. Stock in the Aurora and Reese River mines
advanced riotously.

People became astounded at the fabulous riches of the mines.
King Midas had touched the Great Mountain. It was predicted by
one of the papers that within three years the Territory would produce $150,000,000 and that there would be 100,000 people. These
figures would convince the Congress that Nevada should become
a State.

A small group of businessmen in Sacramento believed in the greatness of Washoe. This new and growing area would need quantities of freight hauled to it. On January 8 of this year, at a momentous ceremony, ground was broken for the commencement of the bold and stupendous task of building the Central Pacific Railroad. To connect the railroad with Virginia City at the Truckee River Crossing (Reno), D. M. Geiger surveyed and constructed the grade which bears his name.

This year was to find every trail and road leading to Nevada jammed with throngs of people—25,000, it was said—rushing over the mountains to Washoe—all from California. The rush to Nevada came from the west. Travel was easier in 1863 than in 1859; transportation was better. Some California towns were almost depleted of their finest, their worst, and their run-of-the-mill people. This new crowd brought money, energy, and ability. In this one year Virginia City became a metropolis. Three stock exchanges were opened, the International Hotel—with an elevator—was enlarged, and gas and sewer pipes were laid. Gas lamps illuminated the main streets. From a miserable tent and shanty town, Virginia City emerged one built of brick, stone, and steel. Three theatres, one seating 1600 people, played nightly to crowded houses; four churches ministered to the religious needs of the people; four daily newspapers reported the news and the progress of the mines; public and private schools educated the young Comstockers; and forty-two saloons kept the throngs from getting thirsty. Daily stages and freight wagons brought in full loads of luxuries—the finest that San Francisco could furnish for this "mad, bad city."

The *Territorial Enterprise* kept pace with this growing community. Why shouldn't it? It had the finest press and the most capable staff on the Lode. Money came in to its owners so fast, it was said, that they carried home their profits every night in buckets. Its power and influence were admitted by everyone. This year made Sam Clemens the greatest reporter in the West—Joe Goodman consented to let him report the proceedings of the 1863 legislature.

There were other reasons why he wanted to go down to Carson City: he always liked to be near his family. On October 2, 1862, Orion proudly went down to San Francisco to meet the steamer which brought Mollie and Jennie to the West. Soon thereafter they were established in their new home in Carson City, built by Orion (and still standing today) at the corner of Spear and Division streets. It was a modest two-story house, gauged by present-day standards. However, it cost $12,000 to build, and the furnishings were several thousand dollars more. "There was no other house in that place that could approach this property for style and cost." It was truly the Governor's Mansion, for Nye had no family in Nevada.

Since Nye was away most of the year 1863, it was "Governor Orion Clemens" most of the time. Mollie enjoyed being a Governor's wife. "No one on this planet ever enjoyed a distinction more than she enjoyed that one. Her delight in being the head of society was so frank that it disarmed criticism, and even envy." [2] When Sam went down to Carson City to report the doings of the legislature, he stayed with Orion and Mollie. Their new house and lavish furnishings must have seemed palatial to Sam after living for two years in cabins and mining camp hostelries.

As a satire on these early hotels, Sam wrote a ditty. It is taken from a scrapbook found in the old Benton Stable in Carson City, Nevada:

MARK TWAIN'S HOTEL

Having lately opened a hashery, I send you these rules and regulations:

This house will be considered strictly intemperate.

None but the brave deserve the fare.

Persons owing bills of board will be bored for bills.

Boarders who do not wish to pay in advance are requested to advance and pay.

Boarders are expected to wait on the colored cooks—for meals.

Sheets will be nightly changed, once in six months, or more if necessary.

Double boarders can have two beds with a room in it, or two rooms with a bed in it, as they choose.

Boarders are requested to pull off their boots if they can conveniently do so.

Beds with or without bugs.

All moneys or other valuables are to be left in the care of the proprietor. This is insisted upon, as he will be responsible for no other losses.

Inside matter will not be furnished editors under any consideration.

Relatives coming to make a six months' visit will be welcomed, but when they bring half of their household furniture, virtue will cease to be forbearance.

Single men with their families will not be boarded.

Dreams will be charged for by the dozen.

Nightmares hired out at reasonable rates.

Stone vaults will be furnished to snoring boarders, and the proprietor will in no ways be responsible for the broken tin-pan-ums of other years.[3]

Sam's reputation for making merry and keeping a party lively made him a favorite guest at the parties in the capital. Many a humorous story is told of his hilarious antics. One evening he escorted a girl to a large ball given at Moore's Opera House. It was the custom in those pioneering days for the girls to provide the refreshments and to furnish the supplies for the banquet. His girl brought a large basket of dishes as her part of the equipment. As they entered the hall, the grand march, which Sam and his lady were to lead, was forming. Without waiting to set down the basket of dishes, he took his girl and went to the head of the line, going through all the intricate figures of the march with that great market-basket on one arm, much to the hilarity of the crowd. It was winter and his girl was wearing galoshes, but he took her right into the march without allowing her to remove them. He laughed with the crowd, for he enjoyed his own jokes.

Among the elaborate pieces of furniture which Mollie and Orion purchased for the "Mansion" was a large square piano. Sam practiced on it until he had learned some chords with which to accompany himself when he sang. Once at an informal neighborhood party he was asked to play and sing something. In those days when invited to perform it was always considered the thing to beg off. Not so with Sam Clemens; he promptly took his place on the piano stool and began to sing in a very loud voice, accompanying himself:

"I had an old horse and he died in the
    wilderness,

Died in the wilderness,

Died in the wilderness;

I had an old horse and he died in the
    wilderness,

'Way down in Alabam'."

He repeated this verse over and over again until, it was said, the other young fellows at the party pulled him off the stool.

Sam was entirely untrained in briefing legislative discussions and recording the parliamentary proceedings in the passing of laws. At first his articles were poorly written. They were not as accurate, perhaps, as they should have been. He never did like to pay attention to exact facts and details. It was for these little omissions that Clement T. Rice, reporter for the Virginia City *Union*, ridiculed him and poked fun at his articles. Rice, who had reported the legislature before, knew the method perfectly. His remarks stung Sam to the quick. Instead of being downcast at the criticism, Sam Clemens came back at Rice with a double-barreled charge in his next letter to the *Enterprise*. He "declared that Rice's reports might be parliamentary enough, but that they were covered with glittering technicalities—the most festering mass of misstatement, and even crime." [4] He vowed that they were wholly untrustworthy, and dubbed the author "The Unreliable," while referring to himself as "The Reliable." This byplay between the *Enterprise* and the *Union* continued throughout the entire session—although Rice and Clemens were in private very good friends and cruised around a lot together. Other Nevada newspapers took up the new names of the reporters, with the result that Rice's name stuck with him for life.

Former meetings of the Legislature also had been reported by William Gillespie, who was the secretary of the 1861 session. Taking pity on Sam, he gave him some lessons in parliamentary matters. For this help Sam christened Gillespie "Young Jefferson's Manual," a title he proudly bore for many years. "Billy" Claggett and A. J. Simmons, prominent members of the Legislature, were good friends of Sam's. They were often seen together, and what with the information they gave him of the political intrigues of the session, and with other data Orion could furnish him, no one could give a better picture of the doings than Sam Clemens. The friendship of these three men has been immortalized in their group photograph.

Sam's articles were not all on the passage, discussion, or defeat of bills. The members came in for their share of burlesque. The delegates from Washoe City and the valley about it were particularly active during this session. Hence Sam decided to polish them off with a little badinage in the form of an article entitled "A Big Thing in Washoe City" or "The Grand Bull Drivers' Convention." The copy of the *Enterprise* in which this article was written is not extant, but it was republished in the *Placer Weekly Courier* of Forest Hill, Placer County, on January 17, 1863. In the foreword this paper said that "The Reliable of the *Enterprise* gives that paper a lively account of a trip he made to Washoe City, and what he saw there." Since this article by Sam Clemens has never been re-published, specimen paragraphs are given here:

Carson, Midnight
December 23d.

Eds., *Enterprise:*

On the last night of the session, Hon. Thomas Hannah announced that a Grand Bull Drivers' Convention would assemble in Washoe City, on the 22d, to receive Hon. Jim Sturtevant and the other members of the Washoe delegation. I journeyed to the place yesterday to see that the ovation was properly conducted. I traveled per stage. The Unreliable of the *Union* went also—for the purpose of distorting the facts. The weather was delightful. It snowed the entire day. The wind blew such a hurricane that the coach drifted sideways from one toll road to another, and sometimes utterly refused to mind her helm. It is a fearful thing to be at sea in a stagecoach. We were anxious to get to Washoe by four o'clock, but luck was against us: we were delayed by stress of weather; we were hindered by the bad condition of the various toll roads; we finally broke the after spring of the wagon, and had to lay up for repairs. Therefore we only reached Washoe at dusk. Messrs. Lovejoy, Howard, Winters, Sturtevant, and Speaker Mills had left Carson ahead of us, and we found them in the city. They had not beaten us much, however, as I could perceive by their upright walk and untangled conversation. At 6 P.M., the Carson City Brass Band, followed by the Committee of Arrangements, and the Chairman of the Convention, and the delegation, and the invited guests, and the citizens generally, and the hurricane, marched up one of the most principal streets, and filed in imposing procession into Foulke's Hall. The delegation, and the guests, and the band, were provided with comfortable seats near the Chairman's desk, and the constituency occupied the body-pews. The delegation and the guests stood up and formed a semicircle, and Mr. Gregory introduced them one at a time to the constituency. Mr. Gregory did this with much grace and dignity, albeit he affected to stammer and gasp, and hesitate, and look colicky, and miscall the names, and miscall them again by way of correcting himself, and grab desperately at invisible things in the air—all with a charming pretense of being scared.

The Hon. John K. Lovejoy arose in his place and blew his horn. He made honorable mention of the Legislature and the Committee on Internal Improvements. He told how the fountains of their great deep were broken up, and they rained forty days and forty nights, and brought on a flood of toll roads over the whole land. He explained to them that the more toll roads there were, the more competition there would be, and the roads would be good, and tolls moderate in consequence.

Mr. Speaker Mills responded to the numerous calls for him, and spoke so well in praise of the Washoe delegation that I was constrained to believe that there really was some merit in the deceased.

Hon. Theodore Winters next addressed the people. He said

he went to the Legislature with but one solitary object in view—the securing to this Territory of an incorporation law. How he had succeeded, the people themselves could tell. . . .

The Chairman, Mr. Gaston, introduced Colonel Howard, and that gentleman addressed the people in his peculiarly grave and dignified manner. The constituency gave way to successive cataracts of laughter, which was singularly out of keeping with the stern seriousness of the speaker's bearing. He spoke about ten minutes, and then took his seat, in spite of the express wish of the audience that he should go on.

Hon. Jim Sturtevant next addressed the citizens, extemporaneously. He made use of the very thunder which I meant to launch at the populace. Owing to this unfortunate circumstance, I was forced to keep up an intelligent silence during the session of the convention. . . .

After this the assemblage broke up and adjourned to take something to drink. At nine o'clock the band again summoned the public to Foulke's Hall, and I proceeded to that place. I found the Unreliable there, and George Hepperly. I had requested Mr. Hepperly, as a personal favor, to treat the Unreliable with distinguished consideration and I am proud and happy to acknowledge he had done so. He had him in charge of two constables.

The Hall had been cleared of the greater part of its benches, and the ball was ready to commence. The citizens had assembled in force, and the sexes were pretty equally represented in the proportion of one lady to several gentlemen. The night was so infernally inclement—so to speak—that it was impossible for ladies who lived at any considerable distance to attend. However, those that were there appeared in every quadrille, and with exemplary industry. I did not observe any wallflowers—the climate of Washoe appears to be unsuited to that kind of vegetation.

In accordance with the customs of the country, they indulged in the plain quadrille at this ball. And notwithstanding the vicissitudes which I have seen that wonderful national dance pass through, I solemnly affirm that they sprung some more new figures on me last night. However, the ball was a very pleasant affair. We could muster four sets and still have a vast surplusage of gentlemen—but the strictest economy had to be observed in order to make the ladies hold out.

The supper and the champagne were excellent and abundant, and I offer no word of blame against anybody for eating and drinking pretty freely. If I were to blame anybody, I would commence with the Unreliable—for he drank until he lost all sense of etiquette. I actually found myself in bed with him with my boots on. However, as I said before, I cannot blame the cuss; it was a convivial occasion, and his little shortcomings ought to be overlooked. When I went to bed this morning, Mr. Lovejoy, arrayed in fiery red night clothes, was dancing the war dance of his tribe (he is President of the Paiute Association) around a spittoon and Colonel Howard, dressed in a similar manner, was trying to convince him that he was a humbug. A suspicion crossed my mind that they were partially intoxicated, but I could not be sure about it on account of everything appearing to turn around so. I left Washoe City this morning at nine o'clock, fully persuaded that I would like to go back there again when the next convention meets.

It is regretted that more of these early letters written about Nevada's politicians are not now extant.

Although the articles which Sam wrote at this time began to be talked about everywhere, and papers all over Nevada Territory and many in the foothill towns and cities of California copied them, the ones now known were written expressly for Washoe consumption. Moreover, they were unsigned. The many other Nevada writers contributing news to Coast papers customarily signed their articles with a pen name—examples of the usual rechristening of the frontier or the mining camps. It is interesting to note that the *nom de plume* usually came at the end of the article. Recognizing that not only approval, but identification, of his work was a needed spur to writing, Sam Clemens decided to adopt such a literary badge. "Josh" would no longer do. It had been abandoned after his return from Aurora.

A number of stories of how Sam Clemens adopted his "Mark Twain" have been told. An old friend and associate in Virginia City gave this version, which was copied in the *Daily Alta California,* on May 13, 1877:

We knew Clemens in the early days and know exactly how he came to be dubbed "Mark Twain." John Piper's saloon on B Street used to be the grand rendezvous for all the Virginia City Bohemians. Piper conducted a cash business and refused to keep any books. As a special favor, however, he would occasionally chalk down drinks to the boys, on the wall back of the bar. Sam Clemens, when localizing for the *Enterprise,* always had an account, with the balance against him, on Piper's wall. Clemens was by no means a Coal Oil Tommy— he drank for the pure and unadulterated love of the ardent. Most of his drinking was conducted in single-handed contests, but occasionally he would invite Dan De Quille, Charley Parker, Bob Lowery, or Alf Doten, never more than one of them, however, at a time, and whenever he did, his invariable parting injunction to Piper was to "Mark Twain," meaning two chalkmarks, of course.

In answer, apparently, to the above explanation, Sam sent a letter to the same paper:

Daily Alta California
June 9, 1877

Dear Sir:

"Mark Twain" was the *nom de plume* of one Captain Isaiah Sellers, who used to write river news over it for the New Orleans *Picayune.* He died in 1863 and as he could no longer need that signature, I laid violent hands upon it without asking permission of the proprietor's remains. That is the history of the *nom de plume* I bear.

Yours,
Samuel L. Clemens

May 29th

He first signed "Mark Twain" to one of his legislative articles on February 2, 1863. It fitted him perfectly; from the very first it had charm, magic, and influence. By no other name thereafter was he called. How many times when he was on the River had he heard the leadsman, when he had sunk his line to the two-fathom knot, call out, "By the mark, twain!" which meant that the boat was safe with twelve feet of water under her—a comforting assurance. As it had sustained him in his Mississippi days, so did it in the years to follow.

Mark Twain's influence increased rapidly in 1863. When he learned the way to get things done in the legislature, he put his pull to good advantage for Orion. Since the organization of the Territory, the Secretary of State had been required to record all mining-corporation and toll-road franchises. For this work Orion received a recording fee. Mark saw where he could manage to increase the Secretary's revenue by having an amendment added to the law, requiring every corporation doing business in the Territory to record its charter *in full* in a record to be kept by the Secretary. Every corporation charter, framed in exactly the same words, was charged for at the rate of forty cents a folio for one hundred words and five dollars for furnishing a certificate of each record. The Secretary was allowed to keep the fees.

Hundreds of toll-road franchises were granted, "so many, they were hanging over the edge of the Territory like a fringe," and thousands of mining companies were chartered. The compliance with this law brought Orion so much business that he had to employ a secretary. His remunerations from this source were easily an average of $3500 a month, more money than he had ever earned before in his life. Orion and Mollie lived handsomely—their home was the "Governor's Mansion." The finest furniture to be bought on the Coast was purchased for it. They were extravagant—there could be no end to the "boom of 1863"!

Mark Twain emerged from reporting this meeting of the legislature one of the most conspicuous figures on the frontier. When a stranger visited Virginia City and was shown the wonders of the Ophir and the Gould & Curry, the visit was not complete unless he had had Mark Twain pointed out to him.

Mark had also learned that a great deal of his popularity came from lampooning someone in his columns. Early that year another paper, the Virginia City *Bulletin,* made its appearance. It, too, came in for the usual witticisms from the *Enterprise* local reporter. But the *Bulletin* came back to poke fun at him:

Sammy Clemens, or as he styles himself, Mark Twain, who scribbles the funny things (Heavens save the mark) for the *Enterprise,* and is not a little addicted to saying hard things about others, as he pretends, in joke, appears to feel it intensely when others turn the joke on him. No man living loves a joke better than ourselves, and we are always as ready to take as to make one. Sammy, it appears, is differently constituted to us in this respect. Perhaps he imagines because he is Sammy that he *has* a right to do what others with less pretensions to character of a wit (?) have not. He does appear to be aware that there is an old adage, that 'those who live in glass houses should be careful when they throw stones.' Merciless himself in perpetrating jokes on others, he winces like a cur with a flea in his ear when others retort, showing conclusively that he has quite misassumed—that of being Washoe's wit! Wit should, like a keen-edged razor, cut without being felt. When acrimony and bitterness is exhibited, wit is no more genuine than a bar of gilded brass is gold. We think the funniest part of poor Sammy's character is his claiming the possession of wit. Drawling stupidity, when well acted by an educated, intelligent man, is indeed comical; but when those features are the natural characteristics of an illiterate and by no means bright intellect, the mouthings of such a one it were a misapplication of terms to call wit. Sammy need give himself no uneasiness about our wishing to deprive him of the "honors" of such a character, which he appears to dread, if we may judge by the bitterness of his remarks in this morning's *Enterprise*.[5]

During the summer of 1863, politics in Nevada became sizzling hot. Delegates to the Constitutional Convention were being selected; and the law setting up the Convention provided that the State officers be chosen at the time the Constitution was submitted to the people. The Union party in Virginia City planned to put a full ticket in the field. There were so many California politicians who thought that Nevada was a fertile field in which to get an office that great numbers of them flocked to this Territory. When the Union party met to choose the nominees, such opposition developed that one faction bolted the caucus. The *Enterprise* supported one faction while the *Union* backed the other one.

While the workmen were getting the new quarters of the *Enterprise* on C Street ready and were working on Joe Goodman's private office, Joe thought it a good time to get in a little trout fishing, his favorite sport, at Lake Tahoe. With a group of his old cronies and well supplied with food and Joe Mallon's whiskey, he hiked off to the mountains for a couple of weeks' vacation. Business was so good at this time and there was so much work to be done that it threw a good deal of responsibility on Mark. When the load became too heavy, he sent for Joe to come home. Joe paid no attention to Mark's pleas. Since Joe got his mail every day, Mark decided to write a red-hot political article solely for Joe's benefit. In the first column of the paper Mark roasted the Democratic candidates. He ran off only one copy of this paper and sent it up to Joe.

As soon as Joe saw the bogus paper, he threw it into the campfire, packed up his things, and hastened back to Virginia, mad as a hornet. Arriving at the office about nine in the morning, he met Mark at the door.

"Who in hell is running this paper?" demanded Goodman.

"Why, you are," Mark meekly replied.

"Well, who wrote that article in the *Enterprise*?" Joe asked.

"What article?" queried Mark.

Goodman grabbed a copy of the paper. After looking through it, he could not find the article that had brought him home in a hurry.

"What is the matter with you?" inquired Mark. Joe was completely nonplused and at a loss to explain his burst of anger. "Why, you are in bad shape," said Mark; "you have snakes in your boots. We will have to look after you. You must have been drinking too much whiskey." Mark never told his boss that he had printed only one copy of the attack on the Democrats. He had accomplished what he wanted: to get Joe back on the paper again.

He continued his byplay with the *Union*—a pastime he so much enjoyed that he wrote his mother and sister: "I have just finished writing up my report for the morning paper and giving the Unreliable a column of advice about how to conduct himself in Church." In spite of all this rivalry with the Unreliable, he was fond of Rice. Together they had a wonderfully good time. Both of these gay young blades were always out for fun.

Some time in the latter part of May, Rice and Mark went to San Francisco on one of the thirteen trips the latter made to that city while he was in Washoe. They stayed at the Lick House, ran around the town from morning until after midnight, took trips to near-by towns, ate luxuriously, "drank champagne and claret, and then do we put on the most disgusting airs. Rice says: 'Oh, no, we are not having any fun, Mark. Oh, no, I reckon not. It's somebody else—it's probably the gentleman in the wagon.' I do *hate* to go back to Washoe." [6]

It was probably at this time that Mark Twain wrote "Those Blasted Children," which he said he thought was a "pearl which ought for the eternal welfare of my race to have a more extensive circulation than is afforded by a local paper." [7] He and the Unreliable, after a full evening, planned to spend much of the next day quietly in their quarters, napping and writing easily. The hotel was full of noisy, romping, boisterous children, who disturbed them endlessly. At length Mark burst into satire:

> . . . Ah me! Summer girls and summer dresses, and summer scenes at the "Willows," Seal Rock Point, and the grim sea-lions wallowing in the angry surf; glimpses through the haze of stately ships far away at sea, a dash along the smooth beach, and the exhilaration of watching the white waves come surging ashore, and break into seething foam about the startled horse's feet; reveries beside the old wreck, half buried in sand, and compassion for the good ship's fate; home again in soft twilight, oppressed with the odor of flowers—home again to San Francisco, drunk, perhaps, but not disorderly. Dinner at six, with ladies and gentlemen, dressed with faultless taste and elegance, and all drunk, apparently, but very quiet and well-bred—unaccountably so, under the circumstances, it seemed to my cloudy brain. Many things happened after that, I remember —such as visiting some of their haunts with those dissipated *Golden Era* fellows, and— Here come those young savages again—those noisy and inevitable children. God be with them! —or they with Him, rather, if it be not asking too much. . . .
> "Hi, Johnny! Look through the keyhole! Here's that feller with a long nose, writing again—les' stir him up. . . ."

Because Mark thought that "Those Blasted Children" should "have a more extensive circulation," he sent it to the New York *Sunday Mercury*. It is believed to be the first article of Mark Twain's to appear in an Eastern paper.

Although Mark and the Unreliable did *hate* to go back to

Washoe, they had to return to their jobs. The *Enterprise* building and the new press were finished on July 31. All hands had to work overtime in straightening out the general confusion, but when everything was in running order, there was a great celebration by the editors, reporters, and pressmen. Congratulations in every form poured into the *Enterprise* office: there were lavish donations of food, and even more lavish gifts of champagne and other fine wines. Mark Twain was not as robust as most of his colleagues— still he tried to keep up with them. In doing so, he fell ill. Between overwork and overcelebrating, his chronic bronchitis laid him up.

Mark's columns had to be filled; so he called on his friend, the Unreliable, to do the work for him while he recuperated. What a chance it was for Rice to get even with Mark! Revenge would be sweet.

The next issue of the *Enterprise* was positively a sensation. The readers of the paper were stunned, dumbfounded, and mystified. Why was Mark Twain so repentant, so contrite, so apologetic? Was this unmitigated wag drunk again, or had he become sober, gone crazy, or what? The article Rice wrote for Mark belongs here:

Aug. 1, 1863

APOLOGETIC

It is said an "open confession is good for the soul." We have been on the stool of repentance for a long time, but have not before had the moral courage to acknowledge our manifold sins and wickedness. We confess to this weakness. We have commenced this article under the head of "Apologetic"—we mean it, if we ever meant anything in our life. To Mayor Arick, Hon. Wm. M. Stewart, Marshal Perry, Hon. J. B. Winters, Mr. Olin, and Samuel Witherel, besides a host of others whom we have ridiculed from behind the shelter of our reportorial position, we say to these gentlemen, we acknowledge our faults and in all weakness and simplicity—upon our bended marrow-bones—we ask their forgiveness, promising that in the future we will give them no cause for anything but the best of feeling toward us. To "Young Wilson," and the "Unreliable," (as we feel that no apology we can make begins to atone for the many insults we have given them). Towards these gentlemen we have been as mean as a man could be—and we have always prided ourselves on this base quality. We feel that we are the least of all humanity, as it were. We will now go in sackcloth and ashes for the next forty days. What more can we do?

The latter-named gentleman has saved us several times from receiving a sound thrashing for our impudence and assurance. He has sheltered and clothed us. We have had a hankering, "my boy," to redeem our character—or what little we have. Tomorrow we may get in the same old way again. If we do, we want it now understood that this confession stands. Gentlemen, do you accept our good intentions?

When Mark Twain read his public apology, it was a sudden and effective cure for his cold. He was embarrassed, perturbed, "confusticated." It was never his intention to apologize. He always stood firmly on his convictions; he never retracted a statement. Rice's one-day substitution for Mark was enough. Something must be done—an explanation followed:

> . . . We are to blame for giving the Unreliable an opportunity to misrepresent us, and therefore refrain from repining to any great extent at the result. We simply claim the right to *deny the truth* of every statement made by him in yesterday's paper, to annul all apologies he coined as coming from us, and to hold him up to public commiseration as a reptile endowed with no more intellect, no more cultivation, no more Christian principle than animates and adorns the sportive jackass rabbit of the Sierras. We have done.

The reporters of the Comstock liked their humor coarse, rough, uncomplimentary. The *Evening Bulletin* a few days later made the following remark:

> At the solicitation of about fifteen hundred of our subscribers, we will refrain from again entering into a controversy with that beef-eating, blear-eyed, hollow-headed, slab-sided ignoramus, that pilfering reporter, Mark Twain.

While Mark was in San Francisco, he arranged with the editors of the San Francisco *Call* to write a weekly letter from Virginia

City for that paper. The first one of them was written on July 5 and published on the 9th. A letter appeared every week for all of July and for the first two weeks of August. There was a good reason why there was no letter for the third week: Virginia City went through its first and one of the most devastating of the fires that were periodically to wipe it out. On the night of the fire Mark, while trying to figure out a way to put it out, took cold again. Mark was then living in the White House, where "I lost my home, my happiness, my constitution, and my trunk. . . . On the day of the fire my constitution succumbed to a severe cold caused by undue exertion in getting ready to do something. I suffered to no purpose, too, because the plan I was figuring at for the extinguishing of the fire was so elaborate that I never got it completed until the middle of the following week." His cold was so bad that his many friends prescribed remedies, some of which he embodied in "How to Cure a Cold."

The first time that Mark began to sneeze, a friend told him to bathe his feet in hot water and go to bed. He followed that advice. It wasn't long before another friend told him to get up and take a shower bath. He took that advice. And before the hour was over, another friend told him that it was a good policy to "feed a cold and starve a fever." Now Mark had both, so he decided to fill himself up for the cold, and "then keep dark and let the fever starve a while."

Mark gave his patronage to a stranger who had just opened a restaurant in Virginia City that morning. He waited on Mark until he had fed his cold, and then he asked him if people in the City were much affected with colds. When Mark replied that they were, the stranger went out and took in his sign. There was no money in feeding people with habitual colds, especially when restaurants operated on the American plan.

On his way down to the *Enterprise* office, Mark met a bosom friend who told him that "a quart of salt water, taken warm, would come as near curing a cold as anything in the world." Although Mark was so full of food that he hardly had room for even an honest drink, he tried the salt-water cure. The result was surprising. He said he thought he "threw up his immortal soul." Warning the public against this remedy for a cold, he said he would "rather take an earthquake than a quart of warm salt water."

When this remedy did not cure, he continued borrowing hand-kerchiefs until he "came across a lady who had just arrived from across the plains, and who said she had lived in a part of the country where doctors were scarce and had from necessity acquired considerable skill in the treatment of 'simple family complaints.'" The old lady, "one hundred and fifty years old," "mixed a decoction of molasses, *aqua fortis,* turpentine, and various drugs"—prescribing a dose every fifteen minutes. Mark took only one dose—that one robbed him "of all moral principle."

After two days he went to doctoring again, following "a few more unfailing remedies." They only drove his cold from his head to his lungs:

> I got to coughing incessantly, and my voice fell below zero; I conversed in a thundering bass, two octaves below my natural tone; I could only compass my regular nightly repose by coughing myself down to a state of utter exhaustion, and then the moment I began to talk in my sleep, my discordant voice woke me up again.
>
> My case grew more and more serious every day. Plain gin was recommended; I took it. Then gin and molasses; I took that also. Then gin and onions, and I took all three. I detected no particular result, however, except I had acquired a breath like a buzzard's.

Not being able to find a remedy in Virginia which could cure him, Mark decided to travel. He and his reportorial comrade from the Virginia City *Daily Union,* "Young" Wilson, went to Lake Tahoe. They went in style by taking the Pioneer Stage Coach, and for such a trip Wilson took all of his baggage with him: "two excellent silk handkerchiefs and a daguerreotype of his grandmother!" They had a wonderful time sailing, hunting, fishing, and dancing by day. At night Mark doctored his cold, which grew steadily worse.

Someone recommended "a sheet-bath." Now Mark had never refused any remedy so far, and it seemed poor policy to begin then. The proper time to take the "sheet-bath," he was told, was at midnight. Although the weather was very frosty, Mark's back and breast were bared and "a sheet (there seemed to be a thousand yards of it) soaked in ice water was wound around" him until he looked like "a swab for a Columbiad," the Big Bertha of the Civil war:

> It is a cruel expedient. When the chilly rag touches one's warm flesh, it makes him start with a sudden violence and gasp for breath. . . . It froze the marrow in my bones and stopped the breathing of my heart. I thought my time had come. . . . Never take a sheet-bath—never.

When the sheet-bath failed to cure the cold, a lady friend advised the application of a mustard plaster. He got one, "a gorgeous one, eighteen inches square." He put it beside the bed where he could reach it, but "Young" Wilson "got hungry in the night, and ate it up. I never saw anybody have such an appetite; I am confident that lunatic would have eaten me if I had been healthy." After Mark had been at Lake Tahoe, he wrote his mother and sister on August 19 from Steamboat Springs (ten miles south of Reno):

> I found the "Lake House" crowded with the wealth and fashion of Virginia, and I could not resist the temptation to take a hand in all fun going. Those Virginians—men and women both—are a stirring set, and I found if I went with them on all their eternal excursions, I should bring the consumption home with me—so I left, day before yesterday, and came back into the Territory again. A lot of them had purchased a site for a town on the Lake shore, and they gave me a lot. When you come out, I'll build you a house on it. The Lake seems more super-naturally beautiful now than ever. It is the masterpiece of the Creation.

Stowe's Hotel [8] at Steamboat Springs was not as crowded as the Lake House. There he took steam baths for his cold, and a "lot more vile medicines." Mark was sure they would have cured him had he not been compelled to go back to Virginia City. It was at this time that he wrote "Information for the Millions," [9] the first history of Nevada.

Finally he decided to go to San Francisco, where again he stayed at the Lick House. The first day he arrived, a lady at the hotel told him to drink a quart of whiskey every twenty-four hours, and another friend at the Occidental Hotel recommended exactly the same thing. "Each advised me to take a quart; that made half a gallon. I did and still live."

Although Mark Twain was getting all kinds of recognition from his writings and was very popular with the men on the Lode, he had not yet "crashed" Virginia City society. Whenever he wrote an article, it generally had a point to it, which was sometimes very sharp. Such was the article he wrote while he was in San Francisco, an article satirizing the fashions of the prominent ladies of Washoe. It was the custom of San Francisco papers to describe in minute detail the coiffure, the dress, the jewels, and the demeanor of the belles at their balls.

Feigning a letter from Washoe requesting a review of the fashions at the "Lick House Ball" and "The Pioneers' Ball," he described the dress of some of the Washoe women: [10] Mrs. William M. Stewart was wearing

> ". . . a gorgeous dress of silk bias, trimmed with tufts of ponceau feathers in the Frondeur style; elbowed sleeves made of chicories; plaited Swiss habit-shirt, composed of Valenciennes, *a la vieille,* embellished with a delicate nainsook insertion scalloped at the edge; Lonjumeau jacket of maize-colored Geralda, set off with *bagnettes,* bayonets, clarinets, and one thing or other—beautiful. Rice-straw bonnet of Mechlin tulle, trimmed with devices cut out of sole-leather, representing *aigrettes* and arastras—or asters, whichever it is."

At "The Pioneers' Ball," Mrs. Stewart "was attired in an elegant *pate de foi gras,* made expressly for her, and was greatly admired."

Mrs. A. W. B. ("Sandy" Baldwin):

> ". . . was arrayed in a sorrel organdy, trimmed with fustians and figaros, and canzou fichus, so disposed as to give a splendid effect without disturbing the general harmony of the dress. The body of the robe was a zero velvet, goffered with a square pelerine of solferino *poil de chevre* amidships. The fan used by Mrs. B. was of real palm-leaf and cost four thousand dollars— the handle alone cost six bits. Her headdress was composed of a graceful cataract of white chantilly lace, surmounted by a few artificial worms, and butterflies and things, and a tasteful tarantula done in jet. It is impossible to conceive of anything

more enchanting than this toilet—or the lady who wore it, either, for that matter."

Mrs. J. B. Winters:

". . . was dressed in a rich white satin, with a body composed of a gorgeously figured Mackinaw blanket, with five rows of ornamental brass buttons down the back. The dress was looped up at the side with several bows of No. 3 ribbon-yellow—displaying a skirt of cream-colored Valenciennes crocheted with pink crewel. The coiffure was simply a tall cone of brilliant field-flowers, upon the summit of which stood a glittering 'golden beetle'—or, as we call him at home, a 'straddle-bug.' All who saw the beautiful Mrs. W. upon this occasion will agree that there was nothing wanting about her dress to make it attract attention in any community."

Mrs. Thomas Fitch:

". . . was attired in an alegant Irish foulard of figured aquamarine, or aqua fortis, or something of that kind with thirty-two perpendicular rows of tulle puffings formed of black zero velvets (Fahrenheit). Over this she wore a rich balmoral skirt—Pekin stripe—looped up at the sides with clusters of field-flowers, showing the handsome dress beneath. She also wore a white figaro postillion pea-jacket, ornamented with a profusion of Gabriel bows of crimson silk. From her head depended tasteful garlands of fresh radishes. It being natural to look charming upon all occasions, she did so upon this, of course."

These articles were written for the *Golden Era* and were published on September 25, 26, and 27. It was said that when they reached the Comstock, the husbands and sweethearts of the women so ridiculously described handled Mark Twain somewhat roughly. Waiting one day for him to take the stage, they lay in wait at an advantageous spot, then stopped and overturned the vehicle. Mark was thrown out and his portfolio was thrown after him. He never told anyone what had really happened to him; to explain his bruises, he turned the incident into "the boldest stage holdup ever to take place in the country."

In his article "The Great Prize Fight" Mark Twain got in some good "digs" at the politicians in California and Nevada, and took a "shot" at the bloody prizefights which were being held clandestinely near San Francisco. The two contestants were Governor Leland Stanford, the Governor of California, and the Hon. F. F. Low, the Governor-elect of California. Stephen J. Field, Supreme Court Justice of California, was Low's second, and "Hon. Wm. M. Stewart (commonly called 'Bill Stewart' or 'Bullyragging Bill Stewart') of the city of Virginia, the most popular as well as the most distinguished lawyer in Nevada Territory, member of the Constitutional Convention, and future U. S. Senator for the State of Washoe, as I hope and believe—[served] on the part of Governor Stanford." It was in this year of prizefights that the San Francisco papers called Mark "The Washoe Giant."

The year 1863 opened with a great rush to Washoe—it matured the Territory to ask for statehood. Before the year was over, a State constitution was framed and submitted to the people. This year revealed that great riches lay buried deep in the bosom of the Great Mountain. Speculation, stock-rigging, dividend-cooking, and wildcat mining ran riot. This year gave birth to "Mark Twain." Over this magic name, he adopted authorship as his life's profession. His writings, appearing in Washoe newspapers at the first of the year, were by the end of it copied all over the West Coast, and Eastern papers were already taking note of him. He had reached the blessed heights of success; he had given America a new kind of literature— a kind that brought about a transition of the literary hegemony of New England to the frontier. It was a year of fulfillment.

Triumphantly Mark Twain wrote his mother:

Ma, you have given my vanity a deadly thrust. Behold, I am prone to boast of having the widest reputation, as a local editor, of any man on the Pacific Coast, and you gravely come forward and tell me "if I work hard and attend closely to my business, I may aspire to a place on a big San Francisco daily, some day." There's a comment on human vanity for you! Why, blast it, I was under the impression that I could get such a situation as that any time I asked for it. But I don't want it. No paper in the United States can afford to pay me what my place on the *Enterprise* is worth. If I were not a naturally lazy, idle, good-for-nothing vagabond, I could make it pay me $20,000 a year. But I don't suppose I shall ever be any account. I lead an easy life, though, and I don't care a cent whether school keeps or not. Everybody knows me, and I fare like a prince wherever I go, be it on this side of the mountains or the other. And I am proud to say I am the most conceited ass in the Territory.[11]

16

DAN DE QUILLE AND MARK TWAIN

THE RUSH AND TURMOIL OF THE 1863 BOOM, THE expansion of the *Enterprise* press, and the new discoveries of ore bodies in the mines swept Joe Goodman's paper into a position of prominence and influence. His limited staff could not keep pace with the increased volume of work on the press. There was no one among the reporters who could write the mining and scientific news. Dan De Quille must be summoned back from Iowa at once. He had been away nine months. Since he had been on the ground from the first shovelfuls of dirt thrown out, no one was better posted on the geology than he was. He had noted and had written about the changes and the development work since 1860.

Joe sent a letter to Dan "posthaste" to return and to resume his old job on the paper. He said everything was "red hot." Indeed, Dan did find everything "red hot," literally and figuratively, when the ship on which he returned steamed into San Francisco Bay. There were a number of Washoe people on board. As the steamer came into the harbor, a lighter went out to meet it. Everyone was anxious to get a newspaper, since they had been weeks without any news. On page one they read that Virginia City was on fire, and that the members of the fire companies had fought with one another for honors in putting out the fire. Several friends of Dan's had been killed. To date the *Enterprise* office had escaped, but everything around it had been burned.

At once there was great excitement on board; the Washoe passengers were anxious about their families and property. They rushed to the newspaper offices and discovered that the city was still in flames. It was midnight before the fire was out. This fire consumed the unsightly, flimsy, wooden shacks which had constantly threatened to burn out the city at any time. Now that they were gone, the city could rise on the ashes in stone, brick, and steel.

Dan returned to the Comstock at once and resumed his job at the old stand, a job that he did not relinquish until the *Enterprise* published its last issue in January, 1893. With his return, the paper had two local reporters: Dan De Quille and Mark Twain. They made a perfect team; Mark disliked the studious detail required in writing up the mining news. In fact, he disliked anything to do with figures, measurements, and solid facts. Hence he covered the informal news of the community, the sensational and social items.

This team had its hands full in giving Joe Goodman what he expected of it. To get everything was impossible—they had to select from the many things that were taking place constantly. Those were the days of daily stage robberies, wonderful discoveries of fabulously rich ore bodies, mining fights, shooting affrays, and new industrial enterprises. Dan De Quille said: "They came tumbling over one another as though playing at leap-frog." While a stage robbery was being written up, a shooting affray started, and before the smoke from the pistol shots had cleared, the fire bells were clanging out an alarm.

The height of this lawlessness came after the fire in August. The crowding of the increased population of this summer into that part of the town which had escaped the fire produced many bloody battles. Fighters, sports, adventurers, and others of the low element of the town, since they were burned out of their old haunts, thronged the remaining saloons, gambling palaces, and hurdy-gurdy houses. Most of them were unwelcome visitors, and, like cats in strange garrets, they battled nightly. Everyone went armed to the teeth; no man was so foolish as to throw away his life with his fists.

Soon after Dan returned to Virginia City, he and Mark took a suite of two unfurnished rooms in the Daggett and Myers Building at 25 North B Street, one of the large buildings which had escaped the fire. Rollin M. Daggett, who occasionally wrote articles for the *Enterprise,* and W. F. Myers, the well-known operator in mining stocks, owned the building, in which only representatives of the best people in the city lived. The larger room of the Twain-De Quille apartment was used as a bedroom, and the smaller one as a sitting room. Joe Goodman superintended the job of furnishing these rooms. From Moses Goldman's furniture store, he selected and had sent up to their rooms several hundred dollars' worth of furniture: a large double bed, piles of fine bedding, good carpets, and other splendid fittings—all quite palatial. Mark said that, since Joe had been "so keen to do the ordering of the furnishings, we'd just let him foot the bill." [1] Whenever the furniture man, "good old Moses Goldman," came after his money, the boys just laughed at him and referred him to Goodman. However, this "passing of the buck" came to an end: old Moses sued them. Mark said that "they ought to have known better than to try such a trick with a man whose front name was Moses and whose rear name was Goldman." [2]

These two roommates agreed. Both of them wanted to read and to smoke about the same length of time after getting into bed. When one of them became hungry and got up to go down town for oyster stew, the other one also became hungry and turned out.

Thomas Fitch, the lawyer, writer, politician, and silver-tongued orator, lived in the same building, just across the hall from Dan and Mark, with his wife, Anna M. Fitch, herself a writer. His sister-in-law and his mother-in-law lived with them also. The neighbors were the best of friends. Mrs. Fitch took pity on the bachelors: "Often when Mark and I got home at night, we found laid out for us in our rooms a fine spread of pie, cake, milk and the like. Mrs. Fitch's pies were perfection. Envious reporters of other papers did not scruple to assert we stole all these good things out of the Fitchs' pantry. We denied the charge at the time, but it was labor lost." [3]

Worse than the pie-stealing accusation was the story by a rival reporter of how Dan and Mark hanged the pet cat of Tom's mother-in-law by tying a cord about its neck and suspending it out of the rear window. "As the good old lady had actually lost her cat, she was a little sour with us for a few days." It later came out that Daggett had thought it a good joke to put the reporters up to publishing a sensational account of the "Secret Midnight Hanging." "For about two weeks no mince pies came forth" until the real truth was out.

The Fitch family came in for other trouble with their neighbors across the hall. Wood in Virginia City was $40 a cord in winter, brought around to the doors of the houses on burros and peddled by Chinamen. One bitterly cold night Dan and Mark found themselves without any wood. Directly opposite their door was Tom Fitch's fuel woodbox. Said Mark to Dan, "We are not going to freeze here with plenty of wood just outside of our door." He went out, gathered up an armful of wood, came back to their door, and threw one stick of wood on the floor. The clatter aroused Tom. Then opening the door noisily, Mark faced about as though he had just come from the inside. Calling out in an angry voice as though speaking to Dan in the hall, he said:

"Dan, d——n it all, don't be taking Tom's wood. It ain't right, and wood so confounded high. It ain't a nice thing to do. Now take that wood right back or there'll be trouble."

Mark then went back to the woodbox and made a racket, but when he threw down one stick, he picked up two. Presently he entered the room with wood piled up to his chin. This load he deposited so carefully that it would not have broken an egg. Soon they had a rousing big fire and plenty of wood to spare for the morning.

Dan was so pleased with their little establishment that he wrote an article about in one of his dispatches to the *Golden Era:*

> We (Mark and I) have the "sweetest little parlor and the snuggest little bedroom" (and it's only three floors from the ground) all to ourselves. Here we come every night and live, breathe, move, and have our being—also our toddies. As Mark has already hinted to the world in his modest way, through the columns of the *Territorial Enterprise,* that "our furniture alone cost $28,000, in Europe," I need add that our upholstery, etc., cost $15,000 more, in—a horn. We have a very good dodge for getting wood; we leave our door open when we go out . . . and the fellows that are hired to carry up wood to the rooms make a mistake nearly every day and pile a lot in our parlor. I never have seen the fellow making these mistakes, but Mark assures me that the wood gets into our parlor that way. I suppose he was right—it looks very plausible—but lately I've been thinking that it was rather strange that the fellow quit making these mistakes the very day that Mark went down to Carson to report the proceedings of the Constitutional Convention.[4]

Mark's and Dan's rooms were the rendezvous for their friends, both reporters and others. It was just as in a modern fraternity house: the doors were always open and the brothers were always welcome. There was plenty of fun "cooking" all the time. A favorite trick of their visitors, all of them inveterate pranksters, was to place all kinds of things in the rooms to annoy the owners.

Mark had a souvenir Japanese sword. One night when the reporters came home, they were startled to see a giant of a fellow standing before them in a menacing attitude with the drawn sword. The perpetrators expected to see Mark and Dan open fire on the intruder, but fortunately they called upon him to surrender. Giving him a chance for his life revealed that he was a stuffed dummy. Another time buckets of water doused them when they opened the

Virginia Dec 13, 1864

Clemens & Wright

To Myers & Daggett Dr

To Rent of Rooms from Oct 28, 1863 to Nov. 28, 1864 — thirteen months — 30$ pr mo. $390.00

1864   Contra —
Jan 11 Cash for Clemens $60.00
March 8   "   " Wright   75.00
July 4   "   " Wright   40.00
Aug. 31   "   " Clemens pr Sale of
           Mining Stock   25.00
                                  $200.00 $390.00
           Amount due $190.00

Room account bill of Sam Clemens and William Wright
(Dan De Quille) to Myers and Daggett
Virginia City, Nevada

door; again bells and clappers rang half the night, while rappings under their bed disturbed their slumber, until they found the secret device bound up in wires and strings.

In these quarters, the gay young reporters had the time of their lives. In later years Mark Twain said, "Those were the days. They will never come again." Such a tidal wave of gold flowed into the coffers of the paper that it seemed to run itself, and in doing so it ran everyone connected with it. "It seemed to take the lead and go right along without thought or care on the part of anyone." All Mark and Dan had to do was to pile as much news into the *Enterprise* as it could hold. Even the money to pay for the subscriptions and the advertisements besieged the office. It was so much fun that Dan said, "We went merrily along, laughing and joking and never feeling the weight of the work we were doing in the whirl and excitement of the times."

Mark Twain was what is called "high-strung" nervously, a condition which his companions delighted in torturing. The glare of the candle—he disliked to care for and to clean a coal-oil lamp—hurt his eyes; so he got an eyeshade. The boys soon learned that if they hid his candle and shade, he would fly into one of his famous rages. In looking for the lost articles he went around and around the room, cursing in a low monotone. Steve, a diminutive compositor on the paper, loved to see Mark go into one of these denunciatory spasms. Once, when Mark was well worked up over these losses and was pacing the floor muttering his anathemas, the Reverend Franklin S. Rising, "the frail, gentle, new fledgling" whom Mark described in *Roughing It* in his Buck Fanshaw episode, appeared at the door. Mark and the minister had become good friends.

Mark was not bothered one whit when he saw the clergyman, but continued cursing the thieves until he had had his say. Then, turning to the Reverend, he said: "I know, Mr. Rising, I know it is wrong. I know I shall certainly go to hell for it. But . . . I know you would say, just as I say, Mr. Rising, G——d d——n their impenitent souls, may they roast in hell for a million years."

The startled clergyman replied: "Maybe I should, Mr. Clemens, but I should try to say, 'Forgive them, Father, they know not what they do!' " [5]

Mark and Dan worked at the same felt-covered table in the office. At Mark's end of it the baize was so slashed from his repeated cutting through the paper in clipping items that there was not much left of the original cloth. Dan said that "in its place appeared what might have passed for a representation of the polar star, spiritedly darting forth a thousand rays."

Whenever Mark was bored, he "doodled." His part of reporting the news consisted of covering the school report, court actions, Coroner's juries, and the meetings of the Board of Aldermen. When a tedious debate occurred during these last, Mark frequently made sketches illustrative of the subjects and persons under discussion—usually in cartoon form.

Dan said that one in particular of Mark's drawings was most amusing. A menagerie show, having many animals, visited the Comstock. The show managers had paid one license to the Commissioners of Storey County, but the City Council wanted them to pay them a license also. When the showmen refused, the Council discussed how it could break up the performances. Mark was so amused over the discussion that he sketched the City Marshal leading away the elephant by its trunk; the Mayor was mounted on a giraffe; one policeman had a lion by the tail; another one captured a rhinoceros; while others marched away shouldering kangaroos, monkeys, and other animals. This sketch was labeled "The Captured Menagerie." After Mark brought his sketches back to the office, he kept them around and touched them up from time to time. How regrettable it is that there are none of these cartoons extant! As the Chinese proverb says, "One picture is worth ten thousand words."

Mark Twain was an inveterate smoker of cigars and of a foul-smelling pipe—the latter usually around the office. His office was just off the composing room, and although printers are not usually squeamish about such things, Mark's pipe bred a revolution. It smelled so bad that it was referred to as "The Remains" and the pipe of "a thousand smells." When the boys could stand it no longer, numerous plots were laid to get it out of the way. However, someone always stopped them because Mark's pipe was valuable, and cherished for its associations.

Because it was clear that something had to be done about the foul-smelling pipe, it was resolved—and even thought justifiable—that he be made the victim of a "pipe joke." Steve Gillis, C. A. V. Putnam, Dennis McCarthy, Dan De Quille, and several other men on the *Enterprise* framed a scheme to present Mark with an imitation meerschaum pipe. They purposely selected one which they knew he would not like on account of its shape. On its German silver mounting this inscription was engraved: "To Mark Twain, from his friends." A cherry-wood stem about a yard long and a genuine amber mouthpiece were procured; the assemblage was all wrapped up with newspaper and made ready for presentation.

It was planned to give Mark his present on a Saturday night at Henry Harris' saloon in Maguire's Opera House, a favorite meeting place for the boys after the paper was up. Charley Pope, the actor, was then playing at the Opera House. He and the *Enterprise* staff had become good friends, as the staff always did with most of the actors and actresses who played Virginia City. Because Charley was dramatic, they selected him to make the presentation speech. Since Dan was in on the joke—and no one loved one better than he —he heightened the enjoyment of it by saying to Mark a few days before the pipe was to be presented:

"Mark, I don't know that I ought to tell you, but the boys are going to make you a present of a fine meerschaum pipe next Saturday night. Charley Pope is to make the presentation speech and, as it will doubtless be rather fine, I have thought it best to post you in order that you may think up a suitable reply."

Mark thanked Dan most cordially for "giving the business away," not suspecting that the boys had made it Dan's part thus to post him in order that they might all have the fun of watching him in his effort to convey the impression that the presentation was a genuine surprise. This was really the "big sell" of the entire affair. Even Charley Pope had been told that Mark knew that he was to receive a pipe, so that the actor could enjoy the victim's pretended unawareness.

The fun began when members of the party tried to entice Mark to the Opera House saloon. Mark acted his part well; he even assumed a degree of coyness when they invited him to go with them. When the victim and all of the conspirators were assembled around the center table in one of the private parlors of the saloon, Pope entered the room carrying a bundle wrapped in newspapers—about a yard long. Advancing to the table, he proceeded to unroll the bundle. After many folds of paper had been peeled off, the ridiculous-looking pipe, with a straight bowl about five inches high and with about a yard of blue ribbon floating from the stem, was produced.

"That is a mighty fine pipe you have there, Charley," said Mark nonchalantly, in an unconcerned tone of voice.

Pope, throwing the newspapers on the floor and taking the pose as seen in the great paintings of "The Pipe of Peace," began his speech.

"Mr. Clemens, on behalf of your friends and admirers that you see here assembled and many others, I present you this magnificent meerschaum pipe as a slight etc., etc., etc. . . ." Charley went on and on for about twenty minutes, "making a really remarkable speech. In parts it was very feeling and again it was witty and jolly. Of course we applauded it from Alpha to Omega."

Then Mark arose. In his hand he held "the mighty calumet." At first he feigned embarrassment, but after a few words he regained his poise and said that he was sorry that he would be unable fittingly to reply to a speech so able and excellent as that of Mr. Pope—a speech that had touched his heart and stirred his bosom feelings. He could not find words to express them. The truth was that he had been taken by surprise; the present was entirely unexpected.

Mark, however, had to play his part for Dan's sake. He couldn't let him down when he had been so good as to "tip him off" that he was to get the pipe. He launched into what everyone knew was his prepared speech. Dan said that "it started with the introduction of tobacco into England by Sir Walter Raleigh and wound up with George Washington." Just how Mark had managed to bring George Washington into the speech Dan could not recall, but he "had him there in the windup, and showed him off to good advantage." Several times in Mark's speech the thunderous applause brought him to a pause. All the way through it he was made to feel that his acceptance speech was a great success. When he had finished, he called the bartender and ordered "Sparkling Moselle" for all hands around; and before the session was over, six bottles at five dollars a bottle had been drunk—on Mark.[6]

A day or two later one of the printers in the *Enterprise* office let the cat out of the bag by telling Mark that his pipe was only a "mere sham." Mark had suspected as much even on the night of the presentation, and was noted examining it critically—as early as the second bottle of Moselle! One day when Dan was alone in the "local room," Mark suddenly entered with the pipe in his hand. He locked the door on the inside and put the key in his pocket.

"I want to know from you now," said Mark, "whether this pipe is bogus?"

"It is just as bogus as they make them," Dan replied.

"Did you know that when you capped me into preparing a speech?"

"Certainly. That was where the fun came in."

"Et tu, Brute!" said Mark in a hollow voice Then he began to pace the floor with his head on his chest. Dan did his best to console him. He knew, he said, that the bogus pipe was to be followed by a really fine one, to be given Mark without ceremony or cost. Mark subsided, but he was by no means satisfied by the business. He *was* given a good meerschaum pipe; but in later years he said that he thought more of the bogus one than he did of the genuine.

No two men ever loved each other more than Dan and Mark did. Probably no two friends got more real pleasure out of playing jokes on each other than these two "live wires." For both pastime and pleasure Dan and Mark took fencing lessons from Professor O. V. Chauvel, who conducted a gymnasium—known as Chauvel's Fencing Club—at 12 North C Street. Chauvel was considered one of the best swordsmen on the Coast and a capable instructor. That Mark and Dan were fast becoming good fencers was noted in the *Gold Hill Daily News:*

> It would appear that our two friends, Mark Twain and Dan De Quille, have little faith in the old saying that the pen is mightier than the sword, as they are taking lessons daily in the latter weapon. It is said to be highly amusing to witness these two "roosters," they sometimes get so terribly in earnest. Then do their blades describe wicked circles, and their nostrils breathe forth wrath. We understand that Dan came out of one of these conflicts minus several buttons and one shirtsleeve, and that Twain was in an almost equally dilapidated state. We should not be surprised if they, one of these days, met with the fate of the Kilkenny cats.[7]

Although Chauvel taught fencing and the use of the broadsword, he also kept a supply of gloves for the accommodation of those sportsmen who liked boxing. Chauvel's school was frequented by the reporters and editors of the newspapers on the Lode. For an hour or two every afternoon this class of patrons took possession of the gymnasium. The men would pair off and have a good work-out with foils, broadswords, or boxing gloves.

Mark nearly always contested with the foils and became quite an expert in his *"stoccado, imbrocata, passada,"* and *"montanto."* In attack it was said that "he was fiery and particularly dangerous for the reason one could not watch his eyes." He habitually half-closed his eyes; at times, it was remarked, they resembled those of an eagle with an inner lid. In defense he was not so good, and would nearly always give ground when hotly pressed.

Boxing was a decidedly different sport from fencing—there were no rules, and the hardest hitter was generally considered the best boxer. Among the boxers at the gym was George Dawson, an Englishman, and at that time an assistant editor on the *Enterprise*. Boxing was his hobby; he prided himself upon being a hard hitter. When he could find no one to box with him, he charged viciously across the hall and hit the sandbag. Dennis McCarthy, who was tall, strong, "long in the reach," and tolerably expert at boxing, was about the only newspaperman who would tackle him. Dawson and McCarthy often boxed; sometimes their sparring reached the angry stage and wound up as a battle for blood.

One day Mark put on the gloves, more for fun than for serious boxing. In his usual playful way he began to mimic boxing motions which he had seen in exhibitions and on the stage. Soon he was capering around the hall, as if in earnest. Dawson kept his eyes on him, watching in an interrogative manner, not certain what his intentions were. Mark, in jest, squared off directly opposite Dawson and began working his right arm like the piston of a steam engine, at the same time stretching out his neck and gyrating his curly head in a very astonishing way. Dawson, taking these gestures as a direct challenge of skill, drew off, and with full force planted a heavy blow squarely upon Mark's nose. Mark was so startled at the move that he made no move to ward off the blow. So hard was he hit that he was lifted off his feet and landed across a settle that stood against the wall on one side of the hall. Dawson, flushed with victory, rushed up and began punching Mark's head, against all rules. McCarthy, Gillis, and others hauled him off and sternly rebuked him. As Mark staggered to his feet, blood spurting from his nose, he went into his usual rage and began looking for a club. He would have killed Dawson if he had been able to find anything with which to hit him.

With his hand and his handkerchief hiding his nose, Mark went to his rooms, leaving a trail of blood along his homeward route. An hour later Dan found Mark in their parlor tenderly ministering to the injured member. Every known application of drugs was employed for the purpose of reducing the swelling, but "that wronged and wounded nose refused to submit to any restraining or ameliorating influences. It was a nose that need not have quailed in the presence of old Antiochus III, that of Mohammed, the great Frederick, or Napoleon I"—moderns might add Cyrano de Bergerac!

Mark was always sensitive about his nose—now more so than ever. He would not even go to the office until it was dark, and then his disposition was bad. A printer, the gentle and amiable William Henry Deane, ventured into the local sanctum in search of copy. Staring at the inflamed organ in "big-eyed astonishment," he cried out: "Why, Mr. Clemens, what is the matter with your nose? It looks like an eggplant!"

"Get out of here, blast you, or I'll make you look like a corpse!" yelled Mark, grabbing a paperweight. "No printer has a d—n bit of right to come into this room, copy or no copy." It is needless to add that little Deane subsided quickly.

At this time the mines around Silver Mountain, near Markleeville, California, were attracting considerable attention. Joe Goodman wanted a reporter to go to this camp to write an article on the newly discovered mines. Mark volunteered to go; he wanted to get his nose out of town. Although he was very well known in Carson City, through which he had to pass, he could "smuggle it through that place" in the stage.

No sooner was Mark out of town than Dan wrote up a ridiculous article for the *Enterprise*, describing Mark's arrival at Silver Mountain. He wrote that, as the stage was entering the town, Mark was observed at the window of the coach. When the alert "suburban inhabitants caught sight of his nose," they cried out that "a freak show" was coming. At once the people of the town dropped everything and flocked about the stage, trying to peer into it as it rolled along. They asked the stage driver if the nose were natural, and where and when the show was to take place. Many boys and men ran ahead to the hotel where the stage was to stop and took up advantageous positions in order to see the "freak" when it emerged. Dan wrote that "three cheers were given as the nose was seen to come out of the stage." But the great public demonstration came when the owner of it, on his way from the coach up to the hotel, passed through a line of admiring citizens. An old lady who stood on the front of the veranda seemed quite fascinated by the phenomenal nose. As Mark passed, the old lady asked permission to touch it. Being gratified in this desire, she took off her spectacles, turned to the crowd, and said that it was the happiest moment of her life.

By the time that Mark had obtained his mining information at Silver Mountain, his nose had returned to its normal size. However, the *Enterprise* containing Dan's story had come down to Carson City, and when Mark arrived there, everyone in town was "kidding" him about his nose. He remarked afterward that all the bums in Carson had annoyed him, and he was obliged to stand treat to shut their mouths. His remark to Dan was that "it wasn't a d—n bit smart."

Mark had to go Dan one better to get revenge. His opportunity soon came. A few days after Mark returned, Dan was riding horseback. Without warning, his saddle turned, landing him on the ground and spraining his knee. That evening the knee became so painful that Dan was forced to go home and leave Mark to write up the local items.

Reporters on the Lode had learned that their readers liked horrible and shocking news. There were many shootings, accidents in the mines, and cutting affrays to set the pattern. Mark Twain delighted in writing up such items.

While Dan was home nursing his knee, Mark distorted the accident for the next morning paper. He said that Dan had been riding a "vicious Spanish horse"; that when returning from American City, "he was coming down the road at the rate of a hundred miles an hour . . . and on turning a sharp corner," found a horse standing in the road blocking his way. Dan, unable to stop his own horse, ran into the other and was "thrown three hundred yards . . . alighting on solid ground, and bursting himself open from the chin to the pit of the stomach; his head was caved in out of sight, and his hat was extracted in a bloody and damaged condition from between his lungs; he must have bounced end for end after he struck first, because it is evident he received a concussion from the rear that broke his heart; one leg was jammed up in his body nearly to his throat, and the other was so torn and mutilated that it pulled out when they attempted to lift him into the hearse . . . both arms were indiscriminately broken up until they were jointed like a bamboo; his back was considerably fractured into the shape of a rail fence. Aside from these injuries, however, he sustained no other damage."

Mark returned home after the paper had gone to press, bringing Dan an orange and a handful of cigars. The next morning, when Dan read the story of his accident in the *Enterprise,* he remarked, "Beware of Greeks bearing gifts!"

"What is it now?" rejoined Mark, trying to look innocent.

"I thought something was up last night when you were so generous with your cigars and oranges."

Mark only laughed and returned: "Now, blast you, maybe you'll hereafter let my nose alone!"

This story had more serious consequences in other parts of the country. The *Enterprise* was always sent to Dan's wife and family in West Liberty, Iowa. Before Dan could write them that the story was greatly exaggerated, the paper reached home. His wife read the shocking story, and when she came to the point where Dan's "hat was pulled out of the wreck of his liver," she burst into great grief. And not until some one of the relatives read the last line— "Our noble old friend is recovering fast, and what is left of him will be around the breweries today"—was she consoled.

As soon as Dan was on his feet and back at the office, three days later, he wrote his own version of the accident. After describing his injury, he stated that "Mark Twain, our confrere and roommate, a man whom we trusted, was our only visitor during our seclusion. We saw some actions of his that almost caused us to suspect him of contemplating treachery toward us, but it was not until we regained in some degree the use of our maimed limb that we discovered the full extent—the infamousness of this wretch's treasonable and inhuman plottings."

Dan then went on to remark that Mark had gone into mourning for him by tying on his arm a small piece of secondhand crepe he had stolen from the doorknob of the Fire Engine House, and had further taken Dan's property, consisting principally of "numerous shares in the Pewterinctum mine, and his toothbrush." Mark had also confiscated other of Dan's valuables by putting on his "only clean shirt and best socks," as well as sporting his cane and smoking his meerschaum pipe. Thus arrayed Mark had gone to the Probate

Court and prayed for letters of administration on Dan's estate. In the meantime Mark had traded Dan's boots and coat to "a nigger saloon-keeper . . . for a bottle of vile whiskey, with which he got drunk; and when the police were about to snatch him for drunkenness, he commenced blubbering, saying he was 'overcome for the untimely death of poor Dan.'"

The Comstock loved this badinage. Eagerly did the readers scan each edition of the *Enterprise* to find an item over which they could roar. Joe Goodman also liked it. He never remonstrated with the locals over their journalistic banter. Each man wrote up his items, hung them on the hook in the composing room, and forgot them. If there were serious repercussions from them, the author had to defend them himself.

Before this particular literary feud was over, Dan took another fling at Mark's proboscis. He opened this article by saying: "We may have said some harsh things of Mark Twain, but now we take them all back. We feel like weeping for him—yes, we would fall on his breast and mingle our tears with his'n. But that manly shirt front of his air now a bloody one, and his nose is swollen to such an extent that to fall on his breast would be an utter impossibility.

"Yesterday he brought back all of our things. . . . This was in the forenoon; in the afternoon . . . he took a first lesson in boxing." Dan related how Mark received a blow on the "snoot" which sent him reeling with "two bountiful streams of 'claret' spouting from his nostrils. At first his nose was smashed out till it covered nearly the whole of his face and looked like a large piece of tripe, but it was finally scraped into some resemblance of a nose, when he rushed away for surgical advice." The article closed with Mark's consideration of what was the best thing to do about his nose—now swollen "to the size of several junk bottles, a vast, inflamed, and pulpy old snoot." None of his friends recognized him. Dan could give him neither advice nor comfort. He remarked that Mark's "nose will never be a nose again. It always was somewhat lopsided; now it is a perfect lump of blubber. Since the above was in type, the doctors have decided to amputate poor Mark's smeller. A new one is to be made for him of a quarter of veal."

The *Golden Era* liked these articles, "Mark Twain and Dan De Quille, Hors de Combat," well enough to reprint them. Comstock

San F, Sept 17.

Dear Dan —

If you will buy my furniture at $55, I'll send you a bill of sale, & then you can sell it to somebody who will suit you better as a bed-fellow than Dawson.

If you consent, go to Parton & Thornburgh, Bankers, & assume a debt I owe them of $55, (provided Harry Blodgett has not already paid it,) & write me word & the bill of sale shall go up by return mail. Mr Daggett cannot prove that I owe him a cent & of course he cannot hold my furniture.

Put has gone back to Sea. Say, look in Cohen's notary book, & tell me how much money he has received from the first beginning. His book is open to inspection by anybody. All's well. Give our love to all — Joe & Dennis. I don't work after 6 in the evening now on the "Call." I got disgusted with night work. Yr old friend

Sam L. Clemens

COPY OF LETTER MARK WROTE TO DAN CONCERNING THEIR FURNITURE
IN VIRGINIA CITY, SEPTEMBER 17, 1864

OVERLAND STAGE ARRIVES IN CARSON CITY, 1863

ORION CLEMENS' HOME, CORNER SPEAR AND DIVISION STREETS, CARSON CITY, NEVADA

humor had seized the Pacific Coast. Items of this kind were copied in most of the leading papers, and Mark Twain was fast becoming the sensation of the age.

Mark Twain and Dan De Quille lived together at 25 North B Street until May 28, 1864, when Mark fled from the law.

17

A SENSATIONAL TRIUMPH

OPHIR! GOULD AND CURRY! JULIA! LADY BRYAN! Wide West! Potosi and Chollar! Queen of Sheba! Everyone was buying Washoe stocks. Frantic buyers and sellers hung around the San Francisco Mining Exchange and the three exchanges in Virginia City in 1863. Purchasers never saw the mine into which they were buying—they knew nothing about its value or worthlessness. It was a mad scramble to buy something that someone else was buying. The gold rush to California brought dozens of speculators, brokers, and mine boosters to the West. They knew how to arouse and to excite the public. California had been played out—many strikes like Fraser River and Gold Lake had been fakes. Washoe was a new field—and silver had not been the California craze. They all rolled up Mount Davidson; it was a magnet that attracted these parasites.

The mad, delirious public went insane when a number of "phony" mines "cooked dividends." These payments went to the favored few on the inside—the result was that the stock went sky-high and the wise boys unloaded on the gullible, unsuspecting public. The practice of salting a mine became common. Endless stories could be related, but the best tale is about the "North Ophir," a remote extension of the rich original Ophir. The only resemblance between the two mines was in the name. The North Ophir organized, and the usual publicity of its wonders made it talked about by everyone.

The most startling claim that the owners of the North Ophir made was the discovery of perfectly "pure silver in small, solid lumps in a shaft six or eight feet deep." A vein of dull, yellowish, unpromising-appearing ore showed up in the bottom of the shaft. When Mark Twain heard about the strike, he, too, went up to take a look at the North Ophir. Given some of the ore, he got out a pan and washed it in a puddle. To his amazement there were "half a dozen black bullet-looking pellets of unimpeachable native silver. Nobody had ever heard of such a thing before; science could not account for such a queer novelty. The stock rose to sixty-five dol-

San Francisco goes Washoe

From Browne's *A Peep at Washoe*

lars a foot. . . . And then it transpired that the mine had been salted . . . in a singularly bold, barefaced, and peculiarly outrageous fashion. On one of the lumps of 'native silver' was discovered the legend '—ted States of,' and then it was plainly apparent that the mine had been salted with melted half dollars." [1]

The hoax-makers had blackened the melted silver half dollars until they looked like native silver, after which they were thrown into the shaft and mixed with the scattered rubbish. As soon as the fraud was discovered, the price of the stock fell at once to nothing a foot. However, this flagrantly salted mine did not deter the public from buying into other salted mines and fabricated ledges. There was such a flood of gambling money that it enabled the gamblers and brokers to "rig" the market and "clean up" on the public through selling their stocks, stimulated by bonanza reports.

That Mark Twain had shares in these salted mines may be assumed. Everyone did, and almost everyone lived to regret his investment. Many certificates were given to reporters for favorable "write-ups" in the mining news. Mark told chuckling how he and Dan wrote up their mining news: The new claim owners went straight to the newspaper office and gave the reporters feet, expecting a good boost. It did not matter what was said, as long as they said something. Consequently they invented every conceivable way of describing a new claim without committing themselves too much. About one they said the "ore resembled the Comstock" and that "indications were good." If the ore were promising, they "used strong adjectives and frothed at the mouth" about it. If a mine were a developed one with no pay ore as yet uncovered, they "praised the tunnel; said it was one of the most infatuating tunnels in the land; driveled and driveled about the tunnel until" [2] they ran out of ecstasies—but never a word was said about the rock. Columns of this stuff were in every mining paper. The gullible public swallowed it and bought the stock. It was reported in San Francisco that a man had been found starved to death, holding a quantity of Washoe stocks.

This frenzy had set Mark Twain to thinking. The San Francisco papers warned the public against these bogus schemes and advised it to buy sound California stocks. Still the public did not heed.

Mark decided to shock the people back to normalcy with a

Stock brokers examine Washoe mining claims

Original sketch by J. Ross Browne

sensational story, in the fall of 1863. Various names have been given to this satire: "Empire City Massacre," [3] "My Bloody Massacre," and "The Latest Sensation." Even in this early part of his career he took an unfailing stand for human justice. In this satire he could help the public and at the same time rid himself of several grudges that he had of late been nursing. Since his articles were unsuppressed, unexpurgated, and unedited, he dared write whatever he pleased.

Mark Twain said that "in my self-complacent simplicity, I felt that the time had arrived for me to rise up and be a reformer." Being a loyal Nevadan, any sneering reference to that Territory by a San Francisco newspaper got an instant reply from an indignant Mark. Although it was apparently simple for him to shift his loyalty, he wrote: "How I hate everything that looks or tastes or smells like California!"

At this particular moment the San Francisco papers were making a great "to do" about the fact that the Daney Silver Mining Company of Nevada had declared a "cooked" or false dividend. In exposing the machinations of this company, the California papers urged the public to sell all their Comstock shares and to invest in "sound and safe San Francisco stocks," giving as an example the Spring Valley Water Company. At the time that the San Francisco papers gave this advice, they were not aware that the Spring Valley Water Company was about to spring the same fraud: "cook" a dividend. Mark Twain "stole upon the public unawares" with a scathing rebuke of this vicious system.

By pure invention Mark contrived the most ridiculous and gory massacre that any human mind could concoct, set it up with real people and well-known places, and published it in the *Territorial Enterprise*. He laid the setting of the gruesome story between Dutch Nick's, a saloon owned by Nicholas Ambrosia in Empire City, and Empire City. This incongruity was expressly used to make the story absurd. Everyone knew that Dutch Nick's and Empire City were one and the same; everyone stopped at this favorite drinking place on the road to Virginia City. The owner was universally liked. He had great hopes for Empire—back of his bar he had drawn the way the future city would look. There were sketches of large buildings, dwellings, and a church with a high steeple.

The narrator of the particulars was no less a person than Abram V. Z. Curry ("Old Curry, Abe Curry, Old Abe Curry"), who was now the warden of the Territorial Penitentiary situated a few miles from Empire City. Abe, of course, still maintained his profitable hotel, in which he operated a bar of which he was very proud. There was considerable rivalry between the hosts of the two places. Mark probably thought it a great joke to have Curry tell this story as taking place at Dutch Nick's.

Curry's tale was about a bachelor by the name of "P. Hopkins or Philip Hopkins" living with his wife and nine children in "the old log house just on the edge of the great pine forest." Hopkins, whose wife had purportedly observed his deranged mental condition and expressed her fears to persons in Carson City, went berserk and killed his wife and seven children with an axe, a knife, and a club. The other two children, Julia and Emma, were desperately injured. He scalped his red-headed wife, severed her head from her body, cut his own throat from ear to ear; then, taking her scalp, he dashed into Carson City on horseback and "fell in a dying condition in front of the Magnolia saloon. Hopkins expired in the course of five minutes, without speaking a word. The long red hair of the scalp he bore marked it as that of Mrs. Hopkins. A number of citizens, headed by Sheriff Gasherie, mounted at once and rode down to Hopkins' house, where a ghastly scene met their gaze." And with studied detail Mark pictured the house full of blood, and brains, and minutely described the instruments with which the outrages had been committed.

"Curry says Hopkins was about forty-two years of age, and a native of western Pennsylvania; he was always affable and polite, and until very recently we had never heard of his ill-treating his family. He had been a heavy owner in the best mines of Virginia and Gold Hill, but when the San Francisco papers exposed the game of cooking dividends in order to bolster up our stocks, he grew afraid and sold out, and invested to an immense amount in the Spring Valley Water Company of San Francisco. He was advised to do this by a relative of his, one of the editors of the San Francisco *Bulletin,* who had suffered pecuniarily by the dividend cooking system as applied to the Daney Mining Company. . . . It is presumed that this misfortune drove him mad and resulted in his killing his family."

Mark made the details so vividly and conscientiously interesting that the readers failed to note the inconsistencies. They did not note that P. Hopkins was a bachelor who everyone knew had no wife and no children. Besides, there was no pine forest at Empire City, nor one any closer than Lake Tahoe, fifteen miles away. Mark thought that surely everyone would perceive the story to be a hoax when he said that Hopkins had cut his throat from ear to ear and had ridden four miles in that condition.

All through the story one could see Mark's desire to take a "crack" at several individuals. For some reason better known to himself, he disliked Hopkins, the owner of the Magnolia Saloon in Carson City. He sold "forty-rod whiskey," so called because it was guaranteed to kill at that distance. "Tarantula juice" was the favorite local name for it. It was said to make the tarantulas and snakes sick when they bit the boys "well charged with this whiskey." A. G. Gasherie, the Sheriff of Ormsby, who mounted and rode to the scene of the crime, had not forwarded the commission Mark so badly wanted when he was out of a job in Aurora. After disposing of the people he wanted to "dig," he slammed at the San Francisco papers that had kept silent about the Spring Valley Water Company's "borrowing money and cooking dividends. . . ."

The story was published in the *Enterprise* on the morning of October 28. The editors of the Gold Hill *Daily News* read the item, failed to detect the absurdities, and got out an extra issue of this paper to republish the sensational incident. This paper commented: "Horrible—the most sickening tale of horror that we have read for years is told in the *Enterprise* of this morning; and were it not for the respectable source from which our contemporary received it, we would refuse it any credence . . . and from our limited space we are compelled to condense it."

As soon as the *Enterprise* and the *Daily News* were distributed to their readers, people began to flock to the newspaper offices to find out more about the horror. Mark said that "in all my life I never saw anything like the sensation that little satire created. It was the talk of the town; it was the talk of the Territory." He might have added "the talk of the papers all over the Coast." So badly was the public fooled by it that Mark had to put it right the next day by publishing a signed statement:

"I take it all back.
  Mark Twain"

The Virginia *Evening Bulletin* was not fooled. The editor of this paper was angry and disgusted. He wrote a scathing rebuke of it in the paper which came out that evening:

A SENSATIONAL ITEM

The *Enterprise* this morning contains a sensational item of the most extravagantly sensational order, referring to a bloody massacre, in which the full particulars of the murder of a whole family, a mother and nine children, and the suicide of the husband and father, who was represented as being the murderer, are given in labored detail. Now we go in for any and all men writing for the press drawing on their imaginations—when they have any—but we are not an admirer of foundationless yarns full of horror, and which by mentioning names and localities, may do much injury without a probability of doing any good.

In matters of fun, or for the purpose of "pointing a moral," we would grant every license to the imagination of a scribe, but in matters that affect the character of a community or an individual, truth is an indispensable necessity. Now in the item referred to, there is not a particle of truth, but unfortunately people at a distance may not be able to detect the self-contradictions that are all through this extraordinary item, and will probably consider this wholesale murder as an "o'er true tale." God knows our Territory has a reputation of being the theatre of scenes of blood and violence that really do occur bad enough to satisfy our bitterest enemies. There does not exist any need to paint our characters any blacker than they really are. Those who have been in this Territory will well know that Dutch Nick's and Empire City are one and the same place, and that there is no pine forest within many miles of that place, nor is there any log cabin, nor any family of nine children of the name of Hopkins living there, or ever did live there. The whole story is baseless as the fabric of a dream.

On October 29, the Gold Hill *Daily News* printed a sizzling rebuke for being sold. It headed the article "That 'Sell' ":

The horrible story of a murder which was yesterday copied in good faith from the *Enterprise* turns out to be a mere "witticism" of Mark Twain. In short a lie—utterly baseless, and without a shadow of foundation. The *Enterprise* is the pioneer newspaper of the Territory, more widely read and known than any other, and having been ably and respectably conducted has heretofore been considered a reliable medium of information. The terrible tale related in its columns yesterday, and copied into ours, was believed true, and will be believed elsewhere— wherever *The News* and *Enterprise* are read. It will be read with sickening horror, and the already bloody reputation of our Territory will receive another smear. When the readers of the soul-sickening story are informed that it was a mere bubble of "wit," they will feel relieved, although they may utterly fail to see the humor of "the point"!

Mark Twain seemed to revel in the way in which he had fooled the public. In his *Sketches New and Old* he related that "few people who could read took food that morning" when the article was published. He and Dan went to breakfast in the Eagle Restaurant; they noticed "two stalwart innocents with that sort of vegetable dandruff about their clothing which was the sign and evidence that they were in from the Truckee with a load of hay." Mark noted that the farmer facing him had the paper folded into a long narrow strip, and that it was the story of his "pleasant financial satire." From the way the farmer was reading the article, it was evident that he was skipping along to reach the gory details as fast as possible, missing the inconsistent points. "Presently his eyes spread wide open, just as his jaws swung asunder to take a potato approaching it on a fork; the potato halted, the face lit up redly, and the whole man was on fire with excitement. Then he broke into a disjointed checking-off of the particulars—his potato cooling in mid-air meantime, and his mouth making a reach for it occasionally, but always bringing up suddenly against a new and still more direful performance of my hero. At last he looked his stunned and rigid comrade impressively in the face, and said, with an expression of concentrated awe: 'Jim, he b'iled his baby, and he took the old woman's skelp. Cuss'd if *I* want any breakfast!' And he laid his lingering potato reverently down, and he and his friend departed from the restaurant empty but satisfied."

When the California papers saw that the "Sensational Satire" was a hoax and that they had been duped, "there was a howl from Siskiyou to San Diego. Some papers demanded the immediate discharge of the author of the item by the *Enterprise* proprietors. They said they would never quote another line from that paper while the reporter who wrote the shocking item remained on its force." All of these remarks worried Mark. Finally he told Dan: "I am being burned alive on both sides of the mountains."

Dan described how Mark felt about these persecutions and related that when they were the worst, he could not sleep. "He tossed, tumbled, and groaned aloud." Dan tried to comfort him. "Mark," said Dan, "never mind the bit of a gale; it will soon blow itself out. This item of yours will be remembered and talked about when all your other work is forgotten. The murder at Dutch Nick's will be quoted years from now as the big sell of these times."

"I believe you are right," replied Mark. "I remember I once did a thing in Missouri, was caught at it, and worried almost to death." He then went on to tell how, when he was attending school in a small town, he had taken part in an escapade. He did not return to that village for three years and, when he did, he was remembered as "the boy who played the trick on the schoolmaster." "He began to laugh and to relax; from that moment he was no longer worried over the results of the satire." But today not one man in a hundred remembers anything written by Mark Twain while he was on the *Enterprise* except the shocking murder at Dutch Nick's.

Although Mark was relieved by Dan's comforting words, he was still concerned about what Joe Goodman thought of the criticisms that the *Enterprise* was getting. He sought an interview with him.

"I'm going back to Aurora. I'm not giving value received," said Mark. "About once a week, I write something worth reading," he continued.

"Admitted," replied Goodman. "But that '*something*' keeps the boys hunting the columns of the *Enterprise* every day until you hit it right again."

"I'll never make a writer," countered Mark.

"You're already one," comforted Goodman.

Some critics said that Mark never intended to quit his job. He merely wanted to find out Joe's real opinion of him as a writer. Mark stayed on as local reporter on the *Enterprise*.

All of these annoyances out of the way, Mark began to enjoy his new notoriety. In an article in the Virginia *Evening Bulletin* of October 30, entitled "A Peculiar Taste," this paper chided him:

The local of the *Enterprise,* after setting the minds of the community in a blaze of indignation by publishing a miserable hoax, says this morning with the greatest *sangfroid,* that he "sits in the shelter and looks out on the storm" which his scandalous hoax has created, "without a pang of remorse."

That fellow's heart must be as callous to all nobler feelings of our nature, as the throat of a whiskey guzzler is to the sense of burning. No remorse for outraging a whole community! And oh! shame, where are thy blushes, that thou tenderest them not to this miserable creature, who actually glories in his deeds, counts them famous, because, forsooth, he—little he—by—what shall we call it, if we didn't say lying?—has set the whole community in an uproar. History publishes but one parallel of a being seeking notoriety, under something similar circumstances, and that is the wretch who destroyed the temple of Diana at Ephesus, in the vain hope of handing his name down to posterity; but the poor fool though he accomplished his infamous purpose, yet failed of his object, for his name has been forgotten for untold ages. So, the author of this hoax, though he has accomplished much to destroy the temple of the fame of the community will himself be forgotten, while Virginia's fame will extend "wide as the poles asunder." It shows a very peculiar taste indeed in one whose feelings would appear to be seared as with a hot iron against all human sympathy to appeal to those whom he has deceived by the allusion to those very feelings he is so evidently destitute of. For him to complain of having his deeds published in 'small caps' badly as he did to the Gold Hill *News* is absurd.

He would have no cause to complain if that paper had recorded in "full-face pica," for it was fooled bad enough to excuse even that sized type to record its folly. And it is an exhibition of even worse taste to suppose that because his contemporaries exposed the malicious hoax, that they did so to injure the *Enterprise* for their advantage. The measuring of the motives of others by our own standard is in his case most unfair. And it exhibits a peculiar taste to coin new terms to abuse those on whom his taunts fall as harmless as do Minié balls on the louvers of a Monitor. The calling of us an "oyster-brained idiot" harms not us, for who can believe anything said by the author of such a hoax as he perpetrated? Were we to retort and say that there is a great difference between an oyster-brained individual and the substance usually employed to hold the materials of a sausage together, doubtless many persons would see the application, but we shall not do so; we shall leave the ambitious scribe to enjoy his peculiar tastes "all alone in his glory," and to the tender mercies of the local of the Gold Hill *News,* who, if he does not give him—Dixie, deserves to be fooled worse than he was this time.

As long as Mark Twain remained in the Territory of Nevada, he was unable to live down the hoax that he had perpetrated on the public. Whenever his name was mentioned in another paper, it brought up something about "My Bloody Massacre."

In the Virginia *Evening Bulletin* of October 31, the editor commiserated with Mark and gave him some solemn and sound advice:

POOR WRETCH, WE PITY HIM

That unhappy mortal, the local of the *Enterprise,* appears to be in a terrible agony at the castigation which he is receiving for the sin he committed in publishing that rascally hoax. Out of pity for the poor wretch's misery, we will not retort upon him and as a mark of the profundity of our pity for his sufferings, we advise him to depart in peace and sin no more. If he will drop that sin of—well, we won't name it—that doth so easily beset him, and leave off going to Chinatown, stop drinking whiskey, pay his washerwoman, get up early in the morning by going to bed early, and not make hideous by howling his sorrows to the winds, he may yet become a partially decent member of society.

"For while the lamp holds out to burn,
The vilest sinner may return."

The same paper dug in after him when he lost a good item to his competitor:

MARK TWAIN

We have always given you the credit of being the best-tempered and most amiable man under the sun, but we find we have been mistaken, for you came out this morning "boiling with rage." We knew you had a splendid item written on those blood-red stains of which we made mention yesterday; but, then, we had a duty to perform, and for the sake of sparing *you,* we could not allow a good opportunity to go by ourselves. Besides, if you did lose one good item, did we not furnish you with a dozen better ones? The night we saw you coming in from Chinatown, with a "feather in your cap" (?), we supposed you had turned Pah-Ute, but we did not imagine you would soon take to the scalping-knife.

Through the years, the "Empire City Massacre" received some editorial changes from the first time it appeared in the *Enterprise* on October 27, 1863. Besides the title changes, other text changes were made. In the *Galaxy* in June, 1870, Hopkins' family was living "in his splendid dressed-stone mansion." Mark went on to comment that "Even the very pickled oysters that came on our tables knew that there was not a 'dressed-stone mansion' in all Nevada Territory." In this comment Mark Twain was entirely wrong. One of the most beautiful "dressed-stone mansions" was constructed in Washoe Valley ten miles north of Carson City in 1863 by Sandy and Eilley Bowers. Not only was the stone in this large house perfectly dressed by stone masons imported from Scotland, but the house itself and its furnishings could have graced Nob Hill, San Francisco, or Fifth Avenue, New York.

The Dutch Nick story was indeed a triumph. It took a dramatic tragedy to get the San Francisco papers *to print the truth.* As for Mark Twain, he had freed himself of a lot of personal grudges; he had exposed the diabolical practice of salting mines and cooking dividends; and he had gone through his own Gethsemane. From this time forward, he struck out boldly and fearlessly when he wanted to take a stand for human justice.

18

GOVERNOR MARK TWAIN

THE BLOODY MASSACRE SENSATION HAD SCARCELY faded out when Mark Twain was to have another triumph. Politics had sizzled in the Territory of Nevada ever since Governor Nye had returned from the national capital successful in convincing the Congress that Nevada should be given statehood. Since the Union party was the only political party of any consequence in Nevada, contests arose within this organization. As a prelude to the Constitutional Convention of 1863, bitter feuds developed in this party in Virginia City. The fight culminated in the editorial rivalry between the Virginia City *Union* and the *Territorial Enterprise*.

Tom Fitch of the *Union,* ambitious politically, bolted the Union party meeting in Virginia City, and later, when he had not been allowed to sit in the Convention, he became abusive in his editorials. Bill Stewart and Sandy Baldwin did the same in expressing their ideas through the *Enterprise*. The latter paper roasted Fitch unmercifully. When the editorial, a composite one written by the reportorial staff, appeared in that paper, Goodman told Fitch that if he were a man, an article of that nature should not go unchallenged. Although Goodman had not written the diatribe, he saw it in proof. His staff, however, assured him that if there were any fighting to be done, they would jointly take care of any challenge which Fitch might send.

The *Enterprise* was published on the morning of September 27, 1863; before the members of the staff could get to their breakfast, Fitch had his challenge in the paper. The avenger sent a formal document worded in correct challenging vernacular: The dueling ground was Ingraham's Ranch in Stampede Valley; the time was nine o'clock in the morning on September 28; the dueling weapons —five-shooters—were to be handed to the duelists by their seconds. After that they were to separate ten paces and at a given signal begin firing at will. Major George Ferrand and Cyrus Brown were "friends" for Goodman; Captain Roe and Captain Fleeson acted as seconds for Fitch.

The locations of dueling contests had to be kept quiet lest the officers prevent their taking place. About one hundred people were up bright and early to follow the principals to the field of combat, some of the spectators going on horseback. Mark Twain was one of these. He and "Young" Wilson hired the fastest riding horses in the town and followed the duelists "at the rate of a mile a minute, since when, being neither iron-clad, nor even half-soled," they "enjoyed more real comfort in standing up than sitting down." It was said that there wasn't a saddle horse left in Virginia City that day—all of them had been hired to go to the duel.

It had been rumored around the Comstock that Goodman had stated he would not fire to hit Fitch above the hips. At the first round, Goodman got the drop on Fitch and sent a ball into his leg. When it struck him, he fell to the ground and Goodman, thinking that he was dangerously, if not mortally wounded, hastily left the field. It was believed that the real reason for the rush was the sight of a stage coming down the hill toward them. Thinking that it contained a sheriff's posse to arrest them, they all departed as quickly as possible.

Whatever may have been the cause of their haste, the Goodman party left without stopping to inquire whether or not the wounded man was killed, or if he were satisfied with the proceedings. After the surgeon had dressed his wound, Fitch arose from the ground and walked to his carriage. It was found that the ball had entered the knee. He was then driven to the Ingraham ranch house, where he remained until he had recovered from the shock. Goodman's party arrived in Virginia City ahead of the stage, which turned out to be from California. The Fitch party came into town at 3:30 o'clock in the afternoon. The wound laid Fitch up for several weeks; and when he finally got out to walk, he had a limp which he carried for the rest of his life. The chief result of the duel was the mutual respect which each editor gained for the other. The two duelists were satisfied, and emerged from the fracas good friends.

The Goodman faction of the Union party sent its delegates to the Constitutional Convention, which was called together in the Masonic Hall in Carson City on October 26. Again Joe Goodman sent Mark Twain to report the proceedings. Mark wrote long

SAMUEL LANGHORNE CLEMENS, 1863
Dan De Quille's favorite of Mark Twain

Courtesy of Irma Wright Morris,
granddaughter of De Quille

MEMBERS OF THE THIRD HOUSE
"Governor" Mark Twain is number five

THE BIBLE GIVEN IN MEMORY OF JANE ("JENNIE") CLEMENS, DAUGHTER OF ORION AND MOLLIE CLEMENS. *Right,* GRAVE OF JENNIE CLEMENS, LONE MOUNTAIN CEMETERY, CARSON CITY

Presented to the 1st Presbyterian church
Carson City, Nevada.

A Memorial
of
Miss Jennie Clemens.

Miss Jennie died February, 1864. Afterwards, it was learned that she had been saving her money to buy a pulpit Bible for the new church. She was ten years of age, and was laid to rest in Lone Mountain cemetery.

DEDICATORY PAGE OF
THE BIBLE ABOVE

articles on the discussions, which were copied in full from the *Enterprise* into the other papers of the Territory. These reports were excellently given. Mark had now begun to make comments on measures adopted and discussions which took place. Politicians, ambitious for favorable mention, sought Mark's friendship. His opinions carried weight and his approval was eagerly sought.

The most controversial subject of the Convention during the framing of the constitution was taxation. Since there were few other industries in Nevada, little agriculture, and only a scattering of settlements, the burden of carrying the financial load of statehood was placed on the mines. Bill Stewart, a member of the Convention and at the same time legal counsel for the largest mines on the Lode, tried to have the tax clauses amended, but he was voted down. He knew that if the development and bed-rock workings were taxed, many of the mines would have to close. During the discussion he made long and boring speeches extolling the virtues of the poor hard-working miner. However, he had other and more sinister reasons for opposing this provision: Bill wanted to be United States Senator. Since the Organic Act had provided that the new officers be elected at the time the voters considered the constitution and Bill was not on the ticket, he wanted *this* constitution defeated.

The Constitutional Convention completed its work at eleven o'clock on the night of December 13. Immediately after the adjournment a "Third House" was organized, a burlesque meeting regularly held in California since 1851. Mark Twain was unanimously elected the President and received the honorary title of "Governor of the Third House." In his own "phonographic report in short-hand," an account of the proceedings has been preserved.[1]

On motion of Mr. A. W. Nightingill, "the rules were suspended and the usual prayer dispensed with, on the ground that it was never listened to by the members of the First House." As soon as Mark was elected, he was conducted to the Chair by James W. Small and William B. Hickok amid a dense and respectful silence, "the former stepping grandly over the desks, the latter walking under them." Governor Twain then delivered his inaugural address:

"Gentlemen: This is the proudest moment of my life. I shall always think so. I think so still. I shall ponder over it with unspeakable emotion down to the latest syllable of recorded time. It shall be my earnest endeavor to give entire satisfaction in the high and bully position to which you have elevated me."

The Governor then appointed the officers for the session and administered the oath to them:

"We do solemnly affirm that we have never seen a duel, never been connected with a duel, never heard of a duel, never sent or received a challenge, never fought a duel, and don't want to. . . ."

The most humorous part of the Third House proceedings was Mark Twain's rulings as presiding officer. By this time he had mastered Jefferson's *Manual*. No longer could anyone poke fun at him as the Unreliable had done when he reported his first legislative session.

When Samuel Youngs tried to speak and had some difficulty in getting his words out, Governor Mark admonished him: "Mr. Youngs, if you have got anything to say, say it, and don't stand there and shake your head and gasp, 'I—ah, I—ah,' as you have been in the habit of doing in the former Convention."

The Governor reported that Mr. Youngs said:

" 'Well, sir, I was only going to say that I liked your inaugural, and I perfectly agree with the sentiments you appeared to express in it, but I didn't rightly understand what——'

"The President: 'You have been sitting there for thirty days like a bump on a log, and you never rightly understand anything. Take your seat, sir; you are out of order. You rose for information. Well, you'll get it—sit down. You will appeal from the decision of the Chair? Take your seat, sir; the Chair will entertain no appeals from its decisions. And I would suggest to you, sir, that you will not be permitted, here, to growl in your seat, and make malicious side remarks in an undertone, for fifteen minutes after you have been called to order, as you have habitually done in the other House.' "

The Governor had considerable difficulty in keeping his unruly House in order and when Mr. Youngs insisted that Jefferson's *Manual* be referred to, the Governor exploded: "D—n Jefferson's *Manual*! The Chair will transact in its own way, sir."

Finally Bill Stewart got the floor and began his long harangue about the poor miner. Addressing the Chair, he began: "Mr. President, I insist upon it, that if you tax the mines, you impose a burden upon the people which will be heavier than they can bear. And when you tax the poor miner's shafts, and drifts, and bed-rock tunnels, you are taxing his property; you are not taxing his substance; you are not taxing his wealth—no, but you are taxing what may become property someday, or may not. . . . In a word, sir, you are taxing his hopes; taxing the aspirations of his soul; taxing the yearnings of his heart of hearts!" When Stewart's ravings threatened to go on *ad infinitum,* the presiding officer could stand it no longer:

"Take your seat, Bill Stewart! I am not going to sit here and listen to that same old song over and over again. I have been reporting and reporting that infernal speech for the last thirty days, and I want you to understand that you can't play it off on this Convention any more. When I want it, I will remember it myself— I know it by heart, anyhow. . . . If you can't add something fresh to it or say it backwards, or sing it to a new tune, you have simply got to simmer down for a while."

Other members of the Third House tried to get the floor in order to talk on taxation, and were "sat on." The Governor completely unnerved Mr. James H. Ralston when he arose to speak:

"Tax! Take your seat, sir, take your seat. I will *not* be bully-ragged to death with this threadbare subject of taxation. You are out of order, anyhow. How do you suppose anybody can listen in any comfort to your speech, when you are fumbling with your coat all the time you are talking, and trying to button it with your left hand, when you know you can't do it? I have never seen you succeed yet, until just as you get the last word out. And then the moment you sit down you always unbutton it again. You may speak, hereafter, Mr. Ralston, but I want you to understand that you have got to button your coat before you get up. I do not mean to be kept in hot water all the time by your oratorical eccentricities."

The Convention proceeded with members trying to speak on Reese River quartz mills, railroads, and free religion. Every one of them was ruled down because he knew little about the subject on which he wished to speak.

The members of the First House having been duly ridiculed, the Governor adjourned the Third House.

"Gentlemen: Your proceedings have been exactly similar to those of the Convention which preceded you. You have considered a subject which you knew nothing about; spoken on every subject but the one before the House, and voted, without knowing what you were voting for, or having any idea what would be the general result of your action. I will adjourn the Convention for an hour, on account of my cold, to the end that I may apply the remedy prescribed for it by Dr. [A. W.] Tjader—the same being gin and molasses. The Chief Page is hereby instructed to provide a spoonful of molasses, and a gallon of gin for the use of the President."

Mark Twain had added another laurel to his rapid accumulation of honors. It was Governor Twain after this meeting, a title which he accepted with pleasure. Following the adjournment of the meeting of the Third House, he returned to Virginia City, where he, Dan, and Artemus Ward had three weeks of unconfined celebrations. This new association gave him a new outlook on the future. He was assured that he was a success as a writer and that soon his articles would be copied in Eastern journals.

Shortly after his return to Virginia City, however, he had once more to return to Carson City to report the proceedings of the regular Territorial legislature of 1864. While this session was in progress, the Presbyterian congregation began raising funds for a church. Orion had become a trustee of this church soon after he arrived in Nevada in 1861; and Mollie and Jennie had been active in its affairs after they came out to live in Carson City the following year. Little Jennie learned that there was no pulpit Bible and began saving her money to buy one. On January 23, 1864, the trustees asked Mark to assist them in a benefit for their church. The request was printed in the Carson City *Independent*:

Governor Mark Twain:
Understanding from certain members of the Third House of the Territorial Legislature that that body will have effected a permanent organization within a day or two, and be ready for the reception of your Third Annual Message, we desire to ask your permission, and that of the Third House, to turn the affair to the benefit of the Church by charging toll road fran-

chises, and other persons, a dollar apiece for the privilege of listening to your communication.

S. Pixley
G. A. Sears
Trustees

Mark Twain answered the request the same day:

Carson
January 23, 1864

Gentlemen:

Certainly. If the public can find anything in a grave state paper worth paying a dollar for, I am willing they should pay that amount or any other. And although I am not a very dusty Christian myself, I take an absorbing interest in religious affairs, and would willingly inflict my annual message upon the church itself if it derive benefit thereby. You can charge what you please, and I promise the public no amusement but I do promise a reasonable amount of instruction. I am responsible to the Third House only and I hope to be permitted to make it exceedingly hot for that body, without caring whether the sympathies of the public and the Church be enlisted in their favor and against me or not.

Respectfully,

Mark Twain

On Monday before the lecture took place, Mark said to a reporter: "You, these fellows want me to deliver a lecture here, for the benefit of the new church. Now if you will work into my hand, we can make a devilish good thing of it. I want you to be doorkeeper, and corral all the filthy lucre, d'ye see. After the performance is over, we will divide—and now understand—we don't let a single 'damn'd Bohemian' in, unless he 'plunges—produces—as it were.'" The lecture was given in the district courtroom of the Ormsby County Courthouse on Wednesday. No account was left of how many attended the lecture or how much money was taken in.

Just one week later, on February 1, Jennie Clemens died of spotted fever. She was only ten years old, a bright and lovely child. Mark was living with Orion and Mollie when Jennie was stricken with this dread mountain disease. Nothing could be done for her, but Mark was consolation to them as he sat with his brother and sister-in-law until the life of their only child had ebbed away. She was buried on February 3, at ten o'clock in the morning. The Territorial legislature adjourned to attend the funeral in a body. When it was learned that Jennie had been saving her money for a Bible for the church, a handsome one was purchased and presented to the church. It has been used continuously ever since she passed away in 1864. The dedicatory page reads:

Presented to the First Presbyterian Church
           Carson City, Nevada
A Memorial
    of
Miss Jennie Clemens
Miss Clemens died February, 1864

(Afterwards it was learned that she had been saving her money to buy a pulpit Bible for the new church. She was ten years of age, and was laid to rest in Lone Mountain Cemetery, Carson City.)

Abe Curry had a stone cut from his quarry for Jennie's grave. It is indeed a lonely grave on Lone Mountain.

When the Constitution of 1863 and the ticket of State officers were submitted to the people, a bitter campaign was waged to defeat them. Bill Stewart and Sandy Baldwin, both ambitious office-seekers, closed their law offices in Virginia City to tour the Territory against them. They traveled to every community and mining camp to raise their voices in protest of a constitution that taxed the "poor miner's shafts, drifts, and bed-rock tunnels." Through the efforts of these two lawyers, aided by an aggressive press, the defeat of the Constitution was overwhelming.

The summer of 1864 looked exceedingly dark for the Union forces. Lincoln himself, in mid-August, thought it "extremely probable" that his administraton would go down to defeat under the repeated military failures. To preserve Republican control of the Congress and to return Abraham Lincoln to the White House, every Republican vote had to be obtained. There were a possible three votes from Nevada for the adoption of the Thirteenth Amendment, also. The people of Nevada wanted statehood with an acceptable constitution—then they could get rid of the Brigade and its corrupt politicians.

Within twenty days another effort was made to give the Territory of Nevada a chance to become a State. There were too many reasons why it should not be allowed to continue in the Territorial status longer. Local reasons furnished the driving force: there were the disappointed office-seekers to push it, and the corruption of the Territorial judiciary was reaching alarming proportions. The people wanted officers whom they could elect themselves; they were through with the Brigade. The Civil War created a need for another State, and the Republican party wanted to have loyal representatives in Congress to keep that party in power. The mining companies were apprehensive about the titles to their mines. Smart Nevada delegates to Congress could get laws passed to recognize the miners' locations on the public domain. Governor Nye again went to Washington to see that the proper legislation for another Organic Act for Nevada was passed.

To obtain publicity in the most powerful political organ in the Territory, the *Territorial Enterprise,* Mark Twain's favor was eagerly sought by ambitious office-seekers. As a means of assuring themselves of his good will, Sandy Baldwin and Theodore Winters, both wanting a national job, gave Mark a handsome gold watch inscribed "To Governor Mark Twain." In those days of one-pound watches, not only was it a manifestation of affection, but it was expensive as well. It cost $200.

Mark continued his reporting of the legislature of 1864 with discerning watchfulness. His editorials were barbed. When a bill needed to be defeated, he lashed out against it; when the act was a momentous one, he was moved to write a satire on it.

Such was the case when the legislature passed a law restricting the number of notaries whom Governor Nye could appoint. There were many who sought appointment to this lucrative position— lucrative, indeed, because of the sale of thousands of shares of stock a day and the requirement that each transfer must be notarized, with a fee for each name in the transaction. Dozens of persons held these appointments, and there were prothonotaries to be appointed, too. To burlesque the way in which these positions were obtained, Mark wrote the sketch "Concerning Notaries" soon after the law was passed. Just what day it appeared in the *Enterprise* is not known, but it was reprinted in the *Golden Era* on February 28, 1864, at which time this paper referred to Mark Twain as the "Wild Humorist of the Sage Brush Hills." Because Mark and the Governor did considerable cruising around together during this session, he capitalized on this companionship in the satire. In one of his letters to the *Enterprise* he ribbed the applicants for notarial appointments and also the legislature for passing such a law.

The *Era* introduced the article as "Washoe Wit":[2]

MARK TWAIN ON THE RAMPAGE

Concerning Notaries

Mark Twain, the wild humorist of the Sage Brush Hills, writes from Carson City to the *Territorial Enterprise,* telling all about the Legislature, Governor Nye, and the rest of mankind at Nevada's capital, He says:

"A strange, strange thing occurred here yesterday, to wit:

"A MAN APPLIED FOR A NOTARY'S COMMISSION

"Think of it. Ponder over it. He wanted a notarial commission—he said so himself. He was from Storey county. He brought his petition along with him. He brought it on two stages. It is voluminous. The County Surveyor is chaining it off. Three shifts of clerks will be employed night and day on it, deciphering the signatures and testing their genuineness. They began unrolling the petition at noon, and people of strong proclivities at once commenced locating claims on it. We are too late, you know. But then they say the extensions are just as good as the original. I believe you."

After writing this introduction, Mark started downtown. He had not gone far when he met "Billson—Billson from Lander [County]," who was a "seedy, ornery, ratty, hang-dog-looking stranger," who had heard of Mark and "had often sighed for an opportunity of becoming acquainted." Billson said, " 'D—n it, old quill driver, you must come and take a drink with me'; and says I, 'D—n it, old vermin-ranch, I'll do it.' "

The two men had a drink, and after Billson charged it with the barkeeper, he opened a carpet-sack. Taking out a shirt-collar and a petition, he began unrolling the latter. After several yards had been exhibited, the petitioner said, "Now, Mark, have you got a good deal of influence with Governor Nye?"

"Unbounded," replied Mark. "When I go and use my influence with Governor Nye, and tell him it will be a great personal favor to me if he will do so-and-so, he always says it will be a real pleasure to him—that if it were any other man, any other man in the world —but seeing it's me, he won't." Mr. Billson was certain after those remarks that Mark was just the man to mention to the Governor that he wanted a notarial appointment.

Mark had no sooner rid himself of the man from Lander than he ran into "old Boreas from Washoe [City]." Greeting Mark, the latter said: "Why, darn it, Mark, how well you're looking! Thunder! It's been an age since I saw you. Turn around and let's look at you. Good! Gad, it's the same old Mark! . . . Every time I come to town, the old woman's sure to get after me for not bringing you out, as soon as I get back. Why, she takes them articles of yourn, and slathers 'em into her old scrapbook, along with deaths, and marriages, and receipts for the itch, and the smallpox, and hell knows what all. . . . But what's the use of fooling away time here? Let's go and gobble a cocktail." Over the drink Boreas mentioned that he wanted a notaryship. Mark promised to use his influence and told him to call for it at the Governor's office in the morning.

Before Mark reached the corner, "a pompous little man with a crooked-handled cane and sorrel mustache" stopped him:

" 'How do you do, Mr. Twain, how do you do, sir? I am happy to see you, sir, very happy indeed, sir. My name is—pardon me, sir, but I perceive you do not entirely recollect me—I am J. Bidlecome Dusenberry, of Esmeralda, formerly of the city of New York, sir.'

" 'Well,' says I. 'I'm glad to meet you, Dysintery, and——'

" 'No, no, Dusenberry, sir, Dusenberry! You——'

" 'Oh, I beg your pardon,' says I; 'Dusenberry—yes, I understand now. . . . I see you have a bale of dry-goods—for me, perhaps.' " Informing Mark that it was only a little petition, and showing him a few acres of it, he told him that he had read Mark's "lucumbrations" and wished him to use his influence with the Governor for his appointment. After he was assured that his commission would be ready as soon as the Governor signed it, Dusenberry "insisted, and insisted, and insisted" until Mark "went and took a drink with him." That made three drinks that Mark had had on the petitioners whom he had helped so far.

On his progress down the street, Mark met Chief Justice Turner, Bill Stewart, Sandy Baldwin, John B. Winters, Judge North, Chinamen, Indians, "and seventy-two other prominent citizens from Storey County, with a long pack-train laden with their several petitions." He examined their documents and promised to use his influence toward getting "notaryships for the whole tribe." He also drank with them. Mark continued for two hours looking over petitions. Finally he saw "a pensive, travel-worn stranger, leaning against an awning-post." Perceiving that he and the stranger were the only persons in the city who were not in "the long procession of petition-laden citizens filing up the street toward the Governor's house . . . going after notarial commissions," he looked at the stranger. The stranger returned his gaze; then Mark opened the conversation:

"Well?"

"Well—well what?"

"Well, I would like to examine your petition, if you please."

The astonished stranger asked for an explanation. Mark told him that there was somewhat of an epidemic in Carson City and proved it by pointing to a large placard on the wall which read:

> "Coaches will leave the Ormsby House punctually every fifteen minutes for the Governor's Mansion, for the accommodations of Notarial aspirants, etc., etc.
>
> "Schemerhorn, Agent."

The newcomer was not only astonished, but swore that he had just arrived and did not want a commission. Mark said that he was so happy to find one person who had not been seized with the disease that "I gazed upon him a moment in silent rapture, and then clasped him to my breast. After which, I told him it was my turn to treat, by thunder."

Mark and the stranger entered "a deserted saloon, and drank up its contents." They lay on a billiard table in a stupefied condition for many minutes. The stranger was seized first, rising up and muttering in "a sepulchral voice":

" 'I feel it—O, Heavens, I feel it in my veins!'

" 'Feel what?' says I, alarmed.

"Says he, 'I feel—O, my sainted mother—I feel—feel—a hankering to be a Notary Public!' "

The exile "tore down several yards of wall-paper" and wrote his petition. Mark was himself at once "seized with the fatal distemper." He attached a copy of the Directory of Nevada Territory to his petition, "so as to save him trouble of getting signers," and the two men "fled down the deserted streets to the Governor's office." [3]

The legislature of 1864 was the last one that Mark Twain was to report. Once when Joe Goodman was in San Francisco, Mark got into difficulties with the editor of the *Union*. Reprisals and counter-reprisals over a considerable period finally resulted in the challenge to a duel. The reform legislature had passed a law against dueling, being a second to a duel, or sending or receiving a challenge. Hence Mark was gone before the Second Constitutional Convention met in July of 1864.

This time the delegates eliminated the objectionable clause taxing the mines. In less than three weeks the Constitution was framed, and Bill Stewart and Sandy Baldwin worked as hard to have the new measure adopted as they had worked to defeat the first one. The new Constitution was overwhelmingly adopted, and the anxious office-seekers had it telegraphed in its entirety to President Lincoln.

On October 31, the President proclaimed Nevada a State. Governor Nye and Bill Stewart were chosen the first United States Senators; and Sandy Baldwin was appointed Nevada's United States District Judge. Inarticulate Orion Clemens lost the nomination for Secretary of State of Nevada.

There was a flood of poetry let loose for the occasion. Joe Goodman, "Nevada's poet laureate," was moved to write this poem commemorating the formation of the State of Nevada:

WASHOE

The mighty tide of Empire dashed
Upon a continent's bold strand,
And rolling back its billows washed
And fertilized a desert land.

They came, the founders of a State,
The men with spirits bold and free,
Who snatched the magic wand of fate,
And shaped their own high destiny.

They smote with it the barren rock—
A silver stream was disentombed;
The mountains sank beneath the shock,
And arid valleys rose and bloomed.

In cañons, deserts, plain and glade,
On mountains towering to the skies,
The broad foundations have been laid
On which our noble State shall rise.

Proud may we be, when God selects
As trusty instruments of fate—
Proud may we be, the architects
Who rear the pillars of a State.

The humblest laborers that toil
Within the tunnels damp and murk
Are clothed with majesty the while
They aid this grand creative work.

Though poor, the legacy they leave
The gifts of wealth and power exceeds;
This greatest boast their sons shall have,
A heritage of noble deeds.

Then lend a stout and willing hand,
And let the stately structure tower,
With its proportions fair and grand
As shaped by superhuman power.

So fair, so grand, that we with pride
Shall list while generous tongues relate,
Where met the West and Eastern tide
Was formed at last a perfect State.

19

"THREE SAINTS—MARK, LUKE, AND JOHN"

THE FRONTIER LOVED ITS FUN, ITS ENTERTAINMENT, its drama. It wanted them boisterous, reckless, absurd, crude, even bawdy. Yet surprisingly enough, Shakespeare was a favorite with the boys. There was so much money in Washoe that every actor and actress wanted to play in its cities; and there were so many bachelors and homeless men who had to be entertained that the show houses were always packed. "Washoe widows" left behind in San Francisco did not know what their men did on the mountain. It was one continuous round of excitement all day and all night. Nothing closed in Virginia City.

Almost as soon as the first impact of the rush to Washoe was felt, a theatre, the Howard House, opened in 1860. Every hall and pavilion built thereafter, and there were many of them, was turned into some kind of a place of amusement: sportsmen's halls, hurdy-gurdy houses, theatres and show palaces. Topliffe built the first big theatre on North C Street in 1862; the following year Thomas Maguire, the proprietor of Maguire's Opera House in San Francisco, opened his Virginia City Opera House in July on D Street. By 1863 there were as many as five companies and six or seven variety troupes showing on the Lode at the same time. Maguire's theatre became the best—it had the prestige of the San Francisco associate. And when Tom Maguire booked a show for San Francisco, he also put it on the Virginia City circuit.

From the time that Joe Goodman took over the *Enterprise,* the paper devoted considerable space to entertainments currently showing in the City. Joe, a real classicist, loved the theatre. He would rather go there than to any other place of amusement. His skill in criticizing the actors and their productions soon attracted the attention of the public in general and the histrionic profession in particular. When Mark Twain and Dan De Quille joined the *Enterprise* staff as local reporters, these two wits and Joe were always seen at the theatre on first nights. After the show was over, they went to the newspaper office where each one of them wrote out his criticism. Then each one read the other critic's reports and a symposium was held. This discussion ended in selecting the article for publication.

So painstaking was this preparation of the final publicity that it was only natural that the articles were copied widely by dramatic journals and other newspapers. Because of the prestige of the *Enterprise* on the Comstock and the Pacific Coast, this paper could make or ruin the reputation of a trouper. There was always great anxiety among the members of the theatrical profession and the managers of each newly arrived company to learn what the *Enterprise* and its staff members thought of them.

Other papers on the Lode were critical, too. From the Virginia City *Bulletin* of July 17, 1863, is taken the following item announcing the arrival of a company to show that tear-jerking play *East Lynne* in the Opera House:

> On Tuesday evening that sickest of all sentimental dramas, "East Lynne," will be turned loose upon us at the Opera House. It used to afford me much solid comfort to see those San Franciscans whinny and shuffle and slobber all over themselves at Maguire's Theatre, when the consumptive "William" was in the act of handing in his checks, as it were, according to the regular programme of "East Lynne"—and now I am to enjoy a season of happiness again, I suppose. If the tears flow as freely here as I count upon, water privileges will be cheap in Virginia next week. However, Mrs. Julia Dean Hayne don't "take on" in the piece like Miss Sophia Edwin; wherefore she fails to pump an audience dry like the latter.

One of Mark Twain's parodies on a play showing in Virginia City was of *Ingomar, the Barbarian*,[1] which was played at the Opera House in the fall of 1863. From the *Golden Era* of November 29, the article, recopied in *Yankee Notions* in New York of April, 1864, was composed of acts and scenes written in Washoe vernacular: Mrs. Claughley, dressed as a "healthy Greek matron," urges her daughter Parthenia to marry Polydor in order that she might save her father from being sold out by the sheriff—"the old man being in debt for assessments." Polydor, however, "a wealthy, spindle-shanked, stingy old stockbroker," is refused by the Greek maiden. "The Comanches capture Parthenia's father . . . and carry him away to Reese River." They want "thirty ounces of silver to get him out of soak."

Mark introduced several local "gags" which only Washoe people could appreciate. The camp of the Comanches was busy "throwing dice for tickets in Wright's Gift Entertainment," a firm which at that time in Virginia City held regular auctions for jewelry and other gewgaws by selling tickets. Ingomar, the chief, and the Comanches go on the warpath; Parthenia arrives; and Ingomar "gets stuck on her." He declares his love, and attempts to embrace her; but she waves him off, gently but firmly, and remarks, "Not too brash, Ing, not too brash, now!" Ingomar subsides, they flee, and from a hilltop they see "the spires and domes of Silver City," a small mining community three miles from Virginia City. Old Myron, Parthenia's father, tells Ingomar that he must dress like a Christian. He is finally tamed. The plot thickens when the chief of police enters, disappears, enters again, gives the Comanches a ranch apiece, and decrees that "they shall build a town on the American Flat," appointing "great Ingomar to be its mayor." A company was at that moment building a $50,000 town at this place as a bid for the future capital site of Nevada.

In the finale, there are "Comanches, police, Paiutes, and citizens generally—Ingomar and Parthenia clinging together in the centre." Ingomar observes: "Two souls with but a single thought," while Parthenia completes the picture by "slinging in the other line, 'Two hearts that beat as one.'"

In recognition of the influence of the *Enterprise* and its generosity in giving considerable space in its columns to theatrical events, Maguire's gave all of its poster advertising and bill printing to this paper. It also reserved some of the best seats—the entire front row of the orchestra to the right of the aisle, a dozen or more—for the *Enterprise* staff. To make sure that no other person occupied these seats, a large sign with an immense eagle and the words "Reserved for the *Enterprise*" painted thereon was stretched across the back of them.

Theatrical history was made on the Pacific Coast when Artemus Ward (Charles Farrar Browne) decided to see the West. He was a lover of traveling and wandering over the country. Arriving in California in 1863 by way of the Isthmus of Panama, he gave his humorous lectures in San Francisco and the California mining camps. He invariably got a laugh from the audience when it first saw him. Going into character on the stage with a solemn, melancholy expression on his face, he affected embarrassment and witlessness. In this attitude of stupidity he ran off the witticisms and chatter which he called his lecture. Mark Twain's description of him was: "He looked like a glove-stretcher; his hair—red and brushed forward" reminded him of "a divided flame. His nose rambled aggressively before his face with all the determination of a cow-catcher, while his red mustache, to follow out the simile, seemed not unlike the unfortunate cow."

Readers in the West had come to know him through *Artemus Ward: His Book*. He wrote in bad English as though he were the proprietor of a traveling show, consisting of "an amoozing Kangaroo and other moral Beests and Snaiks, also Waxwork figures of G. Washington, General Taylor, John Bunyan, Captain Kidd, and Dr. Webster in the act of killing Dr. Parkman, besides several miscellanyous statoots of celebrated Piruts and Murdrers ekalled by few and exceld by none." Although he had never met him, he "interviewed" Abraham Lincoln. The great President was amused by his writings and even opened a Cabinet meeting by reading some of his nonsense to the members before he asked them to consider the Emancipation Proclamation.

Ward had a number of lectures in stock, and even before he arrived in San Francisco, the newspapers were speculating on which of them he would speak. It turned out that "Babes in the Wood" was the one he selected with which to amuse them. His clever manager and advance agent, E. P. Hingston, an Englishman who started Ward on his lecture career, got him a big "build-up" in the newspapers. The result was that on November 13 Ward filled Platt's Hall (Maguire closed his opera house for the night) and scooped in $1624 in gold. Franklin Walker described his disarming way with his audience in *San Francisco's Literary Frontier:*

A very quiet-looking, faultlessly dressed young man with a prominent nose stepped out upon the bare platform. He was very tall and thin, with a touch of red in his hair and in his heavy, drooping mustache. His long, slender hands and soft,

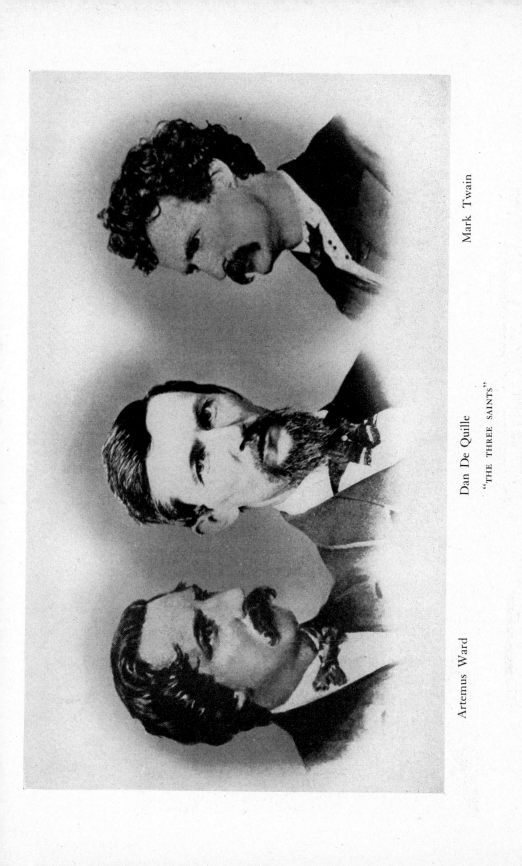

Artemus Ward   Dan De Quille   Mark Twain

"THE THREE SAINTS"

REUEL COLT GRIDLEY
AND THE SANITARY SACK OF FLOUR

MRS. ORION CLEMENS
The first, first lady of Nevada

K. B. ("KETTLE BELLY") BROWN

gentle voice were in keeping with his quiet and subtle technique as a lecturer, and the only suspicion of humor in his face was his mirthful eyes. His lecture was unprecedented; it was humor without any other purpose than to amuse. He didn't even tell what became of the babes in the wood. Instead, for nearly two hours he chatted with his audience, introducing quaint thoughts, whimsical fancies, bizarre notions, ludicrous anecdotes. Atrocious puns were followed by fits of abstraction, during which he appeared to be miles away. Then he would return to his audience and artlessly and unexpectedly come bang up with another side-splitting remark. He was a born showman; he played on his listeners as a musician plays upon an organ.[2]

Two weeks later Mark Twain was announcing Ward's forthcoming appearance in Virginia City. Mark had read about Ward's success, and Ward had made the acquaintance of some people Mark knew in San Francisco. These mutual friends knew the two wits would hit it off famously together—letters of introduction were carried by Ward to Mark. San Francisco had been referring to Mark as "The Wild Humorist of the Sage Brush Hills," and Mark welcomed Ward as "The Wild Humorist of the Plains" to Virginia City. In the *Enterprise* Mark wrote:

We understand that Artemus Ward contemplates visiting this region to deliver his lectures, and perhaps make some additions to his big "sho." In his last letter to us he appeared particularly anxious to "sekure a kupple ov horned todes; alsowe, a lizard which it may be persessed of 2 tales, or any comical snaix, and enny sich little unconsidered trifles, as the poets say, which they do not interest the kommun mind. Further, be it nown, that I would like a opportunity for to maik a moddel in wax of a average size wash-owe man, with feet attached, as an kompanion pictur to a waxen figger of a nigger I have sekured, at an large outlaye, whitch it has a unnatural big hed onto it. Could you also manage to gobbel up the skulp of the layte Missus Hopkins? I adore sich foot-prints of atrocity as it were, muchly. I was roominatin' on gittin' a bust of Mark Twain, but I've kwit kontemplatin' the work. They tell me down heer to the Bay that the busts air so kommun it wood only bee an waist of wax too git us kounterfit presentiment." We shall assist Mr. Ward in every possible way about making his Washoe collection and have no doubt but he will pick up many curious things during his sojourn.

Artemus Ward and his manager arrived on the Comstock early in December to stay three days. On invitation from Ward, Mark had breakfast with him for an interview. In deference to the custom in the mining camp Ward preceded his morning meal with three whiskey cocktails, but Mark said that he would rather not drink one because it would go straight to his head and confuse him. On Ward's insistence, Mark drank "the treasonable mixture under protest." Mark said: "In a minute or two I began to imagine that my ideas were clouded. I waited in great anxiety for the conversation to open, with a sort of vague hope that my understanding would prove clear, after all, and my misgivings groundless."

After an "unimportant remark or two," Ward went into character and delivered an "astounding speech," asking Mark many questions concerning mining, the locations of the veins, and why this and why that about them. He rambled on and on in a most unintelligible manner, ending the speech with "geology has failed to account for, although everything in that science goes to prove that, all things being equal, it would if it did not, or would not certainly if it did, and then, of course, they are. Do not you think it is?"

"Now I just knew how it would be—that whiskey cocktail has done the business for me; I don't understand any more than a clam."

To that confession Mark added:

"I—I—that is—if you don't mind, would you—would you say that over again? I ought——"

"Oh, certainly, certainly! You see I am very unfamiliar with the subject, and perhaps I don't present my case clearly, but I——"

"No, no—no, no—you state it plain enough, but that cocktail has muddled me a little. But I will—no, I do understand for that matter; but I would get the hang of it all the better if you went over it again—and I'll pay better attention this time."

At this point Artemus got more and more impressive "and emphasized each particular point by checking it off on his finger ends." Going into greater detail about seeking information on the subject of mining, he asked about the vein, the lode, the ledge, and the sulphurets of silver, in another long speech. Mark, however, still could not get the hang of the question: "I feel ashamed of myself, Mr. Ward. I know I ought to understand you perfectly well, but you see that treacherous whiskey cocktail has got into my head, and now I cannot understand even the simplest proposition. I told you how it would be."

"Oh, don't mind it, don't mind it; the fault was my own, no doubt—though I did think it clear enough for——"

"Don't say a word. Clear! Why, you stated it as clear as the sun to anybody but an abject idiot; but it's that confounded cocktail that has played the mischief!"

"No, now don't say that. I'll begin all over again, and——"

And Artemus did go over it again, confounding confusion. Suddenly Mark "heard a suspicious noise behind" him and, turning quickly, he saw Hingston, Ward's manager, dodge behind a newspaper, "quaking with a gentle ecstasy of laughter. I looked at Ward again, and he had thrown off his dread solemnity and was laughing also. Then I saw that I had been made a victim of a swindle in the way of a string of plausibly worded sentences that didn't mean anything under the sun."

From that moment forward Mark Twain and Artemus Ward were comrades. Making the *Enterprise* office his headquarters, Ward soon became one of the "gang". The boys initiated him into the Comstock fraternity. For three orgiastic weeks of fun and frolic, they played together, drank together, ate together, and slept together. There were Mac, Joe, Steve, Mark, Dan, Ward, and Hingston, all bachelors and most of them under thirty years of age. Artemus became a familiar figure around town—many times he was "joshed" about his "Babes in the Wood."

Everyone who met him was pleased with his personality. The editor of the Gold Hill *Daily News* met Artemus at the *Enterprise* office and on December 23 described this meeting:

A JOLLY COUPLE

We had the pleasure of an introduction to Artemus Ward last evening in Virginia. He was in company with Dan De Quille, the most witty writer in this Territory. We never saw Artemus before, face to face; but we have often seen him in his books, and we confess that in person he is just about what we had pictured him out in "our mind's eye." In person he is a tall, thin, young man, aged perhaps twenty-seven years; fresh healthy complexion; heavy growth of brown hair on his head; heavy moustache; a mouth not as large as a barn door; eyes that fairly sparkle with wit; and a soul (you can see it!) evidently brimful of the milk of human kindness with a slather of creamy wit floating upon the surface. Artemus is a "brick," and socially as social as the jolliest. Dan De Quille and Artemus Ward! To see the two tipping glasses together! 'Tis worth five dollars to see it.

Since this same paper forgot to mention the most conspicuous part of Ward's make-up, on the following day it wrote: "In describing the appearance of A. Ward, the 'wax-figger' man, . . . we forgot the most prominent feature—*His Nose*. It is a regular Duke of Wellington proboscis—a kind of inverted town pump-handle—(all great men have such noses)—and Artemus looks as if Betsy Jane and the Babes in the Wood had pulled it upon every trifling occasion of a domestic *jar*—it looks so much to be a jar of spiced pickles."

Virginia City fascinated Artemus Ward. He loved the excitement of the greatest and most exciting mining town in history. Mining-camp vernacular intrigued him. He wanted to master it for the purpose of using it in some of his lecturing. Believing that he was familiar enough with it to use it, he was determined to try it out. The greetings among the mining men struck him as something new, and he began practicing by passing himself off as an oldtimer. The looks of astonishment which his efforts in this line called forth in some quarters showed him that the "half-horse, half-alligator" style of greeting was good only with a certain class of people. However, one day when Ward was with Mark, they met one of Mark's clerical friends on the street. Without prefacing the name with "Reverend," Mark introduced Ward to him. Some twinkle in the Reverend's eye led Artemus to believe him to be one of the "pioneers," and he greeted him with: "Well, old Two-Pan-One-Color, is the devil in your dough-dish?" Mark was highly amused and hastened to explain everything. It all ended in a laugh in which Ward joined faintly.

The Paiute Indians and the Chinese filled Artemus Ward with curiosity. He had seen neither race until he had come to the Pacific Coast. While he was in Virginia City, he had a good opportunity to observe the Celestials in a festivity. The occasion was the visit of some Oriental priests to the Chinese inhabitants of Nevada. A large tent was set up on a vacant lot in Chinatown, situated several blocks downhill from the main street. In this primitive "joss-house" the purple-robed priests from San Francisco set up their gods to receive the vows of the faithful.

One night Dan and Mark took Artemus to Chinatown to show him the sights.[3] They went to visit Hop Sing, the head of one tong, and then to old Sam Sing, the champion of the opposition tong. Food, drink, and cordiality always accompanied these festive events. As the trio visited each headquarters, they were treated to "blandy" —rice brandy—and other kinds of fiery drinks. While they were going from one headquarters to another, they narrowly escaped disaster. A fight started between the rival groups. Shots were exchanged, killing one man and wounding two or three more.

Returning up the steep hill from Chinatown to Virginia City, the three bohemians, who were feeling pretty good, decided to take a short-cut. Coming to a row of low frame houses, Artemus said that the nearest cut was over the roofs of these shanties. Crying out, "Follow the leader!" he leaped onto a shed and thence to the roof of a house, where he again shouted: "Come ahead, and we'll go up into town over the roofs of the houses. Follow your leader." Soon they were marching along over the roofs of the houses. They had not gone very far when there came a command: "Halt there or I shoot!" They followed the order and saw a man with a shotgun leveled at them. The man, a night watchman, held the gun on them until they climbed down and marched up to him. As soon as explanations and their names had been given, everything was all right.

In gratitude Artemus remarked, "Right you are. Take a few tickets and come to my show," handing the watchman a handful of tickets. "Thanks!" was the reply, and reaching around to the tail of his long coat, the latter brought forth a bottle that was almost as long as the barrel of his gun. "Good stuff," said he, as he poked the long bottle over the fence to the troupers. There was some anxiety on the part of Dan and Mark over mixing fighting American whiskey with warlike Chinese "blandy," but Artemus was game and took the bottle. As he lifted it to his lips and elevated it toward the North Star, it resembled a telescope. "Splendid," said he, as he lowered the "instrument."

On reaching C Street by the way of Sutton Avenue, the night revelers heard music coming from one of the pavilions in which a hurdy-gurdy show was holding forth. Hurdies were new to Artemus, and he voiced his determination to see the show. On entering the dance hall Artemus announced that they were "Babes in the Wood." By this time he was known by sight to most of the people present, and there were "cheers for Artemus Ward!" "Now," said Ward, "we three have got to have a dance together. It'll be a thing our offspring to the furtherest generation will be proud of!" Selecting three of the most stalwart girls in the show as partners, they danced together to the "unbounded admiration of a large and enthusiastic audience," headed by K. B. ("Kettle-Belly") Brown.

Brown, a powerful man and a gambler and all-round sportsman, took the three merrymakers in hand. He could see that they were in need of a protector. When their party at the show was over, Artemus threw a twenty-dollar gold piece on the bar to pay for the dances and the beer. The barkeeper, seeing that they were in no condition to know what change they were to receive, took out about four times the usual rate. Just as the barkeeper was in the act of raking in Ward's double eagle, Kettle-belly's big hand came down upon the gold piece with a resounding *spat!* "No, you don't!" said Kettle-Belly. "These gentlemen are friends of mine. This twenty don't go into your till until you hand out the right change." Instantly the correct change was handed over to Ward.

Immediately the whole heart and soul of Artemus went out to Kettle-Belly. Said he to their protector: "We are three mere 'Babes in the Wood.' Come along with us. We need you to take care of us." Instead of going home to bed, the three clowns started out again under the guidance and protection of Brown. From the hurdy-gurdies they went to hear the Cornish singers, and then to see some of the big gambling games which were always in progress. At every place they visited they refreshed themselves anew. The fun continued until the first rays of the morning sun were gilding the peak of Mount Davidson. The "Babes" sought some fresh air out in front of Aaron Hooper's saloon, where there happened to be some packing cases. Seated upon one of the boxes, Artemus was trying to get

Virginia City Night Club, 1864

From Browne's *Washoe Revisited*

down a sobering drink of mustard and water, when John A. Collins, the town's pillar of righteousness, happened along on his early morning walk.

"You are early abroad, gentlemen," said the staid old man. (They would have much preferred at that moment to have seen Beelzebub.)

"Yes, Mr. Collins," said Mark, as he saw halted before them the moral patriarch of the Lode, "it is beautiful to see the sun rise. As the poet says:

> " 'Now fair Aurora lifts the golden ray
> And all the ruddy Orient flames with day.' "

This poetical outburst of Mark Twain's aroused the muse in Artemus. Lifting his head with Kettle-belly's aid, he tearfully gazed up at the great reformer and with much feeling and emphasis, declaimed:

> "A man oppressed, dependent, yet a man."

After this final adventure they decided to go to their rooms. All three of them climbed into the big bed together. When they were comfortable, nimble-witted Ward remarked: "Three Saints! Mark, Luke, and John."

There are no copies extant of the *Territorial Enterprise* during the visit of Artemus Ward to the Comstock, but the Virginia City *Evening Bulletin* of December 28, 1863, reprinted an article written by Mark Twain about Ward's lectures, of which it said:

AN INAPT ILLUSTRATION

Mark Twain, of the *Enterprise*, in commenting on the lecture of Artemus Ward says:

"There are perhaps fifty subjects treated in it, and there is a passable point in every one of them, and a healthy laugh, also, for any of God's creatures who hath committed no crime, the ghastly memory of which debars him from smiling again while he lives. The man who is capable of listening to the 'Babes in the Wood' from beginning to end without laughing either inwardly or outwardly must have done murder, or at least meditated it, at some time during his life."

That accounts for the fact of Mark's solemnity of appearance while listening to the lecture. The remembrance of his murder of the Hopkins family must have been preying on his mind; their ghosts, like that of Banquo's, must have appeared in gory horror to his refined and sensitive mind.

Amid all the revelry, Artemus Ward found time to give lectures to the people in the towns up and down Gold Cañon. The last one was given in Gold Hill near the close of the year. After this lecture Ward gave a farewell party at Chauvel's French Restaurant for his friends. It was a great party—Dan, Mark, Joe, and Artemus. As glass after glass was filled and drunk, wits grew sharper and the fun noisier. Toasts were drunk—Artemus arose and proposed: "Gentlemen, I give you upper Canada."

"Why did you give us upper Canada?" asked Joe Goodman.

"Because I don't want it myself," replied Artemus. Mark furnished his part of the fun by singing his one and only song, "There was an old horse and his name was Jerusalem." When it came time for this dinner party to end, Artemus said: "I never, gentlemen, was in a city where I was treated so *well*, nor, I will add, so *often*." And —good sport that he was—he paid the bill of $237 for the night's merriment.

Several years later Mark Twain described the happy times these humorists had during Ward's visit. These memories were still vivid in his mind as he pictured one of their good times together:

"*Scene*—private room in Barnum's[4] Restaurant, Virginia, Nevada: present, Artemus Ward, Joseph I. Goodman (editor and proprietor Daily 'Enterprise'), and 'Dan De Quille' and myself, reporters for same; remnants of the feast thin and scattering, but *such* tautology and repetition of empty bottles everywhere visible as to be offensive to the sensitive eye; time, 2:30 A.M.; Artemus thickly reciting a poem about a certain infant you wot of, and interrupting himself and *being* interrupted every few lines by poundings of the table and shouts of 'Splendid, by Shorzhe!' Finally, a long vociferous, poundiferous, and vitreous jingling of applause announces the conclusion, and then Artemus: 'Let every man 'at loves his fellow man and 'preciates a poet 'at loves *his* fellow man, stan' up!—Stan' up and drink it *stanning*!' (On all hands fervent, enthusiastic, and sincerely honest attempts to comply.) Then Artemus: 'Well—consider it stanning, and drink it just as ye are!' Which was done." [5]

During the more sober moments of Ward's visit to the Comstock, Mark and he had serious discussions which left their stamp on the Westerner. Ward had been successful both on the platform and in writing his book, which was then running into 40,000 copies sold. There can be no doubt that Mark studied Ward's technique. That may account for Mark's solemn face as observed by the *Evening Bulletin's* reporter. Ward advised Mark to seek recognition from Eastern publishers. He promised to write a letter to the editors of the New York *Sunday Mercury* telling them about Mark's literary work in the West.

The friendship between the two great humorists did not end with their parting in Virginia City. Artemus got no farther than Austin, Nevada, before he wrote Mark a letter. His love and affection for Mark is sincere throughout the missive:

Austin, Jan. 1, '64

My dearest love:

I arrived here yesterday A.M at two o'clock. It is a wild untamable place, full of lion-hearted boys. I speak tonight. See small bills.

Why did you not go with me and save me that night? I mean the night I left you after that dinner party. I went and got drunker, beating, I may say, Alexander the Great, in his most drinkiest days, and I blackened my face at the Melodeon, and made a gibbering idiotic speech. G— d—n it! I suppose the *Union* will have it. But let it go. I shall always remember Virginia as a bright spot in my existence, as all others must or rather cannot be, as it were.

Love to Joe Goodman and Dan. I shall write soon a powerfully convincing note to my friends of "The Mercury." Your notice, by the way, did much good here, as it doubtlessly will elsewhere. The miscreants of the *Union* will be batted in the snout if they ever dare pollute this rapidly rising city with their loathsome presence.

Some of the finest intellects in the world have been blunted by liquor.

Do not, sir—do not flatter yourself that you are the only chastely humorous writer on the Pacific slopes.

Good-bye, old boy—and God bless you! The matter of which I spoke to you earnestly shall be just as earnestly attended to— and again with very warm regards for Joe, and Dan, and regards to many of the good friends we met, I am faithfully, gratefully

Yours,

Artemus Ward.[6]

From Austin, Ward went on to deliver a lecture in Salt Lake City. However, while he was there he was taken very ill. When he was able to write, he sent Mark a letter:

Salt Lake City
Jan. 21, '64

My dearest Mark:

I have been dangerously ill for the past two weeks here, of congestive fever. Very grave fears were for a time entertained of my recovery, but happily the malady is gone, though leaving me very weak. I hope to be able to resume my journey in a week or so. I think I shall speak in the theater here, which is one of the finest establishments of the kind in America.

The Saints have been wonderfully kind to me. I could not have been better or more tenderly nursed at home—God bless them!

I am still exceedingly weak—can't write any more. Love to Joe and Dan, and all the rest. Write me at St. Louis.

Always yours,

Artemus Ward.[7]

The *Enterprise* staff did not have an opportunity to recover from the hilarity of the visit of Artemus Ward before it was again taken by storm in the visit of Adah Isaacs Menken and her friend Ada Clare. The former actress was the "pin-up girl" of the 1860's. Posters of her in deshabille, except for thin flesh-colored tights and a wisp of a loincloth, lashed to the back of a "fiery, untamed steed," portraying the Tartar Prince in *Mazeppa*, were plastered all over San Francisco. Her reputation was well known to the theatre-going public of Washoe long before she came up from the Coast to do her strip-tease act in Virginia City. In fact, the local papers were taunting Mark Twain about her as early as November 19, 1863, when the *Union* wrote:

> Adah will perhaps visit the Territory of Nevada next Spring. Mark Twain is writing a bloody tragedy for her, equal to *Mazeppa*—and which will excel *Mazeppa* in many respects. It is to be called 'Pete Hopkins, or the Gory Scalp.' Mark is now training one of Balaam's Arabian steeds especially for this play. Those who have attended the performances of Adah admire her very much—what they have seen of her.

Over in Washoe City *The Old Pah-Utah* gave her another good send-off in describing her act:

> The Menken is a pretty shapely Jewess, considerably more undressed than any actress yet tolerated on the American stage. Her costume in *Mazeppa* consisted of a flesh-fitting suit with the little end of a dimity nothing fastened at the waist. She fences with a strong wrist and a Bowery dexterity. She attitudinizes with statuesque effect. She suffers herself to be strapped on a 'fiery, untamed steed'—both barebacked—and thus be carried up a mountain, over what appears to be a road rough and perilous as the road to Washoe.
> The Menken is a beauty, and believes strictly that 'Beauty unadorned is adorned the most.'

Finally it was announced in the Comstock papers that Adah was really coming to play at Maguire's in March, 1864. In January of that year, the editor of the *Union* wrote the following:

> 'Outstripped!' The Menken and her wild horse of Goat Island are coming! The young gentleman who *does* the local of the *Enterprise* is in ecstasies at the *bare* mention of the fact—notwithstanding he says he has seen on the banks of the O-hi-o all such shows, 'outstripped.' Daniel De Quille, you surprise us— we are amazed at your adventures on the banks of the Ohio! Better view the Menken—she don't 'dive'—nary time. It ain't her forte; besides, the weather is too cold to dive. The show is not intended for exhibition *under* water.

Thus was Washoe prepared for the visit of the greatest actress that had ever come before its audiences. Pictures of Adah began to appear behind the bars, on billboards, and pasted to the cañon walls. Her past life—and she had one—was related; the wags gossiped about the three husbands she had taken. To her current mate, Robert H. Newell—Orpheus C. Kerr was his *nom de plume* in the literary world—she was "a dirty Rebel." Born Dolores McCord, it was said, in New Orleans, and to have been the adopted daughter of old Sam Houston. She had been the "Queen of the Plaza" in Havana. While in Texas she had been captured by Indians, tomahawked by them, and then dramatically rescued by the Texas Rangers. While with them she had learned horsemanship and circus stunts.

Wherever she went, she created a furor: In Baltimore she put the Stars and Bars in the theatre where she was playing; in Ohio she had been dubbed the "Darling of Dayton" and made an honorary captain of the Light Guard. With her sword and epaulettes her picture was hung in their armory. In San Francisco she was known as the "Frenzy of Frisco." What would she do to Washoe?

Adah was at the height of her fame when she came to Sun Mountain. There was great excitement during the days just preceding her arrival. At what hotel was she going to stay? Or was there a private mansion being fitted up for her? All of these questions were answered on the morning of February 27 when she arrived in the stage at about 11:30 A.M. Curvaceous, voluptuous, buxom, black curly-headed Adah sat on the front seat inside the stage with her back to the horses. Along with her were her numerous canine companions. Orpheus Kerr, her husband, was noted as occupying "a decidedly lively and conspicuous position on top of the hind boot." This small, homely, foppishly dressed, pomaded-mustached gentleman with the plug hat wrapped up in a gray blanket looked "either like a troubadour or a Georgia Major, just returned from the war." They went directly to the International Hotel where a large sign read:

"WELCOME TO THE MENKEN AND ORPHEUS!"

Soon after she arrived, the Opera House Band went to the hotel and serenaded her.

Although the Menken's repertoire ran through *The French Spy, Dick Turpin, Jack Sheppard, Lola Montez, The Three Fast Women,* and *Mazeppa*, she was a success only when she played *Mazeppa*. She opened her engagement at Maguire's in *The French Spy* on March 2. The boys did not like it—the papers condemned it. They wanted *Mazeppa*. In this melodrama, she was at her best. Based somewhat loosely on Byron's poem, it was such that she could give it all she had as the play progressed. There were passionate love scenes, brave encounters with the Count in the duel scene, all climaxed by the act in which she was stripped and lashed helpless to the back of an uncontrolled and unbroken steed. The unloosed horse dashed up a pseudo-precipice and disappeared in the sky-flies amidst the roaring, stomping, thunderous applause of the boys. It was the most daring act ever put on by a woman. And there was very little "fake" about it, too. In performances in other cities she had been injured— as when she played *Mazeppa* in Sacramento.

The histrionic three from the *Enterprise* staff were there. They fell completely under her charm—that voice, that form divine, that impenetrable soul! Joe, Dan, and Mark went to the office to write up the Menken. How could they do her justice? Words were frail in expressing their praise of her performance. It was a eulogy, a pæan of praise, their greatest combined effort of approval. The Menken was pleased and delighted that the *Enterprise* boys liked her show. So fervent was their praise of Adah and of Adah *alone* that it excited the jealousy of the other members of the company. Why should they not have received their share of praise as a supporting cast? To show their contempt and disgust for the staff, the less fortunate members of the show interspersed uncomplimentary "gags" directed at Mark and the paper during the next evening's performance. This made the Menken furious. So angry was she that she turned savagely upon the manager. She ordered him to go at once before the audience, even before the performance was completed, and make a public apology to Joe Goodman and his fellow reporters. When the manager declined, she refused to go on with her part. Mark and Dan were embarrassed. They had been too lavish in their praise. She turned to them for the decision; they begged her to resume her role. She, however, was adamant.[8]

On the succeeding night the Menken relented and the play went on. Mark Twain's notice of the play was copied all over the United States. However, at the conclusion of her engagement at the Opera House, the management turned on the *Enterprise* to punish it for its impropriety in the Menken affair. It withdrew its printing, posters, and advertising business and suspended the free tickets for everyone connected with the paper. But the Opera House manager took on too big a fight to handle when he tackled the staff. No one in the theatre business can alienate the press and succeed. The long articles in the *Enterprise* appeared no more. If a good show came, the locals never mentioned it; no one would ever know from them that there was such a place as Maguire's Opera House in Virginia City. But if a poor show came to town, Joe or Dan or Mark would pay his dollar for admission and "then take a hundred dollars' worth of fun or satisfaction out of the hides of the poor actors or actresses."

The Menken loved the Lode. The tintinabulations of the many bells thrilled her heart; the ceaseless and unending whirl of excitement delighted her night and day. The cacophony of noises—the rumbling of the heavy, ore-laden wagons, the shrill shriek of the mill whistles, the groans and scrapings of the hoists, the rat-a-tat-tat of the stamps, the jolting shots of the underground explosions—moved her to poetic expressions. Several of these, set down in her characteristic gigantic handwriting, appeared in the *Enterprise*. So impressed was Mark with her literary ability that he took some of his own productions to her for criticism. In a letter to his mother he wrote:

> I took it [an article] over to show Miss Menken, the actress, Orpheus C. Kerr's wife. She has a beautiful white hand, but her handwriting is infamous; she writes fast, and her caligraphy is of the doorplate order—her letters are immense. I gave her a conundrum, thus:
> 'My dear Madam:
> 'Why ought your hand to retain its present grace and beauty always?'
> (Answer)
> 'Because you fool away devilish little of it on your manuscript.' [9]

Adah "bowled over" all of the boys on the Mountain. Her performances did not end with the daring dash up the zigzag path at the Opera House. They extended to all the "hot spots" of the town. One night after the play she went to the Sazerac saloon where she put on the gloves with "Joggles" Wright, the superintendent of the

Sierra Nevada Mine and a Washoe *bon vivant*. She knocked him out in a couple of rounds, throwing him so hard that he had to be carried out. Taking on two more of the boys who were considered good in the ring, she cleaned them up, too. One of her former husbands, "Benicia Boy" Heenan, had shown her some of the tricks of good boxing.

Nothing on the Lode escaped her. She took in the hurdy-gurdy shows, the bars, the gambling games, and other dens of iniquity. She was accompanied on most of these expeditions by Tom Peaseley, the proprietor of the Sazerac, fire chief, and political boss; he took her underground where she boiled an egg in the scalding subterranean waters, and she danced with him at the Melodeon.

The boys of American Engine Company No. 2 voted Adah an honorary membership in the company and gave her a red morocco fire belt with the emblem of the company encrusted in Comstock silver bullion. The honor of the presentation was given to Tom Peaseley. At the ceremony, which took place on the balcony of the International Hotel, Tom buckled on her belt while the boys below serenaded them. She had been fêted and honored in many cities, but none of them had equalled the Lode. While she was in Virginia, she considered giving up acting. She thought that she might devote her entire time to writing. At one time during her stay she sent for her little, dainty, fluffy, blonde-headed friend, Ada Clare, née McElheny. Ada was not only a Rebel, too, but also a bohemian. A writer of verse, an actress, and an unconventional in her love affairs, Ada Clare made an impression.

While she was in Virginia, Adah Menken decided to give a dinner for the press and her friend.[10] She was in the habit of giving dinners of this kind for the press. She had given a gorgeous one in London and wanted this one to be equally as fine.

There were only four guests at this dinner party given on a Sunday afternoon at her private suite in the International Hotel: Mark, Dan, Ada Clare, and the Menken. Even Adah's ineffectual little husband, whom she was then considering putting back in circulation, was not invited. For this three-hour splurge the finest wines, champagne, and food were ordered. A procession of waiters moved constantly to and from the kitchen to her rooms carrying the viands up two flights of stairs. On their way they passed Orpheus doing patrol duty in front of the rooms in which the feast was being held.

For some reason known only to Adah herself, he was in disfavor for the moment.

The apparent objects of the dinner were to discuss a novel which the Menken was then planning to write, and to talk about a play for Ada Clare. Dan said that "aside from this talk . . . the dinner was rather dull. It was thought to enliven the occasion with some

> 'Short swallow flights of song, that dip
> Their wings . . . and skim away.'

But the Menken was no nightingale, Clare was a sort of wren, and I was a screech owl. Mark enchanted us with his one and only song of

> 'There was an old horse and his name
>   was Jerusalem,
> And he came from Jerusalem,
> And he went to Jerusalem,
>
> 'There was an old horse——'

and so on *ad infinitum.*"

Adah kept her dogs in her rooms, and what with Ada Clare's pets there were about "nineteen dogs of as many breeds, 'mongrel,' puppy, whelp, and hound, and curs of low degree." During the entire feast Clare and the Menken fed "the pampered beasts with cubes of sugar soaked in brandy and champagne. This kind of provender made the animals howlingly hilarious, to the great delight of their mistresses, but to the disgust of Twain, who was seated on Menken's side of the table, where the canine carnival was most rampant." In their revelry one of the darling beasts took "an unwarranted liberty with Mark's leg."

Mark decided to avenge the nip which he had received with a furtive kick at the offender. Guessing, however, at the whereabouts of the culprit under the table, he let go a blow that hit the Menken's pet corn. In agony she leaped from her chair to a lounge and rolled and groaned with pain. This unfortunate incident put a wet blanket on the dinner. Mark became sullen "as though it had been his own corn that was wounded, and even when Menken came limping back to her chair and begged him not to mind, he refused to be conciliated." After this mishap, Mark soon imagined a pressing engagement and begged leave to be excused. As the two guests took their departure, they passed Orpheus still walking up and down the hall. Dan said that "He was not in good humor and scowled and muttered in reply to our salutations." Thus ended the great dinner which had begun so propitiously.

The Menken left her permanent footprints on the Lode: a street was named in her honor, and a newly discovered ledge was named "The Menken." The *Union* quipped with the remark that "We suppose the first work done in that district will be to 'strip the ledges.'" [11] "The Menken Shaft and Tunnel Company" was organized, the stock certificates for which were engraved with a naked siren strapped to a stallion. A new ledge called the "Mazeppa Mounting Ledge" made its appearance in Washoe. She was presented with many shares of stock in mining companies. A bullion bar of silver worth $2000 and suitably inscribed was given to her. Where else, one asks, in the wide world could such performances be repeated? Great actors and actresses were to come to the Lode, but not one of them equalled the Menken.

20

PATRIOTISM VERSUS DUELING

ALTHOUGH WASHOE WAS SEVERAL THOUSAND MILES away from the thick of the fighting in the Civil War, the people were none the less patriotic in raising money, in celebrating Union victories, and in keeping down secessionist sentiment. Every invention was used to raise money for the Sanitary Commission, the Civil War version of the Red Cross. Sanitary balls were given, Sanitary fairs were held, and rich ore was donated, run out into silver bars, and forwarded for this work. In the spring of 1864, several events were held in all of the important towns of the Territory to raise money for the sick and wounded soldiers. It was reporting these events which led to an editorial controversy between Mark Twain, aided and abetted by Steve Gillis of the *Territorial Enterprise*, and James L. Laird and J. W. Wilmington of the Virginia City *Union*.

The "red-hot" editorials and articles which appeared in both papers grew warmer and warmer. Very soon Mark Twain found himself involved in a duel in Virginia City, as well as having to answer to the irate husband of one of the ladies in Carson City who had been prominent in putting on a ball in that city for the same cause. It happened that at this time Joe Goodman was not in Virginia City, and Mark had a free hand in printing whatever he pleased. Not that Joe would have interfered, for only a few months had passed since he and Tom Fitch had had their duel.

On April 20, the ladies of Gold Hill gave an entertainment for the benefit of the Sanitary Fund at the Old Theatre. The leading ladies of the town were on the committee of arrangements. Their boast was that enough money would be raised to "buy a silver brick that will cause the good people of St. Louis and the country round about to stare in astonishment and the hearts of the sick and wounded recipients of the benefit grow glad." In addition to dancing, there was a concert and an elaborate supper, all for five dollars a person. A report of the committee, published in the Gold Hill *Evening News* on April 26, declared that the net proceeds amounted to $3080. The *Enterprise* complimented the ladies on a grand success.

At about the same time that the Gold Hill ladies had their ball, the ladies of Carson City began arrangements for an entertainment in aid of the Sanitary Fund in which "they propose to outdo our fellow-citizens in the amount of funds raised. The Gold Hill ladies will, however, take good care that the high reputation of our town for liberality and patriotism does not suffer in the strife of noble emulation between themselves and their sisters at Carson." In the Carson benefit Mollie Clemens took a prominent part, as she had done in everything since her arrival in the Territory. Some time went by, and no report was forthcoming. The *Enterprise* began twitting the Carson City ladies about the amount raised and the purpose for which the money was to be spent.

However, before Mark Twain got himself hopelessly involved in this affair, he became enmeshed with the editor of the Virginia City *Daily Union* over the contributions made for the Sanitary Fund in auctioning the Sanitary Sack of Flour. No story of the early period of Nevada history is complete without a description of this unique event; and it is also important in the story of Mark Twain in Nevada —it led to his exit from the Territory.

The occasion for the auction of this particular sack of flour was a wager on the outcome of the mayoralty contest over in Austin, about one hundred and fifty miles east of Virginia City on the old Pony Express-Overland Stage route to Salt Lake City. Austin, a city about two years old, and the most recent of the boom towns, was robust, thriving, and pulsating with excitement. When Lander County was set up as the result of the rush to Reese River, Austin was made the county seat, and Governor Nye had unwittingly appointed a number of Secesh to county offices. In fact, these Southern sympathizers were so active in the summer of 1863 that Acting Governor Clemens removed several of them, for which he received the commendation of the *Enterprise* of July 10 when it stated that "Governor Clemens seems to be the right man in the right place. He has acted bravely, patriotically, promptly, and to the extent of his power in aiding to oust treasonable officials." It will be remembered that brother Sam was a reporter on this paper at the time.

A number of "copperheads" were living in the vicinity of Austin, and when the time came for the city election, a full ticket was put in the field. Colonel David E. Buel, an ex-special Indian agent, affectionately nicknamed "Uncle Dave," ran for mayor on the Demo-

The first auction, Sanitary Sack of Flour, Main Street, Austin, Nevada

From Browne's *Washoe Revisited*

cratic ticket. He was a dignified and imposing gentleman six feet four inches in height, large in proportion, and without a fault save that of always being on the wrong side. He was wonderfully attractive to the "honest miner" because of his frank, generous, offhand manner. In fact, he was so popular that it was believed that he would carry a large portion of the Republican vote in the election.

Buel's opponent was Charles Holbrook, a young merchant who had a fine character and who was an excellent businessman. Holbrook was responsible in a large degree for anchoring the floating population of the Reese River Mining District by building a cut-granite store building in upper Austin. He was a Unionist of the ultra brand. There could be no doubt about *his* election; his integrity and loyalty were unassailable.

Formal amusement in these early mining towns was not to be had. To make up for this lack of entertainment, every event, large or small, was played up as much as possible. Any kind of contest was the occasion for much betting, be it a horse race, a badger fight, hopping fleas, or a political contest. Many bets were laid on the outcome of the race for Mayor. The unique one was made between Dr. H. S. Herrick and Reuel C. Gridley: if Uncle Dave were elected, Herrick, supporting Holbrook, was to carry a fifty-pound sack of flour from Clifton to Upper Austin, a distance of about a mile and a half and a stiff upgrade all the way; whereas if Holbrook were elected, Gridley, supporting Buel, was to carry a sack of flour from Upper Austin downgrade to Clifton. The election battle was exciting; Holbrook, the Republican, was elected by a fair majority. Americans voted soundly when their Union was at stake.

Gridley, having lost his bet, prepared to "pay off," and was on hand at the appointed time with his sack of flour, which he had appropriately decorated with small American flags and red, white, and blue ribbon. A big crowd of people gathered in front of Holbrook's hardware store to witness the payment of this novel election bet. A grand procession was formed, led by a band, and followed by the newly elected city officers mounted on horseback. Gridley came next with his sack of flour hoisted on his shoulder, Dr. Herrick carrying his coat, and Gridley's ten-year-old son walking by his side. Crowds of cheering citizens brought up the rear.

As the parade passed through the street on the way to Clifton, the band struck up "Yankee Doodle," but Gridley never flinched.

The mine and mill whistles set up a continuous screech. All along the line of march Gridley sympathizers urged him on with "Go it, Gridley!" "Stick to it, Gridley!" "Never say die, Gridley!" The procession finally arrived at Clifton, whereupon some enterprising genius, anxious both to keep up the excitement and the patriotic demonstration for the Union cause, suggested that the flour be auctioned for the benefit of the Sanitary Commission. The proposition was received with applause commensurate to the occasion. In a moment an empty barrel was rolled into place and an auctioneer mounted upon it. Although the bidding was lively, the crowd had not quite got the infection and the flour brought only $5.

To keep the betting alive, someone else suggested that the sack be taken back up the hill to Upper Austin and re-auctioned. The procession was re-formed and this time the band struck up "Dixie." The "copperheads" were by that time delirious with joy, and both sides gathered enthusiasm on the way back. It was a clever stroke of policy on the part of the Republicans.

This time the crowd stopped in front of the newly elected Mayor Holbrook's store. It soon got around to all the mines and mills in the vicinity that another auction was to take place. It was said that scarcely a living person for miles around was not present—out of the mines, mills, saloons, and bunkhouses came Indians, Chinamen, women, and children—everyone—to see the fun.

Then the sack of flour, now referred to as the "Sanitary Sack of Flour," was once more put up for auction. And *now* everyone caught on to what it was all about. Not only did the sick and wounded soldiers tug at their hearts and their pocketbooks, but also the spirit of competition and the love of excitement stirred them. The people began to bid by the twenties, the fifties, the hundreds; mining stock, city lots, and gold and silver coins were used to get the sack of flour. Every time it was knocked down to the winner, it was returned and re-auctioned. Three thousand dollars was the grand result of the second auction.

On the following day a third auction was held and an additional $1700 was added to the original sum. So proud was the community of its achievement that the Reese River *Reveille* published a long account of it.

Over in Virginia City the story was read with interest and envy. The first-born of the Territory was not going to be outstripped by a little community out on Reese River. A telegram was sent by the boys on the *Enterprise* to Gridley telling him to bring his sack of flour over there and give Virginia City a chance to bid on it.

Sam Clemens had known Reuel Gridley back in Hannibal, Missouri.[1] Although Gridley was some years older than Sam, they had gone to the same one-room school. Gridley had come to the West in the Gold Rush, and later to Nevada in the Silver Rush. One day as he was passing down the main street in Carson City in 1861, he came opposite a group of men and heard what he thought was a familiar drawling voice. Sam was having a difficulty with an editor on the sidewalk. There was only one person in the world who spoke in that slow Missouri twang. Slapping him on the back, Gridley said: "Give him the best you've got, Sam. I'm at your back."

Arranging his business affairs in Austin, Gridley resolved to make an institution of the Sanitary Sack of Flour. He planned an auction tour, of which Virginia City would be merely the first stop after Austin. Arriving unexpectedly on a Sunday, May 15, the sack brought only $580. On the following day, Gridley, seated in an open barouche and accompanied by a band, headed a procession which took off over the Divide and down to Gold Hill with great pomp, waving banners, and the playing of martial music. The Gold Hill *Evening News* said that "Tone was given to the Procession by the presence of Governor Twain and his staff of bibulous reporters, who came down in a free carriage, ostensibly for the purpose of taking notes, but in reality in pursuit of whiskey." Thomas Fitch was along to arouse their patriotism. Large sums of money were raised in Silver City and Dayton. On the way back "The Lord's Army," as the procession had been dubbed by the papers, stopped at Silver City, and a few more sales were made.

Tom Fitch added merriment to the occasion by relating the story of the Sanitary bug: It seemed that some person had observed a small brown bug—it was not a "grayback"—crawling on the pantaloons of Captain Close. In the enthusiasm aroused by the occasion, he caught the specimen of Washoe entomology, placed it on the bar of the saloon, and, describing it to be the "Great Sanitary Bug of Washoe," asked for bids for His Bugship. The idea took; several bids were made, and soon the bug was knocked down for $10. The new owner of the Great Sanitary Bug again put him up for auction, and again the bidding commenced. Just at this time a man who had

Torch light parade, Virginia City, Nevada, 1864. Auction of Sanitary Sack of Flour

From Roughing It

offered $1.50 for the bug asked a bystander for information in regard to it. "What is there about the bug," he inquired, "that makes it so valuable?"

"It is the Great Sanitary Bug," answered the person to whom this question was propounded. "It is only because the money is going to the Sanitary Fund that people are bidding on it."

At this the man who had offered $1.50 showed symptoms of disgust. "Damn the Sanitary Fund!" he cried. "Is that all?"

At once Captain Close confronted him with "My friend, you must not damn the Sanitary Fund here." However, the man, who had been going it altogether on the merits of the bug, insisted upon damning the Sanitary Fund, whereupon Captain Close turned loose upon him and gave him a beautiful thrashing, blacking his eyes handsomely. During the confusion incident to this slight digression from the program, the Great Sanitary Bug was swept away and lost, or His Bugship might have sold ere this for thousands of dollars, and might have had the honor of a glass case and a trip to the Mississippi Valley Fair, labeled "The Great Sanitary Bug from Washoe."

Toward evening the sack of flour, Gridley, and the reporters returned to Virginia City. That evening the second auction took place, which ended in historic controversy. The Virginia City *Union* urged the meeting in a rousing announcement:

> Turn out for the honor of Nevada! Turn out for the sake of loyalty and humanity. Listen to the cry of suffering from our wounded thousands on the road to Richmond, and fill the building with an eager throng of humane, generous-hearted givers.

The *Union* praised the response of the people individually, but scathingly rebuked the large mining companies for their lack of patriotism in not giving what that paper thought they should:

> The contributions of yesterday were, with a few honorable exceptions, made by the miners, merchants, mechanics, and professional men of Nevada. The great companies, which could easily have afforded to donate a quarter of a million from their coffers, were generally most shamefully indifferent.

The discussion about the generosity, or lack of it, in certain groups on the Lode might have ended with the outburst of the *Union*, had not a dispute arisen between the editors of that paper

and Mark Twain, acting editor of the *Enterprise* in the absence of
Joe Goodman, over the donations of the newspaper workers to the
Fund. The *Enterprise* fired the opening gun in the *casus belli* by
making certain accusing statements which thoroughly aroused the
Union. In reply to Mark's editorial the *Union* said:

THE "HOW IS IT" ISSUE

When last the Sanitary Commission called for aid, the publishers and employees of the Virginia *Daily Union* unostenta-
tiously united with their generous fellow citizens and contributed the sum of five hundred and fifteen dollars. We have
paid that sum in gold to the Treasurer of the Sanitary Fund for
Storey County. The *Territorial Enterprise* newspaper has only
pretended to contribute. It has paid nothing of the contributions
which it, with great self-show, promised—always in the presence
of a crowd. This sort of showing-off was not sufficient in itself.
The *Enterprise* must contemptibly boast of its liberality over the
Union, and, in the most unmanly manner, carry its unwarrant-
able assertions so far as to say that the gentlemen in the employ
of the *Union* would not pay their subscriptions. We showed the
utter and unprecedented meanness of the *Enterprise* in this instance, and that paper yesterday returned a string of despicable
stuff knotted so full of lies that there was not left a space sufficient for the smallest thread of truth. Never before, in a long
period of newspaper intercourse—never before in any contact
with a contemporary, however unprincipled he might have
been, have we found an opponent in statement or in discussion,
who had no gentlemanly sense of professional propriety, who
conceived in every word, and in every purpose of all his words,
such a groveling disregard for truth, decency, and courtesy, as
to seem to court the distinction only of being understood as a
vulgar liar. Meeting one who prefers falsehood; whose instincts
are all toward falsehood; whose thought is falsification; whose
aim is vilification through insincere professions of honesty; one
whose only merit is thus described, and who evidently desires
to be thus known, the obstacles presented are entirely insur-
mountable, and whoever would touch them fully should expect
to be abominably defiled.

In the same issue of the *Union*, J. W. Wilmington, a member of the printing force of that paper, prepared a statement giving the workers' point of view:

"HOW IT IS"

Virginia *Daily Union:*

The editor of the *Daily Enterprise* has, during the last two days, in his anxiety to injure a contemporary, seen fit to place before the public in a false light, and slander in a cowardly manner the printers of this city. We refer to his misrepresentation of the circumstance attending our donation to the Sanitary Fund. We wish it distinctly understood that we have no sympathy whatever in any issue between the proprietors of the *Union* and *Enterprise.* Nor do we entertain any feeling of rivalry toward our fellow-craftsmen employed on that paper. We consider that what redounds to our credit is equally due them. The editor of the *Enterprise* has asserted that but for *his* promptings, the employees of the *Union* would never have paid their last contributions. In this he wilfully lies. The employees of the *Union* were in no way instigated to make the donation by their employers, and never contemplated repudiating it. Thursday morning's *Union* gave a full list of the men who had donated the money, and the receipt of Mr. Black, Secretary of the Sanitary Fund, attesting that it ($515) had been paid. This should have removed all doubts, if any existed, as to who were the donors. Why does not the editor of the *Enterprise* accuse Mr. George F. Jones, Mr. De Long, and many other prominent citizens who subscribed repeatedly during the evening, of being influenced to do so by a spirit of rivalry toward this establishment?

We can only view his blackguardism as an attack upon members of our craft. In asserting that we "had not intended to pay the bill, but on secondary consideration, and for the sake of saving an entirely imaginary reputation for virtue and honesty, concluded to do so," he has endeavored to misinterpret the generous, patriotic promptings of laboring men who gave their little mite willingly; and in so doing he has proved himself an unmitigated *liar, a poltroon, and a puppy.*

Printer.[2]

After these two articles appeared in the *Union,* there followed several accusing and challenging notes between Laird and Mark, in which the latter issued the peremptory demand:

Enterprise Office,
Saturday Evening,
May 21, 1864

James Laird

Sir:

I wrote you a note this afternoon, demanding a published retraction of insults that appeared in two articles in the *Union* of this morning, or satisfaction. I have since received what purports to be a reply, written by a person who signs himself "J. W. Wilmington," in which he assumes the authorship and responsibility of one of said infamous articles. Wilmington is a person entirely unknown to me in the matter, and has nothing to do with it. In the columns of your paper you have declared your own responsibility for all articles appearing in it, and any further attempt to make a catspaw of any other individual, and thus shirk a responsibility that you have previously assumed, will show that you are a cowardly sneak. I now peremptorily demand of you the satisfaction due to a gentleman, without alternative.

Sam. L. Clemens

The same evening Laird replied to the challenge with a note in which he explained who Wilmington was. He stated his responsibility for the editorials only. He did say, however, that he would, in the case of future communications, accommodate Mark by giving him the names and addresses of the authors. Among other things in the same note, Laird said:

You demand of me, in your last letter, the satisfaction due to a gentleman, and couple the demand with offensive remarks. When you have earned the right to the title by complying with the usual custom, I shall be most happy to afford you any satisfaction you desire at any time and in any place. In short, Wilmington has a prior claim upon your attention. When he is through with you, I shall be at your service. If you decline to meet him after challenging him, you will prove yourself to be what he has charged you with being, 'a liar, a poltroon, and a puppy,' and as such, cannot, of course, be entitled to the consideration of a gentleman."

Respectfully,

James L. Laird.

It was nine o'clock in the evening of the same day that Mark replied:

"You assume in your last note, that I 'have challenged Wilmington,' and that he has informed me, 'over his own signature,' that he is quite ready to afford me 'satisfaction.' Both assumptions are utterly false. I have twice challenged you, and you have twice attempted to shirk the responsibility. . . . In the meantime, if you do not wish yourself posted as a coward, you will at once accept my peremptory challenge, which I now reiterate."

On the following Monday morning, May 23, Laird accused Mark of evading a meeting with Wilmington and of trying to force one on him. He added that he had "no right under the rulings of the code to meet or hold any communication with you in this connection."

Mark Twain's last fling at Laird was an open denouncement of him as "an unmitigated liar" . . . and "an abject coward"; he ended with: "Finally, he is a fool, because he cannot understand that a publisher is bound to stand responsible for any and all articles printed by him, whether he wants to do it or not."

Other newspapers thought the whole affair of the Laird-Clemens quarrel foolish. The Gold Hill *Evening News* of May 24 under the title of "Hoity! Toity!" had the following to say about it:

The cross-firing that has been going on for a week past between the *Union* and *Enterprise,* concerning a donation made by the employees of the former paper to the Sanitary Fund, has at last culminated in a serious row, and the bloody and barbarous code has been appealed to. Nearly a column of this morning's *Enterprise* is devoted to the publication of the correspondence between Sam Clemens and James L. Laird, and Mr. Wilmington, who comes in as an intervener, and assumes the responsibility of the article for the publication of which Clemens holds Laird to an account. Laird declines to accede to the proposition of Clemens, and the latter proceeds to 'post him,' with all of those epithets in such case by the code made and provided. This is emphatically a bad egg. In the first place, the cause of [the] quarrel was not as calculated to enlist public sympathy; neither did the discussion of the question demand the use of the language which was resorted to. If the matter results in bloodshed, the victim will not be mourned as a martyr in a holy cause, nor the victor crowned with laurel as the champion of right. The sentiment of a civilized community revolts at the appeal to bloody code on every trifling cause of offense. There is another reason, and that a very serious one, why we object to the code being called into requisition on slight occasions among the editorial fraternity. We have noticed that there is a proneness to fire at the legs, and that 'there is a divinity that *un*-shapes our ends,' to the extent that one of the parties is ever afterwards remarkable for the gait vulgarly styled the 'stip and go fetch it.' . . . 'How are you, old limpy?' This thing must be put stop. [*sic*]

(The allusion, of course, was to the Goodman-Fitch duel in which Fitch, it will be remembered, was shot in the knee, because of which he limped the rest of his life.)

Goodman had been in San Francisco .or two months. He returned to Virginia City on May 25, the day after the challenge was issued.

The Sacramento *Union* reprinted the Laird-Clemens notes, and at the conclusion commented that "There was no fighting at last accounts." The San Francisco *Call* on May 28 made light of the whole affair and remarked that "The day has gone by when duels can give any man credit for bravery or honor, wisdom or truth; and to call people fools, cowards, poltroons, liars, puppies, and other flattering names does not make them so, nor prove them so."

Mark Twain made no reference to this affair in *Roughing It*; but Albert Bigelow Paine, in his biography of Mark, told the story of it as it was related to him by Steve Gillis. Mark dictated an account of it to the same author, printed in his *Autobiography*.[3] There was no doubt that Steve Gillis had a big hand in the entire affair, Diminutive Steve, weighing less than one hundred pounds, was the son of "Fighting" Gillis, one of General William Walker's men in his filibustering campaigns in Central America. In fact, the father was killed in the memorable Plaza fight, when a bullet through his eye carried the glass of his spectacles into his skull. Steve had wanted dearly to go along, and so did several of his brothers, but they were too young.

Mark said the challenge was written for him by Rollin M. Daggett, who was on the *Enterprise* staff at the time, and that Steve Gillis, his second, carried the challenge. Steve was the go-between for Laird and Mark in most of the correspondence that passed between them. And Steve took the responsibility of training Mark for the duel. The familiar story about the training for the bout—the account has it that Mark received an undeserved but formidable reputation for marksmanship from an amazing shot, really Steve's, which took off the head of a small bird perched at an impossible distance on a sagebrush twig—makes good reading. It may or may not be fact.[4]

However, there was a serious angle to the affair of honor: After the Goodman-Fitch duel in 1863 had maimed Fitch for life, the Territorial legislature had passed a law making the challenge, the acceptance of a duel, or serving as a second in one a felony, punishable with two years in the penitentiary. Word was sent indirectly to Mark and Steve that they had better leave the Territory at once. They took the outbound stage on May 29, 1864, for San Francisco.

Before they left the Territory of Nevada, another serious matter had to be cleared up, or Mark Twain would have had another duel on his hands. This circumstance concerned the disposition of the proceeds of the Sanitary Ball, referred to in the first part of this chapter, given by the ladies of Carson City. "You see," said Mark, "Laird was not the only person whom I had tried to reform during my occupancy of the editorial chair. I had looked around and selected several other people, and delivered new zest of life into them through warm criticism and disapproval—so that when I laid down my editorial pen, I had four horse-whippings and two duels owing me."

Mr. W. K. Cutler had come up to Virginia City, not only as the representative of the Carson City ladies' committee, but also as the husband of the president of the committee.

In a sharp editorial which Mark Twain wrote in the *Enterprise* on May 18, just a few days before his altercation with Laird, he had aroused the wrath of the ladies of the capital city. In protest to the editorial, the committee had sent a note to the *Enterprise,* which took no recognition of it. The same note was then sent to the Virginia City *Daily Union,* which paper, in turn, printed it.

Carson City
May 18th, 1864

Editors of the *Enterprise:*

In your issue of yesterday, you state "that the reason the Flour Sack was not taken from Dayton to Carson, was because it was stated that the money raised at the Sanitary Fancy Dress Ball, recently held in Carson for the St. Louis Fair, had been diverted from its legitimate course, and was to be sent to aid a Miscegenation Society somewhere in the East; and it was feared the proceeds of the Sack might be similarly disposed of." You apparently mollify the statement by saying "that it was a hoax, but not all a hoax, for an effort is being made to divert those funds from their proper course."

In behalf of the ladies who originated and assisted in carrying out the programme, let us say that the whole statement is a *tissue of falsehoods,* made for *malicious* purposes, and we demand the name of the author. The ball was gotten up in aid of the Sanitary Commission and *not* for the St. Louis Fair. At a meeting of the ladies, held in this city last week, no decision was arrived at as to whether the proceeds of the ball should be sent to St. Louis or New York, but one thing *was decided,* that they should go to the aid of the sick and wounded soldiers, who are fighting the battles of our country, and *for no other purpose* . . . the ladies having the matter in charge consider themselves capable of deciding as to what shall be done with the money, without the aid of outsiders, who are probably desirous of acquiring some *glory* by appropriating the efforts of the ladies to themselves.

Mrs. W. K. Cutler, President.
Mrs. H. F. Rice, Vice President.
Mrs. S. K. King, Treasurer.
Mrs. H. H. Ross, Sec'y San. Ball.

Mollie Clemens had been very active in making the Carson ball a success and was one of the officers of the original committee.

Mark, being very fond of Mollie, did not wish to embarrass her. He learned, however, that the Carson City ladies were taking it out on her for his misdeeds. Not wishing his sister-in-law to be snubbed by them on his account, he wrote Mrs. Cutler a letter explaining why he could not at that particular time come out with an apology. An example of the finer qualities of Mark Twain shows up in this letter to Mrs. Cutler:

Virginia
May 23rd, 1864

Mrs. W. K. Cutler:

Madam:

I address a lady in every sense of the term. Mrs. Clemens has informed me of everything that has occurred in Carson in connection with that unfortunate item of mine about the Sanitary Funds accruing from the ball, and from what I can understand, you are almost the only lady in your city who has understood the circumstances under which my fault was committed, or who has shown any disposition to be lenient with me. Had the note of the ladies been properly worded, I would have published an ample apology instantly—and possibly I might even have done so anyhow, had that note arrived at any other time—but it came at a moment when I was in the midst of what ought to have been a deadly quarrel with the publishers of the *Union,* and I could not come out and make public apologies to anyone at such a time. It is bad policy to do it even now (as challenges have already passed between myself and a proprietor of the *Union,* and the matter is still in abeyance), but I suppose I had better say a word or two to show the ladies that I did not wilfully and maliciously do them a wrong.

But my chief object, Mrs. Cutler, in writing you this note (and you will pardon the liberty I have taken) was to thank you very kindly and sincerely for the consideration you have shown me in this matter, and for your continued friendship for Mollie while others are disposed to withdraw theirs on account of a fault for which I alone am responsible.

Very truly yours,
Sam L. Clemens.[5]

Mrs. Cutler, a celebrated singer and elocutionist, was a teacher in the Sierra Seminary in Carson City, the only private school in the Territory, and, as such, she was influential in the community. Mark avoided Mr. Cutler when he came to Virginia City.

There may have been something significant in the fact that Steve and Mark took the Henness Pass Stage instead of the Johnson Pass route when they fled from Virginia City. The former "bypassed" Carson City and went over the Geiger Grade, where connections were made with the Donner Pass route that took the boys directly to Sacramento and thence to San Francisco.

And thus the years in Nevada Territory came to an end for Mark Twain. He had stayed in the West for almost three years, where at first he had planned to remain only three months. From an observer on Carson Street in the capital he had passed in quick succession to a mine owner, mill hand, speculator, feet owner, and finally to a reporter on the *Territorial Enterprise,* the most influential paper in the intermountain region. His editorials and articles had been printed in the leading papers on the Pacific Coast; and he had received some notice in Eastern journals. His "Empire City Hoax" had made a greater impression on his readers than any other article he had written in Nevada. Indeed, today he is more readily known by that story among the old pioneer mining folk than by any other of his writings. In Nevada he was known by a number of names— "Josh," "Mark Twain," and "Governor Mark Twain"—but all the oldtimers refer to him as Sam Clemens.

The leave-taking of Sam Clemens was noted by the Gold Hill *Evening News* of May 30 under the title of:

AN EXILE

Among the few immortals that have departed—that is, those who departed yesterday morning by the California stage—we notice that of Mark Twain.

We don't wonder. Mark Twain's beard is full of dirt and his face is black before the people of Washoe. Giving way to the idiosyncratic eccentricities of an erratic mind, Mark has indulged in the game infernal. In short, "played hell!"

Shifting the locale of his tales of fiction from the Forest of Dutch Nick's to Carson City; the *dramatis personae* thereof from the Hopkins family to the fair ladies of the Ladies' Fair; and the plot thereof from murder to miscegenation, he stopped. The enormities have been too crushing to be borne by living man, tho' sheathed with the brass and triple cheek of Mark Twain.

"Thrice the wounded cat hath mewed
"Thrice, and once the hedgehog whined . . ."

Thrice the card of the indignant ladies has appeared in the columns of the *Union* and once the Carson *Independent* contained the following: "The Ladies' Sanitary Committee met in the parlor of the Ormsby House on Thursday evening last, for the purpose of ascertaining the amount of funds derived from all sources in aid of the Sanitary Fund. After deducting all expenses, it was found they had just $2000 which was forwarded to Dr. Billows, President of the National Sanitary Committee, yesterday. A vote of thanks was tendered to his Excellency, Governor Nye, for his able lecture delivered in aid of the Fund, and to the *Independent* office for many favors in the way of printing; also to offices of the society and ladies who have assisted in the undertaking. The ladies all seemed pleased with their efforts and we are informed that before adjourning they gave three cheers for the 'immortal four' and three groans for the *Territorial Enterprise.*"

These groans were not for the *Enterprise* in the abstract but for the *Enterprise* as the vehicle of Mark Twain's abominations. He has vamosed, cut, absquatulated; and among the pine forests of the Sierras or amid the purlieus of the city of earthquakes, he will tarry a while and the office of the *Enterprise* will become purified and by the united efforts of Goodman and Dan De Quille once more merit the sweet smile of the ladies of Carson City.

The "Wilmington-Laird versus Clemens" duel took Mark Twain out of Washoe probably only a few months before he would have gone of his own volition. A combination of events was shaping, events which would have impelled him to shake off the alkali dust of the Lode. In the first place there were no more literary worlds to conquer in Nevada—he *was* the recognized humorist of Washoe, and he was the most feared political writer in the Territory. San Francisco already knew him well; papers of many other cities as well had printed some of his sketches. He wrote his mother from San Francisco as early as June 1, 1863: "I suppose I know at least a thousand people here—a great many of them citizens of San Francisco, but the majority belonging to Washoe—and when I go down Montgomery Street, shaking hands with Tom, Dick, and Harry, it is just like being on Main Street in Hannibal and meeting the old familiar faces. I *do hate* to go back to Washoe." [6]

The exhilarating excitement of Washoe had spent itself by 1864. Even by the end of the preceding year many of the smaller mines had closed, and the prices of "wildcats" had dropped to low levels. Dividends from the best-producing mines had fallen far below expectations—scarcely interest on the enormous expenditures. There had been little or no returns from hundreds of other mines on which millions of dollars' worth of development work had been done. The San Francisco mining market was unsteady—rumors that the Ophir and Gould & Curry bonanzas were not holding on the lower levels were spread around. The market needed only a small break to send it down rapidly.

That push was furnished by "reckless, bloody, extravagant Aurora." Early in 1864 the ore in the two leading mines of that camp—the Del Monte and the Wide West—failed at the water level, less than one hundred feet down. And with that crash, Aurora was through as a great mining camp. Before Mark Twain left Virginia City, the newspapers were complaining of dull times: "Merchant and miner, banker and broker, lawyer and doctor, join in the chorus and echo the oft-made assertion that never since 1860 has Virginia been so dull as during the last few weeks—Stocks are down; money is high, and almost impossible to obtain even at the highest rates. . . . From Austin and Aurora and Humboldt the same cry of dull times comes up unceasingly." The stimulus which Mark had felt when he arrived in Nevada had worn off.

When Nevada became a State, there were several candidates for all of the offices, with the possible exception of United States Senator and Secretary of State. Nye was sure of the former and Orion of the latter. However, on the day that the Republican party convention met to name the candidates, Orion was seized with "one of his spasms of virtue" and absolutely refused to go near the convention.

BOOK V

ALUMNUS

21

FAREWELL TO THE ROBBERS

SHORTLY AFTER SAM CLEMENS AND STEVE GILLIS were settled in their San Francisco boardinghouse, Sam got a job as a reporter and Steve as a compositor on the San Francisco *Morning Call*. However, their "quiet" boardinghouse proved to be so noisy that they had to find another one. By the time they had been in San Francisco four months, they had "tried out five boarding-and-lodging establishments and two hotels." How Sam Clemens ever stood the noises in Virginia City as long as he did is more than can be reconciled with his dislike of din. What with the hundreds of stamps pounding on the ore night and day, the shrill shrieks of the mill steam whistles, the constant hammering in the foundries and blacksmith shops, his hypersensitive ears must have been tortured.

In San Francisco Sam not only wrote for the *Call,* but also contributed articles to the *Golden Era* and the *Californian.* In San Francisco he met most of the resident literati and the visiting writers. He enjoyed their companionship and the life in the city, but the routine work of a large city newspaper was not sufficiently interesting for him to remain at this job. "It was fearful drudgery —soulless drudgery—and almost destitute of interest. It was awful slavery for a lazy man." [1]

Seizing a chance to resign his position on the *Call,* he then concentrated on the letters which he had been contributing to the *Territorial Enterprise* in which he rebuked and exposed the political corruption of San Francisco, especially that of the police department. So specific in names and circumstances were these letters that no San Francisco paper dared publish them. Hence Sam sent them to Joe Goodman, who, in turn, published them in full. The San Francisco police were so savagely attacked that the chief filed a libel suit against the Nevada paper. Even this threat, of which nothing came, did not deter Sam from his efforts to bring about social justice.[2]

Unfortunately for Sam, however, when this controversy was

going on, Steve got into trouble with the police. Picking on a big bartender in a saloon fight, Steve, although much smaller, got the best of his adversary. The police arrested him, and Sam went his bail. As soon as Steve was free, he "lit out" for Virginia City, whereupon the police chief promptly brought action against his bondsman. Jim Gillis, Steve's brother, who was in San Francisco at the time, warned Sam to take to his cabin on Jackass Hill. Sam arrived there on December 4, 1864. He spent several months in the California foothill mining towns, where he did some pocket gold mining and gathered literary material. The latter was to become the basis for his literary fortune, for from it he wrote his first story, "Jim Smiley and His Jumping Frog."

This tale was to have been published in a volume of sketches by Artemus Ward, but it did not arrive in New York in time to be included in that volume. The publisher turned it over to the *Saturday Press,* wherein it appeared November 18, 1865. It immediately seized the imagination of the great American public; it was quoted, copied, read, and discussed "up and down the Atlantic Coast, and out over the prairies of the Middle West." And with the "Jumping Frog," Mark Twain leaped to fame. Deference began to be paid him and special honors were bestowed on him, at home as well as in distant parts.

Turning down an invitation to go on the maiden voyage of the new steamer *Ajax* built for the trade with the Sandwich (Hawaiian) Islands, he reproved himself after it had gone. He later found a way to go on the second trip by obtaining a commission from the *Sacramento Union* to write a series of letters for that paper about island life. He wrote fully of this trip to and from the Islands and his stay there in *Roughing It.*

Sailing on March 7, 1865, the *Ajax* took eleven days to make the voyage. Armed with many letters of introduction, Sam met the first missionary and industrial families of the Islands. Several old Washoe friends were there, among them the Reverend Rising, his old friend from Virginia City, in the Islands for his health. To see the Islands properly in those days one had to go on horseback. Once more in Sam Clemens' life in the West he acquired a steed, "Oahu" by name, upon which he encircled and crossed and recrossed the island of Oahu, visiting the important points of interest. He met the American missionaries; he dined with the King's Chamberlain; he called on his royal highness, the King; and he visited the island legislature.

Sam made trips to all of the islands reached by the interisland boats and enjoyed himself immensely. He loved the idyllic life of tropical plantations. During his stay on the island of Maui, he spent two weeks with Mr. Alexander and his wife, the former a bookkeeper at the plantation house in Wailuku. Here a great deal of that portion of *Roughing It* which describes the Islands was written. "He was often welcomed to supper at the Alexander home, and he and Mr. Alexander had jolly times together."

When Sam returned to Honolulu from his trip to Maui, he found a letter from Mollie Clemens awaiting him. So accustomed had she and Orion become to having Sam make major decisions for them that she was now asking him when he expected to go back home, meaning Missouri. He replied: "I set sail again, a week hence, for the island of Hawaii, to see the great active volcano of Kilauea. I shall not get back here for four or five weeks, and shall not reach San Francisco before the latter part of July. So it is no use for me to go home. Go on yourselves. . . ."[3]

After Orion had failed to obtain a State office under the new government of Nevada, he tried to practice law in Carson City; but he obtained so few clients that he finally closed his office. In 1866, he was elected an Assemblyman from Ormsby County. In the legislative session of that year he introduced a bill similar to the one adopted during the Territorial days—namely, to have all corporations doing business in Nevada record their papers fully. He hoped that he might receive the position of recorder and restore the prosperity he had gained from the same source while he was Territorial Secretary; but the measure failed to pass.[4] Shortly after the close of this session he and Mollie sold the "Governor's Mansion," which had cost $12,000, for $3500 in greenbacks, and returned to Keokuk, Iowa.[5] They left little Jennie buried in Lone Mountain Cemetery where one may still see her grave. Her little rocking chair, however, went with her parents wherever they went. It always had a prominent place in their living room.

The great island of Hawaii fascinated Mark Twain, what with its places of historical interest, the active volcanoes, and its peculiar coral formations. He spent a long time riding over its rough terrain. It was at this time, near Waiohinu Kau, that he planted the

"Monkey-pod Tree" which today is well-marked and grown to a prodigious size. Near the end of June, Mark returned to Honolulu, tired from travel and uncomfortable from saddle boils, to rest quietly until he recovered.

While he was recuperating, the *Ajax* arrived from another trip to the States carrying His Excellency, Anson Burlingame, then returning to his post as Minister to China. Other distinguished persons on board were Colonel Rumsey; General Van Valkenburg, Minister to Japan; and Edward Burlingame, son of the Minister to China. Edward had read the "Jumping Frog" story and some other bits of Mark Twain's writing. Upon learning that Twain was in Honolulu and ill, the party sent word to him that it would call on him the next morning. It was event enough in Mark Twain's life to meet such distinguished people, but of even greater importance to him was the aid which Minister Burlingame gave him in "scooping" a big story: the personal narrations of the fifteen survivors of the *Hornet* who had battled the open sea for forty-three days, and had managed to live on ten days' rations. The *Hornet* had set out from New York and taken fire and burned. These few starving wretches had finally drifted to the island of Hawaii, from which place they were brought to Honolulu.

With Burlingame's help Mark took down their story and sent it on the next steamer to the *Sacramento Union* in which it was printed on July 19, and from which it was telegraphed everywhere. For this story he was paid handsomely when he returned to the States, and to Anson Burlingame he was eternally grateful for helping him get the information. The Minister, who was impressed with Mark Twain, gave him some unforgettable advice:

> "You have great ability; I believe you have genius. What you need now is the refinement of association. Seek companionship among men of superior intellect and character. Refine yourself and your work. Never affiliate with inferiors; always climb." [6]

Although it had been four years since he had trudged on foot all of the way from Aurora to Virginia City to take up his first writing job in the West, Mark Twain had come a long way: he had met many people of importance, he had seen many places, and he had been climbing the ladder to fame.

On August 13, 1866, Mark Twain returned to San Francisco full of information on island life which he intended to include in his writings and about which he planned to lecture. His first lecture was given in San Francisco at Maguire's Academy of Music on October 2. It was a great success financially and oratorically. Under the management of Dennis McCarthy, his old friend and former associate on the *Territorial Enterprise,* he lectured in Sacramento and many of the mining towns along the Mother Lode. Every place he went he packed them in. The newspapers in San Francisco and other towns gave him flattering write-ups, and the success of the events was acclaimed everywhere.

Having lectured in most of the important towns in California, he planned to cross the Sierra Nevadas and lecture in the towns of Washoe, his old stamping ground. The advance announcement of his lecture in Virginia City in the *Territorial Enterprise* of October 31, 1866, stated that:

> Tomorrow night our citizens will be afforded an opportunity to gratify their curiosity and offer a fitting testimonial to their fellow-townsman, Mark Twain, who will do up the Sandwich Islands at the Opera House on that occasion.
>
> The enthusiasm with which his lecture was everywhere greeted is still ringing throughout California, and now that his foot is in his native heath, we expect to see the very mountains shake with a tempest of applause.
>
> Our state can justly claim Mark Twain as its own peculiar production. It was while a resident here and associated with the *Enterprise* that he assumed the name of Mark Twain and developed that rich and inexhaustible vein of humor which has made the title famous. True he has since warmed his fancy in tropical climes and expanded his thought by ocean pilgrimage and heated his eloquence in volcanic fires; but all these rest upon the solid foundation which was originally laid in our native alkali and sagebrush.
>
> From present appearances he will receive an ovation seldom if ever equalled in our city and it is pleasing to know that such an event will be equally gratifying to the audience and speaker.

So, with Dennis McCarthy, Mark Twain returned to Nevada. In most of the towns in which he had given lectures, "Mac" had found someone to introduce him; but when Mark reached the Comstock, Joe Goodman, whose guest he was, told him: "Sam, you do not need anybody to introduce you. There's a piano on the stage in the theatre. Have it brought out in sight, and when the curtain rises, you be seated at the piano, playing and singing that song of yours, 'Had an Old Horse Whose Name Was Methusalem,' [*sic*] and don't seem to notice that the curtain is up at first; then be surprised when you suddenly find out that it is up, and begin talking, without any further preliminaries."

This introduction worked perfectly—it started him off "with general hilarity and applause." His old cronies on the *Enterprise* gave him a great write-up the following day.

One of the largest and most fashionable audiences that ever graced the Opera House was in attendance last evening on the occasion of Mark Twain's lecture on the Sandwich Islands. The entire dress circle and the greater portion of the parquette were filled with ladies while all the available space for extra seats and standing room was occupied. It was a magnificent tribute to the lecturer from his old friends. Of the lecture itself we can only speak in general terms as its points are too numerous and varied to admit of special mention.

Combining the most valuable statistical and general information with passages of drollest humor, all delivered in the peculiar and inimitable style of the author in the lecture, it constitutes an entertainment of rare excellence and intelligence. The lecture will be delivered in the principal towns throughout the state, but we are unable at present to mention definitely any time or place.

In a day or two the entire programme will be arranged. Meanwhile our neighboring towns can well afford to wait patiently in anticipation of a rare treat.

Mark Twain was well pleased with his reception in Virginia City and his success at lecturing. After his lecture in this city, he wrote home to his family:

Virginia City
Nov. 1, 1866

All the folks, affectionate greetings:
You know the flush times are past, and it has long been

impossible to more than half fill the theatre here, with any sort of attraction, but they filled it for me, night before last, full-dollar all over the house.

I was mighty dubious about Carson, but the enclosed call and some telegrams set that all right—I lecture there tomorrow night.

They offer a full house and no expense in Dayton—I go there next. Sandy Baldwin says I have made the most sweeping success of any man he knows of.

I have lectured in San Francisco, Sacramento, Marysville, Grass Valley, Nevada, You Bet, Red Dog, and Virginia. I am going to talk in Carson, Gold Hill, Silver City, Dayton, Washoe, San Francisco again, and again here if I have time to re-hash the lecture.

Then I am bound for New York—lecture on the steamer, maybe.

I'll leave toward 1st December—but I'll telegraph you.

Love to all.

Yours,

Mark.

The lecture was so good, in the minds of his friends, that it could have been repeated to packed houses for a week or more. Mark, however, said that he had only one lecture so far and he could not bring himself to repeat it.

His old friends in Carson City also wanted to hear him speak on the Sandwich Islands. While Mark was still in Virginia City, a group of men led by the Governor sent a request to him to come down, to which Mark sent the following reply:

Virginia
November 1, (1866)

His Excellency, H. H. Blasdel, Governor,
and Messrs. A. Helm, O. A. Gilbert, H. F.
Rice, and others:

Gentlemen:

Your kind and cordial invitation to lecture before my old friends in Carson has reached me, and I hasten to thank you gratefully for this generous recognition—this generous toleration, I should say—of one who has shamefully deserted the high office of Governor of the Third House of Nevada and gone into the missionary business, thus leaving you to the mercy of scheming politicians—an act which, but for your forgiving disposition, must have stamped my name with infamy.

I take natural pride in being welcomed home by so long a list of old personal friends, and shall do my level best to please them, hoping at the same time that they will be more indulgent toward my shortcomings than they would feel called upon to be toward those of a stranger.

Kindly thanking you again, gentlemen, I shall gladly accept your invitation, and shall appear on the stage of the Carson Theatre on Saturday evening, November 3d, and disgorge a few lines and as much truth as I can pump out without damaging my constitution.

Yours sincerely,

Mark Twain.

Ex-Gov. Third House, and late Independent Missionary to the Sandwich Islands.

P.S. I would have answered yesterday, but I was on the sick list, and I thought I had better wait a day and see whether I was going to get well or not.

M. T.

His friends, however, thought differently, and planned a way to keep him in Virginia City and to furnish him with a new and different topic. In the two years which Mark Twain had been away from Washoe, he had changed immeasurably—no longer was he the clown that his friends had known in the days when he had first come on the Lode as a reporter. He had "been places" and he had met people of importance—"Never affiliate with inferiors; always climb." Nevada had changed, too. On October 31, 1864, Governor Nye had telegraphed the State Constitution to President Lincoln, who had immediately proclaimed Nevada a State. Gone were the members of the Brigade with their corruption, their incompetency, their inefficiency. In their place the people had elected officers of their own choice. The only appointee to the Territory who had obtained an office under the State was James W. Nye. With the aid of Bill Stewart he was elected the junior United States Senator from the State.[7]

The most important man to emerge from the chaos of Territorial days was Bill Stewart. Almost single-handed he had defeated the proposed constitution of Mark Twain's Third House days. Wishing to represent the State in the National Congress, he worked equally as hard to have the Constitution of 1864 adopted. Successful in controlling the Constitutional Convention of that year, he was elected the first United States Senator from Nevada. At Washington he distinguished himself in Congress by writing the text of the Fifteenth Amendment as it went into the Constitution. He had been sent there, now a millionaire from the handsome fees received as counsel for the leading mining companies in Nevada, to obtain some laws favorable to the mining interests. In this field he was to gain honors by writing and securing the passage of the first national mining laws.

Mining rushes continued after Mark Twain left Nevada; to the east and to the south silver miners rushed. New towns sprang up. Wishing them to be under the laws of Nevada rather than those of the Territories of Utah or Arizona, Stewart succeeded in getting Congress to give Nevada two degrees of area on the east and a like number on the south.

The Lode, however, had changed little since Mark Twain had left it. His old friends were going about their work as usual; new mines were being opened as in the old days; new mills were being built; and new buildings were being erected. The *Territorial Enterprise* was in the same place as when he left it, and it was still prospering. His old pals around the city thought that Mark was just the same, too. Believing that he could take a joke as he had in the old days, Steve and Dennis planned an incident to amuse Mark and to keep him with them a few days longer. This little affair took the form of a holdup on the Divide. It was made realistic; and because there had been an epidemic of robberies at the place where it was planned to stop Mark, he took it seriously. In fact, on the very night that Mark was held up, the Wells-Fargo Express stage was stopped on the Geiger Grade and $14,000 was taken.

The pranksters believed that Dennis and Mark, returning to Virginia City from the Gold Hill lecture, would have the proceeds of their venture with them in a carpet-bag. Just as the two were making the steep climb which separated the two cities, the blowing of a policeman's whistle suddenly cut through the night. Mark was heard to say to Dennis, "I'm glad they've got a policeman on the

Divide. They never had one in my day." Just at that moment, the boys—City Marshal George Birdsall, Pat Holland, Leslie Blackburn, Jimmy Eddington, and Chief of Police John V. B. Perry—with masks over their faces and silver dollars in their cheeks to disguise their voices, stepped out to obey the commands of their general, Sandy Baldwin. The *Enterprise* of November 11 printed a description of the holdup as it was given to the paper by Mark Twain himself. In it the reader's attention is called to Mark's inconsistencies in counting the number of assailants.

"Stand and deliver!"

I said, "My son, your arguments are powerful. Take what I have, but uncock that infamous pistol."

The young man uncocked the pistol (but he requested three other gentlemen to present theirs at my head) and then he took all the money I had (only $20 or $25) and my watch. Then he said to one of this party:

"Beauregard, go through that man!" meaning Mac—and the distinguished rebel did go through Mac. Then the little captain said:

"Stonewall Jackson, seat these men by the roadside and hide yourself; if they move within five minutes, blow their brains out!"

"All right, sir!" said Stonewall. Then the party (six in number) started toward Virginia City and disappeared.

It was a bitterly cold night, a strong north wind was blowing, and the air was full of drifting snow. Clemens' agent, Dennis McCarthy, had no overcoat and had become almost half-frozen while waiting for the robbers to finish their job. As soon as they left, therefore, he said to Clemens, "Come on, Sam, let's get out of this."

"Dennis," said Sam, who had on a heavy overcoat, "that big duffer told us that if we left here in less than half an hour, we would be killed. As I have no desire to leave this world at the present time, I am going to stay here until that half hour is up."

"Why, Sam," said Dennis, "do you suppose they are going to wait to see if we leave or not? Both of them are at the top of the hill by this time, beating it for town [Virginia City]. Come on and get out of this wind and snow. I'm near frozen."

"You may be right, Dennis," Sam retorted, "and you may be

wrong, but I am taking no chances either way and I am not going to move from this spot till I know that I am taking no risk in doing so, and you are going to stay with me."

When the victims of the holdup finally reached the *Enterprise* office, they went into the composing room to warm themselves by the big box stove, in which there was a rousing fire. The other boys, Dan De Quille among them, were there waiting. Steve greeted them with:

"It seems to me that you fellows have been a mighty long time getting here from Gold Hill. What's been keeping you? Been stopping by the roadside to rest?"

"We did stop once by the wayside," answered Sam, "but it wasn't to rest, by a long shot. We met two gentlemen on the Divide who thought we had more than they did, and they argued their claim so convincingly that we let them take it. The long and short of it, boys, is that we've been held up and robbed."

"My gracious, is that so, Sam?" asked Sandy Baldwin. "Did they get the money taken in at the box office?"

"No, a few dollars only. The receipts are in the safe of Wells-Fargo. But, I tell you, boys, Dennis and I had a pretty close call and it looked pretty nasty for a while, with two big guns within six inches of our eyes."

"How many were there, Sam?" asked another of the boys.

"I don't know how many there were in the gang. I saw four, though only two of them had their guns trained on us. But those two big .44's had a mighty persuasive look and were just as effective as a whole battery of cannon, but 'All's well that ends well,' and I am glad that I am back with you fellows instead of at the bottom of one of the old holes out there on the Divide."

"So am I," said Steve, "and I am awful glad that you didn't crawl."

For the next two or three days Sam kept busy recounting his experiences with the robbers. He got his first inkling of the hoax when Sandy Baldwin, the robber chief, halted him on the street one day and ordered, "Hands up!" in the gruff voice of the robber, at the same time pointing a dummy gun at him—and then sprinting upstairs to the composing room.

If ever Sam had been mad, he was mad then. Speechless with fury, he stalked into the office of the *Enterprise,* wrote a check, and started out to find Dennis. He discovered him at Charley Leggett's eating house. Throwing the check on the table, he said, "I do not require any further services from you, sir!" Then he turned and walked away.

Going back to the office, he walked up to Dan De Quille and asked, "Dan, did you know that this confounded fake holdup was going to be put over on me?"

"No, I did not. I knew no more about it that you did," replied Dan.

"Do you think Steve had a hand in it?"

"Well, you know that Steve is always up to any fun among the boys, but I know that he was not one of the robbers because he was at work in the composing room from 5 o'clock until you got back from Gold Hill."

"I hate to think Steve would go back on me like that," Sam announced; "but I'll bet he was in it up to his eyes. And you bet I'll get even with him!"

Sam might have known that a little Southern rebel had planned the holdup. No one but a Confederate would have used "Beauregard" or "Stonewall Jackson" in giving the commands.

Dan had not been taken in on the joke because the perpetrators wanted him to write up the story realistically and thereby create sympathy for Mark. The benefit that was planned to be given him for the loss of his money would be a great success. At the end of that affair, it was intended to return his watch and money before the audience. His friends meant well, but, like other schemes of mice and men, this one did not turn out as conceived.

On November 11, Mark had published a card in the *Enterprise,* along with his description of the holdup, asking the return of his watch:

> "Now I want to write you road agents as follows:
>
> "'My watch was given me by Judge Sandy Baldwin and Theodore Winters, and I value it above anything else I own. If you will send that to me (to the *Enterprise* office or to any prominent man in San Francisco), you may keep the money and welcome. You know, you got all the money Mac had—and Mac is an orphan—and besides, the money he had belonged to me. Adieu, my romantic friends.'"

It was said that Mark Twain was disgruntled over this horseplay, and that on the morning when he was to leave and was at the Wells-Fargo Express Company stage office, he was in a "pretty glum and irritable mood." The long wait on the Divide where the cold winds from the mountains sweep across the ridge had given him a heavy cold, and the loss of his watch and money had provoked him. As the stage was about to start, he noticed a rather large group of men gathered at the office, but he thought nothing of it. When he had bought his ticket, had got into the stage, and had settled himself down for the journey, one of the "robbers" rushed up to Mark and put the money, watch, and masks in his hands; then the "robbers" came into sight around a corner where they had been hiding and gave three cheers for Mark.

After Mark Twain had finished with his lectures on the Pacific Coast, he planned to return to his home in Missouri, the first trip back to his old home in over five years. Before he sailed, he sent a farewell note to his friends in Nevada. Under the date of Friday, December 14, he wrote in the *Daily Alta California:*

SO LONG

Editors *Alta:*

I leave for the States in the *Opposition* steamer tomorrow, and I ask, as a special favor, that you will allow me to say to my highway-robber friends of the Gold Hill and Virginia Divide, and convince them that I have got ahead of them. They had their joke in robbing me and returning the money, and I had mine in the satisfaction of knowing that they came near freezing to death while they were waiting two hours for me to come along the night of the robbery. And at this day, so far from bearing them any ill will, I want to thank them kindly; for their rascality, I am pecuniarily ahead on the transaction. I got a telegram from New York last night which reads as follows:

New York
December 12th

Mark Twain:

Go to Nudd, Lord, & Co., Front Street, collect amount of money equal to what highwaymen took from you.

(Signed)

A. D. N.

I took that telegram and went to that store and called for a thousand dollars, with my customary modesty; but when I found they were going to do it, my conscience smote me and I reduced the demand to a hundred. It was promptly paid, in coin, and now if the robbers think *they* have got the best end of that joke, they are welcome—they have my free consent to go on thinking so. (It is barely possible that the heft of the joke is on A. D. N. now?)

Goodbye, felons, goodbye. I bear you no malice. And I sincerely pray that when your cheerful career is closing, and you appear finally before a delighted and appreciative audience to be hanged, that you will be prepared to go, and that it will be as a ray of sunshine amid the gathering blackness of your damning recollections, to call to mind that you never got a cent out of *me*. So long.

Mark Twain.

22

THE LAST MESSAGE

THE LECTURE TOUR THROUGH CALIFORNIA AND
Nevada was a thrilling success. Mark Twain could now return triumphantly to his family and his friends in Missouri. He did not discover gold or silver in the hills of the West—he found that wealth was in himself. Leaving San Francisco by steamer via the Isthmus route to New York, he went to his old haunts on the Mississippi River. At St. Louis he visited his mother and sister, whom he had not seen since he and Orion had set out for Nevada in July of 1861. There he had a wonderful time renewing old acquaintances up and down the River.

While he was in St. Louis, he saw the announcement of an excursion to the Holy Land on the steamer *Quaker City*. Abandoning the idea of a trip around the world, he decided to take this one instead. At once he wrote the editors of the San Francisco *Daily Alta California* proposing that they send him on this excursion. Mark was to contribute letters about the trip at twenty dollars each. The San Francisco newspaper knew that it was a sound investment to hire Mark Twain as a correspondent. The *Alta* editors wired their New York agents at once to pay his passage of $1250.[1]

With all his expenses paid, and with contracts to write also for the New York *Tribune,* the beloved vagabond sailed with a congenial group of people on June 8, 1867. On the night before the ship left, he wrote a goodbye letter to his mother and sister. In it he expressed worry over Orion, still living in Carson City. In his customary patronizing attitude toward his brother Mark wrote: "I often wonder if his law business is going satisfactorily. I wish I had gone to Washington in the winter instead of going West. I could have gouged an office out of Bill Stewart for him, and that would have atoned for the loss of my home visit. But I am so worthless that it seems to me I never do anything or accomplish anything that lingers in my mind as a pleasant memory. My mind is stored full of unworthy conduct toward Orion and toward you all, an accusing conscience gives me peace only in excitement and restless moving from place to place

. . . and so, with my parting love and benediction for Orion and all of you, I say goodbye and God bless you all. . . ." [2]

The trip to the Holy Land was a glorious adventure. There was very little that Mark Twain missed on this excursion. He was insatiably curious, and because he was at the same time extremely articulate, the world of literature is infinitely richer for his observations. He wrote his letters to the *Alta* and to the *Tribune,* he met some of the most fascinating and companionable people he had ever known in all his life, and he gathered material for later works and articles.

Every writer on the life of Mark Twain selects this event or that incident as the great turning point of his life. Many of them, however, have good reason for selecting this trip as the greatest factor of all. One needs only to keep in mind the advice which Anson Burlingame gave Mark in Honolulu in June, 1866: "You have great ability; I believe you have genius. What you need now is the refinement of association. Seek companionship among men of superior intellect and character. Refine yourself and your work. . . ." His companions on board the *Quaker City* were undoubtedly the most refined with whom he had ever associated in his life. Ministers, deacons, and cultured world travelers were his shipmates for four months. And on this trip he saw for the first time the beautiful and aristocratic face of Olivia Langdon in miniature on ivory. Her devoted brother, Charles Langdon, had it with him on the boat. When Mark first saw it in "Charley's" cabin, he looked at it with great admiration. Thereafter every time that he visited this cabin, he asked to see it. The fine, spiritual face with its delicate features aroused in him a desire to possess not only the miniature, but also the girl. When Olivia Langdon became the life partner of Mark Twain in January, 1870, she brought into his life its greatest refining influence.

Shortly before the *Quaker City* sailed, Mark received a letter from his old Nevada friend, Bill Stewart, now a United States Senator from that State, offering Mark the position of private secretary. Bill was a clever politician. He knew that Mark was popular in Nevada, on the Pacific Coast, in the Mississippi Valley, and all throughout the eastern States. To have him attached to his political menage would mean prestige to Bill in the national capital. Mark made no reply to the offer at the time, but in August he wrote to Stewart from

Naples, Italy, stating that he would accept the position.[3] He reasoned that while he was acting as secretary, he would have time to write; and he also hoped that he could get a government office for Orion. On the day after the boat docked in New York, he went over to Washington to take up his duties.

Senator Stewart went to Washington a multimillionaire, thanks to the handsome fees he had received from the Comstock mining litigation. Mrs. Stewart, who had been educated at a boarding school in Washington while her father, Henry S. Foote, was representing Mississippi in the Senate, was desirous of living permanently in the capital. Bill had purchased a fine homesite near Dupont Circle, on which he planned to build a castle. He had sent Mrs. Stewart with the children to Europe for a visit and to buy furnishings for their new home. While his family was away, the Senator had taken a suite of rooms, which Mark shared with him. They ate their meals at the Willard Hotel.

Mark Twain did not last long as secretary to a United States Senator—in fact, the job lasted only a little over two and one-half months. The arrangements were not satisfactory to either party. Mark had to cover the sessions of Congress all day, answer letters from Nevada constituents, and meet all kinds of people seeking jobs. Socially Mark found himself deluged with invitations to dinners, receptions, and other occasions for speech-making.

The house in which Bill and Mark lived was a rather tumble-down building on the northwest corner of Fourteenth and F Streets N.W. It was kept by a prim and strait-laced old maid of about seventy. Mark made himself at home in Stewart's apartment, helping himself to the cigars and whiskey.

Because Mark had to do most of his writing at night—he was at this time writing his *Innocents Abroad*—he did much prowling around late at night. These nightly escapades nearly frightened the genteel old maid to death. She complained bitterly to the Senator, who warned Mark that he must reform his ways or else he would have to thrash him. Stewart said in later years that Mark Twain was "the most lovable scamp and nuisance who ever blighted Nevada."

What particular incident terminated the association of Bill and Mark was not stated by either party. Apparently at the time it was a friendly one. However, it wasn't long before Mark was publishing stories on the subjects of "My Late Senatorial Secretaryship" and

"Facts Concerning the Recent Resignation," and other incidents relative to the time when he held this position. When *Roughing It* was published, Stewart accused Mark of cheating. In this book Mark printed a picture of the Senator with a patch over his eye, supposedly acquired when Mark had given him a sound thrashing.[4] Politicians cannot afford to be lampooned.

The writer has had the privilege of going over the thousands of letters written by Senator Stewart and an equally large number received by him in his private collections of correspondence. When Mark burlesqued the character of his duties during his secretaryship, he was not stretching the truth very far, particularly when he wrote:

> "I am not a private secretary to a senator any more now. I held the berth two months in security and great cheerfulness of spirit, but my bread began to return from over the waters then—that is to say, my works came back and revealed themselves. I judged it best to resign. The way of it was this. My employer sent for me one morning tolerably early, and, as soon as I had finished inserting conundrums clandestinely into his last great speech upon finance, I entered the presence. There was something portentous in his appearance. His cravat was untied, his hair was in a state of disorder, and his countenance bore about it the signs of a suppressed storm. He held a package of letters in his tense grasp, and I knew that the dreaded Pacific Mail was in. He said:
>
> " 'I thought you were worthy of confidence.'
>
> "I said, 'Yes, sir.'
>
> "He said, 'I gave you a letter from certain of my constituents in the State of Nevada, asking the establishment of a postoffice at Baldwin's Ranch, and told you to answer it, as ingeniously as you could, with arguments which should persuade them that there was no real necessity for an office at that place.'
>
> "I felt easier. 'Oh, if that is all, sir, I *did* do that.'
>
> " 'Yes, you *did*. I will read your answer for your own humiliation.
>
> Washington
Nov. 24
>
> Messrs. Smith, Jones, and others:
> Gentlemen:
>   What the mischief do you suppose you want with a postoffice at Baldwin's Ranch? It would not do you any good. If

any letters came there, you couldn't read them, you know; and, besides, such letters as ought to pass through, with money in them, for other localities, would not be likely to *get* through, you must perceive at once; and that would make trouble for us all. No, don't bother about a post-office in your camp. I have your best interests at heart, and feel that it would only be an ornamental folly. What you want is a jail, you know—a nice substantial jail and a free school. These will be a lasting benefit to you. These will make you really contented and happy. I will move in the matter at once.

Very truly, etc.,

Mark Twain.
For William M. S——,
U. S. Senator.

" 'That is the way you answered that letter. Those people say they will hang me, if I ever enter that district again; and I am perfectly satisfied they *will,* too.' "

In another ruinous letter which Mark wrote in answer to one written by one of the Senator's constituents who was desirous of a road and other post offices, he said:

Washington
Nov. 30

Messrs. **Perkins, Wagner,** et al.:
Gentlemen:
It is a delicate question about this Indian trail, but, handled with proper deftness and dubiousness, I doubt not we shall succeed in some measure or otherwise, because the place where the route leaves the Lassen Meadows, over beyond where those two Shawnee chiefs, Dilapidated-Vengeance and Biter-of-the-Clouds, were scalped last winter, this being the favorite direction to some, but others preferring something else in consequence of things, the Mormon trail leaving Mosby's at three in the morning, and passing through Jawbone Flat to Blucher, and then down by Jug-Handle, the road to the right of it, and naturally leaving it on the right, too, and Dawson's on the left of the trail where it passes to the left of said Dawson's and onward thence to Tomahawk, thus making the route cheaper, easier of access

to all who can get at it, and compassing all the desirable objects so considered by others, and, therefore, conferring the most good upon the greatest number, and, consequently, I am encouraged to hope we shall. However, I shall be ready, and happy, to afford you still further information upon the subject, from time to time, as you may desire it and the Post-Office Department be enabled to furnish it to me.

Very truly, etc.

Mark Twain.

For William M. S——

U. S. Senator.

" 'There—now *what* do you think of that?' Stewart demanded.

" 'Well, I don't know, sir. It—well, it appears to me—to be dubious enough.'

" 'Du—leave the house! I am a ruined man. Those Humboldt savages never will forgive me for tangling their brains up with this unhuman letter. I have lost the respect of the Methodist Church, the Board of Aldermen——'

" 'Well, I haven't anything to say about that, because I may have missed it a little in their cases, but I *was* too many for the Baldwin's Ranch people, General.'

" 'Leave the house! Leave it forever and forever, too.'

"I regarded that as a sort of covert intimation that my services could be dispensed with, and so I resigned. I never will be a private secretary to a senator again. You can't please that kind of people. They don't know anything. They can't appreciate a party's efforts."

Leaving Washington late in December, he went to New York to have a reunion with some of the passengers whom he had known on the Holy Land excursion. Among them was Charley Langdon, who was then in New York with his sister, Olivia, and his father, Jervis Langdon, a wealthy coal mine owner of Elmira, New York. On December 23, 1867, he met for the first time "in reality" the girl with whose miniature he had fallen in love.

When Mark returned to New York, he continued to write for several newspapers: the New York *Tribune,* the New York *Herald,* and the Chicago *Republican.* He kept up on the activities of his old friends out West, and when he heard of something that they had done which invited comment, he fell into the same literary mood that had brought him fame.

In February, he heard that an old friend, Judge McCorkle, was going to be married. It was more than Mark could stand, and this is the way in which he expressed his feelings about it:

"They report that this homely old friend of mine—this ancient denizen of California and Nevada—the wrinkled, aged, knock-kneed, ringboned, and spavined old war-horse of the Plains is to be married shortly to a handsome young Ohio widow worth $300,000. Well! What is the world coming to anyhow? If any woman in her right mind and under 70 would be willing to marry that old fossil—that old tunnel—that old dilapidated quartz mill—I would never, never have believed it. He is a splendid man, you know, but then he must be as much as 92 or 93 years old. He is one of my nearest friends, but what of that? I would remain a bachelor a century before I would marry such a rusty, used up old arastra as he is. I have always considered that I ought to fairly expect to marry about $17,000, but I think differently now. If McCorkle ranges at $300,000 in the market, I will raise my margin to about a million and a half."

Mark Twain apparently did raise his price, for he married a girl whose father was a very rich man. This article was one of the last ones which he wrote in the true frontier vernacular.

While in New York City this time, he made some good publishing contacts. He also turned down for the last time the offer of the San Francisco postmastership, a position which he had been offered before. He made this decision when he heard that the chief editor of the *Daily Alta California* wanted the position.

Although there is no published statement saying that he had told Joe Goodman of his plans to use the *Alta* letters in his forthcoming book, the facts point conclusively in that direction. Joe wired him that the *Alta* publishers had copyrighted his *"Quaker City* Letters" for the purpose of putting them in book form to help compensate them for sending him on that excursion. Immediately Mark telegraphed the paper protesting this action on their part. He followed up the wire with a letter.[5] At the same time he wrote his grievances to Orion:

"I have made a superb contract for a book and have prepared the first ten chapters of the sixty or eighty, but I will bet it never sees the light . . . that thieving *Alta* copyrighting the letters; and now no disposition to let me use them. I have done all I can by telegraph, and now await the final result by mail." He received his reply from the editors, but it was not satisfactory. He decided to go to San Francisco and see those "*Alta* thieves face to face." He left by steamer for the Isthmus route to San Francisco. (Never again did Mark Twain take that stagecoach trip to the West.)

When he did see the editors "face to face," he was successful in persuading them that they had been reimbursed sufficiently for the expense of his trip. The way was now clear for his book, but he needed funds to return to New York. Remembering how remunerative his Sandwich Islands lectures had been, he decided to give talks on the Holy Land in the cities in which he had spoken before.

After he had given several lectures in San Francisco and the California mining camps, he went up to Nevada. His old friends and associates were anxious to see him and to hear him talk again. His friends on the *Enterprise* gave him a good write-up before he arrived. On April 24, 1868, this paper thus announced his coming speech:

MARK TWAIN

This celebrated humorist, after having visited the Holy Land and all the principal cities of the old world, will again once more press his foot upon his native sagebrush this morning. We received the following telegram from him last night dated at Coburn's: "I am doing well, having crossed one divide without getting robbed anyway. Mark Twain."

Owing to the dissatisfaction of many in regard to the smallness of the hall [Athletic Hall], in which it was at first proposed that Mark should lecture, arrangements have been made by which the Opera House is secured for this Monday and Tuesday nights: the Webb sisters having very kindly given their consent to release the house to him for those two nights. This arrangement having been made, he will not lecture on Saturday night as was advertised—he will have enough to do for three or four days to shake hands and swap yarns with his old friends. The box office will open on Monday from 10 o'clock A.M. till 4 o'clock P.M. when seats may be secured for both nights.

Over in Gold Hill, the *Evening News* on the following night announced his coming:

The remarkable Mark, who has been cruising among the far-off Turks, Piutes, Arabs, and outlandish ruins and queer cities of the "Holy Land" and now returns perfectly saturated with interesting information and funny stories relative to his journey and experiences on the famous *Quaker City* where jolly companionship, bright examples, and the joy of social religious intercourse were as a continual "love feast," will "harikari" his immense fund of collected information of a highly pleasing, varied, and interesting nature to crowded audiences at Piper's Opera House on Monday and Tuesday evenings of next week, on each of which occasions an admission fee of one dollar will be charged, and the raid upon the doors will commence precisely at 7 o'clock, just an hour before Mark commences his tribulations, to enjoy which, properly, it is necessary to have good seats, which can be secured on application at the box office of the theatre at 10 o'clock A.M.

Mark arrived at five o'clock on the morning stage "in good health and without meeting a single footpad on the way." Virginia City was proud to claim him as its own, and the *Enterprise* on the Sunday after his arrival wrote:

Mark Twain we have a right to claim as a Washoe humorist, and claiming him let us not fail to do what we can to encourage him by showing him that we appreciate his efforts to amuse and instruct us. He comes back to us after many wanderings by sea and land in foreign countries, with his mind and portfolio enriched with choice collections of fact and fancy gleaned in places holy and not holy. He is a living budget of not the jokes *of* all nations but of jokes *upon* all nations, suggested by their peculiarities of manners, customs, and appearance. We predict for him the most crowded and brilliant audience of the season. All who have ever seen or heard of Mark Twain and his genius as a brilliant descriptive writer, wit, and humorist—and who has not?— will desire to go with him aboard the *Quaker City,* carpet bag in

hand, and gaze on the sleek faces and heads of the pious pilgrims to the Holy Land, all as yet unafflicted with the wilting
nausea of sea-sickness, and looking forward with godly and
courageous eyes toward the sacred soil and cities of the country
in which scriptures were born; all will wish to accompany Mark
to Palestine and ramble with him among the musty old palaces,
churches, and tombs—in short, all will wish to follow him
wherever he goes. As his followers will be many, let those who
do not desire to be left behind on the voyage go early tomorrow
and secure seats for the through trip.

His lectures in Virginia City were brilliant and well-attended.
People who were not disposed to look favorably on Mark when he
lived on the Lode vied with one another to do him honor.

On the Comstock, he was again the guest of Joe Goodman.
At that time the citizens of Carson City, headed by Governor H. G.
Blasdel, sent him an urgent invitation to speak there. A long list of
prominent citizens of the capital signed it, too.

In Carson, he went around the town and called on all of
his old friends, among them Mrs. Curry, and "Old Curry, Abe
Curry, Old Abe Curry." In telling Mrs. Curry of his travels, he mentioned, among other things, that snow from the Lebanon Mountains
was brought to Damascus on the backs of camels. Mrs. Curry
thought that it was just one of Mark's tall tales and said: "Sam,
. . . if you tell that in your lecture tonight, I'll get right up and say
so." That night he did tell the story, for indeed it was a fact. Although Mrs. Curry did not get up and deny it, she shook her finger
at him.

Mark was persuaded, while in Carson City, to repeat his Sandwich Islands lecture for the benefit of the school children who had
not heard him on this subject when he talked there two years
before.[6]

The Carson visit over, he returned to Virginia City to spend
another week visiting with his old friends. And what a week it
was! It must have seemed like old times to Mark to have so much
taking place during the few days that he was there.

On the first day of his lecture the murderer of Julie Bulette was
hanged in Virginia City. The story of her death and of the conviction and hanging of the murderer eminently belongs here:

On January 20, 1867, Julie, one of the "fair but frail" girls living down at D and Union Streets, was found in her little white cubicle, strangled to death by some unknown assassin. Her death was mourned by most of the miners and firemen whom she had befriended in sickness and misfortune. She had nursed them through their illnesses and injuries; she had been charitable and kind to the unfortunate. For all these good qualities and for other reasons, she had been elected an honorary member of the Fire Department. She had gone to all of the fires; and when she was not working at the pumps, she had carried coffee and food to the firemen.

Julie was born a "miscegen" in London about 1832. She was taken to New Orleans where her family remained. As a young girl she had lived in the Vieux Carré, until she went to San Francisco. In the Bay city she was set up in fine style by two rakes who bought her fine clothes, furs, and jewels. However, when the rush to Washoe attracted many of her admirers, she followed them up to Virginia City and skipped her lovers by the sea.

Her murderer was believed to have been hired by her former San Francisco benefactors, for they were known to have come up to Virginia City about the time of her death. They were often seen in the company of John Millian, a Frenchman whose real name was Jean Marie à Villain. When she was discovered dead, all of her furs, good clothes, and jewels, even those on her fingers, were missing.

Virginia City's funerals were something to relate. Julie's ranked among the famous ones. Her "boys" took up a collection and bought her a beautiful casket, while the sixty members of Virginia Company No. 1 arranged for her funeral services at their engine house on B Street. The sermon was preached by the Reverend William M. Marlin; the *Enterprise* said of it: "A more appropriate one we never heard."

Members of the Fire Company, preceded by the Metropolitan Brass Band marching on foot, were followed by eighteen carriages filled with Julie's friends. It was said that as the procession passed by, the ladies above B Street pulled down their window shades.

Her casket was taken to the Flowery Hill Cemetery to the east of Virginia City where today on her lonely grave, surrounded by a picket fence, one may see the headstone which bears simply the name "Julie." When the band and the boys returned to Virginia City from laying their "girl" away, the band played and the boys sang "The Girl I Left Behind."

Julie was kind-hearted, benevolent, and charitable not only to the boys on the Lode: a tradition still exists that down in New Orleans she had contributed generously through her family toward buying freedom from slavery for her black friends.

Millian was not apprehended for some time—in fact, not until he tried to dispose of some of the things which he had taken from Julie. He was arrested and his premises searched; there many of her belongings were found in his trunk.

His French countrymen living on the Lode took up a collection, and employed Charles De Long, one of the best lawyers in Virginia City, to defend him. After the trial had dragged along for several months, Millian was found guilty and sentenced to be hanged. Mark Twain arrived in town the day he was to die.

In those primitive days of administering justice, the counties had to carry out executions. On the appointed day, April 27, almost at dawn, a crowd began to gather about the Court House; and "shortly before ten o'clock the entire area was a living, swaying mass of human beings." Each spectator was intent upon catching a glimpse of the condemned man as he was led from the jail to the carriage to be taken to the gallows. Men, women, children, bucks, squaws, and long-queued, wild-eyed Chinamen pressed against one another as the word was spread around that the prisoner was about to appear.

At last, about 11:30, a carriage with drawn curtains was driven in front of the Sheriff's office, where forty deputies with Henry rifles took up their stations. The National Guard in full uniform marched from the Armory to the jail. On their arrival they fixed bayonets and formed a lane through the crowd. The prisoner, accompanied by Father Patrick Manogue, priest at Saint Mary's of the Mountain, and the Reverend Father Clarke of Carson City, advanced to the carriage. They all walked so rapidly that the crowd caught scarcely a glimpse of anyone.

This carriage was followed by another containing the two physicians required by law to be present at the execution. Then came the reporters of the Virginia City newspapers. It was to be expected that Mark Twain would be along with his associates on the *Enterprise*. The rear of the procession was brought up by a wagon carrying the coffin, draped in black, and the undertaker with his assistants. All along the way people were hurrying to the place where the gallows had been set up. Some three thousand people had gathered on the hillside around the gallows, about one hundred and fifty yards above the Jewish cemetery.

After Millian had kissed his father confessor and shaken hands with the Hall family, for whom he had worked, and with his lawyer De Long, he mounted the scaffold and was soon swinging by his neck. When his body had been cut down and taken away, the crowd went back to town to drink down its atonement for the murder of Julie Bulette. The French colony gave Mr. De Long a solid gold cigar box set in diamonds for his efforts in behalf of Millian. That same evening the same crowd went to the Opera House to hear Mark Twain talk about the Holy Land.[7]

There was another funeral that week over in Gold Hill, when the sorrowing friends of Sandy Bowers, only thirty-five years old, followed his body down the steep Ophir Grade and across Washoe Valley to lay him away on the hillside in back of his mansion. As a dying request Sandy had asked the members of the Miners' Union of Virginia City and Gold Hill to accompany his body as far as they could. Although Sandy was a millionaire then, he had never forgotten his humble origin and his friends, and everyone loved him for it. The Masonic Lodge of Gold Hill conducted the services after his body had lain in state all morning. More than one hundred carriages and as many men on horseback followed the funeral procession to his last resting place. Today hundreds of visitors to Bowers' Mansion climb the hill to see where he is buried.[8]

Before Mark Twain left the Lode, his old friend Conrad Wiegand,[9] the well-known assayer of Gold Hill, presented him with a bar of silver bullion on which was inscribed:

"Mark Twain—Matthew V:41—Pilgrim."

One will recall that the Biblical reference reads: "And whosoever shall compel thee to go a mile, go with him twain."

On Monday, May 4, he said farewell to his friends in Nevada. Although he promised that he would return some future day, he never did.

The life of Mark Twain and the history of Nevada were never again to be connected, but they were curiously and symbolically parallel. Both struck bonanzas which brought fame and fortune, and good luck was succeeded by periods of borrasca for both.

For Mark Twain there was his marriage to Olivia Langdon in

1870, followed by the successful production of many books and writings that brought him a handsome income. He became the father of four lovely children, one son and three daughters. There were many trips abroad, and beautiful homes in America. Universities honored him with degrees, and societies heaped invitations on him to speak. Royalty and nobility entertained him. His cup was full and running over.

Nevada found its richest "pay dirt" from 1870 to 1880. Many mining towns flourished in the State during these years. It was during this period that the Virginia Consolidated Mining Company in Virginia City discovered the Big Bonanza which made multimillionaires out of James Flood, William O'Brien, James Fair, and John W. Mackay. The stock in this mine, which had sold at $1 a share, shot up to $780.

The fame of the Big Bonanza spread around the world. The gambling instinct of Mark Twain welled up again. He sent money to Dan De Quille, directing him to buy "Con Virginia . . . at such a time as John Mackay thinks is best and when he says sell, *sell*, whether at a loss or a profit, without waiting to swap knives." [10]

Dividends from the mines on the Comstock, and in other parts of Nevada, made some very rich men—and many more poor ones. The peak of production came about 1879. From that date borrasca, an unproductive period, followed, and for more than twenty years the fortunes of Nevada declined, and so did the population. The demonetization of silver ruined the silver-mining industry; the condition of the Sagebrush State was deplorable. [11] The mines and mills shut down, and the population of Nevada fell to 42,000 people in 1900. Many of Mark Twain's friends left the State. Although he tried to get Dan to leave and go to California, Dan stayed on in Virginia City until he was too old to work any more. Finally he returned to his old home in Iowa.

In 1894, the fortunes of Mark Twain turned to borrasca when Charles L. Webster & Company, Mark's publishing firm, failed, leaving him over one hundred thousand dollars in debt to creditors, and more than sixty thousand dollars in debt to Olivia, who had loaned him that amount out of her personal fortune. Mark, sixty years of age and in dubious health, promised his creditors that he would pay everything, dollar for dollar.

To accomplish this stupendous task, he decided to make a lecture tour around the world. With "Livy" and his daughter Clara to sustain him on the trip, he set out July 14, 1895. With the receipts of his lectures and the revenues of the books which he published from the material gathered on his tour, he was completely freed from debt by January of 1898.

Nevada regained some of her wealth and fame in November, 1900, when rich silver ore was discovered in Tonopah; and the following year, when an equally rich gold deposit was found at Goldfield. Soon new discoveries were made throughout the State, and Nevada entered into a new age of mining and agricultural prosperity that has continued to the present time.

In all of the years after Mark Twain had gone from Nevada, he was never forgotten by his old friends. They rejoiced in his good fortune. Mark was probably closer to Joe Goodman all of his life than to any other of his Comstock companions. Joe went East and helped Mark write *Roughing It,* which came out in 1871. Two years later Joe sold out his interest in the *Enterprise* for a handsome sum, and moved to California. There he became interested in the civilization of the Mayas, whose ruins he visited. He spent a good deal of his fortune and time in translating the Mayan inscriptions. The publication of these translations is a monument to his efforts.

Joe made several more trips to the East to visit Mark. They corresponded with regularity. Finally Mark became interested in a typesetting machine invented by James W. Paige. He sent for Joe to come and help him organize a stock company to promote this scheme. Two other Nevadans, Senator John P. Jones and John W. Mackay, were also represented in it. This venture, however, proved a failure.

In the early autumn of 1903, Mark decided to take Livy to Florence, Italy, to live indefinitely, in the hope that it would benefit her health. Joe went East to say goodbye to Mark. They enjoyed themselves "in the old way at quiet resorts where they could talk over the old tales." It was the last time these men ever saw each other.

When Joe Goodman was asked in later years what he remembered most about Mark Twain, he replied: "I recall Mark Twain in so many different personal aspects at various periods of our long acquaintance that it is difficult to say in which particular one I remember him best. Of course, there were always the same slight figure, the same noble head, the same gray eyes, the same delicate hands and feet, and the same half-skipping, half-shambling gait. . . ."[12]

* * * * *

Mark Twain had no virtue greater than his love for old friends. Paine says that he "was continually inviting old friends to share his success with him. Any comrade of former days found welcome in his home as often as he would come, and for as long as he would stay."[13] In 1873, Dan De Quille was urged to visit him in Hartford, Connecticut. The two "boys" spent a happy spring together in Mark's luxurious home. (What a contrast it must have been to their little parlor and bedroom at 25 North B Street in Virginia City!) While Dan was there, he planned his book, *History of the Big Bonanza,* which was published by the same firm that was then publishing Mark's works. It was the best book ever written on this period of the Comstock, but it was not a financial success. Dan returned to Nevada, where he remained on the *Enterprise* until it suspended in 1893.

Steve Gillis, Mark's devoted little pal on the Lode, stayed on in California. When Steve grew old and invalid, he wrote that he would have plenty of time to read Mark's books—if he owned them. That was too much for Mark. He autographed and ordered sent to Steve, charges prepaid, an expensive set of his twenty-five volumes of published works. Steve's last message to Mark was sent to him through Albert Bigelow Paine, biographer of Mark Twain, when he visited Steve on Jackass Hill in 1897:

> Tell Sam I'm going to die pretty soon, but that I love him, and I've loved him all my life, and I'll love him till I die. This is the last word I'll ever send him.[14]

When Mark Twain reached "Pier 70" in 1905, there were great honors bestowed on him. In New York, "the flower of American literature gathered at a great dinner to honor him on his seventieth birthday."

Away out in Nevada his old friends did not forget him on this occasion. The city of Reno, which was not in existence when Mark lived in that State, but to which many of his friends had moved, invited him to come West and to let its citizens honor him. To Robert L. Fulton, the writer of the invitation, he replied:

In the Mountains
May 24, 1905

Dear Mr. Fulton:

I remember, as if it were yesterday, that when I disembarked from the overland stage in front of the Ormsby in Carson City in August, 1861, I was not expecting to be asked to come again. I was tired, discouraged, white with alkali dust, and did not know anybody; and if you had said then, "Cheer up, desolate stranger, don't be downhearted—pass on, and come again in 1905," you cannot think how grateful I would have been and how gladly I would have closed the contract. Although I was not expecting to be invited, I was watching for it, and was hurt and disappointed when you started to ask me and changed it to, "How soon are you going away?"

But you have made it all right, now the wound is closed. And so I thank you sincerely for the invitation; and with you, all Reno, and if I were a few years younger, I would accept it, and promptly. I would go. I would let somebody else do the oration, but, as for me, I would talk—just talk. I would renew my youth; and talk—and talk—and talk—and have the time of my life! I would march the unforgotten and unforgettable antiques by, and name their names, and give them reverent "Hail-and-farewell" as they passed: Goodman, McCarthy, Gillis, Curry, Baldwin, Winters, Howard, Nye, Stewart, Neely Johnson, Hal Clayton, North, Root, and my brother—upon whom be peace!—and then the desperadoes, who made life a joy and the "Slaughterhouse" a precious possession: Sam Brown, Farmer Pete, Bill Mayfield, Six-fingered Jake, Jack Williams, and the rest of the crimson discipleship—and so on and so on. Believe me, I would start a resurrection it would do you more good to look at than the next one will, if you go on the way you are doing now.

Those were the days!—those old ones. They will come no more. Youth will come no more. They were so full to the brim with the wine of life; there have been no others like them. It chokes me up to think of them. Would you like me to come out there and cry? It would not beseem my white head.

Goodbye. I drink to you all. Have a good time—and take an old man's blessing.

Mark Twain.[15]

By this time, Mark Twain was indeed a lonely person. His mother had passed away October 27, 1890. She had been living with Orion and Mollie Clemens for a number of years in Keokuk, Iowa. Her three remaining children, Orion, Samuel, and Pamela, took her body to Hannibal, Missouri, for burial.

"Death never came singly to the Clemens family." In 1896, Susy, Mark and Livy's oldest daughter, died; and the following year, on December 11, Orion passed away at the age of seventy-two. He remained to the end the same dreamer of success from his multitudinous projects. Paine says that "To his last day and hour Orion was the dreamer, always with a new plan. It was one morning early that he died. He had seated himself at a table with pencil and paper and was setting down the details of his latest project when death came to him, kindly enough, in the moment of new hope." [16]

Mark and his family were in Europe when he received word of Orion's death. Consolingly he cabled Mollie. Later he wrote her: "He was good—all good—and sound; there was nothing bad in him, nothing base, nor any unkindness. It was unjust that such a man . . . should have been sentenced to live seventy-two years. It was beautiful, the patience with which he bore it."

In 1904, there was a harvest of death in the Clemens family. It began on January 20 when Mollie passed away; on June 5, Mark's beloved Livy died in Florence, Italy; and on the following September 1, his only living sister, Pamela, died. Mark Twain was left with two of his daughters, Clara and Jean. Jean lived with him, but Clara spent most of her time abroad studying for the concert stage.

Over in Carson City, his few remaining friends hoped so much they could see him once more and experience again the good old days gone by.

To them he sent his last message,[17] written on both sides of a correspondence card. It is shown on the facing page.

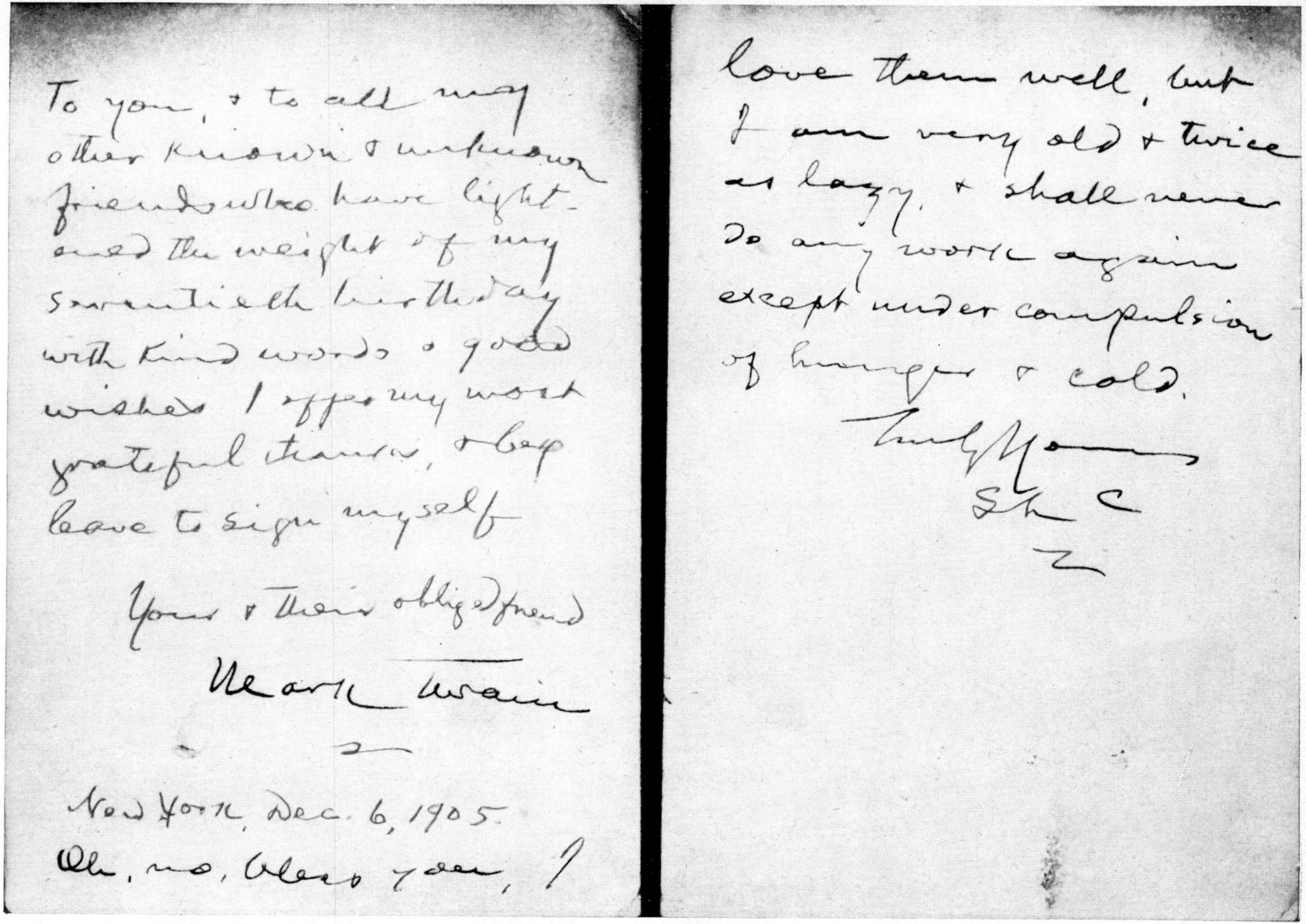

To you, & to all my
other known & unknown
friends who have light-
ened the weight of my
seventieth birthday
with kind words & good
wishes I offer my most
grateful thanks, & beg
leave to sign myself

Your & their obliged friend

Mark Twain

New York, Dec. 6, 1905.

Oh, no, bless you, I
love them well, but
I am very old & twice
as lazy, & shall never
do any work again
except under compulsion
of hunger & cold.

Truly Yours

S L C

FACSIMILE OF
MARK TWAIN'S
LAST MESSAGE
TO HIS FRIENDS
IN NEVADA

NOTES

1. THE LAND OF WASHOE

1. Albert Bigelow Paine, *Mark Twain: A Biography*, I, 203. The full text of this article is not extant. It probably appeared in the *Territorial Enterprise* some time in July, 1862: C. C. Goodwin, *As I Remember Them*, 253. (Mr. Goodwin's book, published in 1915, does not give accurate data. He did not live on the Comstock during the days Mark Twain was there. He was mining in Galena, a small mining camp about twenty-five miles from Virginia City).

2. This oration was supposed to have been delivered by George Turner, appointed by President Lincoln as Chief Justice of the Supreme Court of the Territory of Nevada. His contemporaries said he was a shallow and egotistical politician. Sam Clemens got well acquainted with him during the meeting of the first Territorial Legislature in 1861.

3. Samuel L. Clemens, *Mark Twain's Letters*, I, 55.

4. Dan De Quille, born William Wright, came to Washoe in 1860. He first settled near Silver City where he saw the original assay equipment of the Grosch brothers at the fork of American Flat Ravine and Gold Cañon. He was there early and talked with the original discoverers of the Lode. De Quille became the local editor of the *Territorial Enterprise* in 1862; he remained on this paper until it published its last issue in January, 1893.

5. William Wright (Dan De Quille, pseud.), *History of the Big Bonanza*, 19–20.

6. Effie Mona Mack, *History of Nevada*, 75–77.

7. *Ibid.*, "With Fremont in Nevada," 79–102.

8. Hoffman Birney, *Zealots of Zion*, 292.

9. Samuel L. Clemens, *Mark Twain's Autobiography*, II, 183.

10. Mack, *op. cit.*, 149.

11. Eliot Lord, *Comstock Mining and Miners*, 11.

12. Swift Paine, *Eilley Orrum*, 55–68.

2. MUCHA PLATA! MUCHA PLATA!

1. Mexicans who knew silver ore from having worked in the mines in Mexico recognized that there was silver in the ledges on Sun Mountain. They showed the Grosch brothers the location of these ledges.

2. Myron T. Angel (ed.), *History of Nevada*, 62 ff.

3. *Carson Daily Appeal*, June 29, 1865. The severe winters of this part of Nevada broke the thin slab into two pieces. They were later pieced together and laid flat in cement where the headstone may be seen today.

4. Albert Bigelow Paine, *Mark Twain: A Biography*, I, 94.

5. A good description of the discovery of the Comstock Lode may be found in William Wright (Dan De Quille, pseud.), *History of the Big Bonanza*, 39–55; Eliot Lord, *Comstock Mining and Miners*, 24–65.

3. "A PEEP AT WASHOE"

1. "A Peep at Washoe" by J. Ross Browne appeared first in *Harper's New Monthly Magazine,* December, 1860, Vol. XXII.

2. "A Memorial to 'Snowshoe' Thompson, Hero of the Sierras" (pamphlet), November 14, 1926, Carthay Center, Los Angeles, California. In this year a memorial to Thompson was unveiled at this place.

3. Effie Mona Mack, *History of Nevada,* 455–460.

4. John Ross Browne was born in Ireland in 1817; he died in Oakland, California, December 9, 1875. When he came to America he settled in Kentucky. At eighteen years of age he received a government job as a shorthand reporter in the United States Senate. In 1849, he was given the position of Commissioner of Internal Revenue in San Francisco. But soon after he arrived he succumbed to the gold fever and took part in most of the gold rushes in California and the rush to Washoe in 1860.

5. "Old Tennessee," W. G. Atkinson, was a correspondent from Genoa, Territory of Utah, later Nevada, to the San Francisco *Herald.* The first letter was written in November, 1857. The quoted letter was No. 43.

6. "Some interested journals and newspaper correspondents have handled Ross Browne without gloves, for the glowing pictures he painted for *Harper's Magazine,* of life, times, society and things in general at the Washoe Mines. And yet there never was a more truthful and graphic account of that famous silver district laid before the country. We know from actual observation that Ross Browne's account was but slightly colored."—San Francisco *Evening Bulletin,* April 18, 1861.

4. THE BROTHERS—SAM AND ORION

1. Minnie M. Brashear, *Mark Twain, Son of Missouri,* 104.

2. Albert Bigelow Paine, *Mark Twain, A Biography,* I, 44; Samuel L. Clemens, *Mark Twain's Autobiography,* II, 270.

3. *Ibid.,* 269.

4. Paine, *op. cit.,* I, 89.

5. *The Palimpsest,* October, 1929, X, No. 10, 354.

6. Effie Mona Mack, *History of Nevada,* 221.

7. *The Palimpsest, loc. cit.,* 359.

5. WITHOUT THE LAW

1. Myron T. Angel (ed.), *History of Nevada,* 50–51.

2. Nevada Historical Society, *Papers,* I, 192–193.

3. William Morris Stewart (George Rothwell Brown, ed.), *Reminiscences,* 126–139.

4. Hubert Howe Bancroft, *History of Nevada, Colorado, and Wyoming,* 209–213.

6. GOVERNOR NYE AND HIS BRIGADE

1. San Francisco *Evening Bulletin,* March 29, 1861.

2. Mark Twain, *Roughing It,* 163.

3. *Daily Evening Bulletin,* June 26, July 5, 1861.

4. *Ibid.,* July 22, 1861.

5. Eliot Lord, *Comstock Mining and Miners,* 110.

6. The description of the stage trip to Nevada is told in *Roughing It,* I, Ch. I–XX.

7. Horace Greeley, *An Overland Journey from New York to San Francisco in the Summer of 1859,* New York, 1860.

8. This watch, weighing almost two pounds, is now owned by V. L. McBride, owner of the Old Bucket of Blood, Virginia City, Nevada.

9. Mrs. M. Murphy's boardinghouse was on the corner of Carson and Proctor Streets (*Nevada Directory, 1862*).

10. Mark Twain, *ibid.,* 165–167.

7. THE SHIP IS LAUNCHED

1. Sacramento *Daily Union,* September 20, 1861.

2. Effie Mona Mack, *History of Nevada,* 228–229.

3. Effie Mona Mack, "Life and Letters of William Morris Stewart," *Ms.* Thesis for the Degree of Doctor of Philosophy, University of California. George Dunlap Lyman, *Saga of the Comstock Lode,* quotes extensively from this Thesis.

4. *Sacramento Daily Union,* October 11, 1861.

5. *Ibid.,* October 7, 1861.

6. A person who was illiterate and had to sign his name with an "X" was called a "bucksaw." There were many illiterates who rushed to Washoe. For teaching a person how to write his name the fee was from $80 to $100.

7. Sacramento *Daily Union,* October 21, 1861.

8. Letter written by Mark Twain from Honolulu to the Sacramento *Daily Union,* June 21, 1866.

9. *Nevada Council Journal,* 1861, 46; *Nevada House Journal,* Nevada Laws, 1861, 295.

10. *San Francisco Post,* November 27, 1877.

8. LEGISLATIVE FOOTPRINTS

1. Samuel L. Clemens, *Mark Twain's Autobiography,* II, 305.

2. Mark Twain, *Roughing It,* I, 182.

3. Rufus C. Arick was the first Mayor of Virginia City, elected in 1860 (incorporated under the laws of the Territory of Utah when this part of Nevada was in Utah). In those days the city set up its Mayor in fine style. Four rooms, described as "palatial," were furnished him. The Mayor was the official host and he was supposed to entertain all distinguished visitors who came to the Comstock. He had an office, parlor, sitting room, and bedroom. In his parlor was a sideboard brilliant with cut glass and in its cupboards was a plentiful supply of brandy, whiskey, rum, and gin with which to treat his guests "all on the city."

Arick left the Lode when the mines "went down"; he settled in Bakersfield, California, where he later was elected Superior Judge of the county. He died in that city December 31, 1891. *Territorial Enterprise,* December, 1891.

4. Miriam Michelson, *The Wonderlode of Silver and Gold,* 109–110.

5. *Daily Alta California,* October 24, 1861.

6. Mark Twain cleared up the mystery of the Carson footprints in the Sacramento *Daily Record-Union,* III, No. 27, March 25, 1885.

9. CONFEDERATE, "SECESH," AND "CHIV"

1. The name "Secesh" was the shortened form for Secessionist, and "Chiv" for Chivalries.

2. Effie Mona Mack, *History of Nevada,* 167–171.

3. Myron T. Angel (ed.), *History of Nevada,* 265.

4. *Ibid.,* 578; *Virginia Evening Bulletin,* July 31, 1863.

5. *Nevada Council Journal,* 1861, 87.

10. "GO IT, WASHOE!"

1. Samuel L. Clemens, *Mark Twain's Letters,* I, 53–55.

2. Mark Twain, *Roughing It,* II, 183.

3. Clemens, *ibid.,* I, 60.

4. The Humboldt mines, situated in the Humboldt Mountains east of the Humboldt River on the Overland Trail, were discovered in the spring of 1860 by Louis Barboo, an employee of the Overland Stage Company. The rush to this district started in the summer of 1861.

5. Claggett was elected Representative to the Nevada Territorial legislature from Humboldt September 3, 1862, reelected September 2, 1863.

6. A. W. "Gus" Oliver was appointed Probate Judge December 10, 1861, reelected September 2, 1863, and again January 19, 1864.

7. Mark Twain, *ibid.,* 199–209.

8. *Ibid.,* 210; a warm winter melted the snows in the Sierra Nevada Mountains, sending a great rush of water down the streams. The flood began in December and continued until early spring. "Cosmos," *San Francisco Daily Evening Bulletin,* December 15, 1861.

9. Mark Twain, *ibid.,* 231.

10. Fred W. Lorch, "Mark Twain's Trip to Humboldt in 1861," *American Literature,* X, November, 1938, Number three; Albert Bigelow Paine, *Mark Twain: A Biography,* Vol. I, 182–187.

11. GOVERNOR NYE AND SAM CLEMENS

1. Albert Bigelow Paine, *Mark Twain: A Biography,* I, 189.

2. Samuel L. Clemens, *Mark Twain's Letters,* I, 68.

3. The ranch belonged to Dick Sides (Dick Hyde in *Roughing It*), an early settler in Washoe Valley

4. Mark Twain, *Roughing It,* 240–247.

5. Samuel L. Clemens, *Mark Twain's Autobiography,* II, 305–307.

6. Samuel L. Clemens, *Mark Twain's Letters,* I, 58.

12. SAM SEES THE ELEPHANT

1. The elephant stood symbolically for the entire business of gold hunting in the gold rush days. When a man said he was going "to see the elephant"

he meant he was going to take a fling at mining. Stewart Edward White, *Old California in Picture and Story*, 89.

2. "An Old Landmark," by Bob Howland, *Daily Territorial Enterprise*, December 2, 1879. This cabin was taken apart in large sections and moved to Reno on November 8, 1924.

3. Samuel L. Clemens, *Mark Twain's Letters*, I, 69–70.

4. The boundary line between California and Nevada was not definitely known until 1863. Until this time, Aurora, Esmeralda Mining District, Mono County, was considered a part of California. It was made the county seat of this county. When the boundary line was fixed in 1863, Bridgeport was made the county seat of Mono County, while Aurora was made the county seat of Esmeralda County, Nevada.

5. Clemens, *op. cit.*, I, 72.

6. *Ibid.*, I, 71.

7. *Daily Territorial Enterprise*, January 7, 1872.

8. Paine, *op. cit.*, I, 73.

9. *Loc. cit.*

10. Mark Twain, *Roughing It*, I, 263.

11. Clemens, *op. cit.*, I, 78.

12. *Ibid.*, I, 80.

13. Mark Twain, *op. cit.*, 274.

14. *Ibid.*, 252–262.

15. *Ibid.*, 271–287.

16. Clemens, *op. cit.*, I, 81–82.

17. Samuel L. Clemens, *Mark Twain's Autobiography*, II, 257–262.

18. Mrs. Orion Clemens and daughter, Jennie, arrived in San Francisco by steamer October 2, 1862. *The Daily Silver Age*, October 2, 1862.

19. Clemens, *op. cit.*, I, 76.

20. *Ibid.*, I, 81–82.

21. Sam P. Davis, *History of Nevada*, I, 393; Albert Bigelow Paine, *Mark Twain: A Biography*, I, 203; C. C. Goodwin, *op. cit.*, 253; Rollin Daggett, "Recollections," San Francisco *Examiner*, January 22, 1893.

22. Paine, *op. cit.*, I, 83.

23. *Ibid.*, I, 85.

13. MARK TWAIN'S NEVADA

1. Arthur McEwen, "In the Heroic Days," San Francisco *Examiner*, January 22, 1893.

2. Mark Twain, *Roughing It*, II, 14–15.

3. *Ibid.*, I, 146–148.

4. J. Ross Browne, *Washoe Revisited*, 293, 376.

5. A good account of the United States camel experiment is given in *Camels of Western America*, A. A. Gray, Francis P. Farquhar, and William S. Lewis; and Lewis Burt Lesley, *Uncle Sam's Camels*.

6. C. C. Goodwin, *As I Remember Them*, 301.

7. Samuel L. Clemens, *Mark Twain's Letters*, I, 89.

8. Sam P. Davis, *History of Nevada*, I, 301.

9. Eliot Lord, *Comstock Mining and Miners*, 131–173.

10. William Morris Stewart, *Reminiscences*, 153.

11. Miriam Michelson, *The Wonderlode of Silver and Gold,* 157–158.

12. Hubert Howe Bancroft, *History of Nevada, Colorado, and Wyoming,* 174; Lord, *op. cit.,* 155.

13. Lord, *op. cit.,* 121–123.

14. Davis, *op. cit.,* I, 249.

15. Mark Twain, *op. cit.,* II, 33–34.

16. Swift Paine, *Eilley Orrum,* 113–114, 118–134.

14. WASHOE—LITERARY FRONTIER

1. Albert Bigelow Paine, *Mark Twain: A Biography,* I, 205.

2. "The Passing of a Pioneer," by Dan De Quille, San Francisco *Examiner,* January 22, 1893.

3. See Appendix I for one of these "quaints" by Dan De Quille.

4. Rollin M. Daggett, part Iroquois Indian, was one of the most colorful figures in the early Western days. Born in New York in 1832, he moved with his family in 1837 to northwestern Ohio where he gained a knowledge of printing. When he was seventeen years old he went to California on foot, supporting himself along the way with his rifle. In 1852 he and J. MacDonough Foard founded the *Golden Era;* in 1862 he went to Virginia City and the following year he was elected a member of the Territorial Council. In 1864 he became permanently connected with the *Territorial Enterprise.* Goodman and Dennis McCarthy, owners of the *Enterprise,* had formerly worked on the *Era.* (It will be remembered that Dan and Mark lived in Daggett's building at 25 North B Street, Virginia City.)

In 1876 Daggett was a Presidential elector from Nevada, and in 1878 he was appointed Minister to Hawaii. He represented Nevada in the Forty-sixth Congress, 1879–1881. *Braxton's Bar,* written by Daggett, is said to be the story of his life. He also wrote extensively of the Hawaiian Islands. These writings were published by Charles L. Webster & Co. *The Atlantic,* November, 1944, V. 174, No. 5, p. 100–101.

5. Joseph and John Mallon were the leading liquor merchants in Virginia City during the days Mark Twain was there. In those years liquor was brought into the city in kegs and barrels. The wholesalers generally owned the bar equipment of the saloons. Every day the wholesalers went the rounds of the saloons, picked up the empty bottles, filled them from the barrels and returned them to the saloon shelves. Since there were no special brands of bottled whiskey, it was given the name of the wholesaler.

6. "The Enterprise Poets" by Sam P. Davis, San Francisco *Examiner,* January 22, 1893.

7. The first book with a Nevada imprint bears the name of Orion Clemens: *Laws of the Territory of Nevada for 1861,* 600 pages, printed 1862, San Francisco, Valentine and Company—John Clyde Oswald, *Printing in the Americas,* 455–456.

8. Mark Twain, *Roughing It,* II, 85–89.

9. Douglas Crawford McMurtrie, *A Bibliography of Nevada Newspapers 1858 to 1875 Inclusive.*

10. George Dunlap Lyman, *Saga of the Comstock Lode,* 205.

15. 1863—YEAR OF FULFILLMENT

1. Samuel L. Clemens, *Mark Twain's Autobiography*, II, 309.
2. *Loc. cit.*
3. This article was found in a scrapbook in the old Benton Stables in Carson City and loaned to the author. There was no date on the scrapbook or the article.
4. Albert Bigelow Paine, *Mark Twain: A Biography*, I, 220.
5. *Virginia Evening Bulletin*, April 2, 1863.
6. Albert Bigelow Paine, *op. cit.*, I, 220.
7. Mark Twain, "Those Blasted Children," *Golden Era*, March 27, 1864; Paine, *op. cit.*, 243–244.
8. Stowe's Hotel at Steamboat Springs, about ten miles from Virginia City, was the nearest resort to this mining camp. Hot steam and mineral water pour out of cracks in the ground for a distance of a mile. The medicinal water is beneficial for many ailments. This hotel was famous for its chicken dinners and oyster stew. Whenever a Comstock nabob wished to put on a gay party he hired a fast team and drove down to this resort. It was said that many a mining report was padded with unessential items when really the money was expended for champagne dinners at Stowe's. Mark Twain stayed at this hotel when he was at Steamboat Springs. The resort burned May 8, 1866.
9. See Appendix for "Information for the Millions." It is the first history of Nevada.
10. *Golden Era*, September 27, 1863.
11. Samuel L. Clemens, *Mark Twain's Letters*, I, 91–92.

16. DAN DE QUILLE AND MARK TWAIN

1. The writer is indebted to Irma Wright Morris of West Liberty, Iowa, granddaughter of De Quille, for information she has concerning the time Dan and Mark lived together in Virginia City.
2. Moses Goldman and Company had the finest stock of furniture, upholstering, carpets, and crockery in Virginia City during the early days of the camp. The business was situated on West C Street near Taylor Street.
3. "Salad Days of Mark Twain," by Dan De Quille, San Francisco *Examiner*, March 19, 1893.
4. *Golden Era*, December 6, 1863.
5. "In the Heroic Days," by Arthur McEwen, San Francisco *Examiner*, January 23, 1893.
6. "Early Journalism in Nevada," by Alf Doten, *The Nevada Magazine*, I, No. 3, October, 1899, 182–184.
7. Gold Hill *Daily News*, April 16, 1864.

17. A SENSATIONAL TRIUMPH

1. Mark Twain, *Roughing It*, II, 20–23.
2. *Ibid.*, II, 18.
3. *Territorial Enterprise*, October 28, 1863; San Francisco *Bulletin*, October 31, 1863.

18. GOVERNOR MARK TWAIN

1. Myron T. Angel, *History of Nevada*, 82–84.
2. *Golden Era*, February 28, 1864.
3. The writer has a collection of Nevada notary petitions and notarial seal impressions for 1862–1863. Although most of the petitions bear many names as Mark Twain described them, the longest one measures two and one-half feet of foolscap paper pasted together. There are two columns of signatures on this one. The notarial impressions vary with the individual appointee. They run from Masonic emblems to Latin mottoes, national symbols, geometric figures, and the seal of the Territory of Nevada which Orion Clemens designed. Gold, silver, copper and different colored papers as well as wax were used on which to make the impressions. This collection includes many which bear the filing date and signature of Orion Clemens when he was the Secretary of Nevada Territory. These evidences prove that Mark Twain's article "Concerning Notaries" was justified.

19. "THREE SAINTS—MARK, LUKE, AND JOHN"

1. *Golden Era,* Nov. 29, 1863.
2. Franklin Walker, *San Francisco's Literary Frontier,* 161.
3. "Salad Days of Mark Twain," by Dan De Quille, San Francisco *Examiner,* March 19, 1893.
4. Barnum's Restaurant was situated on the corner of North B Street and Sutton Avenue.
5. Samuel L. Clemens, *Mark Twain's Letters,* I, 183.
6. *Ibid.,* I, 93–94.
7. *Loc. cit.*
8. Sam P. Davis, *History of Nevada,* II, 719–720.
9. Albert Bigelow Paine, *Mark Twain: A Biography,* I, 248.
10. "Salad Days of Mark Twain," by Dan de Quille, *San Francisco Examiner,* March 19, 1893.
11. *Virginia Daily Union,* March 23, 1864.

20. PATRIOTISM VERSUS DUELING

1. Samuel L. Clemens, *Mark Twain's Autobiography,* II, 216–217.
2. *Virginia City Union,* May 21, 1864.
3. Clemens, *ibid.,* I, 350–360.
4. *Ibid.,* I, 357.
5. George D. Lyman, *Saga of the Comstock Lode,* Ch. LV, fn. 1.
6. Samuel L. Clemens, *Mark Twain's Letters,* I, 97–98.
7. Samuel L. Clemens, *Mark Twain's Autobiography,* II, 318.

21. FAREWELL TO THE ROBBERS

1. Albert Bigelow Paine, *Mark Twain: A Biography,* I, 257.
2. *Ibid.,* 264–269.

3. Samuel L. Clemens, *Mark Twain's Letters,* I, 105–106.

4. *Daily Silver Age,* February 27, 1866.

5. Samuel L. Clemens, *Mark Twain's Autobiography,* I, 309. This home, a modest two-story house, is still standing in Carson City today in an excellent state of preservation. The writer is indebted to Dorothy Mackey Ingram of Reno for this information. The Mackey family owned and lived in Orion Clemens' home for a number of years.

6. Paine, *op. cit.,* I, 287.

7. Nye and Stewart were elected the first two United States Senators from Nevada in 1864. These men drew by lot for their terms. Nye drew the two-year term, Stewart, the four-year term. Nye was reelected in 1866, Stewart in 1868. Senator Nye died in White Plains, New York, December 25, 1875. Senator Stewart retired from the Senate in 1875 to practice law. In 1886 he reentered politics and was elected to the United States Senate for three more terms. He died in Washington, D. C., April 23, 1909.

22. THE LAST MESSAGE

1. Albert Bigelow Paine, *Mark Twain: A Biography,* I, 310.

2. Samuel L. Clemens, *Mark Twain's Letters,* I, 127–128.

3. Paine, *ibid.,* I, 346–347.

4. Mark Twain, *Roughing It,* 310; *Sketches New and Old,* 190–196.

5. Paine, *op. cit.,* I, 359–360.

6. Carson City *Silver Age,* April, 1868.

7. *Territorial Enterprise,* April 27, 1868.

8. Bowers' Mansion, Washoe Valley, twenty miles south of Reno.

9. See Mark Twain, *Roughing It,* Appendix C.

10. Letter from Mark Twain to Dan De Quille loaned to the writer by Irma Wright Morris, granddaughter of De Quille.

11. Effie Mona Mack, *History of Nevada,* 455–460.

12. Sam P. Davis, *History of Nevada,* II, 707.

13. Paine, *op. cit.,* I, 544.

14. *Ibid.,* III, 1377.

15. The original of this letter was loaned to the writer by Helen Fulton Peterson, daughter of Robert Fulton. When Mr. Paine, biographer of Mark Twain, was in Nevada gathering material for this part of his volumes, he made the Fulton home, 146 West First Street, Reno, his headquarters. The letter is also quoted in Paine, *op. cit.,* III, 1247.

16. Paine, *op. cit.,* II, 1053.

17. The original of this message, inscribed on both sides of a correspondence card, was loaned to the writer by Dorothy Mackey Ingram, to whose father it was written.

APPENDIX I

WASHOE RAMBLES *

By Dan De Quille
A Trip among the Mountains, Lakes, and Deserts to the Eastward

SINK STATION—SPIRITED KEEPER

13th Topic. We reached the Sink Station a little before sundown, and unsaddling our animals, drove them out to the margin of the lake to graze. The Station consists of a one-story house, surrounded by an adobe wall enclosing a plot of ground some six rods square. This wall is eight feet high, and three feet thick at the bottom by one at the top, with loopholes for muskets. The stables are also within the walls. This Station is on the west side of the lake and within a few rods of the shore. It is a stopping-place, both for the Overland Mail Line and the Pony Express. There being nothing in the firewood line to be found at this Station, the keeper very kindly invited us to come into his kitchen and make use of his stove or anything else we might need. This politeness on his part so warmed Tom's heart toward him that he brought forth our basket-flask and gave him a "pull" at the cocktail. Station-keeper departed—smacking his lips—within the walls of the fortification, and very shortly after came forth a red-nosed individual.

"Have you sich a thing as any kind of speerits 'long o' you?" queried the red-nosed etc.

The fact was that "speerit" wasn't very abundant with us. Tom heaved a most heart-rending sigh and replied, "A *very* little."

Red-nosed individ' began to look scared, but mustered courage to say in a most doleful, coaxing voice: "I've been out in the hot sun all day, and drank a heap o' nasty alkerli water, and now I feel bad in my stummick—a lettle speerit might do ma a power o' good."

"Ye-a-as," replied Tom, "that's bad. We've been traveling all day in the hot sun and not a bite to eat, to speak of, since yesterday noon, and have drank several canteens full of the worst alkali water *we have seen,* and now we ain't well ourselves."

* *The California Magazine and Mountaineer,* Vol. VI, No. 2, Whole No. 62, September, 1861. Dan De Quille referred to these articles as his "quaints."

As Tom finished this hint, he suddenly clapped his hand to his side, threw his head back, shut his eyes, and opened his mouth as though he had experienced a sudden dart of pain; while I clapped both hands upon my bread-basket, hung down my head, shut my eyes, and ground my teeth.

For a moment red-nosed etc. gazed upon our solemn visages and looked frightened; however, his thirst and courage soon revived.

"If you could only spare me the last drop," persisted red-nosed individ', "I *do* think it would be good for my stummick."

"Well," said Tom, "if a very *little* will do you any good, I suppose we might spare it."

Red-nosed etc. is glad from ear to ear.

He receives the precious flask; inserts the top of it just below the finis of his blazing nose; elevates the bottom. As the bottom of the flask goes up, the pair of jaws belonging to Tom and I expand. He still elevates the bottom of the flask; continues to elevate it gently— his ears work up and down slowly—nostrils expanded—features rigid. Bottom of flask still slowly rising. Gentle elevation and depression of the ears; nervous twitching about nostrils; the rigid corrugations near the eye relax and we catch a faint glimpse of the twinkling pupil; cheeks and neck growing a deeper purple; great distention about the windpipe. He can hold out no longer—the bottom of the flask lowers, he withdraws it from the loving embrace of his lips, and heaves a deep, long-drawn sigh—ditto Tom and I.

Red-nosed individual still holds the flask in his left hand, and— to Tom and I—alarmingly near his mouth; looks as though about to make a second attack, but Tom stretches forth his hand and red-nosed etc. relinquishes his hold, heaves another toward either of us, says, "Thank'ee," turneth on his heel and departeth. Tom shook the flask, took off the top, and looked into it. We both sighed; neither of us spoke—our hearts were too full for words.

APPENDIX II

INFORMATION FOR THE MILLIONS *

A young man anxious for information writes to a friend residing in Virginia City, Nevada, as follows:

> Springfield, Missouri
> April 12.

Dear Sir:

My object in writing to you is to have you give me a full history of Nevada. What is the character of the climate? What are the productions of the earth? Is it healthy? What diseases do they die of mostly? Do you think it would be advisable for a man who can make a living in Missouri to emigrate to that part of the country? There are several of us who would emigrate there in the spring if we could ascertain to a certainty that it is as much more a country than this. I suppose you know Joel H. Smith? He used to live here; he lives in Nevada now; they say he owns considerable in a mine there. Hoping to hear from you soon, etc., I remain,

> Yours truly,
> William ——

The letter was handed in to a newspaper office for reply. For the benefit of all who contemplate moving to Nevada, it is perhaps best to publish the correspondence in its entirety:

Dearest William:

Pardon my familiarity—but that name touchingly reminds me of the loved and lost, whose name was similar. I have taken the contract to answer your letter, and although we are now strangers, I feel we shall cease to be so if we ever become acquainted with each other. The thought is worthy of attention, William. I will now respond to your several propositions in the order in which you have fulminated them.

* Text is taken verbatim from *The Celebrated Jumping Frog of Calaveras*, pp. 144–152. Regarded as the first history of Nevada. Written while Mark Twain was at Steamboat Springs, August, 1863.

Your object in writing is to have me give you a full history of Nevada. The flattering confidence you repose in me, William, is only equalled by the modesty of your request. I could detail the history of Nevada in five hundred pages octavo, but as you have never done me any harm, I will spare you, though it will be apparent to everybody that I would be justified in taking advantage of you if I were a mind to. However, I will condense. Nevada was discovered many years ago by Mormons, and was called Carson County. It only became Nevada in 1861, by an act of Congress. There is a popular tradition that the Almighty created it; but when you come to see it, William, you will think differently. Do not let that discourage you, though. The country looks something like a singed cat, owing to the scarcity of shrubbery, and also resembles that animal in the respect that it has more merits than its personal appearance would seem to indicate. The Grosch brothers found the first silver lead here in 1857. They also founded Silver City, I believe. Signify to your friends, however, that all the mines here do not pay dividends as yet; you may make this statement with the utmost inflexibility—it will not be contradicted from this quarter. The population is about 35,000, one-half of which number reside in the united cities of Virginia City and Gold Hill. However, I will discontinue this history for the present, lest I get you too deeply interested in this distant land, and cause you to neglect your family or your religion. But I will address you again upon the subject next year. In the meantime, allow me to answer your inquiry as to the character of the climate.

It has no character to speak of, William, and alas! in this respect, it resembles many, ah! too many, chambermaids in this wretched world. Sometimes we have the seasons in their regular order, and then again we have winter all the summer, and summer all winter. Consequently, we have never yet come across an almanac that would just exactly fit this latitude. It is mighty regular about not raining, though, William. It will start in here in November and rain about four months, and sometimes as much as seven days on a stretch; after that, you may loan out your umbrella for twelve months, with the serene confidence which a Christian feels in four aces. Sometimes the winter begins in November and winds up in June; and sometimes there is a bare suspicion of winter in March and April, and summer the balance of the year. But as a general thing, William, the climate is good, what there is of it.

"What are the productions of the earth?" You mean in Nevada, of course. On our ranches here anything can be raised that can be produced on the fertile fields of Missouri. But ranches are very scattering—as scattering as lawyers in Heaven. Nevada, for the most part, is a barren waste of sand, and fenced in with snow-clad mountains. But these ghastly features were the salvation of the land, William; for no rightly constituted American would have ever come here if the place had been easy of access, and none of our pioneers would have stayed after they got here, if they had not felt satisfied that they could not find a smaller chance for making a living anywhere else. Such is man, William, as he crops up in America.

"Is it healthy?" Yes, I think it is as healthy here as it is in any part of the West. But never permit a question of that kind to vegetate in your brain, William, because as long as Providence has an eye on you, you will not be likely to die until your time comes.

"What diseases do they die of mostly?" Well, they used to die of conical balls, and cold steel, mostly, but here lately erysipelas and the intoxicating bowl have the bulge on those things, as was very justly remarked by Mr. Rising last Sunday. I will observe for your information that Mr. Rising is our Episcopal minister, and has done as much as any man among us to redeem this community from its pristine state of semi-barbarism. We are inflicted with all the diseases incident to the same latitude in the States, I believe, with one or two added and half a dozen subtracted on account of our superior altitude. However, the doctors are about as successful here, both in killing and curing, as they are anywhere.

Now, as to whether it would be advisable for a man who can make a living in Missouri to immigrate to Nevada, I confess I am somewhat mixed. If you are not content in your present condition, it naturally follows that you would be entirely satisfied if you could make either more or less than a living. You would exult in the cheerful exhilaration always produced by a change. Well, you can find your opportunity here, where, if you retain your health, and are sober and industrious, you will inevitably make more than a living, and if you don't, you won't. You can rely upon this statement, William. It contemplates any line of business except the selling of tracts. You cannot sell tracts here, William; the people take no interest in tracts; the very best efforts in the tract line—even with pictures on them—have met with no encouragement. Besides, the newspapers have been interfering; a man gets his regular text or so from the Scriptures in his paper, along with the stock sales and the war news, every day now. If you are in the tract business, William, take no chances on Washoe; but you can succeed at anything else here.

"I suppose you know Joel H. Smith?" Well, the fact is, I believe I don't. Now isn't that singular? Isn't it very singular? And he owns "considerable" in a mine here, too. Happy man! Actually owns in a mine here in Nevada Territory, and I never heard of him. Strange—strange—do you know, William, it is the strangest thing that ever happened to me? And then he not only owns in a mine, but owns "considerable"; that is the strangest thing about it. He is a lucky dog, though. But I strongly suspect that you have made a mistake in the name; I am confident you have; you mean John Smith—I know you do; I know it from the fact that he owns considerable in a mine here, because I sold him the property at a ruinous sacrifice on the very day he arrived here from over the plains. That man will be rich one of these days. I am just as well satisfied of it as I am of any precisely similar instance of the kind that has come under my notice. I said as much to him yesterday, and he said he was satisfied of it, also. But he did not say it with that air of triumphant exultation which a heart like mine so delights to behold in one to whom I have endeavored to be a benefactor in a small way. He looked pensive a while, but, finally, says he, "Do you know, I think I'd a been a rich man long ago if they'd ever found the d—d ledge?" That was my idea about it. I always thought, and I still think, that if they ever do find that ledge, his chances will be better than they are now. I guess Smith will be right one of these centuries, if he keeps up his assessments— he is a young man yet. Now, William, I have taken a liking to you, and I would like to sell you "considerable" in a mine in Washoe. Let me hear from you on the subject. Greenbacks at par is as good a thing as I want. But seriously, William, don't you ever invest in a mining stock which you don't know anything about; beware of John Smith's experience!

You hope to hear from me soon? Very good. I shall also hope to hear from you soon, about that little matter referred to. Now, William, ponder this epistle well—never mind the sarcasm here and there, and the nonsense, but reflect on the plain facts set forth, because they are facts, and are meant to be so understood and believed.

Remember me affectionately to your friends and relations, and especially to your venerable grandmother, with whom I have not the pleasure to be acquainted—but that is of no consequence, you know. I have been in your town many a time, and all the towns of the neighboring counties—the hotel-keepers will recollect me vividly. Remember me to them—I bear them no animosity.

Yours affectionately.

BIBLIOGRAPHY

Manuscripts, newspapers, magazines, and books have been examined at the following libraries: Bancroft Library, University of California, Berkeley; Nevada State Library, Carson City; University of Nevada, Reno; Mark Twain Museum, Hannibal, Mo.

The books and articles listed below will aid in reading more widely on this period of history:

Alexander, Mary Charlotte. *William Patterson Alexander, in Kentucky, the Marquesas, Hawaii.* Honolulu, 1934. (Privately printed.)

Angel, Myron T. (Ed.). *History of Nevada.* Thompson & West, Oakland, California, 1881.

Bancroft, Hubert Howe. *History of Nevada, Colorado and Wyoming,* Works. Vol. XXV. The History Company, San Francisco, 1890.

Becker, George Ferdinand. *Geology of the Comstock Lode and the Washoe District.* Washington, 1882. 1 vol. and atlas. (U. S. Geological Survey Monographs, III.)

Benson, Ivan. *Mark Twain's Western Years.* Stanford University Press, Stanford, California, 1938.

Birney, Hoffman. *Zealots of Zion.* The Penn Publishing Company, Philadelphia, 1931.

Brashear, Minnie M. *Mark Twain, Son of Missouri.* University of North Carolina Press, Chapel Hill, North Carolina, 1934.

Brooks, Van Wyck. *The Ordeal of Mark Twain.* E. P. Dutton & Co., rev. ed., New York, 1933.

Browne, J. Ross. "A Peep at Washoe," in *Harper's Monthly Magazine,* vol. 22, New York, December, 1860—February, 1861.

Clemens, Cyril (Ed.). *Mark Twain Anecdotes.* Mark Twain Society, Webster Groves, Missouri, 1929.

Clemens, Samuel L. *Mark Twain's Autobiography.* With an introduction by Albert Bigelow Paine. 2 vols. Harper & Brothers, New York, 1924.

———. *Mark Twain's Letters.* Selected and annotated by Albert Bigelow Paine. 2 vols. Harper & Brothers, New York, 1935.

———. *Mark Twain's Notebook.* Prepared for publication with comments by Albert Bigelow Paine. Harper & Brothers, New York, 1935.

———. *Mark Twain's Speeches.* With an introduction by William Dean Howells. Harper & Brothers, New York, 1910.

———. *Mark Twain's Works,* Hillcrest Edition. Harper & Brothers, New York, 1904.

———. *The Washoe Giant in San Francisco.* Edited by Franklin Walker. George Fields, Publisher, San Francisco, 1938.

———. *The Writings of Mark Twain,* Author's National Edition, New York and London, 1917.

Cummins, Ella Sterling. *The Story of the Files.* Issued by World's Fair Commission of California Columbian Exposition, San Francisco, 1893.

Daggett, Rollin M. *Braxton's Bar.* Harper & Brothers, New York, 1892.

Dana, Charles A. *Recollections of the Civil War; with the Leaders in the Field in the Sixties.* Appleton and Company, 1898.

Dane, G. Ezra (Ed.). *Letters from the Sandwich Islands written for the Sacramento Union, by Mark Twain.* The Grabhorn Press, San Francisco, 1937.

Davis, Sam P. *History of Nevada.* 2 vols. The Elms Publishing Company, Los Angeles, 1913.

De Groot, Henry. *Sketches of Washoe Silver Mines.* Mining and Scientific Press, San Francisco, 1906.

De Voto, Bernard. *Mark Twain's America.* Little, Brown & Co., Boston, 1932.

Drury, Wells. *An Editor on the Comstock Lode.* Farrar & Rinehart, New York, 1936.

Gillis, William R. *Gold Rush Days with Mark Twain.* Albert and Charles Boni, New York, 1930.

Goodwin, C. C. *As I Remember Them.* Salt Lake Commercial Club, Salt Lake City, 1913.

Gray, A. A., and others. *Camels in Western America.* California Historical Society. Vol. IX, No. 4, December, 1930, San Francisco, 1930.

Greeley, Horace. *An Overland Journey, from New York to San Francisco in the Summer of 1859.* H. H. Bancroft & Co., 1860.

(Gridley.) *Tribute to the Memory of Reuel Colt Gridley—compiled and published for the purpose of raising money to aid in building a monument to his memory and establishment of a fund for his family.* A pamphlet. Stockton, 1883.

Hingston, Edward P. *Genial Showman.* Hotten, London, 1871.

Johnson, Merle. *A Bibliography of the Works of Mark Twain, Samuel Langhorne Clemens.* Harper & Brothers, New York and London, 1910.

Julian, George Washington. *Political Recollections, 1840–1872.* A. C. McClurg & Co., Chicago, 1894.

Kelley, J. Wells. *Directory of Nevada Territory.* San Francisco, 1862.

King, Joseph L. *History of the San Francisco Stock and Exchange Board.* J. L. King, San Francisco, 1910.

Lesley, Lewis Burt. *Uncle Sam's Camels.* Harvard University Press, Cambridge, 1929.

Lord, Eliot. *Comstock Mining and Miners.* Washington, 1883. (U. S. Geological Survey Monographs, LV.)

Lyman, George D. *The Saga of the Comstock Lode.* Charles Scribner's Sons, New York, 1934.

Mack, Effie Mona. *History of Nevada.* Arthur H. Clark Company, Glendale, 1935.

———. "Life and Letters of William Morris Stewart." MSS. 1930.

Marye, George T. *From '49 to '83.* A. M. Robertson, San Francisco, 1923.

McMurtrie, Douglas Crawford. *A Bibliography of Nevada Newspapers 1858 to 1875 Inclusive.* Gutenberg-Jahrbuch, Mainz, 1935.

Michelson, Miriam. *The Wonderlode of Silver and Gold.* The Stratford Company, Boston, 1934.

Mighels, Henry R. *Sage Brush Leaves.* Edward Bosqui & Co., San Francisco, 1879.

Nevada Historical Society. *Biennial Report, 1909–1910.* State Printing Office, Carson City.

———. *Papers. 1907–1924.* State Printing Office, Carson City.

Paine, Albert Bigelow. *Mark Twain: A Biography.* 3 vols. Harper & Brothers, New York, 1912.

Paine, Swift. *Eilley Orrum, Queen of the Comstock.* The Bobbs-Merrill Company, Indianapolis, 1929.

Richtofen, Ferdinand Paul. Wilhelm, Freiherr von. *The Comstock Lode, its Character, and the Probable Mode of its Continuance in Depth.* Mining and Scientific Press, San Francisco, 1866.

Seitz, Don C. *Artemus Ward. A Biography and Bibliography.* Harper & Brothers, New York, 1919.

Shinn, Charles Howard. *Mining Camps: A Study in American Frontier Government.* Charles Scribner's Sons, New York, 1885.

——. *The Story of the Mine as Illustrated by the Great Comstock Lode.* D. Appleton and Company, 1908.

Smith, Grant M. *The History of the Comstock Lode, 1850–1920.* Vol. XXXVII, No. 3, University of Nevada Bulletin. State Printing Press, Carson City, 1943.

Stewart, William Morris. *Reminiscences.* Edited by George Rothwell Brown. Neale Publishing Company, New York, 1908.

——. *Stewart Scraps, 1887–1905.* MSS, Letters, and Newspaper Clippings, Nevada Historical Library, Reno.

Swift, John Franklin. *Robert Greathouse.* Carleton Publisher, New York, 1870.

Van Sickle, Henry. "Utah Desperadoes." MS., Bancroft Library, 1883.

Wagenknecht, Edward. *Mark Twain: The Man and His Work.* Yale University, New Haven, 1935.

Walker, Franklin. *San Francisco's Literary Frontier.* Alfred A. Knopf, New York, 1939.

Ward, Artemus (Charles Farrar Brown). *Artemus Ward, His Travels.* Harper & Brothers, New York, 1864.

White, Stewart Edward. *Old California in Picture and Story.* New York, 1937.

Wilson, Neill C. *Silver Stampede.* The Macmillan Company, New York, 1937.

Wren, Thomas. *A History of the State of Nevada, its Resources and People.* The Lewis Publishing Co., Chicago, 1904.

Wright, William (Dan De Quille, pseud.). *History of the Big Bonanza.* American Publishing Company, 1876.

INDEX